SCRIPTURE,
THE GENESIS
OF
DOCTRINE

DOCTRINE AND SCRIPTURE IN EARLY CHRISTIANITY

VOLUME ONE

SCRIPTURE, THE GENESIS OF DOCTRINE

FRANCES M. YOUNG

WILLIAM B. EERDMANS PUBLISHING COMPANY
GRAND RAPIDS, MICHIGAN

Wm. B. Eerdmans Publishing Co.
4035 Park East Court SE, Grand Rapids, Michigan 49546
www.eerdmans.com

© 2023 Frances M. Young
All rights reserved
Published 2023

Book design by Lydia Hall

Printed in the United States of America

29 28 27 26 25 24 23   1 2 3 4 5 6 7

ISBN 978-0-8028-8298-1

Library of Congress Cataloging-in-Publication Data

A catalog record for this book is available from the Library of Congress.

To all who along the way have opened my eyes

Contents

Foreword by David F. Ford		xiii
Preface		xxiii
List of Abbreviations		xxv

1. Doctrine and Scripture:
   Mutually Coinherent? What Are the Problems? ... 1

   1. A Widening Gap? ... 1
   2. The Developmental Model ... 3
   3. Hellenization of the Gospel ... 7
   4. Changed Perspectives ... 11

2. Rethinking the Context:
   The School-Like Character of Early Christian Groups ... 14

   1. Christianity: A Religion or What? ... 15
   2. Synagogues and Schools ... 19
   3. The Sociological Turn ... 22
   4. Schools within "Fractionated" Churches: Two Key Examples ... 27
      - 4.1. Rome in the Second Century ... 27
      - 4.2. Alexandria in the Second and Early Third Centuries ... 29

	5. Hellenization or the Acculturation of a Distinct Identity?	37
	5.1. Acculturation as a Network of Schools	37
	5.2. A School with a Distinct Identity?	38
	6. Conclusion and Prospect	41
3.	**Reading Texts, Asking Questions: Key Second-Century Conclusions**	44
	1. Scripture and Its Exegesis	45
	1.1. Marcion's Biblical Criticism and Its Context	49
	1.2. Ptolemaeus's Letter to Flora	53
	1.3. Justin's Reading of Scripture	55
	2. God and Creation	58
	2.1. Marcion and the God of the Scriptures	62
	2.2. Marcion's Good God and the God of the Beyond	64
	2.3. From Marcion's Duality to God's Monarchia	69
	3. Conclusion	73
4.	**Summing up Scripture: From Gospel of Truth to Canon of Truth**	74
	1. Gnosticism	75
	1.1. The Gospel of Truth	75
	1.1.1. Overview	76
	1.1.2. Saving the Lost: Gospel of Truth 31–34	78
	1.1.3. Jesus as Revealer: Gospel of Truth 18.7–20.2 and 30.35–31.35	80
	1.1.4. Names in the Book of the Living: Gospel of Truth 19.34–23.31 and 37.35–43.22	83
	1.2. Behind and Beyond the Gospel of Truth	85
	1.2.1. The Gospel of Truth and the Valentinian System	85
	1.2.2. The Gospel of Truth and Scripture	87

2.	The Canon of Truth	90
	2.1. *Irenaeus's* Demonstration of the Apostolic Preaching and the Rule of Faith	91
	2.2. Proof from Prophecy	92
	2.3. The Threefold Shape of the Rule of Faith / Canon of Truth	93
	2.4. The Names	95
	2.5. The Rule of Faith and Rule of Life	97
	2.6. The Rule of Faith as the Hypothesis of Scripture	98
	2.7. Irenaeus's Reading of Scripture in the Light of Scripture's Hypothesis	99
3.	So Was It Gnosticism That Provoked Definition of the Scriptural Canon and the Canon of Faith?	104
	3.1. Irenaeus and the *Gospel of Truth*: Parallels and Contrasts	104
	3.2. Did Gnosticism Provoke Canonical Definition?	105
	3.2.1. On God and Creation	106
	3.2.2. On Recapitulation	107
	3.2.3. On the Scriptural Canon	108
4.	Conclusion	108

5. Divine Pedagogy: Unearthing the Intent of the Holy Spirit — 110

1.	**Doctrine as Pedagogy**	110
	1.1. Different Levels and the Learning Journey	110
	1.2. The Intent of the Divine Author	114
	1.3. *Paideia and* Dogma	117
2.	**Right Doctrine, Right Reading**	122
	2.1. Against Celsus—*Replaying the Second-Century Arguments*	124
	2.1.1. Oracles and Prophecies	125
	2.1.2. God's Knowledge of Us: Judgment, Providence, and Creation	128

		2.1.3. Our Knowledge of God: Knowing and Worshipping the One Unknowable Creator of All	131
		2.1.4. Scripture: Wrong Doctrine, Wrong Reading	134
		2.1.5. Conclusion	136
	2.2. First Principles: *Toward a "Single Body of Doctrine"*		136
		2.2.1. The Rule of Faith	137
		2.2.2. Inquiries into Meaning and Truth	139
		2.2.3. From Scripture to Doctrine: The Holy Spirit	141
		2.2.4. From Doctrine to Scripture: God	145
		2.2.5. Beyond Doctrine and Scripture	149
3.	**Retrospect and Prospect**		152
	3.1. *Doctrine and Scripture*		152
	3.2. *Divine Pedagogy*		154

6. Creeds: From Confession to Dogma — 156

1. **Cyril of Jerusalem: Scripture Digested for Catechesis** — 157
    1.1. *What Did Cyril Mean by "Summary"?* — 158
    1.2. *Cyril's Scriptural Proofs and Quotations* — 160
    1.3. *So What about Alternative Readings?* — 161

2. **"Holy Dogmas": Scriptural Roots, Doctrinal Legacies** — 163
    2.1. *God* — 163
    2.2. *Lord Jesus Christ, Son of God* — 170
    2.3. *Born of the Virgin Mary* — 176
    2.4. *Crucified under Pontius Pilate, Was Dead and Buried* — 183
    2.5. *Resurrection and Ascension* — 191
    2.6. *Judgment* — 195
    2.7. *Sin* — 197
        Excursus: Original Sin — 199

  2.8. Final Clauses: *The Church, the Resurrection of the Body, and the Last Things*   209

   2.8.1. Bodily Resurrection and Eternal Life   209
   2.8.2. The Church   213
    2.8.2.1. Images of the Church Deriving from Scripture   214
    2.8.2.2. Cyprian: *The Unity of the Catholic Church* and Beyond   217

  2.9. Conclusion   220

 3. Christian Teaching as Dogmatic Truth Grounded in a Plain Reading of Scripture   221

  3.1. Epiphanius: Creedal Dogma and Scripture   222
  3.2. Dogma and the Reaction against Allegory   223
  3.3. Conclusion   225

7. Scripture, the Genesis of Doctrine: Conclusions and Consequences   226

 1. Augustine's *Teaching Christianity*: Context and Purpose   227

  1.1. From Augustine's *Inventio* to Canon Criticism   230
  1.2. From Augustine's "Signs" to Scriptural Language and Doctrinal Concepts   234
  1.3. From Augustine's Pedagogy to the Twenty-First-Century Renaissance in Theological Interpretation of Scripture   240

 2. Beyond That Gap: An Interim Report   243

Bibliography   249

Index of Authors   261

Index of Subjects   264

Index of Scripture and Other Ancient Sources   271

Foreword

It is a rare experience to be able to witness the creation of a *magnum opus* step by step. Beginning slowly before the Covid-19 pandemic, increasing in frequency during it, and now finally completed, I have been receiving from the author chapter after chapter of *Doctrine and Scripture in Early Christianity*. It has been a scholarly, historical, hermeneutical, theological, and spiritual feast. It has also been a culmination to Frances Young's *oeuvre*, whose range and depth were already astonishing, embracing biblical studies, early Christian history, literature and theology, ecumenical and interreligious engagement, theological method, contemporary Christian theology on all the main doctrines, theology and disability, spirituality, preaching, and poetry. Yet that is not all.

A Magisterial, Field-Encompassing Culmination

The originality and long-term importance of the present two volumes is in their core achievement: they bring to a critical and constructive culmination more than two centuries of modern scholarly and theological engagement with the early centuries of Christianity. Those early, identity-forming centuries are still of immense significance for more than two billion Christians in the twenty-first century—above all through giving them their core text, the Bible, but also through showing how earlier Christians worked out basic, long-lasting ways to understand the Bible and discern its essentials for Christian life and thought.

Yet recent centuries have also delivered one shock after another to mainstream, traditional Christian ways of reading the Bible and of receiving the history and theology of the early church. In volume 1 Frances Young gives some account of this radical shaking, and she is alert to it through both volumes. She describes the responses to it by such figures as John Henry Newman and Adolf von Harnack and acutely analyzes their inadequacies. She then sets herself the massive task of giving better answers to the fundamental questions:

> Is it possible to construct a new account of the arguments that produced dogmatic discourse, particularly of the ways in which appeals to scripture functioned as new questions were raised? Can we find another way of telling the story that acknowledges that, in the process of forming a distinct identity, there is inevitable tension between "acculturation" on the one hand and, on the other, self-conscious challenge to the all-pervasive cultural milieu—this challenge, in the case of the early Christians, being grounded in certain key convictions ultimately deriving from scripture? These two volumes on *Doctrine and Scripture in Early Christianity* constitute a perhaps rash attempt to produce such an account. . . .
>
> Then, maybe, through the dynamic of an "ethical reading,"[1] which respects the text while acknowledging the tension between the reader's difference from and identification with the material in view, we may find insights that might affirm or challenge our own hermeneutics and our own use of scripture in doctrinal and ethical debate—after all, as Newman noted, Christians have always engaged in justifying their theological and ethical commitments from scripture. Can we clear a path through early Christian argument by recognizing how the definition of doctrine was a process of making sense of scripture in terms of the rationality of that time? And then, perhaps, make a parallel journey of sensemaking in our very different intellectual context . . . ? (12–13 below)

All her academic life Frances Young has wrestled with such questions, refusing to avoid their immense complexity and implications, not least for Christian living and thinking today. She has circled around them, approaching them from one angle after another, and she has discerned more and more clearly how to respond to them with both scholarly and theological integrity and wisdom. She has written articles and monographs that have opened fresh ways of engaging

---

1. For "ethical reading" see Frances Young, "The Pastoral Epistles and the Ethics of Reading," *JSNT* 45 (1992): 105–20; and "Allegory and the Ethics of Reading," in *The Open Text: New Directions for Biblical Studies?*, ed. Francis Watson (London: SCM, 1993). In her introduction to *God's Presence* (see below) she describes "ethical reading" as "being as true as possible to texts from the past, while also being true to ourselves" (1).

with them and has written textbooks and edited authoritative works of reference that helped to define and shape the field.² And the field to which she is contributing is far wider than that of the early church and its thinking: in particular, she has something vital to say to any Christian theology that wants to draw on the Bible in its thinking today and to practice faith seeking understanding.

Now, finally, these summative volumes give a rich, mature account of how in the twenty-first century we can both learn the many lessons and avoid the many pitfalls of recent centuries, in order to arrive at a retrieval of early Christianity that rings true with thorough scholarship, sophisticated hermeneutics, and theological wisdom.³ Not only is the time right for her to distill her understanding from a lifetime in the field, which began as a classicist steeped in the history and culture of the early Christian centuries in the Hellenistic world. The time is also ripe for the field of early Christian life and thought, which has been much divided by different disciplinary approaches and by conflicts of many sorts, to be given a detailed yet coherent response to those key questions she identifies. There is probably no one else in the field so well equipped to do so, and this is probably also the first time in recent centuries that there are the scholarly, hermeneutical, and theological resources available to let it be done convincingly.

---

2. Specifically on scripture and doctrine, her main specialist books relating to early Christianity have been *Biblical Exegesis and the Formation of Christian Culture* (Cambridge: Cambridge University Press, 1997); *Exegesis and Theology in Early Christianity* (Farnham: Ashgate, 2012); and *Ways of Reading Scripture: Collected Papers* (Tübingen: Mohr Siebeck, 2018). Her principal textbooks and works of reference are *From Nicaea to Chalcedon* (London: SCM, 1983; 2nd ed. 2010); *The Making of the Creeds* (London: SCM, 1991); *The Cambridge History of Early Christian Literature*, coedited with Lewis Ayres and Andrew Louth (Cambridge: Cambridge University Press, 2004); and *The Cambridge History of Christianity*, vol. 1, coedited with Margaret M. Mitchell (Cambridge: Cambridge University Press, 2006).

3. A key event in my own theological formation was a five-year collaboration in teaching and writing about Paul's second letter to the Corinthians, which resulted in our coauthored work, Frances M. Young and David F. Ford, *Meaning and Truth in 2 Corinthians* (London: SPCK, 1987). That work's interweaving of scholarship, hermeneutics, theology, and spirituality, developed in conversation with Frances Young, has informed my thinking since then. During the final years of work on *The Gospel of John: A Theological Commentary* (Grand Rapids: Baker Academic, 2021), I was reading *Doctrine and Scripture in Early Christianity* as it was being written, and it is part of the hidden background of the commentary. One way of seeing the commentary is as an attempt to combine scholarship, hermeneutics, theology, and spirituality by interpreting the Gospel of John (which has probably been the single Christian biblical text that has most deeply shaped Christian thinking) in ways that have learned from Frances Young's *oeuvre*. As she says in the preface to her second volume, "this work would appear to endorse the recent turn to theological commentaries on biblical texts."

The result is a magisterial achievement by one person that is also epochal in its significance for the field. Frances Young, who is not only steeped in the modern field of early Christian studies but also acutely aware of its inadequacies and its fragmentation, has produced a fresh, rigorous, and deep integration of it that can act as the paradigm best suited to understanding it today. It is to be hoped that these volumes will soon become a standard textbook for those studying early Christianity during the rest of this century.

An Earlier Culmination: God's Presence—a Contemporary Recapitulation of Early Christianity

Doctrine and Scripture in Early Christianity is not the first culminating work by Frances Young. A decade ago she published *God's Presence: A Contemporary Recapitulation of Early Christianity*.[4] That too is summative, but with a central concern for intelligent, imaginative, and wise Christian faith today, arising out of dialogue with the leading teachers of the early church.

God's Presence is essential reading if one is to understand the extensive twenty-first-century implications of the present two volumes. Rowan Williams says of it:

> No-one but Frances Young could have written a book like this. It combines an immense professional expertise in the literature of early Christianity with intense personal and pastoral reflection, an insightful perspective on contemporary theological concerns, and an interweaving of sermons and poetic meditations that remind us of Frances' stature as a spiritual guide. It is a book of exceptional human maturity as well as intellectual challenge. Frances Young has always combined these elements in a rare way, but this book is a summation of all that has been most fruitful and nourishing in both her academic and her pastoral ministry. It is a treasury of real wisdom, both authoritative and vulnerable.[5]

God's Presence is a lively, attractive account of how one can be alert simultaneously both to two millennia of Christian life and thought and also to such recent factors as developments in the natural and human sciences; challenges of modern and postmodern hermeneutics of suspicion; new forms of interreligious engagement; feminism; racism; and big changes in politics, economics,

---

4. Cambridge: Cambridge University Press, 2013.
5. From the cover.

technology, and warfare. The book is a rewritten and expanded version of Frances Young's acclaimed Bampton Lectures at Oxford University, and, like *Doctrine and Scripture in Early Christianity*, it is a search for integration with integrity in the course of a journey through modernity into whatever we might call the twenty-first century—"late modernity"? "post-modernity"? "chastened modernity"? The integration sought is not just intellectual but also embraces church life,[6] public life,[7] and personal life.[8] Seeking to do justice to these leads her into daring to communicate through ways less conventionally academic, such as poetry, storytelling, the visual arts, prayer, liturgy, sacramental spirituality, personal testimony, "snapshots" of everyday living, and preaching.

All of this is in line with what she draws on again and again: the history and theology of the early centuries of Christianity. She summarizes the recurrent motifs rooted there as "reading of the Bible as essentially a transformative text"; God's creativity and human creatureliness; "the wisdom of intellectual humility"; the transcendent God working "through particularities and the constraints of history, paradoxically exercising power through weakness"; "the sacramental perspective which seems to shape and unite the incarnation, the scriptures as Word of God, the eucharist, the church, enabling discernment of the Creator through the creation, of the Spirit in ordinary, physical dailiness, of God in God's human image and the human community of the Body of Christ"; the overarching narrative of fall and redemption with all its ambiguities, and its realism about how things go wrong; true love, modeled on God's love, as beyond power and possessiveness; "the significance of facing the 'other' for theological, ethical and spiritual transformation"; the "otherness" of God and "the paradox of God's concurrent absence and presence"; and "the mystery of the Trinity as the all-embracing, overflowing wisdom of divine love."[9] There is one further motif on her list, intrinsic to that core mystery of the Trinity, which recurs in her daring, Augustinian postscript to the second volume of *Doctrine and Scripture in Early Christianity*: "the inseparability of truth, beauty, and goodness."

---

6. ". . . the search for an understanding of theology that can affirm and celebrate different histories, relationships and identities, including the ministry of women, within an ecumenical horizon" (*God's Presence*, 3).

7. ". . . the search for an understanding of Christian theology which is robust enough to discern the presence of God in a post-Christian, pluralist society, within a globalised world dominated by science and technology, and on a planet subject to humanly induced climate change" (*God's Presence*, 3).

8. ". . . from long, and sometimes desperate, searching for answers to the discovery that questions of theodicy cease to engage as over forty years of caring for a profoundly disabled son gives privileged access to the deepest truths of the Christian religion" (*God's Presence*, 3).

9. *God's Presence*, 5–6.

The importance of those motifs should be enough to convince anyone concerned with the meaning, truth, and practice of Christianity today that it is still vital to learn from those early centuries. Yet until *Doctrine and Scripture in Early Christianity* she had not brought together in one work her key insights and overall "sense-making" of the Bible and the early Christian centuries. It is fascinating to see how she has now gone about this.

Doctrine and Scripture in Early Christianity: Key Elements

The basic twofold approach is indicated in the titles of each volume.

Volume 1, *Scripture, the Genesis of Doctrine*, tells the story of the early Christian church as it worked out its identity amid the complexities of the pluralist Roman Empire, in which it did not fit any of the available categories.

The Christian communities would have seemed more like a network of schools than a religion:

> Teaching and learning were their business, and they were both like and unlike other schools. They were dissimilar from these schools in that all comers were welcome—the poor, slaves, women, outcasts, orphans, widows. But they were like other schools in other respects, in that their teachers advocated a particular lifestyle and grounded ethics in an account of the truth: truth about the way things are, about God, about human destiny. And sooner or later they would argue for distinctive positions with respect not just to ethics but to such topics as cosmology, physics, and metaphysics. Again, like other schools, this one distilled wisdom concerning these branches of philosophy from ancient written texts, albeit stylistically crude texts that came from a "barbarian" source rather than the classics. (41–42 below)

Those "crude," strange texts testified to the distinctive "good news" of Christianity, believing and trusting in which was at the heart of this community's distinctiveness.[10] The rest of volume 1 narrates (with critical attention to alternative narratives) how the priority given to the Bible was the subject of

---

10. The work of a younger scholar, Teresa Morgan (who, like Frances Young, combines classics, scholarship on scripture and early Christianity, and theology), on *fides* and *pistis* in the Roman Empire, Hellenistic Judaism, the Septuagint, and the New Testament is a rich, corroborating accompaniment to *Scripture, the Genesis of Doctrine*. See especially Teresa Morgan, *Roman Faith and Christian Faith: Pistis and Fides in the Early Roman Empire and Early Churches* (Oxford: Oxford University Press, 2015), and *The New Testament and the Theology of Trust: 'This Rich Trust'* (Oxford: Oxford University Press, 2022).

much debate and conflict and resulted in the recognition that, while reading and interpreting scripture was the highest study in the community, it also required the guidance of teaching—dogma or doctrine ("teaching" in Greek is *dogma*, in Latin *doctrina*)—distilled over many years and embodied in the rule of faith (leading to the creeds) and in catechetical teaching. So scripture and doctrine belong together in a school-like environment.

The surrounding culture was one where education was based on a canon of ancient literary and philosophical texts in which were found indicators both to a right way of life and to the truth about the way things are. Christians adapted many of classical culture's methods of textual interpretation in learning from their own scriptural texts a way of life and an understanding of reality. There was both "acculturation" and a distinctive, scripture-centered identity that challenged the culture through believing and trusting in the one Creator God who is the Father of Jesus Christ. The debates were of course carried on with the modes of reasoning learned through their culture, and in response to the questions and events of their time, but the distinctiveness is irreducibly scriptural. Scripture was thus the genesis of doctrine, and the kind of "teaching" discerned was a response to current intellectual questions about life, the universe, and everything. This complex, culturally shaped yet culturally transformative coinherence of scripture and doctrine is the basic lesson of volume 1. Some of its detailed lessons for our century are worked out in *God's Presence: A Contemporary Recapitulation of Early Christianity*.

Volume 2, *Scripture in Doctrinal Controversy*, concentrates mainly on issues relating to the two core questions that dominated much theological discussion and controversy in the early church and are still utterly central to Christian life and thought: Who is Jesus Christ? and Who is God?

Christians today still read the Bible as their primary way of trying to answer them, and the answers affect all other key teachings. But the way the early church arrived at their answers and expressed the coinherence of scripture and doctrine has often been dismissed by modern biblical scholarship. As Frances Young says, "Their basis in scripture was and remains far from self-evident: they emerged out of conflict and debate over the implications of the biblical material, and modern biblical scholarship has largely treated them as anachronistic models for interpreting the canonical texts."[11]

Faced with this challenge, one response is to ignore it and to reaffirm the early church approach and conclusions, or even to ignore both modern scholarship and the ways the early church wrestled with scripture and try to bypass both by going back to the "plain text" of the Bible. Another response is to take

---

11. Volume 2, preface.

modern historical-critical scholarship as the primary guide, leading to the contemporary irrelevance of the early church engagement with scripture.

Frances Young argues strongly against both responses. She is a historical-critical scholar both of the Bible and of the early Christian centuries, but is also acutely aware of (and has written extensively about) the limitations of that modern method when it comes to the sort of questions being pursued by both early and contemporary Christians, above all concerning who Jesus Christ is and who God is. As she states in the prefaces to both volumes, "Ultimately we seek on this journey to move beyond the estrangement between doctrine and scripture brought about by modernity and the historico-critical method, so as to rediscover how scripture and doctrine have the kind of theological coinherence that the fathers of the church attributed to them" (xxiv below).

To move beyond this estrangement, while doing justice to both sides, is a complex task, with no simple affirmation or negation of one side or the other. It is, as she says, a journey, and it is one in which the experience along the way is essential to where one arrives at the end. It is tempting in any large book to jump to a summary of the conclusions. That would be especially unfortunate with these volumes. Immersion in the particularities of how scripture, historical and cultural context, and doctrine were shaped through their inseparable interaction over several centuries is the only way to appreciate both the significance of what happened during those centuries and their profound relevance today. Frances Young's achievement is not only to guide readers on that journey through the formative centuries of what is now the world's largest religion, but also, especially in *God's Presence: A Contemporary Recapitulation of Early Christianity*, to give an example of how learning from those centuries can inspire an analogous coinherence of scripture and doctrine for our century. But to be in a position to understand and assess her achievement it is essential to engage with the particularities of her work, in both its historical and its contemporary aspects. The centuries covered in the current work deserve the hours of slow reading and reflection that the two volumes demand.

A Third Culmination: Augustine, the Future of the Text, and the Christian Future

Both volume 1 and volume 2 conclude with reflections on major texts of Augustine. In volume 1, *Teaching Christianity*, Augustine's summative discussion of the interpretation of scripture, is the theme; in volume 2 it is his *The Trinity*. Augustine emerges as a consummate practitioner and creative developer of the coinherence of doctrine and scripture, exemplifying Frances Young's decisive verdict:

Surely the burden of these two volumes has been that the doctrinal articulation of scripture's overall meaning was both vital and valid, and the continuing identity of Christianity depends upon our capacity to embrace this coinherence. It is from this reading that the one God comes to be identified as Father, Son, and Holy Spirit, the three names into which every believer is baptized. At the end of *The Trinity*, Augustine prays: "Directing my attention toward this rule of faith as best as I could, as far as you enabled me to, I have sought you and desired to see intellectually what I have believed."[12]

Augustine prayed these words as his civilization faced collapse, and his "doctrinal articulation of scripture's overall meaning" was to prove formative and generative for many, not only during the coming traumas of his own civilization, but also during later centuries. One of Frances Young's hermeneutical concepts for such generativity is "the future of the text," and she argues for the wisdom and appropriateness of the ways in which the future of the biblical text was, through much debate, trial, and error, opened up during these centuries, not least by Augustine. Her detailed discussion of elements in his writing (such as his use of allegory, proof-texting, and christological reading of the Old Testament), which have in recent centuries been seen as most problematic, is integrated into a robust justification of his central concern with the overarching scriptural narrative. For him, and for Frances Young, the Bible rings truest when it is read in line with the conclusions of both volume 1, where the decisive interpretative guidelines in *Teaching Christianity* are love of God and love of neighbor, and volume 2, where the decisive guidelines in *The Trinity* are the rule of faith; who Jesus Christ is— incarnate, crucified, resurrected; and who God is—Father, Son, and Holy Spirit. Doctrine and scripture are complementary ways of attending to the truth.

Frances Young, too, writes and prays in a century facing massive civilizational challenges, to several of which she has responded theologically and prophetically. In the midst of these challenges, Christian churches easily lose touch with the depths of scripture, as opened up through those guidelines. But Augustine by no means has the last word, and the future of the Bible needs to be opened up afresh—continually, critically, and creatively. In the final chapter of volume 2, her retrieval of Augustine leads into three further "words" that together offer a Christian wisdom for the twenty-first century.

The launchpad is the hypothesis that Augustine's "distinction between 'intellectual cognisance of eternal things' and 'rational cognisance of temporal things' might perhaps anticipate the kind of insight we need to both characterize and close the gap . . . between doctrine and scripture."

---

12. Chapter 6 of volume 2.

First, she gives a fascinating autobiographical account of three stages in the intellectual journey toward her present position on how to describe and how to close that gap. She begins in the 1970s with her strongly historical-critical contribution to *The Myth of God Incarnate*. Next, in the 1990s, comes her interrelation of the historical-critical approach with a more synthesizing, imaginative mindset, as in her inaugural lecture, "The Critic and the Visionary." Then, in the early twenty-first century, the neuroscientist, psychiatrist, and philosopher Iain McGilchrist helps to stimulate a fuller integration of analysis and synthesis, as seen in *God's Presence: A Contemporary Recapitulation of Early Christianity*. The gap is closed when rational knowledge both is affirmed and becomes wisdom.

The second "word" (the final one in the final chapter) is worship. There she finds the performance of the coinherence of doctrine and scripture and the lived reality of transcending any gap between them. The final subheading, "Worship: Where Scripture and Doctrine Truly Coinhere," brings her to the heart of her own tradition: "At this point my Methodist self cannot resist the temptation to demonstrate how deeply both scripture and the doctrines of incarnation and Trinity are embedded in the hymns of Charles Wesley."

Yet that is not all. The demonstration of her position through verses from some profound, little-known hymns of Charles Wesley overflows into three remarkable meditations, one "after Augustine," one "after Augustine with McGilchrist," and the last "after Augustine, with Gregory Nyssen." They are an invitation to readers to enter more and more deeply, wisely, and wholeheartedly into what the two volumes have opened up—that is, into who Jesus Christ is; who God is; and the truth, goodness, and beauty in God and created by God. It is a daring, doxological culmination:

> *Father, we adore you, lay our lives before you, how we love you.*
> *Jesus, we adore you, lay our lives before you, how we love you.*
> *Spirit, we adore you, lay our lives before you, how we love you.*[13]

DAVID F. FORD

---

13. Terrye Coelho (1972).

Preface

Many of my books over the years have been responses to requests, and these two volumes on *Doctrine and Scripture in Early Christianity* are no exception. This particular project I have come to welcome wholeheartedly. It has afforded me several new insights along the way as I have pulled together the threads of the major interests of my research career. Doctrinal interests long since sidetracked my PhD thesis from its original proposal to explore early Christian exegesis of Hebrews, while at a later stage my appointment to teach New Testament studies drew me back to focussing on the church fathers' approach to biblical hermeneutics. So the request to consider how they understood the relationship between doctrine and scripture could hardly have been more apposite. Yet this request came when I thought my final work had been completed—without it there is no doubt these volumes would never have been conceived, let alone undertaken. I have reason to be grateful to James Ernest for his suggestion and his persistence.

Barely had I begun work on the project when the COVID-19 pandemic struck and other commitments closed down—time and opportunity seemed given, yet the closures included libraries, of course. So I have largely been reliant on the resources I have personally assembled over the years, with occasional more recent brief forays to check references once the library world opened up again. I hope these circumstances have not had a detrimental effect on the result by causing me to miss significant and pertinent discussions of which account should have been taken.

I have in any case largely worked directly from key early Christian writings. Most of the texts discussed are available in translation, no doubt an advantage for that part of my potential readership whose focus is on the current theological implications of these matters as distinct from early Christian studies as such. I am particularly grateful to David Ford, Emeritus Regius Professor of Theology in the University of Cambridge, UK, for undertaking to write the foreword. This will, I hope, encourage that wider theological constituency to engage with this account of how in those formative years Christian doctrine came to be articulated simply because of the passionate need to make sense of the scriptures and their teaching within the intellectual frameworks available in the culture of the Greco-Roman world. To clarify the process whereby doctrine expressed what scripture was about, while scripture provided doctrinal proof, is surely relevant to efforts in our own time to engage in a similar intellectual journey in a profoundly different intellectual context. Christians have always searched the Bible for answers to questions, metaphysical or ethical, to which the books of the Bible give no obvious, clear, or consistent response without deduction, debate, and argument, and it is that process and its outcome in the formative early centuries that claims our attention in these volumes.

With the appeal to scripture at the center of attention, volume 2 will concentrate on the crucial controversies that contributed to the formation of the doctrine of the Trinity and classic Christology, focusing largely on the period from Nicaea to Chalcedon. This initial volume will first trace the sociocultural context in which "dogma," "doctrine," and even books took on an importance in Christianity largely unprecedented in other religions of antiquity (books and their interpretation lay at the core of Judaism, of course, but not doctrine as such). Then certain determinative doctrinal fundamentals that were arrived at before the end of the second century will be identified. Finally, it will sketch the trajectory from searching for the truth embedded in scripture, together with a certain acceptance of intellectual inquiry, to increasing anxiety as to where that inquiry might lead and the advent of an ecclesial mindset to which the common English usage of "dogmatic" becomes appropriate.

Ultimately we seek on this journey to move beyond the estrangement between doctrine and scripture brought about by modernity and the historico-critical method, so as to rediscover how scripture and doctrine have the kind of theological coinherence that the fathers of the church attributed to them.

FRANCES M. YOUNG
Birmingham, UK
December 2022

Abbreviations

The abbreviations of biblical books follow the conventions established in the *SBL Handbook of Style*, second edition.

Ancient and Late Antique Sources

1 Clem. 1 Clement

Alcinous
Did. *The Handbook of Platonism*

Athanasius
C. Gent. *Against the Pagans*
Inc. *On the Incarnation*

Athenagoras
Leg. *Embassy for Christians*
Res. *On the Resurrection*

Augustine
Civ. *The City of God*
Doctr. chr. *Teaching Christianity*
Gen. imp. *On the Literal Interpretation of Genesis*
Gen. Man. *On Genesis against the Manichaeans*
Retract. *Retractations*

Basil

De Spir.   On the Holy Spirit
Ep.   Letters

Clement of Alexandria

Strom.   Miscellanies

Cyprian

Unit. eccl.   The Unity of the Catholic Church

Cyril of Alexandria

Comm. Jo.   Commentary on John

Cyril of Jerusalem

Cat. orat.   Catechetical Homilies
Procat.   Procatechesis

Ephrem

Hymn. eccl.   Hymns on the Church

Epiphanius

Anc.   Ancoratus
Pan.   Panarion

Eusebius

Hist. eccl.   Ecclesiastical History

Gos. Truth   Gospel of Truth (Nag Hammadi)

Gregory of Nanzianus

Orat.   Theological Orations

Gregory of Nyssa

De hom.   On the Making of Humankind

Herm. Mand.   Shepherd of Hermas, Mandate

Hippolytus

Haer.   Refutation of All Heresies
Trad. ap.   Apostolic Tradition

Ignatius

Ign. *Eph.*	*To the Ephesians*
Ign. *Phld.*	*To the Philadelphians*
Ign. *Smyrn.*	*To the Smyrnaeans*
Ign. *Trall.*	*To the Trallians*

Irenaeus

Epid.	*Demonstration of the Apostolic Preaching*
Haer.	*Against Heresies*

Josephus

Ant.	*Jewish Antiquities*
C. Ap.	*Against Apion*

Justin Martyr

1 Apol.	*1 Apology*
Dial.	*Dialogue with Trypho*

Maximus of Tyre

Dis.	*Dissertations*
Or.	*Philosophical Orations*

Melito of Sardis

Pasch.	*On Pascha*

Methodius

Sym.	*Symposium*

Origen

Cels.	*Against Celsus*
Comm. Jo.	*Commentary on John*
Hom. Sam.	*Homilies on Samuel*
Hom. Matt.	*Homilies on Matthew*
Princ.	*First Principles*

Plutarch

An. procr.	*On the Generation of the Soul in the Timaeus*
Def. orac.	*On the Failure of Oracles*
E Delph.	*The E at Delphi*

Is. Os.	*On Isis and Osiris*
Pyth. orac.	*The Oracles at Delphi*

Tertullian

Herm.	*Against Hermogenes*
Marc.	*Against Marcion*
Nat.	*To the Heathen*

Theophilus

Autol.	*To Autolycus*

SECONDARY SOURCES

ANF	*Ante-Nicene Fathers*
BETL	Bibliotheca Ephemeridum Theologicarum Lovaniensium
CCSG	Corpus Christianorum: Series Graeca
CCSL	Corpus Christianorum: Series Latina
CSEL	Corpus Scriptorum Ecclesiasticorum Latinorum
FC	Fathers of the Church Series
GCS(NF)	Die griechischen christlichen Schriftsteller der ersten [drei] Jahrhunderte (Neue Folge)
JEH	*Journal of Ecclesiastical History*
JSNT	*Journal for the Study of the New Testament*
JTS	*Journal of Theological Studies*
LCL	Loeb Classical Library
LXX	Septuagint
NHC	Nag Hammadi Codices
NPNF	*Nicene and Post-Nicene Fathers*
OECT	Oxford Early Christian Texts
PG	Patrologia Graeca [= Patrologiae Cursus Completus: Series Graeca]. Edited by Jacques-Paul Migne. 162 vols. Paris, 1857–1886
PTS	Patristische Texte und Studien
SC	Sources Chrétiennes
SJT	*Scottish Journal of Theology*
StPatr	Studia Patristica
VCSup	Supplements to Vigiliae Christianae
WUNT	Wissenschaftliche Untersuchungen zum Neuen Testament

Doctrine and Scripture

MUTUALLY COINHERENT? WHAT ARE THE PROBLEMS?

1. A Widening Gap?

It was an illuminating moment. At a session of the weekend course in theology once run by the Centre for Black and White Christian Partnership,[1] the pastor of a black-led Pentecostal church was presenting the doctrine of his "Jesus only" tradition. As one of the tutors of the course, I was in the audience. In the "Jesus only" or "Oneness" Pentecostal tradition, baptism is performed in the name of Jesus, as attested in the book of Acts, rather than in the name of the Father, the Son, and the Holy Spirit, as directed in Matthew 28:19. During this presentation this practice was being justified doctrinally: there is only one God, one divine Spirit, variously revealed as Father and Son, but essentially *one*. Polemically framed against a Trinitarianism that seemed tritheistic, this modalist position was argued for, and grounded in, key biblical texts: Isaiah 44:6—"I am the first and the last, and besides me there is no other," and John 10:30—"I and the Father are one," not to mention the first commandment—"I am the Lord your God . . . you shall have no other gods before me" (Exod 20:2; Deut 5:6–7).

As I listened, I realized that I was hearing in late twentieth-century England a replay of arguments that raged in the mid-third century when Monarchians insisted on the oneness of the sole Sovereign, the sole first principle, the one God known as Father and also revealed as Word and Spirit. Furthermore, the exact same appeal was being made to the exact same scripture texts. Doctrine

---

1. A course run at the Selly Oak Colleges, Birmingham UK, and leading to a Certificate in Theology under the auspices of the University of Birmingham School of Continuing Education.

concerning the nature of God was emerging from scripture through a process of deductive argument. The assumption was that scripture and doctrine were coinherent and mutually consistent, and that scripture could substantiate as truth those theological propositions. Yet, from the point of view of what became the mainstream Christian doctrine of the Trinity, the theological outcome in the case of both the Monarchians and my Pentecostal student was the wrong and, indeed, a heretical position, a point all the more telling since the mainstream Christian view also deduced doctrine from biblical texts and presumed that scripture and doctrine were coinherent, mutually consistent, and could substantiate theological propositions as truth.

Given the fact that, using the same procedures and resting on the same assumptions, rival dogmatic constructions could and can be argued from scripture, the relationship between the two must surely be regarded as not entirely self-evident. Tracing in the early church the complexity of the interaction and tension between scripture and doctrine, between dogmatic argument and biblical hermeneutics, is one object of this work. For the notion that the relationship involves straightforward development from Gospel narrative to creedal affirmation can hardly be sustained in the face of such rival outcomes.

Furthermore, the problem of the relationship between scripture and doctrine has been markedly exacerbated by the rise of historical consciousness and modern biblical criticism. No New Testament scholar would now assert that there is anything quite like the doctrine of the Trinity in the New Testament, nor would any New Testament author recognize talk about the two natures of Christ. Just as we have to acknowledge that our world is very different from past worlds, so we need to recognize that the thought-forms of fourth- and fifth-century gentile Christians were far removed from those of first-century Jewish followers of Jesus. Conceptual changes through movement from one culture to another or one era to another must mean a gap of some sort between later Christian doctrine and the scriptures on which it purportedly rests. The wedge was driven even deeper by Maurice Wiles's suggestion that "the existence of a basic outline of doctrine, related, of course, to the Scriptures but existing now *in its own right in practical independence of them*" (my italics) was what enabled "the church to come to terms with a thoroughgoing critical treatment of the Scriptures."

> In the faith of Nicaea and of Chalcedon belief in God the Father, the incarnation and saving work of the Son, the reality of the Holy Spirit's presence in church and sacrament and Christian believer, the substance of the church's

faith seemed able to dwell secure and unscathed, whatever the scholars might discover in the course of their critical investigations of the Bible.[2]

The gap, it would seem, has been widening.

2. The Developmental Model

The gap has been bridged, for a century and more, by the developmental model; if that "basic outline of doctrine" was there in germ in the New Testament, then tracing the story of doctrinal development could plug the gap, the embryonic character of New Testament theology becoming apparent from the perspective of later doctrine.

However, the fact is that two opposing evaluations of the process of development have held the field since the mid-nineteenth century. One emphasizes implicit continuity from the beginning, the seeds of later dogma already being inherent in the earliest *kerygma*. John Henry Cardinal Newman represents this approach. His *Essay on the Development of Christian Doctrine* was pioneering, though often treated with a certain suspicion, not least because his essay coincided with his conversion to Roman Catholicism in 1845. As such, his aim was apologetic and his argument affirmed the Roman Church as the one faithful outcome of the process. But he did produce a "theory" of development, and his basic premise that later doctrine is already latent in the earliest Christian material surely undergirded the confidence of which Maurice Wiles wrote.

Exploring first the way in which big "ideas" develop within the mind of individuals and take hold of a society, Newman then applies this model to Christianity, regarding it as such an "idea." What he meant by "idea" seems to include a whole complex of concepts, beliefs, and practices—one might almost compare it to the development of a *Zeitgeist*. Ironically, Newman unconsciously reveals himself as embedded in the nineteenth century *Zeitgeist* in which evolutionary and developmental notions were affecting the study of both biology and history.

For Newman, "the church's creed and rite are the complete, if inadequate and symbolic, expression of the eternal 'idea' of Christianity."[3] Yet, "his de-

---

2. Maurice Wiles, "Looking into the Sun," in *Working Papers in Doctrine* (London: SCM, 1976), 148–63.
3. Nicholas Lash, *Newman on Development: The Search for an Explanation in History* (London: Sheed and Ward, 1975), 59.

scription of doctrinal history takes into account its dialectical nature" for "a living 'idea' becomes many, yet remains one."[4] In other words, there are variations, and perversions or corruptions can seem much like such variations. Indeed, perversions can even arise from a conservative refusal to move on rather than "changing in order to remain the same," for "here below to live is to change, and to be perfect is to have changed often." But the whole point is to discern "true" development where the fundamental "idea" remains essentially the same in that it is still based on the same principles. Newman explores seven tests for such "true" development, as the essential "idea" interacts with different circumstances and societies. "All parties appeal to Scripture, that is, argue from Scripture; but argument implies deduction, that is, development." "All bodies of Christians develop the doctrines of Scripture." "Luther's view of justification had never been stated in words before his time."[5]

So, the "fact" of development is an alternative hypothesis to "immutability" or "corruption."[6] "Homogeneous evolution" as the ideal encourages the use of organic language: the growth of doctrine arises from its vitality or its "life," its seeds in scripture, its fruit in later creeds and definitions.[7] Time is necessary for all this to unfold,[8] but the whole circle of doctrine is in some sense already present from the beginning of Christianity; from the first stage of Christianity its teaching "looked towards" or "tended towards" the teaching of the later period, even as obscurities were clarified and dogmatic statements elaborated.[9] Traces of the development to come can be found in the early period, and Newman takes it for granted that the process of its elaboration in the history of the church is the fruit of meditation on scripture.[10]

However, for Newman scripture is basic but also problematic. Not only can its interpretation give rise to many different opinions, but its "structure and style" is "so unsystematic and various," "so figurative and indirect," that "it cannot, as it were, be mapped, or its contents catalogued"; it must remain for us forever "an unexplored and unsubdued land, with heights and valleys, forests and streams, on the right and left of our path and close about us, full

---

4. Lash, *Newman*, 33.

5. John Henry Newman, *An Essay on the Development of Christian Doctrine*, Pelican Classics (1845; repr. Harmondsworth: Penguin, 1974). Quotations in this paragraph from 119–22, 131, and 150. Cf. Lash, *Newman*, 251.

6. Lash, *Newman*, 56.

7. Lash, *Newman*, 71.

8. Newman, *Essay on Development*, 90. Cf. Lash, *Newman*, chapter 5.

9. Newman *Essay on Development*, 188–89. Cf. Lash, *Newman*, 103.

10. Lash, *Newman*, 90.

of concealed wonders and choice treasures."[11] So we depend on the fourth and fifth centuries:

> As to Scripture, former centuries certainly do not speak distinctly . . . but still we see in them, as we believe, an ever-growing tendency and approximation to that full agreement which we find in the fifth.
>
> Indeed, all doctrines together are "members of one family, suggestive, or correlative or confirmatory, or illustrative of each other," making up "one integral religion."[12]

Scripture, then, is not in itself adequate as a guide, liable as it is to be "read in contrary ways." Yet, the whole Bible is written on the principle of development: prophecies, indeed, are "pregnant texts," while the parables of leaven, or seeds and growth, anticipate Christianity's progressive expansion "through the use of reflection, argument and original thought."[13] Indeed:

> the divines of the Church are in every age engaged in regulating themselves by Scripture, appealing to Scripture in proof of their conclusions, and exhorting and teaching in the thoughts and language of Scripture. Scripture may be said to be the medium in which the mind of the Church has energized and developed.[14]

So, despite its problematic nature as a guide, meditation on scripture is what gives rise to doctrine.

As noted, the key thing for Newman is how to identify true versus false doctrinal development. In the end, however, despite his recounting of many examples that illustrate his seven tests for true development, this is not really worked out through textual proofs or logical argument, but on the basis of his assumption of providential continuity upheld by proper authority. So, unless one accepts his conclusion (i.e., conversion to Rome), the problem of the relationship between doctrine and scripture remains ultimately unresolved. Traces of future doctrine may be identifiable in the New Testament in hindsight, but there is a real possibility that finding them involves projecting back those later conceptions onto apparently similar language. So the ques-

---

11. Newman, *Essay on Development*, 162.
12. Newman, *Essay on Development*, 188, 198–99.
13. Newman, *Essay on Development*, 155, 163–64.
14. Newman, *Essay on Development*, 336–37.

tion remains: do those classic doctrines actually reflect the implications of the New Testament?[15]

Doctrines were, indeed, deduced through exegesis of biblical texts, honed in debate and argument, and then given liturgical expression. But doctrines constitute "discourse," and discourse surely does not develop as an oak tree grows from an acorn—propositions and concepts do not organically "evolve" from a "primitive" form to one more mature. Just as Platonism shaped the intellectual context in the days of Origen, so evolutionary models are now all-pervasive and we need to name our culturally determined presuppositions. They may conspire with those who want a teleological—even providential—account of the emergence of Christian doctrine, or conversely with those who would like to treat Christian doctrine as historically relative, but surely they obscure the reality that doctrine arose out of discourse and argument. Doctrines were the result of trying to make sense of scripture, of reading scriptural texts with particular questions in mind, those questions often being entirely new issues:

> questions generated by the socio-political and cultural-philosophical context in which early church leaders and thinkers found themselves. To that extent it is a conceptual superstructure built on the foundations of the New Testament. Rather than using organic models we need to take yet more seriously the dialectical process of shaping the building blocks, and the factors which contributed to that shaping.[16]

To undertake this task is to be disturbed. There are several reasons for this. The first is that Christian doctrine begins to look as if it might simply be the product of particular cultural pressures—the Neoplatonic Trinity, for example, parallels the Christian Trinity and is a response to many of the same intellectual questions. Second, the reading of scripture on which the eventual doctrinal edifice depends is profoundly different from anything modern scholars would regard as valid. Newman himself asserts that the mystical or allegorical interpretation of scripture is vital, indeed, "one of the characteristic conditions or principles on which the development of doctrine has proceeded."[17] System-

---

15. The following two paragraphs reflect my discussion in "The Trinity and the New Testament," in *The Nature of New Testament Theology: Essays in Honour of Robert Morgan*, ed. Christopher Rowland and Christopher Tuckett (Oxford: Blackwell, 2006), 286–305.
16. Young, "Trinity and New Testament," 288.
17. Newman, *Essay on Development*, 336.

atic theology today, by simply accepting the traditions of Christian doctrine and trying to make them intellectually plausible in our (post)modern world, conveniently overlooks the shaky foundation on which the doctrinal tradition rests, at least from the point of view of the different intellectual world in which we operate and our very different estimate of what constitutes valid interpretation. Third, as my opening anecdote reveals, it is not inconceivable that an entirely different outcome could have held the field.

3. Hellenization of the Gospel

So what about the other long-standing way of approaching the development of doctrine? Taking historical relativity to the extreme, one might say, this approach argued that dogma was the outcome of the Hellenization of the simple gospel, thus appearing to sever the connection between scripture and doctrine. This view was the conclusion of Adolf von Harnack in his multivolume *History of Dogma*, first published in 1885.[18] Interestingly, Harnack did not claim that Neoplatonism had a *direct* influence on the "ecclesiastical dogmatic," but this was because Christianity "already possessed the fundamental features of its theology," having developed these "contemporaneously and independent of Neoplatonism" (Harnack 1:358–59). "Living faith" was "transformed into a creed to be believed," into doctrine based on "the philosophic spirit of the Greeks," through "the detachment of the Gospel from the Jewish Church" (Harnack 1:45–46). The burden of his argument is that "in these later dogmas an entirely new element has entered into the conception of religion"; indeed, "dogma in its conception and development is a work of the Greek spirit on the soil of the Gospel" (Harnack 1:17). "Biblical theology is not the presupposition of the history of dogma" (Harnack 1:51).

It was Gnosticism that Harnack famously named "the acute secularizing or Hellenizing of Christianity." Indeed, the gnostics were the "theologians of the 1st century," "the first to transform Christianity into a system of doctrines (dogmas), and the first to work up tradition systematically" (Harnack 1:226–27). Opposition to the gnostics was the catalyst: tradition and philosophy aided Irenaeus, Tertullian, and Hippolytus in their opposition to Gnosticism, from which "they undoubtedly learnt very much." As Harnack continues to write:

---

18. Adolf von Harnack, *History of Dogma*, trans. Neil Buchanan et al., 3rd ed., 7 vols. (London: Williams and Norgate, 1894–1898). Hereafter in this section, page references to this work will appear in the text.

If we define ecclesiastical dogmas as propositions handed down in the creed of the Church, shown to exist in the Holy Scriptures of both Testaments, and rationally reproduced and formulated, then they [Irenaeus, Tertullian and Hippolytus] were the first to set up dogmas—dogmas but no system of dogmatics. (Harnack 1:9).

The development of Logos-theology in response to Gnosticism was what hastened doctrinal development, according to Harnack, though it did not give a new direction. For, of course, "the essential premises for the development of Catholicism were already in existence" before Gnosticism—"the great Apostle to the Gentiles himself . . . transplanted the Gospel into Greek modes of thought" (Harnack 1:216–17). It was the apologists, however, in their attempt "to represent the Christian religion as a philosophy, and to convince outsiders that it was the highest wisdom and the absolute truth" (Harnack 2:170) who produced "on the basis of the Logos doctrine" a Christianity "conceived and formulated from the standpoint of the Greek philosophy of religion" (Harnack 2:14) with revelation and *dogmata* at its heart.[19] We cannot here follow through the whole story Harnack tells, but as one reads his account of the fourth- and fifth-century debates, it becomes clear that the contradictions he identifies in, for example, the works of Arius and Athanasius have their roots in this earlier adoption of Logos-cosmology, the initial Hellenizing move.[20] As a result of what the apologists did, Greek philosophy "was to attain victory and permanence by the aid of Christianity," while Christianity became "heir to antiquity," and "the specific content of traditional Christianity" was "thoroughly neutralized" (Harnack 2:172, 200–201). Later, Harnack describes Clement of Alexandria as the one through whom "the highest philosophy of the Greeks was placed under the protection and guarantee of the Church, and the whole Hellenic civilization was thus at the same time legitimized within Christianity" (Harnack 2:328).

Nevertheless, the Greek spirit "never became quite master of the situation; it was obliged to accommodate itself to it," "it" being a Christianity that had to be "in harmony with the rule of faith and the canon of New Testament Scriptures" (Harnack 2:8–9). This too was a response to Gnosticism. Harnack's initial contrast between Gnosticism and Catholic Christianity focuses on their respective rejection or conservation of the Old Testament (Harnack 1:226). Yet, "the authority of Holy Scripture frequently appears in the Fathers as some-

---

19. See chapter 4 of volume 2 of Harnack, *Dogma*.
20. See volume 4 of Harnack, *Dogma*.

thing wholly abstract or despotic," he suggests (Harnack 3:207). As one works through Harnack's version of one doctrinal controversy after another, or his interpretation of one theologian after another, it is noticeable how he identifies the extent to which the initial gospel, the rule of faith, and the scriptures are, or are not, overlaid by or transformed into ideas or formulae. Some examples include the following:

1. Harnack suggests that Christianity, defined as knowledge of God, produced "an inability to discover a specific significance for the person of Christ within the sphere of revelation" (Harnack 2:203).
2. Harnack can only give qualified affirmation to the correspondence of the Christianity of Clement of Alexandria to the gospel (Harnack 2:329).
3. "It is of the highest interest to notice how far . . . the speculative interpretation of the Rule of Faith had taken the place of that rule itself," he notes as he quotes the letter to Paul of Samosata from the bishops of Palestine and Syria (Harnack 3:47). Such interpretations may claim to be expounding the faith received from the beginning, but what they then produce "*as 'the faith' and furnished with proofs from Scripture, was the speculative theology*" (italics original), namely, affirmation of God as unbegotten, one, without beginning, unseen, unchangeable, and so on; and of the Son as the Only-begotten, image of the unseen God, firstborn of all creation, wisdom and Word, and power of God, and so on.
4. "Almost every trait which recalls the historical Jesus of Nazareth was erased," he says of Athanasius's position (Harnack 4:45).

Thus Harnack appraises material according to its conformity to the Jesus of history, the gospel, the rule of faith, or the scriptures.

So Harnack, like Newman, betrays a point of view. His program at first sight implies the kind of gap between scripture and subsequent doctrinal development that might be expected of a Protestant, and indeed he does intimate that "the revolution which was characterized by the isolation of the Bible, its deliverance from the authority of ecclesiastical tradition, and the annihilation of the latter, only took place in the 16th century, and even then it was, we know, not completely successful" (Harnack 2:207). Here, then, the thesis of Hellenization apparently serves the Protestant call back to origins, to *sola scriptura*, and in the process shockingly unecumenical assessments (at least from our current perspectives) are made of Eastern Orthodox and Roman Catholic traditions. Yet Harnack's position proves to be even more radical. The prolegomena to the whole project notes that "the dogmas of the fourth and fifth centuries have more influence today in wide circles of Protestant churches, than all the doctrines which are concentrated around justification by faith." Indeed, according to Harnack, "dogma, that is to say, that type of Christianity which was formed in ecclesiastical antiquity, has not yet been suppressed even in Protestant churches, has really not been modified or replaced by a new conception of the Gospel." Yet, "who could further call in question, that, in consequence of the reforming impulse in Protestantism, the way was opened up for a conception which does not identify Gospel and dogma?" (Harnack 1:20). So Protestants are free to reconsider the classic doctrines of the creed and return to the pristine simple gospel. Even scripture, given that its canon was authorized by the institutionalized church, proves not to be the ultimate stopping point in the unpacking of subsequent developments.

So what is this pristine simple gospel that is so quickly overlaid? It is not dogma but a "message," a "form of life," and a "new religion" focused on "the overpowering personality" of Jesus Christ, who leads people into "a new communion with God," and sets forth "in his own person a holy life with God and before God." A message, not a doctrine—but it must surely strike us as basically the nineteenth century liberal Protestant portrait of the Jesus of history, the one who, according to the now conventional characterization, taught "the Fatherhood of God and the brotherhood of man." This approach to the development of doctrine, then, not merely exacerbates the gap between doctrine and scripture, but even truncates scripture for the sake of a particular, questionable historical reconstruction.

It would seem, then, that neither scripture nor creed "is immune from that historicity to which all human grasp of truth is subject,"[21] and the gap between scripture and doctrine is unlikely to be bridged through either of those developmental models. There has, of course, been much research and discussion since those nineteenth-century contributions, but those two basic maps, subsequently nuanced it is true, have endured in early Christian studies. The early twenty-first century has seen John Behr's three-volume work on *The Formation of Christian Theology*[22] take on Harnack from a standpoint that, though Orthodox, is not dissimilar to that of Newman: "It is not the transformation of the primitive Gospel into Greek metaphysics, the development of something not there from the beginning, but is rather the deepening understanding of what is given once and for all."[23]

---

21. Lash, *Newman*, 15.
22. John Behr, *The Formation of Christian Theology*, 3 vols. (Crestwood, NY: St. Vladimir's Seminary Press, 2001–2004).
23. Behr, *Formation*, 1:6–7.

Meanwhile, the twentieth century saw the influence of the Harnackian approach pervade the field of New Testament studies, with the key questions about Judaism and Hellenism, the pre-Christian Hellenization of Judaism, and Gnosticism dominating research and discussion, and all that without mentioning its implicit shaping of such controversial volumes as *The Myth of God Incarnate*.[24] Harnack's general perspective has also been mirrored in the tendency to give primacy to the "experience" of the "fact" of Jesus and the religious response of faith to it, and to turn the development of doctrine into a process whereby a "second order" account was reached. But surely, however far back we go, only "second order" accounts are available.

4. Changed Perspectives

The above comment arises from the way in which postmodernism has shifted perspectives on historical narrative.[25] We now recognize that there are no "facts" without interpretation. History is a narrative construct, which is formed by interpretation, by selection of what is significant, by discernment of cause and effect. In other words, we "create" history by telling the story, and that means the way it is told is affected by our own interests and concerns. Passing on the past, however, usually belongs to a community; it is a social construct related to identity formation. As each generation or interest group "reconstructs" the story, there will be no end to new versions.

Here "create" does not, of course, mean "invent." Reconstructions may be more and less responsible, depending on how far proper attention has been given to the available evidence and how far allowance has been made for potential distortion through prior commitments or inappropriate presuppositions. The past cannot be changed, and anachronism should not appropriate it in such a way that its "pastness" is compromised. This surely was the motivation for the insistence on "fact." The postmodern change in perspective just recognizes that no account will be complete or entirely neutral and that the eyes of different researchers will be caught by different aspects. Indeed, even if a "bare event" were accessible to us, it would have no sense or relevance without context or interpretation.

---

24. John Hick, ed., *The Myth of God Incarnate* (London: SCM, 1977).
25. The following paragraphs reflect my discussion in the introduction to my *The Making of the Creeds* (London: SCM, 1991), in which I explained how the book's perspectives were different from those of Alan Richardson in his *Creeds in the Making* (London: SCM, 1935), the book I had been asked to update.

Nor can experience be separated from the sensemaking process. Experience is captured in the language through which we name things and events, and this language is a social and cultural construct that we learn. This was true for the first Christians too. So response was already involved in their experience of the so-called fact of Jesus—already it was in process of interpretation, and nothing of significance could have been grasped or communicated without it. The formation of doctrine or creed is not therefore second order but rather continuous with forging the community identity grounded in "Jesus-responded-to-and-understood." Encounter with Jesus belonged exclusively neither to the category of religion nor dogma.

Hermeneutics, influenced by the sociology of knowledge as well as by linguistic philosophy and structuralism, has contributed to this change in perspective. It has been observed that we live in "symbolic worlds" mediated by our culture; this makes certain ideas plausible and others implausible. Furthermore, it is not simple and straightforward to differentiate "literal" meaning from "metaphor," "symbol," or "myth," nor to state the "real" meaning of figurative language. How we assess early Christian thought and scriptural exegesis is bound to be affected by this. Somehow we have to enter the world of discourse of that time, the mindset, the assumptions, the mode of argument.

Looking back, we can see that my account of both Harnack and Newman bears out the fact that neither offered a neutral account. No historian is free from presuppositions and prior commitments. However, if possible, we surely could do with a more open reexamination of the relationship between doctrine and scripture in the early church—hopefully, one more ecumenical and less anxious about the outcome. Is it possible to construct a new account of the arguments that produced dogmatic discourse, particularly of the ways in which appeals to scripture functioned as new questions were raised? Can we find another way of telling the story that acknowledges that, in the process of forming a distinct identity, there is inevitable tension between "acculturation"[26] on the one hand and, on the other, self-conscious challenge to the all-pervasive cultural milieu—this challenge, in the case of the early Christians, being grounded in certain key convictions ultimately deriving from scripture? These two volumes on *Doctrine and Scripture in Early Christianity* constitute a perhaps rash attempt to produce such an account. This first book will explore

---

26. It is perhaps worth noting that even though "inculturation" is often used for adopting another culture's norms, it is also used for the natural inculturation of a person growing up, being schooled, etc., in what might be called their own cultural ambience, while "acculturation" refers to the former process of adoption or adaptation to an initially alien culture.

the extent to which doctrine was generated by the need to make sense of scripture, a diverse collection of scrolls or codices with initially ill-defined limits. The second volume will consider the argumentation, especially the appeal to scripture, which over time led to the articulation of the core Christian doctrines of the Trinity and the two natures of Christ. Thus we will endeavor to construct a plausible account of the genesis of doctrine from scripture through the early church's search for a viable biblical hermeneutic.

Then, maybe, through the dynamic of an "ethical reading,"[27] which respects the text while acknowledging the tension between the reader's difference from and identification with the material in view, we may find insights that might affirm or challenge our own hermeneutics and our own use of scripture in doctrinal and ethical debate—after all, as Newman noted, Christians have always engaged in justifying their theological and ethical commitments from scripture. Can we clear a path through early Christian argument by recognizing how the definition of doctrine was a process of making sense of scripture in terms of the rationality of that time? And then, perhaps, make a parallel journey of sensemaking in our very different intellectual context so that secure bridges may again span the perceived gap between doctrine and scripture?

---

27. For "ethical reading," see Frances Young, "The Pastoral Epistles and the Ethics of Reading," *JSNT* 45 (1992): 105–20; and Young, "Allegory and the Ethics of Reading," in *The Open Text: New Directions for Biblical Studies?*, ed. Francis Watson (London: SCM, 1993).

2

Rethinking the Context

THE SCHOOL-LIKE CHARACTER OF EARLY CHRISTIAN GROUPS

We began the first chapter with an illuminating moment. Let me continue by sharing three other such moments:[1]

1. A colleague in classical studies once said to me that understanding religion in the ancient world is a hard task simply because Christianity has so dramatically shifted and shaped our perceptions of what a religion is that it is hard to interpret what material we have, saturated as it is with assumptions we do not share.[2]
2. Something important struck me years ago when reading an old classic, Edwin Hatch's late nineteenth-century work, *The Influence of Greek Ideas on Christianity*.[3] The word "aura" he never actually used but that word seemed to me to capture what he was saying. His point was the profound respect accorded to written texts in antiquity, simply on the grounds that they seemed

---

1. Along with some other points made in this chapter, the incidents I am about to recount I used previously in my article "Books and Their 'Aura': The Functions of Written Texts in Judaism, Paganism and Christianity during the First Centuries CE," in *Religious Identity and the Problem of Historical Foundation: The Foundational Character of Authoritative Sources in the History of Christianity and Judaism*, ed. Judith Frishman, Willemien Otten, and Gerard Rouwhorst (Leiden: Brill, 2004), 535–52; republished in Frances Young, *Ways of Reading Scripture*, WUNT 369 (Tübingen: Mohr Siebeck, 2018), and used again here with permission.

2. I owe this remark to my colleague, Ken Dowden, of the Classics Department in the University of Birmingham; see further his *Religion and the Romans* (London: Duckworth, 1992).

3. This work was republished in 1957 as a Harper Torchbook (New York: Harper and Brothers); Hatch's Hibbert Lectures of 1888 had been edited from the unfinished manuscript by A. M. Fairbairn and published posthumously by Williams and Norgate, London.

to defy mortality. Though no longer present, the absent authors of the past could still speak, and later generations had access to their wisdom. It is well known that in Rome's classical period novelty was suspect and truth was regarded as enshrined in old traditions, so it is hardly surprising how important the ancient written classics were.

3. I was intrigued when a Jewish colleague observed in a seminar how processing the Torah scrolls around the synagogue was comparable to the way an idol would have been processed at pagan festivals.[4] Reflection on that remark provoked observations on Christian practice: such pagan ceremonies must surely be the precursors of not only festivals in which images of the Virgin are processed, but also the way the Gospel is processed and incensed prior to being read in some church traditions (though the latter could, of course, have come about more indirectly via synagogue practice). If so, what are the implications? Does this not suggest that the Torah scrolls or the Gospel, being the word of God in scripture, were in some sense equivalent for Jews or Christians to the presence of the divine in pagan images?

Directly or indirectly, these remarks alert us to certain key features that need to be taken into account as we engage in rethinking the context.

1. Christianity: A Religion or What?

Christianity began life looking less like a religion and more like a school.

At first sight this bald statement might seem surprising. But Jesus gathered disciples (Gk. *mathētai*, "pupils, learners") around him, and when one stops to think about it, *dogma* (Greek) and *doctrina* (Latin) simply mean teaching. The school context is where teaching and learning, together with the reading of books, has always belonged. This was markedly true of education in the ancient world where classical literature provided the very basis of schooling at all levels. The scriptures were a collection of written texts read and studied at Christian gatherings, so surely the centrality in Christianity of scripture together with dogma must derive from such an initial school-like character. That, then, is where we should look to bridge the gap identified in the first chapter, indeed, to uncover the fundamental connection between them.

---

4. This was Dr. Martin Goodman, latterly of the University of Oxford. If I have inadvertently misrepresented his remark, I take full responsibility while acknowledging my source.

It is important to disabuse ourselves of assumptions about schools drawn from our experience in modern societies. In antiquity schools were not institutions. Greek cities did provide salaries for some teachers to offer public education, but the majority of teachers operated on a "freelance" basis, gathering groups of students, with group size depending on their popularity. Their classes might be held in the gymnasium or another public place, or at their own house or some other private location. Classical literature provided the very basis of schooling, beginning with reading and writing with the *grammaticus* and continuing with speech-making, effective argument, and civic virtues with the *rhetor*—all pursued through reading, copying, exegeting, and imitating texts. A pupil might then proceed to some philosopher, so advancing to physics, metaphysics, and ethics, but again focusing on truth found in authoritative texts.[5] When one philosophical teacher followed another as his successor, the word "school" is sometimes used for this continuous succession—the best-known case being the Academy that stemmed from Plato and lasted several centuries. But schooling in general took place in gatherings of pupils around a particular master.

In due course this chapter will consider analogies between ancient schools and early church practices. First, however, we need to indicate how odd early Christianity was in its contemporary social context if considered as a religion. The distinctive Jewish origin of this network of little Christian communities accounts for some of that oddity, but by no means all of it. Conscious as I am of my colleague's remark about the difficulties of understanding religion in antiquity, let me hazard a sketch of religious practice in the ancient Mediterranean world. The anomalous character of Christianity as a religion of "belief" in certain "dogmatic propositions," which were ultimately derived, as they claimed, from written texts (i.e., the scriptures), will then become evident.[6]

Pervading all social life, religion was everywhere.[7] Ancestral or household gods were acknowledged at home by habitual rituals. Trades and clubs honored their own deities with gifts in the hope they would look after their interests. Each city had elected officials and priests responsible for servicing the worship of its divine patrons, with public space dominated by their temples and great public festivals providing occasions for communal rejoicing. Military standards involved religious honors, not to mention the imperial ruler

---

5. See further below in section 4.2.

6. In fact, the anomaly persists. Christianity remains the only major religion to set such store by creeds and doctrines, as noted in my book, *Making of the Creeds*, 1.

7. The following summary reflects chapter 3 of Morna Hooker and Frances Young, *Holiness and Mission: Learning from the Early Church about Mission in the City* (London: SCM, 2010); cf. Dowden, *Religion and the Romans*.

cult, which also affected civil society—cities in Asia Minor would compete in temple-building and offering honors to the Roman emperor.[8] Famous healing shrines attracted people to go and sleep there in the hope of miracle cures or answers to prayer in the form of prescriptions given in dreams. Besides this, all kinds of exotic foreign gods and mystery cults spread around the Roman Empire with promises of benefits for their worshippers, including immortality. People sometimes took out multiple divine insurances, though they would generally be mocked as superstitious. And while critiques of the gods and their myths were offered by intellectuals, in the end they would go along with conventional liturgies because they recognized the importance of religion to society. The Latin word *pietas* (Gk. *eusebeia*) meant respect for gods, rulers, ancestors, even parents, and the conventional practices that expressed that virtue. Religion was not a matter of belief but of the habits and binding duties (the root meaning of the word *religio* lies here) that kept families attached to their ancestral gods and the state bound to the deities that had made Rome great.

Temples, images, altars, sacrifices, offerings (including not just animal sacrifice but firstfruits, olive oil, cakes, libations of wine, etc.), priests, processions, festivals, and feasts (public and private) constituted the normal accoutrements of the multiplicity of religious cults practiced by different ethnic groups across the empire, including the Jews up to 70 CE when the Jerusalem temple was destroyed. Indeed, the indispensability of such things for religion is evidenced by the activities of the late fourth-century emperor Julian, known as the Apostate. Not only did Julian attempt to revive the traditional pagan rites after more than a generation of decline under the increasingly Christianized empire, but he also tried to rebuild the temple at Jerusalem for the Jews so as to undercut Christian supersessionist arguments; implicitly this act is an indication of how Christians were indeed a religious anomaly, for they had eschewed all accepted religious practices.

Christianity, then, was not obviously a religion. Christians had long since been dubbed "atheists" because of their refusal to participate in all the everyday religious activities around which social life revolved. Nor were faith and belief (*pistis* in Greek, *fides* in Latin) particularly religious values:

> Varro, one of the few ancient systematists of religion, categorizes Roman religious matters under priesthoods, holy places, festivals, rituals and gods, but not beliefs. In Cicero's *On the Nature of the Gods* (3.5), the Academic

---

8. On the imperial cult, see S. R. F. Price, *Rituals and Power: The Roman Imperial Cult in Asia Minor* (Cambridge: Cambridge University Press, 1984).

Cotta divides them even more simply into rituals, auspices, and warnings. In his own voice at the start of that work (1.14), Cicero offers a longer list of elements of *religio*, religious observance, which depend on human understanding of the nature of the gods: reverence, piety, holiness, ritual, *fides*, the swearing of oaths, temples, shrines, solemn sacrifices, and auspices. Even this taxonomy, though, is not usually seen as encompassing statements of belief.[9]

Indeed, the presence of *fides* in Cicero's list is generally taken to mean not so much "belief" as "trustworthiness."

So, you could privately think what you liked as long as you carried out the appropriate duties and did not seem to undermine the important social cement and moral sanction such practices helped to sustain.[10] There was no official doctrine or dogma, no belief system or creed, no books exclusively containing religious truth. Collections of oracles were in circulation—clearly they had a religious origin, and they might be consulted for advice about undertaking an operation such as a dangerous journey or going to war, but they were in no sense "official" or particularly associated with any religious practices or institutions. Books of philosophy or revelation might contain religious material, but they circulated through networks or schools and not religious organizations. As literature they carried the culture and offered wisdom; but, for all their "aura," such books belonged to contexts other than religion.

Religion, then, was a plethora of traditional local practices, in the home and family, in clubs and associations, in the civic arena, at regional holy sites, all deeply embedded in various ancient ethnic customs, yet embraced within the Roman imperial framework. Rome respected the ancestral religions of the peoples over which it ruled, including that of the Jews. Ethnicity and antiquity guaranteed the respectability of a religion. Christianity stood outside those criteria, and furthermore lured people away from their proper religious obligations whether Jewish or otherwise. In other words, Christians were an anomaly in the social world of the Roman Empire's cities. One imperial edict reflects the difficulty of categorizing them by calling them a nation (*ethnos*), then a superstition (*deisidaimonia*), and then a cult (*thrēskeia*).[11] They simply

---

9. Teresa Morgan, *Roman Faith and Christian Faith: Pistis and Fides in the Early Roman Empire and Early Churches* (Oxford: Oxford University Press, 2015), 125–26.

10. Cicero, *De natura deorum* is the classic exposition of this view. For the Latin text and English translation, see H. Rackham, trans., *On the Nature of the Gods: Academics*, LCL (Cambridge: Harvard University Press, 1933).

11. Eusebius, *Hist. eccl.* 9.9; noted by Martin Goodman, *Mission and Conversion: Proselytizing in the Religious History of the Roman Empire* (Oxford: Clarendon, 1994).

did not fit obvious categories, though Christians did combine several to some degree. Embracing the nickname the "third race," they belonged neither to the polytheistic majority nor to the exception that proved the rule—the Jewish community, which would not compromise or conform on ancient and traditional grounds.[12]

Christianity was not obviously a religion at all—and its eventual success not only displaced other religious practices but also modified forever the understanding of what religion is, as my colleague indicated. Its claim to teach the truth, along with its attachment to scripture, made it much more like a philosophical school. But it was not entirely alone in that: in being school-like, Christian *ekklēsiai* were anticipated by Jewish *synagōgai*.

2. Synagogues and Schools

Up until the destruction of the Temple in 70 CE Jewish rites were comparable to those of other peoples: sacrifices took place at a temple, to which Jews would make special pilgrimages for festivals. But given there was just the one and only temple in Jerusalem, the local synagogue had become the locus of everyday cultural and religious life for Jews.[13] Here prayer and the reading of books replaced the usual religious practices, such as the offering of sacrifice.

Assimilation of the gods of Greeks, Egyptians, Romans, and others had been occurring over several centuries.[14] Such syncretism had its positive aspects, tending as it did to unify the polytheisitc religious landscape into a philosophy of a single divine Being to which the pluralism of religious practices pointed in different ways. The trouble with Judaism was its exclusiveness and refusal to participate in such practices. Nothing that implied apostasy from their one God could be countenanced by loyal Jews, and they cherished their distinct identity through the practice of circumcision and adherence to Torah.[15]

---

12. Tertullian, *Nat.* 1.8; cf. "Excursus: Christians as a Third Race" in Adolf von Harnack, *The Mission and Expansion of Christianity in the First Three Centuries*, trans. James Moffatt (London: Williams and Norgate, 1908), 266–78.

13. The bibliography on the synagogue is vast. There is useful material and bibliography in Emil Schürer, *The History of the Jewish People in the Age of Jesus Christ*, ed. Geza Vermes, Fergus Millar, and Matthew Black, rev. ed. (Edinburgh: T&T Clark, 1979), and Lee I. Levine, *The Ancient Synagogue: The First Thousand Years* (New Haven: Yale University Press, 2000).

14. This section reflects my article, "Books and Their 'Aura,'" cited above in note 1.

15. For an overview, see Lee I. Levine, *Judaism and Hellenism in Antiquity* (Peabody: Hendrickson, 1998). See also the large bibliography in volume 2 of Schürer, *History*.

Jews were respected by some ancient people; through their commitment to monotheism and morality they came to be seen as philosophers.[16] Accepted as an ethnic group with their own proper ancient practices and so having as much right to preserve their traditions under Roman law as any other people, their position was strengthened by a treaty made between Rome and the Maccabees against the Syrian Hellenistic dynasty.[17] However, living alongside other citizens in the diaspora, their refusal to assimilate could be found disturbing. Especially in Alexandria, but by no means exclusively, Jews found themselves faced with anti-Semitism and subject to riot and pogrom.[18]

The community gathering place would function as school as well as prayer center, the reading of books being essential to both. Literacy seems to have been more widespread among Jews, and synagogues are compared to schools by Josephus as well as Philo. Indeed, Josephus states that the weekly meeting on the Sabbath was for "the learning of our customs and Law."[19] For, just as the classics preserved Greek culture and traditions, so Jewish customs and culture were enshrined in books. But Jewish writings were sacred, having a religious role such that, when deprived of access to the temple, the actual practice of sacrifice might be replaced by reading about it or by spiritualizing it in fasting, prayer, and meditation.[20] Indeed, God's word was in the Torah, and as the teaching of their God its precepts were to be practiced. So it was vital to read and reproduce the Torah accurately; a Greco-Roman reader might speak from memory, but for the ritual reading of Torah eyes were always on the text, and there was tight control over its reproduction—it was always done by meticulous copying from a master roll, never by dictation.[21] It was an act of piety to study Torah; to follow its commandments was to obey God. The word *nomos* (law) was used to translate "Torah" into Greek, and that carried the implication that Moses was parallel to someone like Solon, the legendary Athenian lawgiver who provided a constitution and legal code for his people. Torah, however, also meant revelation more widely. The ritual reading of scripture enabled

---

16. Aristotle is the most frequently cited case; cf. Josephus, *C. Ap.* 1.176–182.

17. Schürer, *History*, 1:171–72.

18. H. I. Bell, *Jews and Christians in Egypt* (London: British Museum, 1924).

19. Harry Y. Gamble, *Books and Readers in the Early Church: A History of Early Christian Texts* (New Haven: Yale University Press, 1995), 191, quoting Josephus, *Ant.* 16.43.

20. See Frances M. Young, *The Use of Sacrificial Ideas in Greek Christian Writers from the New Testament to John Chrysostom*, Patristic Monograph Series 5 (Cambridge: The Philadelphia Patristic Foundation, 1979).

21. Gamble, *Books and Readers*, 78.

encounter with God, the hearing of God's word in a direct way. So, the scrolls themselves acquired "aura"—indeed, holiness—within synagogue worship, and a permanent architectural feature for housing the scrolls, known as the "ark of holiness," would eventually replace the moveable chest of books.[22]

Interpretation, however, was essential. In synagogue schools, the young would learn to read the unpointed Hebrew text in the accustomed way, and that in itself carried not just the customary chant but the traditional construal of the text. Also in the course of the Sabbath service, a Targum (an interpretative translation) and possibly a homily would be offered. It seems likely, however, that in the context of the Hellenistic diaspora often only the Greek version of the scriptures was read. Furthermore, the methods of Hellenistic scholarship were exploited by Jewish scholars. Philo is the obvious case, but rabbinic techniques also seem to have been developed under Hellenistic influence. True, the extent to which that is the case is debated, but one may admit that Jewish interpretation had ancient traditional roots while also acknowledging that its Hellenistic environment led to a certain systematization of those traditions in a rationalistic way.[23] This influence affected not just the rules of exegesis: parallels are found in the development of similar systems of critical marks, and Hellenistic works concerned with the interpretation of dreams parallel the techniques of haggadah. Games like gematria, whereby symbolic meanings were derived from the numeric value of letters, along with other tricks for deciphering riddles, were apparently very old, but it was under the influence of the Greeks that they became systematized.[24]

Jewish apologists made parallels between Jewish groups such as Sadducees, Pharisees, and the Essenes and the philosophical *haireseis* (Gk. options): Platonism, Stoicism, Epicureanism, and so on. They also presented their own literature as having parallel genres to those of the Greeks: law books, history, poetry, collections of oracles, and books of wisdom and philosophy. Inter-

---

22. Gamble, *Books and Readers*, 190–91.

23. Regarding this debate, see Karlfried Froehlich, *Biblical Interpretation in the Early Church* (Philadelphia: Fortress, 1984), 4. With respect to the middot (the exegetical rules that guided Jewish exegetical traditions), Daube is said by Froehlich to have "convincingly argued that all these rules reflect the logic and methods of Hellenistic grammar and forensic rhetoric." Cf. David Daube, "Rabbinic Methods of Interpretation and Hellenistic Rhetoric," *Hebrew Union College Annual* 22 (1949): 239–64. That position is, however, somewhat more extreme than that of Saul Lieberman, *Hellenism in Jewish Palestine* (New York: Jewish Theological Seminary of America, 1950), though there is a sense in which they reached a somewhat similar nuanced position.

24. See further Lieberman, *Hellenism*.

preters like Philo brought the techniques of the Hellenistic schools to bear on the Jewish scriptures, just as philosophers did with Homer and Plato. And yet there was the additional dimension that religious practices and traditions had Torah at their heart and the everyday lives of the Jewish people were shaped by halakic interpretation; this had no parallel in Hellenism. Of course, rabbis disagreed and debated proper Torah interpretation, and the books might be overridden by appeal to the oral Torah, but still in Judaism books had acquired an authority and an "aura" of sanctity that transcended the "aura" of respect generally accorded to them in the Greco-Roman world.

The Jewish roots of Christianity certainly explain the centrality of scripture and also the school-like character of its activities, but Judaism was never a "dogmatic" religion with a claim to "truth"—and certainly not universal truth—for it was the religious tradition of a particular *ethnos*. It was an orthopraxy rather than an orthodoxy. We need something further to account for the way in which Christianity derived right doctrine, rather than correct practice, from scripture.

3. The Sociological Turn

A major growth area in New Testament studies in the 1980s was what is variously called the "sociology," "social history," or "social world" of early Christianity. Already sociological categories, such as Weber's contrast between charismatic leadership and institutionalized structures, had made their mark on the subject, but now questions about role and status, class and mobility, riches and poverty, began to suggest new possibilities for understanding the texts and their background, and indeed provoked some revision of accepted estimates of the social composition of early Christian communities in their urban settings around the Mediterranean. Most relevant to our present inquiry is research that has asked what kind of a social entity those communities were by employing social models drawn from the period as yardsticks for assessing the best contemporary analogies.[25] Such work has quickly revealed that no social comparand is a perfect fit, although aspects of several are illuminating.

Clearly a prime model was the Jewish synagogue.[26] It seems that the Jew

---

25. E.g., Wayne A. Meeks, *The First Urban Christians. The Social Context of the Apostle Paul*, 2nd ed. (New Haven: Yale University Press, 2003).

26. See further James Tunstead Burtchaell, *From Synagogue to Church: Public Services and Offices in the Earliest Christian Communities* (Cambridge: Cambridge University Press, 1992).

Paul began his mission by going to the synagogue in each city he visited. But he was not well received, and those he first attracted were gentiles, likely God-fearers already on the fringes of the synagogue. What this probably meant was that those who followed Paul would effectively decamp from the household where the synagogue met and accept hospitality from another householder.

This immediately takes us to one evidently significant social model: namely, the household, a model whose validity is reinforced by the familial language adopted by Christians to address one another and also by the very terminology that became fixed for Christian leaders during the postapostolic age. The so-called Pastoral Epistles are particularly instructive here.

According to 1 Timothy 3:15 (and also 1 Pet 4:17), the church is "the household of God," and the recipient of the letter is told, "When you put these instructions before the *brothers and sisters*, you will be a good *servant* of Christ Jesus" (1 Tim 4:6). An older man is to be addressed as *father*, younger ones as *brothers*, older women as *mothers*, younger women as *sisters* (1 Tim 5:1–2). Here household codes, mirroring typical Hellenistic ethical teaching patterns already used in earlier Pauline letters such as Colossians (3:18–4:1) and Ephesians (5:22–6:9) as well as 1 Peter, are adapted to the new ecclesial context. The *episkopos* is the *oikonomos theou*, God's steward, the overseer or superintendent, the head servant charged with running the household on God's behalf. The *diakonoi*, probably both men and women, are the servants or slaves in God's household, no doubt with gender appropriate functions. Widows have exemplary roles and are to be protected, while elderly men (*presbyteroi*) have special status and duties, perhaps because their age and experience meant they conserved the community's memory.[27] Exactly what these early texts imply about the development of clerical functions is much debated, not least because the codes focus mainly on qualities of character rather than tasks, but it is unnecessary to pursue that further here. The point is that there is strong evidence pointing to the household as a societal analogy illuminating the form and function of early Christian communities.

Potential objections to this analogy may be met by other aspects of ancient social norms surrounding the household:

1. A typical household, it has been reckoned, was made up of about fifty persons, including not just the extended family with their servants and slaves, but also clients, tenants and other hangers-on. So the householder hosting

---

27. See my discussion in chapter 5 of *The Theology of the Pastoral Epistles* (Cambridge: Cambridge University Press, 1994).

an eclectic mix of people is not so strange as we might think—though it might well be for all of them to share the same table.

2. Studies of slavery in the ancient world have shown how misleading it is to transfer our assumptions to ancient society.[28] Slaves could be of all ranks, and the *oikonomos* or steward held high status; he could even be entrusted with the master's seal, so being empowered to be his agent and representative in business transactions, management, and so on. Paul proudly called himself the slave (*doulos*) of Christ (Rom 1:1; picked up in Titus 1:1), a point obscured by most English translations!

An early Christian community was clearly self-consciously analogous to a household, and indeed dependent on the hospitality of a householder for space to meet. Nevertheless, it was not literally a household. We need to explore further.

Just as synagogues were often based in households, so too were other comparable social groupings such as *collegia*, which were clubs or voluntary associations with particular common interests—craft or professional guilds, or those with interest in sport, philosophy, politics, literature or anything else. These *collegia* would meet for meals and social events and would perform their own private rituals. Some, indeed, specifically met to engage in private religious cults, while many made provision for the burial of members and the remembrance of their dead. The catacombs are evidence that Christian groups behaved like *collegia* of that kind, and the initiation rite (baptism) and the Eucharist indicate that these Christian groups, like other *collegia*, had religious features.

Furthermore, the household context and *collegium*-like character does not undermine the proposal that Christians belonged to something very like a school of philosophy. In important articles heralding the "sociological approach" to the New Testament, E. A. Judge argued that the church of Paul was to be understood less as a religious group and more as a "scholastic community."[29] He designated Paul a "sophist," a term justified by Paul's travelling and preaching behavior. He notes that Paul was sponsored by about forty patrons, and another forty or so persons can be identified among his professional fol-

---

28. Dale B. Martin, *Slavery as Salvation: The Metaphor of Slavery in Pauline Christianity* (New Haven: Yale University Press, 1990).

29. E. A. Judge, "The Early Christians as a Scholastic Community," *Journal of Religious History* 1 (1960): 1–8, 124–37; Judge, "St. Paul and Classical Society," *Jahrbuch für Antike und Christentum* 15 (1972): 19–38.

lowing. He writes that Paul "is always anxious about the transmission of the *logos* and the acquisition of *gnosis*. . . . The Christian faith, therefore, as Paul expounds it, belongs with the doctrines of the philosophical schools rather than with the esoteric rituals of the mystery religions."[30] The parallels between Paul and travelling preachers of the Cynic-type have since been explored further by Abraham Malherbe.[31]

Judge was quite clear that his case was not invalidated by the fact that the sociological parallel to the early church most commonly accepted is the household. Ancient society, he suggested, was not made up of classes (high, middle, working, etc.), but competing vertical hierarchies: most people were in some sense dependent or "hangers-on"—the clients, employees, tenants, servants, slaves, ex-slaves, and kinsfolk beholden to a head of household. In such a society, Judge suggests, philosophical ideas did not circulate widely through the formal tradition of the great classical schools, or even through street preachers, but through the talk that took place in household communities. This is confirmed by a standard *topos* in ancient ethical texts that the head of the household provides education and instruction for those belonging to his little empire (and that word was not used inadvertently, for another standard *topos* was the analogy between the household and the state—indeed, the civil service was "Caesar's household"). To fulfill their teaching obligation, however, heads of households might employ a kind of philosopher chaplain to guide their own lives and to ensure that proper training for life through ethical precept was offered to the society over which they presided.

We are observing a society, then, in which there was a fascination with instruction, and where, even though few would attend philosophical schools, many set themselves up as travelling philosophers offering teaching about life and proper conduct. Such teachers, wearing the well-known mantle, were familiar figures on the street and in the household. That Paul would have been recognized as such a teacher, and that the church was a kind of philosophical school based in local households, has thus been cogently argued.

Once again the Pastoral Epistles are instructive, for this is the social background behind their obvious interest in teaching. In 1 Timothy 3:14–16 the church is not only called the household of God but "the pillar and bulwark of the truth." The persistent theme of these epistles is "sound teaching"; eight times we find concern for the "health" of teaching or words, or anxiety that

---

30. Judge, "Early Christians as a Scholastic Community," 135–36.

31. For several of Malherbe's essays on the subject, see *Paul and the Popular Philosophers* (Minneapolis: Fortress, 1989).

church members be "healthy" in faith. There is concern about "teaching otherwise" (*heterodidaskalein*)—indeed, from the opening sentences of 1 Timothy to almost the last words of Titus, warnings about false teaching keep appearing. The noun *didachē* and the verb *didaskō*, in both simple and compound forms, punctuate the text, while the word *didaskalia*, "teaching, instruction," occurs fifteen times in these three little letters. The urgency that church officials be *didaktikoi*, "apt for teaching," appears twice, and Paul is twice described as *didaskalos*, "teacher," alongside the usual *apostolos*. The bulk of these letters is *paraenesis*, ethical advice and exhortation—teaching, in other words. The purpose for which Timothy and Titus are delegated is to instruct or to exhort; training (*paideia, paideusis*) and discipline are thus important. Metaphors of athletic training also punctuate the letters: stripping (as in a gymnasium for physical training) is for *eusebeia*, the practice of piety (1 Tim 4:7–8); the man of God is to run the great race of faith, as the usual translations put it, but the Greek implies struggling in any athletic contest, even a wrestling match. The vocabulary highlighted in this summary comes straight from the schools, especially the implied reference to the ideal of *paideia*—the training of body and mind.

Timothy's own education in the scriptures is recalled, as the usefulness of every inspired written text for teaching, reproof, reformation, and "training" in righteousness is affirmed (2 Tim 3:14–17). Thus, we find here the connection we have been looking for between doctrine and scripture: the "usefulness of every inspired written text" for instruction appears alongside the overall focus on both teaching (often translated "doctrine") and "knowledge of the truth," along with resistance to other claims to truth.[32] Most of the teaching is about ethics, about correct relationships, duties, and obligations, or the development of a proper Christian character, but providing warrant for it are some key truths found in hymn-like passages and in the "faithful sayings" that punctuate these little texts:

> There is one God; there is also one mediator between God and humankind, Christ Jesus, himself human, who gave himself a ransom for all. (1 Tim 2:5–6 NRSV)

---

32. Heine notes that the "usefulness of a text" was a standard discussion point between teacher and pupil; see R. E. Heine, "The Introduction to Origen's *Commentary on John* Compared with the Introductions to the Ancient Philosophical Commentaries on Aristotle," in *Origeniana Sexta: Origène et la Bible. Actes du Colloquium Origenianum Sextum, Chantilly, 30 août–3 septembre 1993*, ed. G. Dorival and A. Le Boulluec, BETL 118 (Leuven: Peeters, 1995), 3–12.

In the presence of God, who gives life to all things, and of Christ Jesus, who in his testimony before Pontius Pilate made the good confession, I charge you to keep the commandment without spot or blame until the manifestation of our Lord Jesus Christ, which he will bring about at the right time— he who is the blessed and only Sovereign, the King of kings and Lord of lords. It is he alone who has immortality and dwells in unapproachable light, whom no one has ever seen or can see; to him be honor and eternal dominion. Amen. (1 Tim 6:13–16 NRSV)

The ethics are theological ethics, God is the God of the universe to whom all are accountable, and the way of life is the divine will revealed in Christ and the scriptures, potentially the universal way for all good citizens to follow. As a household-based *collegium* with some religious features, this community is more school-like than anything else, teaching like the philosophers the truth about the way things are and the lifestyle to be adopted in response to the truth about the universe.

4. Schools within "Fractionated" Churches: Two Key Examples

The value of this sociological approach to rethinking the context, namely, the circumstances in which scripture and doctrine became so central to early Christianity, is borne out by the fascinating light shed on the second century church in Rome by the research of Peter Lampe.[33] Alongside this example we will explore what information can gleaned about competing schools in Alexandria.

4.1. Rome in the Second Century

Lampe's book, *From Paul to Valentinus*, details the evidence we have for the quarters of Rome where the Christian population concentrated. It draws out links with trading routes into the city and highlights the extent to which migrants made up the Christian house-churches dotted about in these generally poorer quarters. Putting archaeological and textual evidence together, he concludes that there was little central control over the various "Christian islands scattered around the capital city," though they were "aware of being a spiritual

---

33. Peter Lampe, *From Paul to Valentinus: Christians at Rome in the First Two Centuries*, trans. Michael Steinhauser (London: T&T Clark, 2003).

fellowship with one another, of perceiving themselves as cells of one church, and of being united by common bonds."[34] This communion and fellowship seems to have been assured by sending the Eucharist to one another, and by other common activities such as collaboration for support of the poor or communication with churches in other cities.[35]

Lampe suggests that some of these "islands" appeared as households where "parties" took place at the invitation of the host, presumably implying *agapē* or Eucharist. Others appeared more school-like—indeed, this was recognized by the medical philosopher, Galen, who around the end of the second century compared Christianity to a philosophical or medical school, though he criticized the tendency toward "faith in authority and tradition" and "neglect of proofs and evidence."[36] Certainly Justin wore the philosopher's mantle and drew students to his home as a private teacher. Other groups, too, "crystalized around a teacher": Tatian, Cerdo, Apelles, Valentinus are cited by Lampe, though he wonders if the last example had some features more like a mystery cult.[37] Furthermore these circles seem to have acted "very autonomously": according to the account of his martyrdom, Justin stated before his judge, "I live above the baths of Myrtinus" and "I do not know any other place of assembly, only the one there. Whenever anyone wished to come to me, I shared with him the words of truth."[38]

Lampe deduces from this that "Justin and his followers do not go on Sundays to another location and another house community for the worship"; rather his group "conducts its own worship services." It is unlikely, then, that there was any kind of rigid demarcation between different styles of gathering. Justin describes reading from the prophecies and the memoirs of the apostles as characteristic of Christian gatherings as well as sharing bread in commemoration of Jesus (*1 Apol.* 66–67). Some gatherings would be "aligned according to their country of origin," such as "the Montanists, who came from Asia Minor, and the Quartodecimans, who continued to foster in Rome their Asia Minor fasting and Easter practices."[39] This simply parallels the alignment

---

34. Lampe, *From Paul to Valentinus*, 397–98.

35. Lampe, *From Paul to Valentinus*, 385–86.

36. Lampe, *From Paul to Valentinus*, 273–74 n. 65. On "faith" as the mark of the Christian school see below, section 5.2.

37. Lampe, *From Paul to Valentinus*, 376–77.

38. *Acta Justini* 3. For text and English translation see H. Musurillo, *The Acts of the Christian Martyrs*, OECT (Oxford: Clarendon, 1972).

39. Lampe, *From Paul to Valentinus*, 382.

to geographical origin of Jewish synagogues in Rome, not to mention other migrant communities.[40] To imagine this situation of "fractionated" and diverse Christian communities, each led by a presbyter or teacher and held together by a rather informal association, is to grasp better the social setting in which a variety of versions of the truth could be promulgated. Boundaries between churches and schools must have been fairly fluid and ill-defined.

Around the middle of the second century, there came to Rome those three teachers about whose activities we have some tantalizing knowledge. They apparently became part of this "fractionated" Roman church, arriving presumably with recommendations through the network. Marcion, a rich shipowner, contributed a huge sum to the treasury for charitable work among widows and orphans. He came from the Black Sea.[41] The other two, Justin and Valentinus, came, respectively, from Samaria and Alexandria in Egypt. Of the three, Justin became a revered teacher whose works were not only saved but pseudonymously added to over the centuries, while the other two would eventually be excommunicated for false doctrine. As we have seen, Justin practiced as a professional philosopher, wearing the traditional mantle and hosting a school, apparently without any particular ecclesiastical office or *imprimatur*. The shipowner, Marcion, got his money back when excommunicated and founded his own church, an organization that spread across the then known world and lasted for some centuries. Valentinus, the other "heretic," had followers who seem to have continued to operate in association with the church in esoteric study groups, first in Rome, and then in various locations from Gaul to Egypt. The careers of these three characters, Justin, Marcion and Valentinus, show something of both the coherence and the diffuse nature of the Christian community. All three were concerned with the right reading of scripture and the right doctrine to be deduced from the right books, as we shall see in subsequent chapters. They each attracted followers to their particular "school."

4.2. Alexandria in the Second and Early Third Centuries

Valentinus came to Rome from Alexandria, the hotbed of Hellenistic scholarship and the locus of the famous "catechetical school" said to have been headed by Pantaenus, Clement, and Origen. To that context we now turn.

---

40. Lampe, *From Paul to Valentinus*, 383.
41. See Lampe, *From Paul to Valentinus*, 241–44; but also H. Wendt, "Marcion the Shipmaster: Unlikely Religious Experts of the Roman World," StPatr 99 (2018): 55–74.

For me yet another illuminating experience was the discovery of Walter Bauer's work, *Orthodoxy and Heresy in Earliest Christianity*.[42] Published in German in the 1930s, it was only after its appearance in English translation in 1971 that it became widely influential. The thesis was, first, that "in earliest Christianity, orthodoxy and heresy do not stand in relation to one another as primary and secondary, but in many regions heresy was the original manifestation of Christianity."[43] Second, Bauer's thesis stated that it was the influence of Rome that gradually asserted uniformity of belief and practice. Thus, the age-old view that a pristine original Christianity was constantly under threat from heretical deviation was challenged. The proposition was supported by a series of case studies, Alexandria being one of the most significant.[44] Bauer attributed our meager knowledge of the earliest Christianity in Egypt to later suppression of its essentially gnostic early forms. Although plausible given that the earliest teachers we know of in Alexandria were the gnostics Valentinus, Basileides, and Carpocrates, this theory nevertheless proves somewhat problematic given the likely Alexandrian provenance of non-gnostic texts, such as the Epistle of Barnabas and various fragments of non-gnostic apocrypha, as well as evidence from the papyri.

However, Bauer's work did provoke recognition that early Christianity was not homogeneous from the beginning. It would seem very likely that the church in Alexandria was as "fractionated" as the church in Rome and, as there, so here too it was only toward the end of the second century or even well into the third century that a single bishop became in any sense a focus of unity and authority. Christian teachers, gnostic or not, assembled "schools" alongside each other; such schools consisted of "small groups of disciples drawn to a magnetic personality who led them in the reading and interpretation of texts considered important in the Christian community."[45]

Eusebius's succession lists, both for bishops and teachers, must have been created by hindsight. It is necessary to probe his account to find this earlier, and by his time lost, institutional fluidity. That fluidity is instructively exemplified, however, by what we can discern of the teaching activities of Origen and his supposed predecessors. Furthermore, this is where we find some of the

---

42. Walter Bauer, *Rechtgläubigkeit und Ketzerei in ältesten Christentum* (Tübingen: Mohr Siebeck, 1934); English translation in *Orthodoxy and Heresy in Early Christianity*, ed. and trans. Robert A. Kraft and Gerhard A. Kroedel, 2nd ed. (Philadelphia: Fortress, 1971).

43. See Georg Strecker's preface to the 2nd edition of Bauer, *Orthodoxy and Heresy*, xi.

44. See chapter 2 on Egypt in Bauer, *Orthodoxy and Heresy*, 44–60.

45. Ronald E. Heine, *Origen: Scholarship in the Service of the Church* (Oxford: Oxford University Press, 2010), 51; cf. 48–51 on "Christian Schools in Second Century Alexandria."

strongest evidence for the claim that the early churches should be regarded as more like a network of schools than a religion.

Eusebius may have used a variety of sources to construct his account of Origen's life and teaching activities.[46] In any case, Eusebius's attempts to order his material chronologically rather than topically resulted in a rather episodic narration broken up by the insertion of other material. Several different descriptions are apposite to our inquiry:

1. After his father's martyrdom, the family was destitute but a rich woman became Origen's patron so that he could pursue his studies, and he rapidly reached the stage where he could earn well as a *grammaticus* (*Hist. eccl.* 6.2).[47] This woman was "the devotee of a notorious heretic," one named Paul from Antioch, and known as her "adopted son." Eusebius insists on Origen's orthodoxy "from the start," this dubious connection already having been raised against him in his lifetime. This initial teaching experience as a *grammaticus* implies that Origen offered private teaching of the usual Hellenistic elementary curriculum, including reading and writing based on the Greek classics.

2. During the persecution, all the Christian catechists had left Alexandria. Various pagans approached Origen for instruction in the word of God. So, at the age of seventeen he was appointed head of the catechetical school by the bishop, Demetrius. Origen came under increasing pressure as soldiers were posted around the house where he was living because of the large numbers who came to him for elementary instruction in the faith, and he had to keep moving from house to house. Responsibility for catechesis was entrusted by Demetrius to Origen alone, we are told, and again it is emphasized that he soon saw pupils coming to him in ever increasing numbers. He decided that this responsibility was not compatible with being a *grammaticus*, so he sold his library of classical literature in order to gain some financial independence and devoted himself to study of the scriptures (*Hist. eccl.* 6.3). All this suggests he had some kind of official church position as a teacher.

3. After a trip to Rome, Origen decided that his catechetical work was too distracting from his scholarly work on the scriptures and his study of theology. So he divided up his pupils and entrusted the introductory lessons to Hera-

---

46. To some extent the following account reflects my discussion in *Origins to Constantine*, vol. 1 of *Cambridge History of Christianity*, ed. Margaret M. Mitchell and Frances M. Young (Cambridge: Cambridge University Press, 2006), 485–500.

47. Greek text in Eduard Schwartz, ed., *Eusebius Werke: Die Kirchengeschichte*, 2 vols., GCS 9 (Leipzig: Hinrichs, 1908). English translation by G. A. Williamson, trans., *The History of the Church* (Harmondsworth: Penguin, 1965).

clas, one of his most promising students, while concentrating on the higher education of more advanced pupils (*Hist. eccl.* 6.15). Eusebius speaks of the many educated people who came to Origen's school, including heretics and philosophers, where, after preparatory studies including geometry and arithmetic, he instructed them in Greek philosophy, discussing the different systems of the philosophers and giving many a general grounding that would stand them in good stead for study of the scriptures. Among these, it would seem, was one Ambrosius, who "shared the heretical opinions of Valentinus," but "was refuted by the truth which Origen expounded, and, as if light had dawned on his mind, accepted the orthodox teaching of the church" (*Hist. eccl.* 6.18).

4. Later we learn that this Ambrosius sponsored Origen's commentaries on scripture by supplying him with seven shorthand writers and a similar number of copyists as well as girls trained in penmanship (*Hist. eccl.* 6.23). This all suggests that Origen was operating more like a philosopher with his own "freelance" school.

So what was this "catechetical school"? Eusebius suggests that Origen succeeded Pantaenus and Clement as head of what sometimes seems more like an "academy." His previous description of Pantaenus certainly suggests something other than catechesis prior to baptism:

> At this time the school for believers in Alexandria was headed by a man with a very high reputation as a scholar, by name, Pantaenus, for it was an established custom that an academy of sacred learning should exist among them. This academy has lasted till our own time, and I understand that it is directed by men of high standing and able exponents of theology, but we know that Pantaenus was one of the most eminent teachers, being an ornament of the philosophic system known as stoicism. (*Hist. eccl.* 5.10)

Eusebius tells of Pantaenus's Christian mission to India, and then continues:

> He himself, after doing great work, ended up as principal of the academy in Alexandria, where both orally and in writing he revealed the treasures of the divine doctrine.

The next paragraph tells of Clement, "noted at Alexandria for his patient study of Holy Scripture." Eusebius states that Clement refers to Pantaenus in his writings as his teacher (*Hist. eccl.* 5.11; 6.12). However, it is not until he is well into his account of Origen that Eusebius mentions Clement again, now claiming that "Pantaenus was succeeded by Clement, who remained principal of the school of instruction at Alexandria long enough to include Origen among his pupils" (*Hist. eccl.* 6.6).

The notion of something like an academy, of which there was a series of well-known heads, both prior and subsequent to Origen's tenure, is probably imposed on the material by hindsight, though it may represent Eusebius's attempt to identify the lineage of orthodox teachers in a context where heterodox teachers also practiced, all of these being "freelance" instructors. Eusebius's account of Origen's teaching activity suggests that an emergency prompted the bishop to ask Origen to undertake the necessary catechesis of converts, and that in response to demand Origen combined duties for which he was patronized by the bishop with the development of a more advanced program undertaken freelance. In other words, Origen engaged in different levels of teaching activity concurrently, at least until he split the work with Heraclas. There remained considerable institutional fluidity.

Later, of course, after tensions arose with bishop Demetrius, Origen moved to Caesarea. Here too Origen attracted students. According to Eusebius, "his services were in constant demand not only by the local people but also by innumerable foreign students who left their own countries" (*Hist. eccl.* 6.30). One of these students even left us a panegyric on his teacher that gives access to Origen's curriculum.[48] Through this panegyric (known as the *Oratio Panegyrica*), Eusebius's brief outline of his more advanced teaching in Alexandria may be filled out from this account of his program in Caesarea (*Hist. eccl.* 6.18). Having received the usual education with *grammaticus* and *rhetor*, the author was on his way to study Latin and Roman law in Beirut when, coming across Origen, he was attracted to studying with him. What Origen gave this pupil apparently followed the pattern of the established *enkyklios paideia*, the equivalent of tertiary education.[49]

Origen's pupil was persuaded to stay in Caesarea, giving up his intended career, his homeland and friends, by Origen's conviction that philosophy was

---

48. Greek text is from H. Crouzel, ed., *Grégoire de Thaumaturge: Remerciement à Origène suivi de la letter d'Origène à Grégoire*, SC 148 (Paris: Cerf, 1969). Attribution of the work is to Gregory Thaumaturgus, though it has been suggested it was rather by one named Theodore; see *The Oxford Handbook of Origen*, ed. Ronald E. Heine and Karen Jo Torjesen (Oxford: Oxford University Press, 2022), 125 for brief discussion.

49. For the classic study of ancient education, see H. I. Marrou, *A History of Education in Antiquity*, trans. G. Lamb (New York: Sheed and Ward, 1956). This work is an English translation of *L'histoire de l'éducation dans l'antiquité* (Paris: Seuil, 1948). More recently see R. A. Kaster, *Guardians of Language: The Grammaticus and Society in Late Antiquity* (Berkeley: University of California Press, 1988).

the foundation for true piety toward God. Taken into Origen's household as a pupil and offered friendship, a spark of love was kindled in his soul—the "type" of David and Jonathan is rehearsed, though he admits to then not yet knowing of this case in the scriptures. Apart from the odd occasional departure, such as this use of a biblical type, the whole panegyric follows the *topoi* of Hellenistic rhetoric. The author likens Origen's skill as a teacher to a gardener's work taming an uncultivated plot or nurturing and pruning a wild plant. Origen took time to find out what knowledge the pupil already had. When he found potential, he prepared the ground for irrigation so as to develop the initial growth; when he came across thorns and weeds, he cut them out. His ruthless questioning and argumentation were Socratic. As a trainer tames unbroken horses Origen tamed his pupils. Once the soil was softened, he began planting seeds of truth. He encouraged them to search within themselves, and avoid sophistry.

Assuming that this describes the teaching of logic and dialectics, the curriculum may be traced beneath the rhetoric and moralizing. Next came natural philosophy—the ancient sciences of physics, geometry, and astronomy. Origen sought to shift his pupils beyond mere amazement and wonder at creation to a rational perception of its order and "economy"—its providential design, we might say. Then came ethics, imparted through example and not only words. The key elements of his ethical teaching consisted of the four cardinal virtues of Greek philosophy, but they were given a new twist: prudence was understood as the capacity to judge between good and evil, temperance as the ability to select what is good, justice as the capacity to give every aspect of the moral life its due, and courage as the strength of character to live out the virtues. Origen, then, recommended that his pupils study Greek philosophy but offered a fresh take on it through his Christian lifestyle. His desire was to "imitate the perfect pattern." Although presenting Origen as exemplary, the author of the panegyric refrains from calling him the perfect pattern: not only is he explicitly careful not to go beyond the truth, but one also senses that he knew without saying that Christ was the pattern for Origen's life. After all, "know yourself" had long been the classic maxim of Greek wisdom—the soul thus beheld itself as in a mirror and reflected in itself the divine mind. Still following standard *topoi*, our author confesses that, given the pupil's dull nature, Origen never managed to instil all the virtues into him, but his teacher did turn him into a lover of virtue and did get him to understand that the ethical life is founded on piety, which is only reached through divine grace. To become like God is the aim, to draw near to the divine and abide within it.

The climax of all these studies, then, was theology. His pupils, Origen thought, should study the writings of the philosophers and the ancient poets, except for works by the atheists who deny both God and providence (a reference, no doubt, to the Epicureans). Philosophers come up with many different theories, of course, each school having its own set of dogmas, and each philosopher being confident that he is right and less than willing to listen to the opinions of others. Origen's pupil suggests that such thinkers are caught in a quagmire or labyrinth from which they cannot escape, and to save his pupils from such a fate Origen made a virtue of eclecticism by not introducing them only to a single school of philosophy. He set before them what was useful and true from all the various options. In the end Origen's students were not to attach themselves to any human teacher, but rather devote themselves to God and to the prophets.

Indeed, the highest study of all was scriptural interpretation. For this all the study of philosophy was a preparation. The prophets often wrote words of a dark and enigmatical character especially unclear to those who have wandered far from God. Origen's pupil reckons his teacher was a skilled and discerning listener to God able to elucidate the obscure because the divine Spirit had befriended him and given him the gift of investigating and explaining the divine oracles. Inspiration was required to interpret scripture. The pupil finally demonstrates that he had learned something about the scriptures from Origen by comparing his own departure to Adam leaving paradise, to the Prodigal going off to a far country, and the deportation of the Jews to Babylon.

It seems that the philosophical education Origen offered was little different from that which Origen had himself received—allegedly from the Platonist, Ammonius Saccas, though the likelihood of this being correct is slim.[50] (More likely it was another Ammonius, known as a Peripatetic, a point which perhaps demands some reassessment of Origen's teaching.)[51] Nevertheless, that Origen himself had undertaken philosophical studies and regarded them as essential prolegomena for a proper intellectual approach to interpreting scripture cannot be denied. As we have seen, the basic structure comprised the usual three disciplines of dialectic (or logic), physics, and ethics. Preserved in the *Philocalia* is a letter Origen himself wrote that lists the subjects ancillary to philosophy and also Christianity: geometry, music, grammar, rhetoric, astronomy—*enkyklia mathēmata* for the interpretation of scripture.[52] As the Egyptians were

50. *Hist. eccl.* 6.19. Here Eusebius quotes and "corrects" Porphyry's account. Ammonius was the teacher of the Neoplatonist, Plotinus.

51. Mark Edwards, "Ammonius, Teacher of Origen," *JEH* 44 (1993): 169–81; reproduced in Mark Edwards, *Christians, Gnostics and Philosophers in Late Antiquity* (Farnham: Ashgate, 2012).

52. Known as the *Letter to Gregory*, the Greek text may be found in Crouzel, *Grégoire de Thaumaturge*; English text in *ANF* 10:388–90.

despoiled of treasures for the worship of God and adornment of the tabernacle (Exod 12:35–36; 31:1–11), so, suggested Origen, it was legitimate for Christian teachers to appropriate the classical *paideia* into their curriculum. Yet the goal for Origen was to provide foundations for theology and biblical study. Christianity, for Origen as for Justin before him, fulfilled not just the scriptures but was the true culmination of the philosopher's intellectual quest.

This, however, he held in tension with his constant claim that the proof of Christianity was that it could school all kinds of people into goodness. In Caesarea he had been ordained to the presbyterate, and there he regularly gave homilies in church. Much of his extant exegetical work survives not in commentaries but in sets of homilies working through particular biblical books, notably on the Pentateuch and the Song of Songs. Origen treated the homily as a genre distinct from the commentary, "more hortatory, much more concise, less technical and less speculative." As Joseph Trigg writes, "as a teacher, Origen recognized that he was not speaking to the learned audience at the eucharistic gathering, but, as a teacher, he also sought to make his hearers a bit more like himself by initiating them into the transformative study of scripture."[53]

Even in church, then, his teaching activity was systematic and school-like—he was educating the whole congregation, including the poor, slaves, women, outcasts, orphans, and widows, not abandoning "the lower classes," but teaching "the true doctrines" so as to help as many people as he could.[54] Writing his response to Celsus, the second century critic of Christianity, Origen made this clear:

> It is the task of those who teach the true doctrines to help as many people as they can, and as far as it is in their power to win everyone over to the truth by their love to mankind—not only the intelligent, but also the stupid, and again not just the Greeks without including the barbarians as well.... On the other hand, all those who have abandoned the uneducated as being low-class and incapable of appreciating the smoothness of the literary style and an orderly description, and who pay attention only to people educated in learning and scholarship, confine what should be of benefit to the community to a very narrow and limited circle. (*Cels.* 6.1)

53. Joseph W. Trigg, *Origen* (London: Routledge, 1998), 39.

54. *Cels.* 6.1; Greek text in P. Koetschau, ed., *Die Schrift vom Martyrium, Buch I–IV gegen Celsus* and *Buch V–VIII gegen Celsus, Die Scrift vom Gebet*, Origenes Werke 1–2, GCS 2–3 (Leipzig: Hinrichs, 1899); English translation quoted throughout (sometimes altered for inclusive language) by Henry Chadwick, *Against Celsus* (Cambridge: Cambridge University Press, 1965).

In Origen's eyes the capacity of Christianity to turn all kinds of people into "reformed characters," even those who "believe without thought" and are "converted with simple faith," is a sign of divine providence (*Cels.* 1.9). The fact that the apostles were uneducated shows that "they succeeded in bringing many to obey the word of God by divine power" rather than through "human wisdom" (*Cels.* 1.62).

Origen's teaching activities surely uphold the thesis of this chapter that the early church in the social world of the ancient Mediterranean would appear to be more like a school than a religion.

5. Hellenization or the Acculturation of a Distinct Identity?

So back to the questions raised by Harnack: Was it Hellenization that put doctrine at the heart of Christian identity?

5.1. Acculturation as a Network of Schools

In the heyday of "Hellenization," New Testament scholarship made much of the analogy with the so-called mystery religions; doubtless some parallels can be justifiably drawn, despite the fact that the "mysteries" were a well-kept secret and our sources tell us very little about them! Harnack, however, had already concluded that

> the parallel between the ecclesiastical dogmas and those of ancient schools of philosophy appears to be in point of form complete. . . . The theoretical as well as the practical doctrines which embraced the peculiar conception of the world and the ethics of the school, together with their rationale, were described in these schools as dogmas. Now, insofar as the adherents of the Christian religion possessed dogmas in this sense, and form a community which has gained an understanding of its religious faith by analysis and by scientific definition and grounding, they appear as a great philosophic school in the ancient sense of the word.[55]

It is evident that for Harnack the analogy with philosophical schools is the key to his "Hellenization" thesis.

55. Harnack, *Dogma*, 1:15.

In the previous chapter I asked whether we could find a new way of telling the story that acknowledges the tension, in the process of forming a distinct identity, between "acculturation," on the one hand, and, on the other, a self-conscious challenge to the all-pervasive cultural milieu. In the above outline of Jewish particularity such a nuanced position was implicit: sociologically speaking, Jewish synagogues were "acculturated" to the world of ancient society and looked like philosophical schools or *collegia*-like assemblies based in households, but they also had their own identity and culture enshrined in their own literary heritage, the scriptures. Not surprisingly, Christian assemblies (*ekklēsiai*) were quickly "acculturated" to their social environment, made up as they were of mostly gentiles, who were in any case "encultured" into gentile social conventions by their upbringing. But that does not mean that they were assimilated to it, for their distinct identity was self-consciously important to them, and that identity was enshrined in a distinct "barbarian" (i.e., non-Greek) body of literature, which was the purveyor of distinct "truth" about the world and the way to live. They offered one among many different "options" (*haireseis*). Interestingly, in the book of Acts this word *haireseis*, which came to mean "heresy," is used not only of Sadducees (Acts 5:17), Pharisees (15:5; 26:5), and Nazoreans (24:5), but also of the Christians, who are treated as a "sect" or "faction" by outsiders (24:24; 28:22).

5.2. A School with a Distinct Identity?

How then did this particular *hairesis* differentiate itself from others? What constituted its distinct identity? Harnack continues:

> they differ from such a school insofar as they have always eliminated the process of thought which has led to the dogma, looking upon the whole system of dogma as a revelation and therefore, even in reception of the dogma, at least at first, they have taken account not of the powers of human understanding, but of the divine enlightenment which is bestowed on all the willing and virtuous.[56]

Such an estimate might seem confirmed by the suggestion that from very early on Christians self-identified as "the faithful" or "the believers."[57] Outsid-

---

56. Harnack, *Dogma*, 1:15.
57. Morgan, *Roman Faith and Christian Faith*. Hereafter in this section, page citations of this work will appear in the text.

ers were "unbelievers," and "faith" was a crucial marker of community identity. The dominance in early Christian texts of the word group *pistis, pisteuō* is not only characteristic but also distinctive, for "faith" as such was no more characteristic of philosophy than it was of religion. Indeed, critics like Galen and Celsus picked up on this distinctive trait, and both found it hard to take seriously claims to truth based on faith rather than knowledge.[58] The likelihood is that a brief investigation into the distinctive implications of "faith" for the Christian *ekklēsiai* could both cast light on the relationship between doctrine and scripture and also prove significant for assessing Harnack's suggestion that dogma as divine revelation, rather than as human wisdom, was the distinctive feature of this school. Were early Christian claims to teach the truth based on some kind of "leap of faith"?

With the help of Teresa Morgan's magisterial study, a number of observations may be made:

1. Christian usage of *pistis* must originate "somewhere within the range of concepts and practices in use at the time"—indeed, in some respects "early churches replicate the shape of *pistis/fides* in the wider Graeco-Roman world; in some ways they subvert it, in some they negotiate with it, and in a few ways they extend it" (Morgan, 502).

2. The semantic range of *pistis* in Greek and *fides* in Latin largely overlaps, covering "trust," "trustworthiness," "honesty," "credibility," "faithfulness," "good faith," "confidence," "assurance," "pledge," "guarantee," "credit," "proof," "credence," "belief," "position of trust/trusteeship," "legal trust," "protection," "security" (Morgan, 7). These words were deployed in everyday relationships, family and friendships, legal, political and military contexts, among others.

3. There were some specialized uses, which may or may not have influenced Christian usage. In Plato's epistemology, *pistis* ranked lower than "knowledge," and is associated with the unreliability of sense perception. In Greek rhetoric *pistis* meant "proof," "argument," or "belief rooted in persuadedness"—in other words, in educational contexts, it could easily be associated either with a credulous "taking things on trust," or, conversely, with accepting things as trustworthy because of the strength of argument or the authority of a trustworthy source.

4. The question of whom or what to trust was built into all social interactions in the ancient world, as in our own. Faith and trust were ever vulnerable

---

58. *Cels.* 1.9–11; for Galen see p. 28 above.

and reasons for confidence were often needed, including guarantees or legal contracts. Suspicion of the rhetorical skill to make lies plausible was endemic in the culture. This is presumably why Paul insists that he is not a skilled speaker (2 Cor 10:10)—he needs to present himself as credible and worth believing rather than able to pull wool over the eyes of his hearers. Faith was no leap into the dark, then, but rather confidence in the reliable testimony of the apostles, not to mention that of scripture: these guaranteed what was believable.

5. However, everyday usages with respect to social relationships are less evident in early Christian texts; indeed, "the *pistis* lexicon is used almost exclusively in the New Testament of relationships between human beings and the divine" (Morgan, 235).

6. Both Jew and Greek placed confidence in the trustworthiness of God or gods—indeed divine beings guaranteed trust in human relationships through such things as oaths and social contracts. Christian usage is distinctive, not because of a different understanding of the concept, but because "the shape of the divine-human and intra-human relationship and community that are formed by *pistis* . . . is not quite like that of any other community of which we know in the first century" (Morgan, 509).

7. The common appeal in New Testament scholarship to the difference between "believing in" and "believing that" cannot ultimately be sustained—for, to trust someone implies accepting that that person, and what that person says, is trustworthy, just as knowing a person also involves knowing facts about them. Ultimately, then, trust and belief are intimately related. In Christian texts, relational meanings dominate, but propositional belief is "increasingly invoked in disputes between Christians and outsiders or between different groups of Christians" (Morgan, 508). In the Pastoral Epistles one saying after another is introduced as *pistos* (faithful)—an appeal is thus made to reliable tradition.

So why did the adherents of Christianity, which began life as a distinctive *hairesis* within the Jewish matrix, self-designate as "believers" from very early on? Teresa Morgan suggests it might go back to the teaching of Jesus and his call to put faith in God (Morgan, 238–41). Or perhaps it was adopted to distinguish Christians from other groups such as the Pharisees. But given the above observations one might hazard a guess that the earliest Christians were those (credulous?) Jews who believed that Jesus was the fulfillment of the prophecies—indeed the Messiah (despite apparent failure)—or those who accepted as true the (preposterous?) claim that Jesus was raised from the dead.

After all, Paul's attribution to Abraham of a faith reckoned as righteousness (Rom 4) is precisely Abraham's (preposterous?) faith that God could bring life out of death: Abraham was himself as good as dead from advanced age, not to mention the deadness (*nekrōsis*) of Sarah's womb. It is this kind of faith that Paul describes as analogous to that of Christians who believe that God raised Jesus. The big question had to be: Is this good news or fake news?

Doubtless the gradual emergence of Christianity's distinctive focus on trust/belief has multiple roots, but according to Teresa Morgan, the "complexity and elasticity of meaning" of the word group, "together with its familiarity and multidimensional resonance for both Jews and Gentiles, made it a superb tool through which to explore the new divine-human relationship in which followers of Christ found themselves" (Morgan, 239).

So up to a point Harnack is right that Christian truth claims were based on revelation not human wisdom: they were matters of "faith" rather than "knowledge." But this faith was a form of knowledge; it was knowledge coming from proofs and arguments grounded in the trustworthy testimonies of the apostles and the scriptures, a point already made clear in the New Testament itself (cf. Luke 1:1–4 and 1 John 1–4). So, surely, it is not true that the Christian schools "eliminated the process of thought which led to the dogma," for, as Harnack admits, the community "gained an understanding of its religious faith by analysis and by scientific definition and grounding." In particular, it was by asking questions about the true meaning of both the scriptures and the apostolic testimony that propositions about the truth were defined, and "faith" became "the faith." It is this dialectical and hermeneutical process that connects scripture and doctrine, as case after case to be explored in this book will show. In a school-like environment there emerged patterns of teaching (i.e., doctrine) concerning the truth of the ways things are and the right way of life, which were believed to be apostolic and grounded in the word of God, that is, the scriptures correctly understood.

6. Conclusion and Prospect

In this chapter we set out to rethink the context in which doctrine and scripture became so fundamental to the nature of Christianity. We have observed features suggesting that in its contemporary context early Christianity appeared less like a religion and more like a network of schools. Teaching and learning were their business, and they were both like and unlike other schools. They were dissimilar from these schools in that all comers were welcome—the poor, slaves, women, outcasts, orphans, widows. But they were like other schools in other respects, in that their teachers advocated a particular lifestyle and grounded ethics in an account of the truth: truth about the way things are, about God, about human destiny. And sooner or later they would argue for distinctive positions with respect not just to ethics but to such topics as cosmology, physics, and metaphysics. Again, like other schools, this one distilled wisdom concerning these branches of philosophy from ancient written texts, albeit stylistically crude texts that came from a "barbarian" source rather than the classics.

There can be little doubt that in the earliest Christianity a massive rereading of scripture took place. At first it was driven by the claim that Jesus was the fulfillment of the prophecies—to this the New Testament itself offers abundant witness. Luke explicitly traces it back to the risen Christ,[59] first in the story of the Emmaus road:

> "Oh, how foolish you are, and how slow of heart to believe all that the prophets have declared! Was it not necessary that the Messiah should suffer these things and then enter into his glory?" Then beginning with Moses and all the prophets, he interpreted to them the things about himself in all the scriptures. (Luke 24:25–27)

And later at his final appearance, as he commissioned them to be his witnesses:

> Then he said to them, "These are my words that I spoke to you while I was still with you—that everything written about me in the law of Moses, the prophets, and the psalms must be fulfilled." Then he opened their minds to understand the scriptures. (Luke 24:44–45)

The movement from the Jewish environment to the pluralist and syncretistic gentile world, however, clearly necessitated more explicit teaching about the nature and identity of the God whose prophecies were fulfilled and who had raised Jesus Christ from the dead. We already observed such a summary in the Pastorals:

> There is one God; there is also one mediator between God and humankind, Christ Jesus, himself human, who gave himself a ransom for all. (1 Tim 2:5–6)[60]

---

59. In John's Gospel it is implicitly traced to Jesus's accusations that the Jews do not believe the testimony of the scriptures about himself (John 5:39, 45).

60. See above, section 3, p. 26.

According to 1 Thessalonians, probably the earliest extant Christian text, the believers were those who had "turned from idols to serve a living and true God" (1:9); and Paul told the Corinthians that

> even though there may be so-called gods in heaven or on earth—as in fact there are many gods and many lords—yet for us there is one God the Father, from whom are all things and for whom we exist, and one Lord Jesus Christ, through whom are all things and through whom we exist. (1 Cor 8:5–6)

These topics—scriptural interpretation and the one God, particularly as Creator of all—foreshadow the areas of questioning and debate that would emerge in the second century, a process that reinforced the importance both of the scriptures and of true, rather than false, teaching: doctrine or dogma, in other words. Thus, alternative construals and rival theories were turned into "heresies" as we now understand the word, and for Christianity's future identity right thinking (ortho-doxy) was coupled together with right reading of scripture.

3

Reading Texts, Asking Questions

KEY SECOND-CENTURY CONCLUSIONS

Scripture and doctrine did indeed hang together for Marcion: "his reading of Scripture as the reliable record of the Creator God of whom it speaks matches neatly his extreme distrust of that same God, which . . . belongs within a wider cosmological world view."[1]

That statement may come as a surprise. We all think we know about Marcion. At first sight the rejection of the Old Testament, on the grounds that it presents a God of wrath and justice whereas the gospel is about a God of love, seems attractive, and not a few Christians today have sympathy for that viewpoint. But it would seem that Marcion did not reject the scriptures generally used by Christians of the time so much as engage with them to find true doctrine there. What Marcion rejected was the Creator God. Was it a case of reading the scriptures to confirm an already held position? Or did his reading of scripture itself provoke what would rapidly be judged a perverse doctrine of God among most of those claiming to be Christian?

Reading Judith Lieu's magisterial study of Marcion was yet another illuminating experience for me. Having demonstrated how our picture of him is filtered through the rhetoric and interests of his opponents, her attempt to set Marcion in his second-century context provides an excellent starting point for considering the contentious questions of the time. For her conclusion is that he "is a product of his age and of its preoccupations," including preoccupation with "the nature of the authority by which answers to those preoccupations could be given." As Lieu writes:

---

1. Judith M. Lieu, *Marcion and the Making of a Heretic: God and Scripture in the Second Century* (Cambridge: Cambridge University Press, 2015), 366.

He is also a thoroughly "Christian" thinker, with an account of human need, with a proclamation of divine intervention narrated through the life, death, and resurrection of one who alone could bring salvation because he was not constrained by the chains of that human need, and with a summons to those who responded to that proclamation to live in a way that demonstrated that they also were free from those same constraints. His authorities are, it would seem, the established authorities of Christian preaching and apologetic, the received Scriptures and the emergent yet sometimes competitive or contested writings that were increasingly shaping the network of Christian communities.[2]

So, rooted in Christian assumptions and debates, Marcion may provide an instructive portal, providing access into the ways in which scripture and doctrine interacted at the time. For informing this revised appraisal are wider perspectives on the period: (1) the Roman church being "fractionated" (as discussed in the last chapter) with divergent schools set up in various neighborhoods and different immigrant communities making up its many house churches; (2) the focus of second-century discussion being true teaching about God, God's relationship with humankind, and with the origins of the universe; and (3) scriptural exegesis being shaped by contemporary exegetical procedures and assumptions. The latter topics we will pursue in reverse order and with a sharp eye on their interaction.

1. Scripture and Its Exegesis

Marcion, Lieu claims, accepted the scriptures as a "reliable record," and thereby found himself challenging the continuity between the gospel and that old record. On the face of it, however, Marcion might simply have radicalized an existing tendency to relativize the "ancient records." For prior to Marcion there appears to be a certain ambivalence in early Christian appropriation of the sacred writings of the Jews, perhaps not surprising given Paul's rejection of Torah. As Ignatius put it earlier in the century:

> Certain people declared in my hearing, "Unless I can find a thing in our ancient records, I refuse to believe it in the Gospel"; and when I assured them that it is indeed in the ancient scriptures, they retorted, "That has

---

2. Lieu, *Marcion*, 434.

got to be proved." But for my part, my records are Jesus Christ; for me the sacrosanct records are His cross and death and resurrection, and the faith that comes through Him. And it is by these, and by the help of your prayers, that I am hoping to be justified. (Ign. *Phld.* 8)[3]

The phrase translated "sacrosanct records" (*ta athikta archeia*) is a remarkable echo of the rabbinic definition of sacred books as those which defile the hands—*athikta* means "untouchable." When he speaks of those "ancient records" Ignatius is surely referring to the Torah, if not the written scriptures of the Jews in general.[4] Thus the gospel, long before written Gospels were current, has for Ignatius superseded the scriptures. In fact, the story of Jesus Christ constitutes the only "sacrosanct record." Maybe this makes it less surprising that Papias preferred the "living voice" to things out of books.[5] The word written and read in Christian assemblies had lost its status except insofar as it had become written testimony to Christ used to confirm the oral testimony.

The concrete reality of early Christian book culture would seem to confirm this observation. The discovery of what we may call the conundrum of early Christian preference for the codex was another significant moment for me.[6] It seems that our earliest surviving remnants of early Christian texts come from

---

3. Greek text in *The Apostolic Fathers*, ed. R. H. Lightfoot, 2 vols. (London: Macmillan, 1885, 1890); English translation: Maxwell Staniforth, trans., *Early Christian Writings*, ed. Andrew Louth, rev. ed. (London: Penguin, 1987), 95.

4. So William R. Schoedel, *Ignatius of Antioch: A Commentary*, Hermeneia (Philadelphia: Fortress, 1985), 208, referring to Josephus, *C. Ap.* 1.29. In a private communication, Ron Heine contests this, suggesting that it refers to the Torah alone: Ignatius couples the Prophets with the gospel in *Phld.* 5 and *Smyrn.* 6–7, and cf. Justin, *1 Apol.* 67, which links reading the "memoirs of the apostles" with reading the Prophets. That puts Ignatius's viewpoint in line with the Pauline rejection of the Law and would not relativize the Prophets in the same way as they provide testimony to Christ. This is certainly plausible. But does it invalidate my overall argument here? Surely the sanctity and authority of both the Law and the Prophets shifted in early Christianity, a fact made concretely evident in the shift in book culture: see further below.

5. Eusebius, *Hist. eccl.* 3.39. The precise implications of Papias's remark are not entirely evident; cf. the comment by Carol Harrison, *The Art of Listening in the Early Church* (Oxford: Oxford University Press, 2013), 5, suggesting that this should be taken "not as a rejection of literacy but as a preference for the first-hand immediacy of the oral, which was shared by pagans and Christians alike in antiquity." In other words, it does not necessarily downgrade written scriptural testimony in the way that might be supposed.

6. C. H. Roberts, "The Codex," *Proceedings of the British Academy* 40 (1954): 169–204; with T. H. Skeat, *The Birth of the Codex* (Oxford: Oxford University Press, 1983); and Gamble, *Books and Readers*.

codices, that is, papyri that were folded to make pages of a primitive book as opposed to being pasted together into the standard literary format of the scroll. Now the extraordinary thing is that Christian texts show this preference from the beginning, indeed, a century or more earlier than the switch took place for other texts; and, for the Jewish scriptures, the switch never took place in the context of ritual reading of scripture in the synagogue. The conundrum lies in the why and wherefore of this apparently distinctive feature of Christian book culture; text-critical scholars have largely focused on that issue and have come up with various theories to explain it. The codex was certainly handier for reference and for carriage, and the early use of notebooks to assemble testimonies to Christ from the scriptures may have contributed to the preference. Or there may have been significant exemplars, such as an early collection of apostolic letters or a Gospel, which stimulated this.[7] But for my purposes the point lies not so much in the search for explanation as it does in the extraordinary implications of this shift.

True, it is partly about social setting: the early Christians were not on the whole members of the literary elite, and codices were the standard format for business records and notebooks, especially the kind used in schools. But it also bespeaks an attitude diametrically opposed to that in Jewish synagogues: for Christians the books have apparently lost their sacredness and been reduced to something like practical aids for school-like activities. Their principal function has become witness to Christ. This being the case, the interesting question is how they regained status and how far they really became scriptural canon in a way comparable with the Jewish scriptures.

The earliest Christians were Jews. On the whole they were likely to be literate but unlikely to possess copies of the scriptures; it would be in the synagogues that they would be used to hearing and reading them. They would have respected the scriptures in the way described in the last chapter. But the Jews were a people, and as with any society there was much pluralism within an essentially identifiable common framework. The earliest Christians were a new group that clearly interpreted the scriptures as largely a collection of prophesies and oracles, which they claimed had been fulfilled in Christ, though they argued over the implications of this. If Acts presents the arguments as a relatively peaceful debate resolved by compromise, the Pauline Epistles, especially Galatians, suggest it was not as easy as that! The situation was no mere theoretical matter: it centered on the immediate and practical

---

7. Roberts changed his mind on this several times; for further discussion see Gamble, *Books and Readers*.

question whether non-Jews had to become Jews in order fully to join the Jesus movement—in other words to become circumcised and keep Torah. I need not rehearse what all theological students must have grappled with in their New Testament study. But again, it is worth teasing out the implications of this.

The debate was about books and their interpretation. Those books had authority to determine how people lived and what practices they adopted. Fulfillment did not necessarily mean annulment. Moses was not necessarily superseded by one who fulfilled the prophecies. I once heard a rabbi from the Hebrew University in Jerusalem argue that when Jesus summed up the Law and the Prophets in the two famous dominical commands, he did not mean that they constituted the whole of the Law and made the rest irrelevant—like other rabbis producing such a summary he meant the whole Law remained valid, whereas Paul, using the same summary in Romans, did mean that these new commandments superseded the Torah.[8] Be that as it may, the Pauline Epistles are a testimony to the authority of those books and the crucial importance of their interpretation. Paul's use of prooftexts is clear as the issues are argued out (Galatians, Romans); his allusions to scripture are all-pervasive and subtle in those epistles which are less directly argumentative (e.g., the Corinthian correspondence).[9] He assumes that non-Jewish readers are persuadable with a rhetoric grounded in this "foreign" literature. The authority of Torah as God's revelation is not questioned; rather a new key to understanding that revelation is advanced, namely Christ.

So what has happened a century later? Ancient Jews generally have rejected this novel form of their tradition. The majority of early Christians are non-Jewish converts. This in itself probably reflects a lower level of literacy and raises questions about the availability of the scriptures in full, official copies. The Jewish scriptures have in practice become a collection of oracles pointing to Christ. Key prooftexts appear to have been abstracted from the scriptures and passed down in testimony books, presented in notebooks or codices, listed out of context with their Christian fulfillment implicit or explicit, and apparently subjected to the vagaries of memory and casual translation so that textually they do not exactly conform to the Septuagint or any other known

---

8. The exact implication of Paul's arguments has come under renewed debate since E. P. Sanders, *Paul and Palestinian Judaism* (London: SCM, 1977); cf. J. D. G. Dunn, *Jesus, Paul and the Law* (London: SPCK, 1990); and Dunn, *The Parting of the Ways between Christianity and Judaism and Their Significance for the Character of Christianity* (London: SCM, 1991).

9. See chapter 3 of David Ford and Frances Young, *Meaning and Truth in 2 Corinthians* (London: SPCK, 1987).

biblical version.[10] Christian use of the codex rather than the scroll suggests that books have been "desacralized," at least to some extent, and now have an "aura" only insofar as they point to Christ. Christ has become God's revelation, and this affects the way the Law and the Prophets are received. Yet, in the mid-second century the Jewish scriptures, directly or indirectly received, remain authoritative for the Christian communities in some sense; there are as of yet no other authoritative texts generally accepted, though "memoirs of the apostles"[11] seem to have been proliferating.

Marcion was clearly initiated into this Christian book culture, and Lieu's argument is that he was one of a number of budding scholars to engage in serious critical study of the literature that so ambiguously lay at the heart of Christian teaching.

1.1. Marcion's Biblical Criticism and Its Context

Marcion is consistently described by his opponents as having mutilated Luke's Gospel and cut up Paul's Epistles. Whatever we make of his *Antitheses*—possibly some kind of preface to the Gospel—quotations show he did set up contradictions within scripture and between the scriptures and Luke's Gospel.

---

10. The use of testimony books was originally a hypothesis arising from quotations in the NT. It has been confirmed by close study of the text of Justin Martyr's quotations. Oskar Skarsaune (*The Proof from Prophecy. A Study in Justin Martyr's Proof-Text Tradition: Text-Type, Provenance, Theological Profile* [Leiden: Brill, 1987]) found two forms of text in Justin's work, both of which, since he makes comments on the basis of each, must be original to his texts rather than introduced by copyists. Generally speaking, the same prooftexts are used in the *Apology* and in the *Dialogue with Trypho*, but in the latter work they are quoted at greater length and, unlike in the former, in the LXX version. The christological meaning Justin takes for granted, whichever version he quotes, and in the *Dialogue* he "often neglects discrepancies between his inherited exegesis and the LXX text he quotes. But sometimes he tries to adjust his interpretation to the LXX text." So Skarsaune argues that Justin must have received his testimonies in a textual form traditional to Christianity, along with the christological interpretation of each testimony. Furthermore, Justin appears to have believed this to be the LXX, but in fact it was not. When Justin quotes longer versions that do correspond with the LXX, he treats these texts as "Jewish." This full text Justin got from a scroll, suggests Skarsaune, and at this date such scroll texts originated from Jews. So Justin suspected "hebraising" recensions. The source of the variant text, to which Justin accords greater authority, would appear to have been one or more testimony books, to which the legend concerning the origin of the LXX, which we know from the Letter to Aristeas, has been attached. The supposition is, then, that Justin knew as authoritative a codex or codices containing Christianizing targums.

11. Justin's phrase in *1 Apol.* 66–67.

However, this activity was not perhaps quite as straightforwardly unusual or necessarily so "heretical" as it has been taken to be. It would depend on what deductions were made from the endeavor.

It is important to go behind later reports to Marcion's actual situation. For it is likely that he simply had a different version of Luke than that known later to his critics, Irenaeus and Tertullian: the Gospel texts were only fixed gradually, and it is very likely that Marcion's version was one of a variety of Gospel texts circulating in the mid-second century.[12] Secondly, in the classroom of the *grammaticus* it was normal for differences between handwritten manuscripts to be picked up and discussed and emendations suggested. Scholars regularly found problems in classical texts, some of which could be dealt with by positing corruption of the text, identifying interpolations or omissions, or suggesting misinterpretation. Correcting the text was regarded as restoring the original. Marcion may well have assumed that this was what he was doing.

Besides this, there is a continuous tradition of "question and answer" traceable from Hellenistic times to the Byzantine period.[13] The genre is less than easy to define.[14] Byzantine grammarians of the twelfth century invented the term, *erotapokrisis* (critical questioning), but there is older Greek terminology, such as *zētēmata* (inquiries), *aporiai kai lyseis* (puzzles and solutions), or *problēmata* (problems), with the Latin equivalents *quaestiones* or *quaestiones et responsiones*.

The oral roots of the literary question-and-answer form are evident in Plutarch's *Table Talk*; here we find literary puzzles canvassed alongside philosophical topics with various solutions. In school classrooms, however, the purpose of questions could be simply didactic; for example, a papyrus (PSI 19) cited by Marrou shows how questions were used to reinforce rote learning:[15]

---

12. See David Parker, *The Living Text of the New Testament* (Cambridge: Cambridge University Press, 1997). For scholarly debate, including the radical view that Marcion's Gospel was the first Gospel as such, see E.-M. Becker and M. Vinzent, "Marcion and the Dating of Mark and the Synoptic Gospels," StPatr 99 (2018): 5–33.

13. The following reflects my discussion in "Teasing out Meaning: Some Techniques and Procedures in Early Christian Exegesis," StPatr 100 (2020): 3–18.

14. Annelie Volgers and Claudio Zamagni, eds., *Erotapokriseis: Early Christian Question and Answer Literature in Context* (Leuven: Peeters, 2004).

15. Quoted by Christian Jacob, "Questions sur les questions: Archéologie d'une pratique intellectuelle et d'une forme discursive," in Volgers and Zamagni, *Erotapokriseis*, 37, referencing H.-I. Marrou, *Histoire de l'éducation dans l'Antiquité* (Paris: Seuil, 1981); English translation: *A History of Education in Antiquity*, trans. G. Lamb (London: Sheed and Ward, 1956), 252.

Q: Who are the gods favourable to the Trojans?
R: Ares, Aphrodite, Apollo, Artemis, Leto and Skamandros.

Q: Who was the king of the Trojans?
R: Priam.

Q: Their general?
R: Hector.

And so on. Here standard answers are clearly meant to be learned and regurgitated, as in the case of a traditional catechism. However, critical questions arising from inconsistencies and improbabilities found in the Homeric epics can be found from Aristotle's *Aporemata Homerica* through the Homeric Scholia. Thus, the text was problematized, the way was opened to propose various solutions or emendations, and the pleasure of intellectual gymnastics encouraged.

Maren Niehoff's fascinating study, *Jewish Exegesis and Homeric Scholarship in Alexandria*, traces the impact of this on Jewish biblical scholarship in Alexandria.[16] In the works of Philo she discovers disparaging accounts of colleagues or predecessors indulging in critical and comparative analysis of scripture, alerting to incompatibilities between earlier practices of the patriarchs and later Mosaic legislation and engaging in textual and stylistic criticism of the books of Moses. In other words, Philo takes issue with those who problematized the biblical literature as was customary in Homeric scholarship. Yet Philo likewise capitalized on such questions, in his case so as to develop sound and consistent theological meanings through allegory rather than denigrate or laugh at the holy books. Indeed, his *Allegorical Commentary* is meant for an academic readership engaged with such questions. However, his *Questions and Answers on Genesis and Exodus*, a work that actually takes the shape of the *quaestiones* literature, is didactic, providing proper answers from a teacher with authority rather than engaged in inquiry.

In the fourth and fifth centuries CE we find this form adopted by Christians for examining scripture. Followed by others such as Theodoret, Ambrosiaster, and Augustine, Eusebius is credited with first using the specific genre, whether for didactic or apologetic ends, as a way of harmonizing the Gospels or providing answers to objections raised by Porphyry. Theodoret sums up how the

---

16. Maren Niehoff, *Jewish Exegesis and Homeric Scholarship in Alexandria* (Cambridge: Cambridge University Press, 2011).

technique could be used either to problematize the text or to defend it in his Preface to the work known as *The Questions on the Octateuch*:[17]

> Previous scholars have promised to resolve apparent problems (*zētēmata*) in holy Scripture by explicating the sense (*nous*) of some, indicating the background (*aitias*) of others, and, in a word, clarifying whatever remains unclear to ordinary people. . . . [But] you should know that not all inquirers share the same purpose. Some inquire irreverently, believing they find holy Scripture wanting; in some cases, not teaching right doctrine, in others, giving conflicting instructions. In contrast others, longing to find an answer for their question, search because they love learning.

Theodoret goes on to claim that his aim is to provide solutions to the questions, proving scripture's consistency and showing the excellence of its teaching.

Use of the tradition of critical questioning, if not the genre itself, is found in earlier Christianity. Origen, for example, in his treatment of *aporiai* (brainteasers) in scriptural texts, would seem to be pursuing Philo's approach. Now Judith Lieu has suggested that, earlier still, Marcion's critical engagement with the scriptures belonged to this *zētēmata* tradition.[18]

Tertullian occasionally allows us to glimpse specific examples from Marcion's antitheses. He pointed out, apparently, that the law prohibited touching a leper, whereas Christ touched him in order to heal, reinforcing this with the point that Elisha needed water, applied seven times, to heal Naaman, whereas Christ healed the leper by a word only (*Marc.* 4.9).[19] Marcion also contrasted the responses of David and Jesus to blind people: David was offended at the blind person who blocked his entrance to Jerusalem (2 Sam 5:6–8), whereas Christ succored the blind, thus demonstrating that he was not David's son (*Marc.* 4.6). Such examples may seem trivial, but may also be an important clue. For many of the Marcionite arguments cited by Tertullian were objections to the character and behavior of the God depicted in the Jewish scriptures, as we shall see.

The point is that Marcion read scripture "as the reliable record of the Creator God of whom it speaks," as Judith Lieu puts it.[20] He did not reject these

---

17. Theodoret of Cyrus, *The Questions on the Octateuch*, ed. John F. Petruccione, trans. Robert C. Hill, (Washington, DC: Catholic University of America Press, 2007).

18. Lieu, *Marcion*, 306–11, 319, 357–66.

19. Latin text and English translation in E. Evans, ed., *Adversus Marcionem*, OECT (Oxford: Clarendon, 1972).

20. See p. 44 above, citing Lieu, *Marcion*, 266.

books but examined them. He treated them as having some authoritative status, though the effect of his critique would be to downplay their significance for Christians. By engaging in critical inquiry and discovering contradictions, he concluded that the God of those scriptures which would become the Old Testament could not be the same God as the God revealed in the written Gospel he knew. The effect of Marcion's problematization was not only to drive a wedge between this unknown God and the Creator (of which more later), but to introduce discontinuity between Jesus's brand-new revelation of God the Father and the received scriptures, between the Gospel and the Law and Prophets. His doctrinal position corresponded with his scriptural hermeneutic.

1.2. Ptolemaeus's Letter to Flora

Marcion was not alone in asking such questions and coming up with such answers. In his compendium of heresies known as the *Panarion* the fourth-century bishop Epiphanius preserves a letter to a woman named Flora from one Ptolemaeus, who is described as a follower of Valentinus.[21] In this text the question raised is the source of scriptural Law:

> For some say that it was given by God the Father, while others turn the opposite way and insist that it was given by the adversary, the devil who causes perdition, just as they attribute to him the fashioning of the world, saying he is the father and maker of the universe. (Epiphanius, *Pan.* 33.3.1 [Amidon])

This latter suggestion goes further than Marcion in identifying the Creator and God of the Law with the devil. However, according to this letter, neither side of the argument is right. The imperfect Law could not have come from God the Father who is perfect (*Pan.* 33.3.4)—something with which Marcion would certainly have agreed. But then "it is equally clear . . . that a law which does away with wrongdoing is not to be attributed to the injustice of the adversary." Besides, the apostle attributes creation "not to a God who causes perdition, but to one who is just and hates evil" (*Pan.* 33.3.5). So Ptolemaeus concludes that "these people have failed to attain the truth. Each side has failed in its own way, the one because it does not know the God of justice, and

---

21. See Epiphanius, *Pan.* 33.3–7; Greek text in Karl Holl, ed., *Epiphanius: Ancoratus und Panarion*, 3 vols., GCS 25, 31, 37 (Leipzig: Hinrichs, 1915, 1922, 1933). English translation, unless otherwise noted, from Philip R. Amidon, SJ, trans. and ed., *The Panarion of St. Epiphanius: Selected Passages* (Oxford: Oxford University Press, 1990), 119–23.

the other because it does not know the Father of all, who has been revealed by the only one who knows him, the only one who has come" (*Pan.* 33.3.7). Marcion would agree that only by the one who has come has the Father of all been revealed, but he would himself be charged with failing to appreciate the God of justice who gave the Law.

Here, then, we have direct access to an original text showing how, in the way we presume Marcion must have operated, others too deduced true doctrine by critical engagement with scripture, reaching similar though by no means identical conclusions. For this epistle goes on to reach a more complex conclusion as to the origin of the Law: "that law as a whole which is contained in the Pentateuch of Moses" cannot be attributed to one source (*Pan.* 33.4.1). Indeed, "some commandments in it are of human origin" and in fact the "Savior's words teach us to divide it into three parts." The author proceeds to use first the debate about divorce recorded in Matthew 19 to distinguish between what Moses allowed and what God intended, and then the critique of the tradition of the elders in Matthew 15 to show how that tradition was used to make God's law void. Thus three parts are deduced: "we have found in it legislation of Moses himself, of the elders, and of God himself" (*Pan.* 33.4.14).

But this is not yet the end of the analysis, for the Law that comes from God is itself divided into three parts: first, the part fulfilled by the Savior identified with the Decalogue; second, the part that is abolished—and Matthew 5:38–39 is used to identify a commandment that is "mixed with injustice" (an eye for an eye); and third "another part . . . which has been transposed and changed from the bodily to the spiritual; this is the symbolic part" that was "legislated in the image of things superior."

> Now his disciples and the apostle Paul too pointed out these three parts: the part concerning images, as we said, by means of the Passover and the Feast of Unleavened Bread which are for us; the part of the law mixed with injustice by speaking of "making void the law of commandments with precepts" [Eph 2:25]; and the part of the law unmixed with what is inferior by saying, "The law is holy, and the commandment is holy and just and good" [Rom 7:12]. (*Pan.* 33.6.6)

This text then recognizes partial annulment and partial fulfillment—the very ambiguity already implicit in the New Testament.

So now the epistle returns to the initial question about the source of the Law and resolves it in the light of the analysis given. "It remains for us to consider who this God is who made the law." If it was neither the perfect God nor the devil, it must have been "the demiurge and maker of the whole world and of what is in it." Being between the perfect God and the devil, this being is "intermediate." The perfect God is good "in his own nature," and therefore, as the one the Savior revealed, "there is only one good God, his Father"; and the devil is just plain bad. So the one "located between them, being neither good nor bad nor unjust, may peculiarly be called 'just' as presiding over his own kind of justice. This God will be inferior to the perfect God and to his justice ... and of a substance and nature different from the substance of these two others" (*Pan.* 33.7.5–6).

The conclusions are not identical to those of Marcion, but the parallels are striking, and they arise from similar questions about how Christians are to make sense of the scriptures. This text provides clear evidence that such debates were alive in the "fractionated" cells of the Roman church in the mid- to late second century. One thing particularly striking in both these solutions to the problem of the Law is the "demotion" of the Creator: the Law-giver is the Creator, but not the ultimate God. So doctrines about God were being generated by asking questions of scripture.

1.3. Justin's Reading of Scripture

The problematization of the Law by such critics as Marcion and Ptolemaeus undermined the Christian claim that all the scriptures were fulfilled in Christ. Justin, by contrast, invested everything in Jesus's continuity with the inspired scriptures, though he was equally focused on finding true doctrine through their correct reading.

Justin believed he was handing on the apostolic exposition of the scriptures, and this apostolic exegesis ultimately derived from Christ's own instruction. Christ appeared to the apostles after his resurrection and taught them to consult the prophecies, in which everything was predicted (*1 Apol.* 50).[22] Justin thought it quite impossible that anyone could grasp the meaning of the cryptic prophecies that Christ would suffer and then be Lord of all before Christ himself demonstrated to his apostles that the scriptures did indeed predict this (*Dial.* 76).[23] For Justin the "grace to understand," without which none can un-

---

22. Greek text in Miroslav Markovich, ed., *Iustini Martyris Apologiae pro Christianis*, PTS 38 (Berlin: de Gruyter, 1994); English translation in *ANF* 1. Text and translation are also available in Denis Minns and Paul Parvis, eds., *Justin, Philosopher and Martyr: Apologies*, OECT (Oxford: Clarendon, 2009).

23. Cf. *1 Apol.* 49; *Dial.* 53. Greek text of the *Dialogue with Trypho* from Miroslav Mar-

derstand the scriptures (*Dial.* 92.1; 119.1), is not some supernatural gift but "*the apostolic proof from the Scriptures*, taught by Christ and transmitted to all Christians."[24] The reference of the text, once understood, illuminates its true meaning so that text and reference confirm one another and conviction follows.

The biblical prophecies were a key plank in Justin's apologetic enterprise. Responding to the charge that Christ merely appeared to be Son of God by performing mighty works through magic, he shifts the argument to the proof from prophecy. For him "the strongest and truest evidence" lies in the precise way in which events already predicted actually occurred. He explains that there were "among the Jews prophets of God through whom the prophetic Spirit made known beforehand things that were to come to pass." These prophecies were collected in books in the original Hebrew, then Ptolemy, the king of Egypt, heard of them and, endeavoring to create a comprehensive library, obtained these books from Herod (an anachronism on Justin's part, of course), and had them translated. Justin suggests that even though Jews all over the world have these books, they do not really understand them and are hostile to Christians. Yet in these books of the prophets, "we found Jesus our Christ foretold as coming, born of a virgin, growing up to adulthood, and healing every disease and every sickness, and raising the dead, and being hated, and unrecognised, and crucified, and dying and rising again, and ascending to heaven, and being called, Son of God" (*1 Apol.* 30–31).

Justin proceeds to quote Genesis 49:10–12, showing how it applies to Christ. The fact that "the sceptre shall not depart from Israel . . . until . . . the obedience of the Gentiles is his" is fulfilled by the Jews having kings until Christ appeared but not subsequently while people in every nation now look to him to return. Moreover, Justin reads "binding his foal to the vine" and washing "his garments in wine and his robe in the blood of the grapes" as referring to the triumphal entry and passion. This introduces a collection of prophetic texts through which the gospel story is told, including Isaiah 7:14 (birth from a virgin) and Micah 5:2 (birth at Bethlehem), through Isaiah 9:6 (unto us a child is born), Psalm 22 (the passion), and Zechariah 9:9 (the king riding on a donkey). For Justin these prophetic texts clearly constitute the prime authority as witness to Christ, even to the life of Jesus.

It is important to realize that Justin was addressing a culture steeped in oracles and accustomed to unpacking riddles and metaphors to discern predic-

---

covich, ed., *Iustini Martyris Dialogus cum Tryphone*, PTS 47 (Berlin: de Gruyter, 1994); English translation in *ANF* 1.

24. Skarsaune, *Proof from Prophecy*, 12.

tions.²⁵ Romans had long made decisions, such as whether to go to war, on the basis of books of Sibylline Oracles. Plutarch's *Moralia*, in particular the *Pythian Dialogues*, illuminate this situation, demonstrating how, in treating the scriptures as a collection of oracles to be deciphered, the hermeneutics of Justin, his predecessors, and his successors had absorbed contemporary cultural norms. Plutarch raises two questions: "Why are there fewer oracular shrines active than there were in the past?" and "Why do oracles now come in prose not verse?" Despite explanations that turn to human factors or natural phenomena, the fundamental conviction remains that one providence orders the universe and everything in it, so predictions through oracles are not at all unexpected.²⁶

These attitudes were deeply entrenched in the culture and also in the mind of Justin. It is by interpretation of symbols and riddles that one discerns the true reference of the scriptures, adopting philosophical reasoning as a guide and trusting in the overarching providence of the one Creator God. In a sense the argument sketched in *1 Apology* provides the project for his *Dialogue with Trypho*: Justin needed to deal with the objection that Jews did not read the scriptures in the same way. The opening narrative of how he worked through various philosophies, never quite being satisfied until he met the old man by the sea, finds its climax in his acknowledgment of the prophets, inspired by the Holy Spirit, as the only sources that can assist the mind to see God. In subsequent discussion with Trypho, the Holy Spirit of prophecy is invoked as pointing to Christ, in Psalms as well as the prophets, often announcing events by parables and similitudes, so interpretation is needed to spot the reference. Compared with the prophetic prooftexts of the New Testament, Justin's dossier is remarkably "Jewish," containing those texts which appear as messianic most often in the Talmud (Isa 11:1–4; Mic 5:1–4; and Ps 72:5–17), as well as others evidenced in Jewish tradition: in Targum Onqelos, for example, Genesis 49:10 and Numbers 24:17 are treated as messianic, neither of which appears in the New Testament, but both of which are treated by Justin. It has been suggested that the initial New Testament prooftexts were collected on the basis of needing to show that the unexpected features of Jesus's life were predicted, so they focus on the crucifixion, resurrection, and ascension while later strata, like the birth narratives, begin to incorporate traditional messianic prophecies. Justin

---

25. See further Frances Young, "Riddles and Puzzles: God's Indirect Word in Patristic Hermeneutics," StPatr 91 (2017): 149–55. On the Sibylline Oracles, see Dowden, *Religion and the Romans*, 32–36.

26. See the Greek text and English translations of *De Pythiae oraculis*, *De defectu oraculorum*, and *De Iside et Osiride* 378 in F. C. Babbitt, ed., *Moralia V*, LCL (Cambridge: Harvard University Press, 1984).

provides evidence of this continuing process. It was increasingly important to show that the traditional messianic prophecies reached their fulfillment in Christ, not just the testimonies initially collected in notebooks.[27]

It is in the *Dialogue with Trypho* that Justin exploits the same critical techniques as Marcion, suspecting "hebraising" recensions where Trypho's text differs from the traditional Christian reading, demanding that inquiries be pursued to discern the true reference and meaning. Here, like Marcion, he betrays awareness of textual fluidity, the need for emendation, and especially the detection of additions or excisions.[28]

> Justin assumes that the debate over the Scriptures with Trypho can be settled by a series of questions or investigations addressed to them; he charges his opponent with failing to recognise that the renaming of Joshua (= Jesus) by Moses demanded an analysis and explanation, and with reopening issues that had already been extensively demonstrated and agreed.[29]

Justin, of course, uses these techniques as Theodoret would claim he did centuries later—namely, to demonstrate the consistency of scripture and the excellence of its teaching, while providing solutions to the difficulties.

Justin's project, then, demands the unpacking of riddles and the assumption of nonliteral meaning to discern the truth, whereas Marcion's literal reading of scripture "as the reliable record of the Creator God of whom it speaks matches neatly his extreme distrust of that same God, which . . . belongs within a wider cosmological world view."[30] It is to their contrasting theological deductions from scripture, and the broader context of those deductions, that we now turn.

2. God and Creation

As Judith Lieu writes, "According to Justin Martyr, Marcion was responsible, firstly, for proclaiming 'another God', 'greater' than the maker of all, and, secondly, for slandering ('blaspheming') and denying the Creator (1 *Apol.* 26; 58)."[31]

27. See further p. 49 n. 10 above.
28. E.g., *Dial.* 72; cited by Lieu, *Marcion*, 184.
29. Lieu, *Marcion*, 308, referencing *Dial.* 68.3; 71.2; 113.1; 123.7 for Justin's use of the language of questioning, investigating, and proving.
30. Lieu, *Marcion*, 366, quoted on p. 44 above.
31. Lieu, *Marcion*, 324.

Marcion, as we have seen, was not alone in denigrating the Creator God. My argument in this section will be that the first defined Christian doctrine—in our sense of the word rather than the general meaning, "teaching" so far adopted—was *creatio ex nihilo*, creation of everything out of nothing by the One and only God, a position that would materially shape later doctrinal outcomes.[32] It was in the second century cauldron of debate about scripture that this doctrine emerged as a direct challenge to certain philosophical presuppositions. We need first, however, to go behind those debates to get a feel for earlier Christian assumptions.

From 1 Thessalonians, probably the earliest Christian document, we have already discovered how the recipients "turned from idols, to serve a living and true God" (1 Thess 1:9–10).[33] The identity of this God, taken for granted as long as the distinctive Christian *hairesis* remained within the Jewish matrix, increasingly had to be taught more explicitly. By 1 Timothy, as again already noted, this God is more lavishly characterized as "the blessed and only Sovereign, the King of kings and Lord of lords," who "alone has immortality and dwells in unapproachable light, whom no one has ever seen or can see," and who is the "one God" who "gives life to all things." What soon becomes evident is that for this Christian "school" the one God is the Creator to whom all are accountable.

First Clement, an epistle written at some point in the late first century and sent from Rome to the Christian community in Corinth, was occasioned by disunity caused apparently by some upstarts challenging the older leadership.[34] Here the interesting aspect of this text lies in its characterization of God and the prominence of creation in its argument. It is worth reviewing a few sections:

1. 1 Clement 19–21: Urged to hasten on to the goal of peace, readers are encouraged thus: "Let us turn our eyes to the Father and Creator of the universe, and when we consider how precious and peerless are his gifts

---

32. An earlier version of the following key points, including my treatment of 1 Clement, appeared in my article "Creation: A Catalyst Shaping Early Christian Life and Thought," in *Schools of Faith: Essays on Theology, Ethics and Education in Honour of Iain R. Torrance*, ed. David Fergusson and Bruce McCormack (London: T&T Clark, 2019), 23–33, used here with permission. See further chapters 1 and 2 in volume 2.

33. See the end of the previous chapter.

34. Greek text of 1 Clement from R. H. Lightfoot, ed., *The Apostolic Fathers*, 2 vols. (London: Macmillan, 1885, 1890). English translation quoted (modified occasionally for inclusive language) from Staniforth, *Early Christian Writings*.

of peace, let us embrace them eagerly for ourselves." The cosmos is then surveyed: "The heavens, as they revolve beneath His government, do so in quiet submission to Him. The day and the night run the course He has laid down for them, and neither of them interferes with the other. Sun, moon, and the starry choirs roll on in harmony at His command, none swerving from its appointed orbit." From there the passage goes on to speak of the earth teeming with abundance for humans, animals, and all living things, all without dispute. Then the epistle deals with the ocean and the seasons following the ordinances of the Lord, along with the winds and springs, the emphasis again being their adherence to their allotted places in harmony and peace, and so to the climax: "Upon all of these the great Architect and Lord of the universe has enjoined peace and harmony, for the good of all alike, but pre-eminently for the good of ourselves who have sought refuge in His mercies through our Lord Jesus Christ. To him be glory and majesty for ever and ever, Amen."

2. 1 Clement 33: The readers are to hasten to do every good deed with energy and enthusiasm. "Even the Architect and Lord of the universe takes a delight in working. In His supreme power He has established the heavens, and in His unsearchable wisdom set them in order. He divided the earth from the waters around it, and settled it securely on the firm foundation of His will, and at His word He called to life the beasts of the field that roam its surface. He formed the sea and its creatures, and confined them by His power." The climax is the fashioning of humankind, "in virtue of its intelligence" the "chiefest and greatest of all His works," made "with His own sacred and immaculate hands," the "very likeness of His own image." Quotations from Genesis confirm this along with the blessing accorded to the human race.

3. 1 Clement 38: Here creatureliness undergirds injunctions to care for the weak, help the poor, and be humble minded. "For just consider, my brothers, the original material from which we took our being. What were we, pray, and who were we at the moment of our first coming into the world? Our Maker and Creator brought us out of darkness into His universe as it were out of a tomb; even before our birth he was ready with His favours for us. To Him we owe everything, and therefore on every count we are under the obligation to return thanks to Him. Glory be to Him for ever and ever, Amen."

4. 1 Clement 59–61: Toward the end of the epistle we find a prayer. God is addressed as "the God of all flesh," the one who sees everything and helps those in danger. Clearly God is conceived as the Creator and Overseer of everyone, for the prayer seeks not just the good of Christians but that

"the nations of the earth" may know "that thou art God alone." "Thou, O Lord, by thine operations didst bring to light the everlasting fabric of the universe, and didst create the world of humankind. From generation to generation thou art faithful, righteous in judgment, wondrous in might and majesty. Wisely hast thou created, prudently hast thou established, all things that are."

It would seem from these passages that the notion of one Creator God is axiomatic yet also needs constant reinforcement. This impression is bolstered by repeated reference to the One who made us, to the *Pantokratōr* (the Almighty), the *Despotēs* (master) of the universe, the *Dēmiourgos* (the demiurge or craftsman), the Father, the King, the all-seeing God. Thus, according to 1 Clement, at the heart of Christian belief and practice is the all-encompassing power of the one and only source of everything.

This life-giving God is the *episkopos*, the one with oversight over everything and to whom all will be accountable in the end. Indeed, the doxology noted above (1 Clem. 21) is immediately followed by a passage emphasizing how closely this Creator and Master of everything knows everything to do with us. It alludes to Proverbs 20:27, saying, "The spirit of the Lord is a candle searching the inward parts of the body," and continues: "let us keep in mind the nearness of His presence, remembering that not a single one of our thoughts or reasonings can ever be hidden from Him." This picture of an omniscient and omnipresent Creator who is a "searcher of thoughts and desires" reinforces what we might call the interiority of Jesus's teaching. Indeed, Jesus Christ appears as the agent of this God, bringing salvation and initiating resurrection, but the title "Lord" is ambiguous and the dominant focus is on the Master and Lord of all, the one Creator God. This, the earliest Christian text we have that was not eventually included in the biblical canon, seems to be aware of some New Testament writings but fundamentally appeals to the Jewish scriptures as authoritative. The common Septuagint address to God, *Despota Kyrie* (Master Lord) has obviously influenced its language. From the start the biblical affirmation of God as Creator mattered deeply to Christian identity.

In the Hellenistic and early Roman Empires ethics was the primary focus of philosophical schools, but as warranty for their ethical program they also taught theories about the way the world is: physics, cosmology, and metaphysics, usually including a philosophical monotheism. The Christian school gradually embraced much of the same discourse, but from the beginning it had distinctive features. The abstract divine of the philosophers was not the all-seeing searcher of hearts to whom all were accountable, a feature rubbed home in other texts in the group known as the Apostolic Fathers. Nor was this the one who gives life to all creatures, nor the exclusive Lord of all who alone was to be worshipped and served, his identity being revealed by the narratives and prophecies of the Jewish scriptures. This conception of God was in some respects congruent with, and in other respects divergent from, that of the philosophers and this would generate second-century questions and the beginnings of dogmatic definition.

2.1. Marcion and the God of the Scriptures

Justin was the first to accuse Marcion of teaching another God greater than the Maker of all, and of blaspheming the Creator (*1 Apol.* 26; 58). Later reports confirm this, equating the "good God of Marcion" with this greater God, and the Creator with the God proclaimed in the Law and the Prophets.[35] This suggests disquiet about the scriptural God as the "maker of evils." Indeed, Tertullian's detailed arguments suggest that Marcion's critique was focused on the character and behavior of the God depicted in the Jewish scriptures. The scriptural God is immoral, inciting the Hebrews to defraud the Egyptians, for example (Tertullian, *Marc.* 2.20). That same God is fickle and unstable: there are contradictions in the laws concerning Sabbath (*Marc.* 2.21). Likewise the election and rejection of Saul shows inconsistency, as does God changing the divine mind about the Ninevites as well as Saul (*Marc.* 2.23–24). Again, that biblical God is ignorant: God had to call out "Where are you?" to Adam and asked Cain where his brother was (*Marc.* 2.25). It is striking how closely Marcion's objections to the God of the Law and Prophets parallel the philosophical critique of the gods of Greek mythology—his Christian near-contemporaries, Theophilus of Antioch and Tatian, would bring a similar raft of criticisms against the many gods of the Greco-Roman world.

But, even worse, the God depicted in the scriptures appeared to Marcion to be malignant, a punishing God not a saving God, angry and jealous. The fact that Marcion made such charges, implying that the biblical narratives depicted a God unworthy to be the Father of Jesus Christ, is made the more plausible by the lengths others would go to find ways of countering the points Marcion made: Tertullian constantly affirms the importance of discipline, and the fact that love and judgment are two sides of the same coin, while Origen over and over again allegorizes the wrath of God, suggesting that irrational passion should not be attributed to the divine but rather the goodness of a physician

---

[35]. E.g., Irenaeus, *Haer.* 1.27.2; 2.1.2; Lieu, *Marcion*, 324–32.

who causes pain in order to heal. These reactions indicate the seriousness of Marcion's exegetical challenge. Tertullian summed up the point early on, indicating that the God of the Gospel is, for Marcion, different from the God of the Law (*Marc.* 1.19).

The somewhat parallel moves made by the *Epistle to Flora* make it plausible that Marcion's differentiation between the Creator and a greater God arose out of engagement with scripture, the issue being reinforced by questions for Christians about the Law. However, the way a text is read can hardly be divorced from the general intellectual ambience: "Philosophical presuppositions and the reading of texts work in dialogue with each other."[36] The idea of differentiating between the Creator and the ultimate, transcendent Deity was already in the wind—indeed, in this period far from confined to Christian debate and speculation. In Platonism the fundamental distinction between being and becoming, between knowledge and faith, encouraged such a differentiation.[37] The created order known through sense perception was transient and material, inferior to the eternal world of "ideas." The demiurge of the *Timaeus*, causing things to come into being by shaping matter according to "forms" or "ideas" that belong to the noetic (intellectual) sphere, must surely be inferior to the transcendent perfect One of the *Parmenides*. The second-century Neopythagorean, Numenius, certainly made a distinction between the supreme God, the One who is goodness and intelligence, and the second God who is good by participating in goodness and is engaged in contemplating the first God and the intelligibles, looking to the "ideas" for guidance in creating and administering the visible world.[38] This second God presides over the realm of becoming and is known to humankind; the first God is unknown.

Marcion, it seems, was not primarily concerned with cosmological questions, but in his time exegetes were equating the Creator God of Genesis with the demiurge of the *Timaeus*. So, like Numenius, Marcion and Ptolemaeus differentiated between this Creator God and the Supreme God. Justin, like the Jewish philosopher Philo before him and other Christian apologists, did not differentiate in that way; rather they identified this Creator with the transcendent divine One—after all, Plato had said the "father and maker of the

---

36. Lieu, *Marcion*, 324.

37. For a full account of philosophical developments in this period see John Dillon, *The Middle Platonists*, rev. ed. (London: Duckworth, 1996).

38. See P. Merlan, "The Pythagoreans," in *Cambridge History of Later Greek and Early Medieval Philosophy*, ed. A. H. Armstrong (Cambridge: Cambridge University Press, 1967), 100. For Greek fragments of Numenius, see E. des Places, SJ, ed., *Numénius: Fragments* (Paris: Les Belles Lettres, 1973); Dillon, *Middle Platonists*, 366–72.

universe" was hard to know, and they too had philosophers, such as Plutarch, on their side of the debate. For Plutarch regarded God as the only one who truly is and is truly one, whereas everything else becomes and is many, at the same time attributing the exercise of providence to this transcendent, unchangeable One, "simple and free from all otherness."[39] Some Platonists understood Plato to mean that the cosmos "depends on some higher principle for its cause," but thought it "has always been in the process of becoming"—in other words the *Timaeus* captured an eternal process.[40] But Plutarch thought the cosmos originated in time, the one God ordering matter according to the "ideas." That Plato meant that the universe had a beginning was, of course, the option taken by Philo and the early Christian apologists. Indeed, some of the apologists claimed that Plato got his teaching from Moses; the one God was the demiurge who fashioned the world from matter, which was taken to be the equivalent of the chaos in Genesis.

The point for our discussion is this: Marcion and Justin, and indeed Ptolemaeus, were all alike reading scripture and trying to make sense of it in terms of the then current intellectual scene, the rationality into which they were at various levels encultured; and each took their own option (*hairesis*) with respect to issues under debate and developed their own teachings (*dogmata*) through that deductive process.

2.2. Marcion's Good God and the God of the Beyond

Marcion's "other God" is both good and utterly transcendent, an unknown and even "strange" God, until the coming of Jesus. This God would appear to share some characteristics with the ultimate One of the philosophers, though Marcion himself seems to have been largely uninterested in the issues that produced their apophatic theology. Again, the impact of reading the Gospels in tension with the older scriptures may have had as much, if not more, influence on him than current philosophical speculations.

What is interesting here, however, is the reaction of Marcion's opponents. They ridicule the idea of a completely unknown God with no back history suddenly engaging in self-revelation out of nowhere, and they defend the Creator, identifying the God of creation as the God transcending everything. This

---

39. See P. Merlan, "The Later Academy and Platonism," in Armstrong, *Cambridge History*, 60; Dillon, *Middle Platonists*, 199.

40. Merlan, "Later Academy," 68, referring to Albinus, *Isagoge* 14 (now Alcinous, *Didaskalikos* 14; see note 41 below).

was the natural outcome of their correlation of the God of the scriptures with the God of philosophy, a "Hellenizing" move often criticized as betraying the "personal" God of the Bible. What I want to suggest, however, is that it was scripture that radicalized the *via negativa* in the Christian tradition. Justin and others saw the radical otherness of the one God as biblical truth, whereas Marcion found the God of the scriptures too anthropomorphic, too susceptible to the philosophers' critique of the typical gods of myth and religion. Both sides alike, however, recognized that revelation through the coming of Jesus Christ was the only access to knowledge of the true but unknowable God, whereas the philosophical tradition always assumed that there were rational ways in which the ultimate, transcendent God could be known. We need to explore those philosophical traditions further.[41]

The pre-Socratic philosophers initiated criticism of popular anthropomorphism, Xenophanes in particular. Interestingly Clement of Alexandria is the source for many of the fragments of his work. Notably Xenophanes argued that humans made gods in their own image:

> Ethiopians make their gods black with turned up noses, Thracians make them with red hair and blue eyes; mortals think that gods are born and have their own food, voice and shape; but if oxen or lions had hands and could draw or produce images like men, horses would draw the shapes of the gods like horses, oxen like oxen, and they would produce such bodies as the bodily frame they have themselves.[42]

Fragments from elsewhere reveal criticism of Homer and Hesiod for depicting the gods as stealing, committing adultery, and deceiving one another,

---

41. The following reflects the discussion in my article "The God of the Greeks and the Nature of Religious Language" in *Early Christian Literature and the Classical Intellectual Tradition: In Honorem Robert M. Grant*, ed. W. R. Schoedel and R. L. Wilken, Théologie Historique 53 (Paris: Beauchesne, 1979), 45–74; republished in Frances Young, *Exegesis and Theology in Early Christianity* (Farnham: Ashgate, 2012). However, that early article of mine depended on scholarship then current, such as A. J. Festugière, *Le Dieu Inconnu et la gnose*, vol. 4 of *La révélation d'Hermès Trismégiste* (Paris: Gabalda, 1954) and the 1977 edition of Dillon, *The Middle Platonists*. Since then, although an account of the principal features of Middle Platonism would remain much the same in most respects, a key treatise, at the time attributed to Albinus and generally known as the *Didascalikos* (though previously sometimes referred to as the *Eisagoge*), has been restored to the name found in the manuscript tradition, namely Alcinous. See Dillon's afterword in the 1996 edition of *The Middle Platonists* and the edition and English translation cited in note 46 below.

42. H. Ritter and L. Preller, *Historia Philosophiae Graecae* (Gotha: Perthes, 1888), #100.

and for myths about the births of the gods—this blasphemy was no less serious than the blasphemy of those saying that the gods die.[43] Clement reports that Xenophanes insisted there must be one god quite unlike mortals in form and thought, and other accounts describe this god as eternal, unoriginated (*agenētos*) and impassable (*apathēs*), as one and everything, as neither finite nor infinite (*apeiron*), neither moved nor at rest, but the greatest and best of all things.[44] Of course, these later descriptions may be the result of reading Xenophanes in their own terms, but it is surely significant that an anticipation of Parmenides's One was discerned here, not to mention Platonism's apophaticism. Thus radical criticism of anthropomorphism generated apophatic theology.

So critique of anthropomorphism, along with the moral objections that Plato had advanced against the gods of Greek mythology, contributed to the development of the kind of monotheism found in later Platonism; namely, the doctrine of a transcendent Being with attributes negating the world of "becoming." This God—who had no beginning or end, was beyond time and place, had no needs and, being perfect, was unchangeable—stood in deliberate contrast to the gods of popular religion and mythology. We can find the resultant concept of God summed up in Maximus of Tyre's eleventh discourse entitled, "Who is God according to Plato?"

> It is this intellect [which] is the Father and Begetter of all. He [Plato] does not tell us its name for he does not know it. He does not tell us its complexion for he has not seen it. He does not tell us its size, for he has not touched it. All these are physical properties, grasped by the flesh and the eye. The divine cannot be seen by the eye or spoken of by the tongue or touched by the flesh, or heard by the ear; it is only the noblest and purest and most intelligent and subtlest and most venerable aspect of the soul that can see it in virtue of their similarity and hear it in virtue of their kinship, grasping it all at once in a simple act of comprehension. (Maximus of Tyre, *Or.* 11)[45]

God, then, is indescribable but can be perceived by the intellect. This concept of the divine can be found also in Alcinous, Apuleius, Celsus, and Nume-

---

43. Ritter and Preller, *Historia*, ##98, 99.
44. Ritter and Preller, *Historia*, ##100, 102, 106a.
45. Text in George Leonidas Koniaris, ed., *Maximus Tyrius. Philosophoumena–Dialexeis* (Berlin: de Gruyter, 1995), 124–42; English translation by M. B. Trapp, trans., *Maximus of Tyre: The Philosophical Orations* (Oxford: Clarendon, 1997), 93–106.

nius. Direct intuition might give a kind of religious knowledge, but there is no possibility of religious language because there is no category allowing speech about God. Alcinous stated that:

> God is ineffable and graspable only by the intellect, as we have said, since he is neither genus, nor species, nor differentia, nor does he possess any attributes... Further he is not part of anything, nor is he in the position of being a whole which has parts, nor is he the same as anything or different from anything; for no attribute is proper to him.... Also he neither moves anything nor is he himself moved. (*Did*. 10)[46]

Such a Being is beyond description, analysis and definition. None of the categories of human logic are applicable. Plato's famous remark was much quoted: "To discover the Maker and Father of this universe is no light task; and having discovered him, to declare him to all men is impossible" (*Tim*. 28e).

So how is God known by the mind? Platonism recognized three ways of knowing God: synthesis, analysis, and analogy. Alcinous describes the three ways in *Didaskalikos* 10 thus:[47]

1. Synthesis involves starting from the beauty of physical objects, proceeding to the beauty of the soul, from there to the beauty of customs and laws, and on to the vast ocean of the beautiful, so advancing to the good, lovable, and desirable.
2. Analysis works by abstraction, in the same way as the concept of a point is reached by removing the idea of surface, then of line.
3. Analogy means the sort of move Plato made when, in book 6 of the *Republic*, he deployed the simile of the sun.

These three ways enabled the Platonist tradition to assert the possibility of knowing God. Apophatic theology is obviously the outcome of the way of analysis, but it is offset by the more constructive ways by which human experience may be not just purified but enlarged so as to attain an intuitive grasp of, or mystical union with, the divine. Such an outcome depends on the assumption that the soul through the intellect has kinship with God. God is unknown and

---

46. Greek text in John Whittaker and Pierre Louis, eds., *Alcinous: Enseignement de doctrines de Platon* (Paris: Les Belles Lettres, 1990); English translation: John Dillon, ed., *Alcinous: The Handbook of Platonism* (Oxford: Clarendon, 1993).

47. Cf. Maximus of Tyre, *Dis*. 11.

indefinable when compared with our knowledge of material realities, but that presumed kinship makes it possible to overcome bit by bit the constraints of the physical world so that the intellect can reach immediate grasp rather than discursive knowledge of the divine.

Platonism, then, did not embrace the idea of God's utter incomprehensibility or the associated idea of God's infinity.[48] There are hints of this in Plato. In the *Symposium* (210e–211b) absolute beauty is described as beyond time, change, relativity, definition or knowledge. In the *Parmenides* (142a) we read that the One is neither named nor defined nor conjectured nor known nor sensed, a text already understood by the Neopythagoreans in the first century CE to refer to the supreme God. There is also the passage in Plato's *Seventh Letter* (341c–d) that Plotinus would interpret to mean that the One is only knowable by a mystical union that cannot be communicated: "it cannot in any way be expressed in words, . . . but is brought to birth in the soul suddenly, like a light that is kindled by a leaping spark from a fire." But prior to Neoplatonism, there was resistance to the idea that God is infinite (*apeiron*) or incomprehensible because of the danger of likening God to matter or "nonbeing," for formless matter was infinite, that is, without boundaries, so incomprehensible and irrational.[49] So with respect to God, appeal was usually made to the possibility of the mind's intuition of the divine, despite the recognition that, if indescribable, God is hard to grasp and certainly not comprehensible by naming, defining, representing, or categorizing.

For Christians, however, there were other sources.[50] In the prophetic tradition there had been a parallel critique of idolatry, not to mention fulmination against inadequate popular notions of, for example, God's reactions to sacrifice. To think one could live as one liked, regardless of the covenant law, and then bribe God with sacrificial gifts was the butt of Amos's criticism, while a century or more later the prophet whose words are recorded in the later chapters of Isaiah produced a brilliant parody of idolatry:

> The carpenter stretches a line; he marks it out with a pencil; he fashions it with planes, and marks it with a compass; he shapes it into the figure of a man. . . . He cuts down cedars. . . . Half of it he burns in the fire. . . . He

---

48. There has been debate about this since Eduard Norden, *Agnōstos Theos* (Leipzig: Teubner, 1913): see e.g., A. J. Festugière, *Le Dieu inconnu*, chapter 6, and E. Mühlenberg, *Die unendlichkeit Gottes bei Gregor von Nyssa* (Göttingen: Vandenhoeck and Ruprecht, 1966).

49. See further discussion on p. 70 below.

50. See also the discussion in Mark Julian Edwards, *Origen against Plato* (Aldershot: Ashgate, 2002), 60–61.

roasts meat. . . . Also he warms himself and says, "Aha, I am warm, I have seen the fire!" And the rest of it he makes into his God . . . and worships it . . . he prays to it and says, "Deliver me, for thou art my god!" (Isa 44:13–17)

The Jews never pronounced God's name, never made images of God, and used scriptures which asserted that the greatest prophet of all could not see God's face, "for no one can see God and live" (Exod 33:20). Indeed Moses, despite God speaking with him "face to face as one speaks to a friend" (Exod 33:11), was hidden in a cleft while God's glory passed by, and could only see God's back parts (Exod 33:17–23). All this undoubtedly contributed to "negative" Jewish theology. Words emphasizing God's otherness and incomparability seem to have been particularly characteristic of Hellenistic Judaism, and so entered Christian tradition: God is unapproachable, untraceable and inscrutable, and thus incomprehensible.[51] Philo grounds this in Exodus 3:34, "I am who I am"; it is only possible to say what God is not.[52] In fact, Jewish fear of blasphemy, respect for the unnameable God, and a deep religious sense of the transcendent holiness and otherness of God went further than Greek philosophy toward recognizing God's infinity and essential incomprehensibility: "My thoughts are higher than your thoughts, and my ways than your ways" (Isa 55:8–9). Yet this transcendent holy God, utterly other than creatures, was consistent and faithful, just, and incorruptible.

It was the congruence of Platonic and Hellenistic Jewish motifs that would contribute to the Christian understanding of God. Marcion's opponents had good grounds for correlating the God of the scriptures with the transcendent God of the philosophers, and this gave them scriptural grounds for challenging his "strange" God appearing from nowhere. But both sides of the argument had to recognize that the philosophical critique applied also to the anthropomorphic features of the biblical God. Hence Marcion's reduction of that God to an inferior position and his opponents' defensive response to his way of reading the scriptures.

2.3. From Marcion's Duality to God's Monarchia

Marcion, it would seem, devalued matter and everything created from it, though this may have been exaggerated by his opponents who, perhaps unjustifiably, correlated his inferior Creator God with the demiurge of gnostic

---

51. E.g., 1 Tim 6:16; Rom 11:33; Eph 3:8; cf. LXX, Philo, Josephus.
52. See e.g., Edwards, *Origen against Plato*, 16–18.

groups, deducing thereby similar hostility on his part to the material world.[53] Whether Marcion was interested in wider cosmological questions is a moot point, but certainly his critics attributed to him an ethic of rigorous asceticism and a docetic view of the appearance of Jesus Christ. The issue here is the ambivalence about matter in debates of the period.

In Platonism matter was the recalcitrant medium, the receptacle of "forms" as the demiurge shaped it into "things." As already noted, the characteristics attributed to formless matter, or nonbeing, were incomprehensibility and irrationality, for formlessness meant infinity, which meant boundlessness so unknowability. As Numenius put it, reflecting a common Platonist view, "If matter is infinite, it is unlimited; if it is unlimited, it is irrational; if it is irrational, it is unknown."[54] Plato in the *Sophist* (238c) describes nonbeing as "incomprehensible and inexpressible and unspeakable and irrational." Until formed it was "nonbeing," indefinite yet an indispensable "some-thing." For "nothing comes from nothing" was a Greek commonplace, and implied that anything coming from nothing was a sham! Typical is the view of Plutarch:

> For creation does not take place out of what does not exist at all but rather out of what is in an improper or unfulfilled state, as in the case of a house or a garment or a statue. For the state that things were in before the creation of the ordered may be characterised as lack of order (*akosmia*); and this lack of order was not something incorporeal or immobile or soulless, but rather it possessed a corporeal nature which was formless and inconstant, and a power of motion which was frantic and irrational.[55]

It was very easy to correlate this with the "chaos" of the Genesis creation narrative, and that is precisely what Justin did, as did Athenagoras, Hermogenes, and other early Christians. God brought order to preexistent matter to create the universe. Thus Middle Platonism became married with Jewish tradition without any sense of tension. Indeed, the Wisdom of Solomon and, probably, Philo had made the same correlation, though debate has raged about Philo's position since he also uses the language of *ex ouk ontōn* (out of nonexistent things). But that, of course, was ambiguous, matter itself being regarded as "non-being." Various earlier texts use the same ambiguous language, but they seem to understand it simply in terms of the production of things that

---

53. See further in chapter 4.
54. See des Places, *Numénius: Fragments*, 4a.
55. Plutarch, *An. procr.* 1014b; as quoted by Dillon, *Middle Platonists*, 207.

were not there before without attending to the question whether this involved ordering existing "stuff" or not.[56]

It has been claimed that the first to affirm unambiguously the notion of creation *ex ouk ontōn* was the gnostic Basileides.[57] According to Hippolytus (Irenaeus's account of Basileides is different):

> There was a time, says he, when there was nothing; not even the nothing was there, but simply, clearly, and without any sophistry there was nothing at all. When I say there was, he says, I do not indicate a Being, but in order to signify what I want to express I say, says he, that there was nothing at all. (*Haer.* 7.20)[58]

> There was nothing, no matter, no substance, nothing insubstantial, nothing simple, nothing composite, nothing non-composite, nothing imperceptible (*Haer.* 7.21)

These statements appear to recognize the ambiguity of nonbeing—the ease with which no-thing could be turned into some-thing—and to be attempting to be categorical about the real nothingness from which everything was created. But we need to look at the whole context. Basileides spoke of the nonexistent God producing a nonexistent world out of the nonexistent (Hippolytus, *Haer.* 10.10). What did he mean then?

When it comes to his nonexistent God, the sense would appear to shift. It has been suggested that the driving force of Basileides's logic is a notion of radical transcendence, a *via negativa*, a critique of human analogies—the ultimate God, who is the Creator in the Hippolytan version of Basileides's teaching, is not to be thought of as an anthropomorphic craftsman or world builder. The demiurgical model of creation does not work for the transcendent God. But what about the resulting creation, that is, Basileides's nonexistent world? The sense of nonbeing shifts again: the only world that could come into being from nothing was the world of appearances, which is transient and a sham for "nothing comes from nothing," and everything we know is only notional. So in the end Basileides, like others known as gnostics, had a deep sense of

---

56. 2 Macc 7:28; Rom 4:17; Heb 11:3; Herm. Mand. 1.

57. Gerhard May, *Creatio ex Nihilo: The Doctrine of Creation out of Nothing in Early Christian Thought*, trans. A. S. Worrall (Edinburgh: T&T Clark, 1994).

58. Greek text in Paul Wendland, ed., *Hippolytus Werke: Refutatio omnium haeresium*, GCS 26 (Leipzig: Hinrichs, 1916). English translation of *Refutatio omnium haeresium* in ANF 5 and selections in Werner Foerster, *Gnosis: A Selection of Gnostic Texts*, vol. 1, *Patristic Evidence*, trans. R. McL. Wilson (Oxford: Oxford University Press, 1972).

alienation from the material world; its reality is in question, and his version of creation out of nothing retains the ambiguities associated with nonbeing.

Quite different are the arguments found in Theophilus of Antioch. For him, "creation out of nothing" was fundamentally about God's power and sovereignty. It was also an explicit challenge to Platonist assumptions. He criticizes Plato for regarding matter as uncreated and therefore equal to God, arguing for God's *monarchia*, a word that could mean not just "sovereignty," but something more like "sole first principle." The demiurgical model has to be "stretched" when applied to God's creativity. As a human craftsman creates out of preexistent material, Theophilus suggests there is nothing remarkable about God doing likewise; the power of God is evident in making whatever God wants *ex ouk ontōn*, out of the nonexistent, meaning absolutely "out of nothing."[59] Later, Tertullian in his *Against Hermogenes* would tackle Hermogenes, a second-century Christian universally described as a Platonist, who had apparently set out the alternatives: either God created out of God's self or out of eternal coexisting matter. Tertullian in response argues that it was neither out of God's self nor out of some-thing, so it must have been out of no-thing (*Herm.*).[60]

So Theophilus and Tertullian were both confronting Hellenistic assumptions. Preexistent matter would mean that the *monarchia* of God was challenged, and there was a second eternal first principle alongside God. It appears that second-century debate provides the context in which the issue explicitly arose and a clear theory *ex ouk ontōn* emerged.[61] The alternative hypotheses, "out of the divine self" or "out of matter," indicate a self-conscious differentiation from philosophical assumptions of the time. It meant that God was no longer conceived as ontologically intertwined with the world, as he was in Stoicism, in Pseudo-Aristotle's *De Mundo*, and in most other contemporary cosmologies. Nor was God simply the active principle in relation to a passive principle; God was able to produce whatever substrate was needed for creation of all that is other than God's self. God became independent of the cosmos as its sole *archē*, its sovereign as well as its beginning. Furthermore, God was not

---

59. Theophilus, *To Autolycus* 1.6–7; 2.4, 10; Greek text and translation in Robert M. Grant, ed., *Theophilus of Antioch: Ad Autolycum* (Oxford: Clarendon, 1970).

60. Latin text in Frédéric Chapot, ed., *Contre Hermogène*, SC 439 (Paris: Cerf, 1999). English translation in *ANF* 3.

61. For reasons why this teaching is unlikely to have been simply inherited from Judaism, see further my article "'Creatio Ex Nihilo': A Context for the Emergence of the Christian Doctrine of Creation," *SJT* 44 (1991): 139–52; republished in Young, *Exegesis and Theology*. The teaching first appears clearly in a late second-century discussion between Gamaliel II and a philosopher recorded in Midrash Genesis Rabbah; cf. Gerhard May, *Creatio ex Nihilo*, 23. Other material from the article cited is generally reflected here in this section.

subject to necessity but free, and that was a better and more biblical grounding for transcendence than a mere adoption of Platonic axioms. Soon this God would be conceived as containing all things while not being contained, and thus would a positive concept of God's infinity begin to be grasped.

The *monarchia* of God seems the inevitable outcome of these second-century debates, given the character of the one Creator God we already found expressed in 1 Clement, so it is hardly surprising that what we know as the doctrine of *creatio ex nihilo* quickly caught on among Christian thinkers. New issues demand new linguistic statements and new discourse forged in the fires of controversy. The development of this distinctively Christian doctrine of God and creation is a clear sign that Christian intellectuals were not captured by Greek philosophy, but both challenged and radicalized philosophical assumptions because of theological thinking shaped by the scriptures. They read the biblical texts and asked questions about truth with their minds shaped by the current rationality, which was inevitable, and distinctive Christian doctrine was the result.

3. Conclusion

In this chapter we have used the controversial figure of Marcion as a portal for exploring second-century engagement with scripture within the particular intellectual context and questioning of the period. So far the issue of "Gnosticism" has only hovered in the background, though gnostics were grappling with similar questions and coming up with some answers sufficiently like those of Marcion, such that he was sometimes counted among them. Still, it does seem that in important ways neither their teaching nor their approach to scripture was the same; whereas Marcion took the biblical picture of God literally, deducing that this was an unworthy deity, gnostics read the texts symbolically and allegorically to unveil the spiritual world to which they really belonged, and they also created new texts. The next chapter will pay attention to scriptural elements in teaching labeled "gnostic," and then focus on the identification of "yardsticks" for determining what truly belongs to scripture, and how scripture was to be truly read. For teaching felt to be erroneous was being deduced from the scriptural texts, and this demanded a response. How was true "teaching" to be found in scripture and false "options" rejected? *Haireseis* and *dogmata* were beginning to acquire the meaning that the words "heresies" and "doctrines" now carry in our normal usage.

4

Summing up Scripture

FROM GOSPEL OF TRUTH TO CANON OF TRUTH

Three teachers arrived in Rome in the mid-second century—not just Marcion and Justin but Valentinus as well. A century ago Valentinus would have been considered the classic example of a Christian gnostic teacher and, as in the case of Marcion, most of what was then known about him would have come from his critics, Irenaeus and subsequent heresiologists. The situation changed radically during the twentieth century with the discovery of original gnostic texts, the widespread acceptance that *gnosis* was not simply a Christian heresy and might well have had pre-Christian origins, and the recognition of its highly syncretistic character. The very applicability of the name "gnostic" was contested, for sometimes it was used to describe a widespread existentialist mood of the period, embracing thinkers from the apostle Paul to Plotinus[1]—a recipe for lack of clear definition.[2]

According to Harnack, as we saw in chapter 1, the gnostics were "the first to transform Christianity into a system of doctrines (dogmas), and the first to work up tradition systematically"—in other words, the "Theologians of the 1st century." The result was "the acute secularising or Hellenising of Christianity." Can Harnack's assessment still be sustained in the light of this new situation? And was Gnosticism the catalyst he supposed for the development of doctrine?

First, this chapter will explore an example of how one "gnostic" group discerned the true meaning of the gospel, and later evaluate the extent to which

---

1. E.g., Hans Jonas, *The Gnostic Religion: The Message of the Alien God and the Beginnings of Christianity* (Boston: Beacon, 1958).
2. Cf. Christoph Markschies, *Gnosis: An Introduction*, trans. John Bowden (London: T&T Clark, 2003).

resistance to gnostic claims stimulated the definition of criteria for true doctrine and true reading of scripture. Second, it will ask how it could be that the rule of faith was treated as a summary of scripture, ignoring as it does most of the narrative that scripture presents—it says nothing about the patriarchs, the exodus, the exile, or even the healing and teaching mission of Jesus. Irenaeus's *Demonstration of the Apostolic Preaching* will enable us to see how the rule of faith (or canon of truth) constituted the *hypothesis* of scripture, and so only its deployment as a hermeneutical key could deliver proper understanding.

1. Gnosticism

1.1. The Gospel of Truth

"The gospel of truth is a joy for those who have received from the Father of truth the gift of knowing him."[3] So opens one of the treatises found in the codices discovered at Nag Hammadi in Egypt in 1946. Now Irenaeus tells us that Valentinians used a Gospel of Truth (*Haer.* 3.11.19).[4] It is scarcely surprising, then, that many accept this as probably a Coptic version of a work by Valentinus. As Irenaeus already noticed, it is not a narrative like the four canonical Gospels—rather its genre is more reflective or homiletic, directly addressing its readers or hearers and offering "good news."

So what do we hear? Basically a call or a promise:

> He who is to have knowledge . . . knows where he comes from and where he is going. He knows as one who having become drunk has turned away from his drunkenness. (Gos. Truth 22.14–18)

> Those who are to receive teaching [are] the living who are inscribed in the book of the living. They receive teaching about themselves. (21.3–5)

---

3. Quotations of the Gospel of Truth are generally taken from the translation by George W. MacRae in *The Nag Hammadi Library in English*, ed. James M. Robinson (Leiden: Brill, 1977), 37–49. Also consulted is the translation by Bentley Layton in his *The Gnostic Scriptures: A New Translation with Annotations and Introductions* (London: SCM, 1987), 250–64. His alternative renderings are noted or used from time to time in the discussion below. I confess I am reliant on these translations for access to the Coptic text.

4. Latin text in *Sancti Irenaei episcopi Lugdunensis libros quinque adversus Haereses*, edited by W. W. Harvey, 2 vols. (Cambridge: Typis Academis, 1857). English translation used throughout from *ANF* 1.

Two preliminary observations may be apposite: (1) The knowledge offered does not apparently consist of philosophical or doctrinal propositions (pace Harnack), but is, on the one hand, "self-understanding," and, on the other, "acquaintance" with the Father (in his translation Bentley Layton consistently uses "acquaintance" where others prefer "knowledge," presumably to bring out the "relationship" flavor of the term). (2) The phrase "the book of the living" already hints that the language and imagery of scriptural texts may be in play. Indeed, what we shall find is a reconfiguration of texts, including those used in common with other Christians, for deeper, spiritual meanings.

1.1.1. Overview

So, let us start from the beginning again: the gospel of truth is joy because that gift of knowing the Father of truth came from

> the Word that came forth from the pleroma [= fullness]—the one who is in the thought and the mind of the Father, that is, the one who is addressed as the Savior . . . [For he was to act for] the redemption of those who were ignorant of the Father. (Gos. Truth 16.34–17.1)

Revelation and redemption were necessary. For, alongside "drunkenness," we find the text saturated with images of fog, mist, oblivion, and forgetfulness as the ignorance of the Father is contrasted with hope and discovery, while anguish and terror give rise to Error, which, not knowing the truth, "fashioned its own matter foolishly" and "set about making a creature . . . the substitute for truth" (17.10–21). Creation, it seems, was somehow a mistake arising from that ignorance and oblivion. Yet, prior to this, "the all went about searching for the one from whom it (pl.) had come forth, and the all was inside of him, the incomprehensible, inconceivable one who is superior to every thought" (17.5–9).

"The all," or "the entirety" (Layton's consistent translation), is both created by and internal to this transcendent one: "the inconceivable, uncontained, the father, who is perfect, who created the entirety" (18.31). "It is he who created the entirety, and the entirety is in him" (19.7). Return of the all to unity with the ultimate, transcendent, unknowable Father proves to be the redemption offered as we learn from where we have come and to where we are going. It is a return, since the all came forth from him. So now we know why Tertullian canvassed, alongside the ideas of preexistent matter and nothingness, the option of everything being created from Godself.[5] There is something deeply monistic, rather than dualistic, about this text.

Quickly, then, we are introduced to the overall perspective of this work, and we begin to sense something of its style. As Layton puts it: "Though carefully controlled the rhetoric of *GTr* is not linear but atmospheric, just as its cosmology is not linear but concentric: *GTr* aims not to argue a thesis by logic, but to describe, evoke, and elicit a kind of relationship."[6]

Also, we already notice here ideas of fall and redemption as well as concepts much like Logos-theology.[7] Indeed, the focus on knowledge makes reflection on the Word a natural move and alerts us to the possible influence of the Johannine material. This text would seem to reflect a similar scriptural ambience to other early Christian literature: potential allusions echo the Gospels, Pauline Epistles, and Revelation as well as the book of Genesis.

It would be a major undertaking to review all possible reminiscences of scripture, not least because pinning them down is often a challenge. Take this passage, for example, which appears to be a hymn or poem, full of potential, but hardly actual, scriptural allusions:

> his wisdom contemplates the Word,
> his teaching utters it,
> his knowledge has revealed it,
> his forbearance is a crown upon it,
> his gladness is in harmony with it,
> his glory has exalted it,
> his image has revealed it,
> his repose has received it into itself,
> his love has made a body over it,
> his fidelity has embraced it. (23.19–31)[8]

Despite the difficulties of identifying scriptural material, it is surely worth working through some key sections where clusters of scriptural reminiscences are gathered.

---

5. See the previous chapter.
6. Layton's introduction to the Gospel of Truth in *Gnostic Scriptures*, 251.
7. For discussion of Logos-theology see chapter 1 of volume 2.
8. This quotation uses the words of the MacRae translation, but in Layton's arrangement.

1.1.2. *Saving the Lost: Gospel of Truth 31–34*

After affirming that the appearance of the Son gave those awakened the means to comprehend, the text continues with an apparent allusion to John 14:6 followed by an incontestable reference to Matthew 18:12–14:

> He became a way for those who were lost and knowledge for those who were ignorant, a discovery for those who were searching . . . He is the shepherd who left behind the 99 sheep which were not lost. He went searching for the one which was lost. He rejoiced when he found it, for 99 is a number that is in the left hand which holds it. But when the one is found, the entire number passes to the right (hand) . . . and thus the number becomes 100. (Gos. Truth 31.27–32.16)

To make sense of this riddle you need to know that hand signals were then used to signify numbers; here the transfer from left to right is understood as a symbol of perfection and so identified with the Father. Now Matthew's parable about the sheep is developed by allusion to another sheep saying from Matthew 12:11:

> Even on the Sabbath, he laboured for the sheep which he found fallen into the pit. He gave life to the sheep, having brought it up from the pit in order that you might know interiorly—you, the sons of interior knowledge—what is the Sabbath, on which it is not fitting for salvation to be idle, in order that you may speak from the day from above, which has no night, and from the light which does not sink because it is perfect. Say, then, from the heart that you are the perfect day and in you dwells the light that does not fail. (32.18–34)

The sense of both parables is transformed as their language is used to refer to the gnostic discovery of interior knowledge. There is allusion to Revelation 21:25—the vision of the city of God where there is no night—with implied reference to the pervasive notion of light in the Johannine material, and maybe the day "from above" owes something to John 3:31.

The passage continues with echoes of canonical Gospel material—all of which one suspects, given the introductory sentence, are meant to be taken metaphorically:

> Speak of the truth with those who search for it, and (of) knowledge to those who have committed sin in their error. Make firm the foot of those who

have stumbled and stretch out your hands to those who are ill. Feed those who are hungry and give repose to those who are weary, and raise up those who wish to rise, and awaken those who sleep. (32.35–33.8)

This is then capped by an apparent allusion to 2 Peter 2:22, coupled with a strange take on "where moth and rust corrupt" (Matt 6:19) and where "worms do not die" (Mark 9:48):

Be concerned with yourselves; do not be concerned with other things which you have rejected from yourselves. Do not return to what you have vomited to eat it. Do not be moths, do not be worms, for you have already cast it off. Do not become a (dwelling) place for the devil, for you have already destroyed him. (33.11–21)

The point surely lies in resisting reversion to corruption, for the destruction of the devil has already happened, perhaps an allusion to Ephesians 4:27. This is surely a transmutation of familiar language into an unfamiliar landscape with the implicit claim that that is what scripture is all about.

There is yet more for, as we are urged on, Matthew's Gospel seems again to hover behind the text: "So you, do the will of the Father, for you are from him. For the Father is gentle and in his will there are good things" (33.30–34). Compare "how much more will your Father in heaven give good things to those who ask him" (Matt 7:11). Then there is a reference to "fruits," perhaps echoing Matthew 7:16–20; in any case it introduces a lengthy and intriguing reflection on the imagery of fragrance in 2 Corinthians 2:14—that "sweet smell" which, as Paul suggested, both repels and attracts, as God spreads everywhere the fragrance of knowledge of himself:

For by the fruits does one take cognizance of the things that are yours because the children of the Father are his fragrance, for they are from the grace of his countenance. For this reason the Father loves his fragrance and manifests it in every place. (33.37–34.5)

The passage offers further complex reflection on this fragrance. Attraction to and submersion in the fragrance of the Father is contrasted with the fragrance that grows cold and causes division; "the warm pleroma of love" does away with the division to prevent cold coming again so that "there should be the unity of perfect thought." Again it would seem that scriptural phrases are being mutated by their transference into a new framework of understanding.

As we move on through the text (Gos. Truth 35–36) other allusive motifs occur: the notion that "the bringing back is called repentance," and that "the physician runs to the place where sickness is" (cf. Matt 9:12); the association of "anointing" with Christ; recurrent references to the "children" as the ones loved by the Father. Throughout the treatise there is the frequent promise of "repose" in the "resting place" when the Father is within them and they are in the Father (John's Gospel comes to mind again), and behind the constant emphasis on reaching perfection and on the "perfect Father" is surely Matthew 5:48. We begin to discern what the author of this work understands as the true meaning of the gospel.

1.1.3. Jesus as Revealer: Gospel of Truth 18.7–20.2 and 30.35–31.35

Here we consider two passages that speak of Jesus appearing as revealer, beginning with this statement in Gospel of Truth 18:

> Since oblivion came into existence because the Father was not known, then if the Father comes to be known, oblivion will not exist from that moment on. This <is> the gospel of the one who is searched for, which <was> revealed to those who are perfect through the mercies of the Father—the hidden mystery, Jesus, the Christ. Through it he enlightened those who were in darkness. Out of oblivion he enlightened them, he showed (them) a way. And the way is the truth which he taught them. (18.7–21)

Johannine echoes again seem evident, especially John 14:6. But there is also Colossians 1:25—the "hidden mystery." Elsewhere also we find the secret revealed and identified with the Son, alluding again, it seems, to Colossians 1:25–26 (Gospel of Truth 27.9) and Ephesians 3:9 (24.9). It is the following sentences, however, which are particularly teasing:

> For this reason error grew angry at him, persecuted him, was distressed at him, (and) was brought to naught. He was nailed to a tree; he became a fruit of the knowledge of the Father, which did not, however, become destructive because it <was> eaten, but to those who ate it gave (cause) to become glad in the discovery. For he discovered them in himself, and they discovered him in themselves, the incomprehensible, inconceivable one, the Father, the perfect one, the one who made the all, while the all is within him and the all has need of him. (18.21–35)

The cross is taken seriously, then, though the Gospel of Truth suggests an interpretation of it that seems to reverse the meaning of Genesis: eating the fruit from the tree to which Christ was nailed involves ingesting knowledge of the Father. Thus one discovers one's unity with that Father who is the origin of all and within whom exists everything, despite lacking knowledge of him. This paradox seems to imply a loss of the Father's perfection in the differentiation of the all from the infinite unity to which the all belongs—a loss, lack, or deficiency made up by returning to him. With the earlier hint of Colossians 1:25 the possibility is that Colossians 1:15–20 lies behind this passage, for there "through him and for him all things were made," while the climax is God making peace through the Son's death on the cross, bringing back to himself all things on earth and in heaven. Reflection on the Pauline and Johannine material seems to undergird this understanding of the gospel.

As we read into Gospel of Truth 19 we find that because the all needed knowledge of the Father, he (presumably the Christ) became a guide—a pedagogue, a teacher of the word, and those who were wise in their own estimation put him to the test: "But he confounded them because they were foolish. They hated him because they were not really wise. After all these, there came the little children also, those to whom the knowledge of the Father belongs" (19.24–30). Gospel stories of disputes with the scribes and Pharisees seem echoed here, along with sayings about becoming as little children

At Gospel of Truth 20 the text moves into a complex amalgam of motifs to which we will return.[9] Here we shall pick out some phrases concerning Jesus: "the merciful one, the faithful one, Jesus, was patient in accepting sufferings . . . since he knows his death is life for many," and "[j]ust as there lies hidden in a will before it is opened the fortune of the deceased master of the house . . ." so "[f]or this reason Jesus appeared . . . he was nailed to a tree," and "he published the edict of the Father on the cross" (20.10–27). Here we pick up echoes of Hebrews 2:1, Matthew 20:28, Hebrews 9:17, and Colossians 2:14, and this is followed by an apparent allusion to 1 Corinthians 15 (vv. 50–57 especially): "O such great teaching! He draws himself down to death though life eternal clothes him. Having stripped himself of the perishable rags, he put on imperishability" (20.28–32).

Shifting attention now to Gospel of Truth 30, we find that those awakened from sleep "leave [the works of ignorance] behind like a dream in the night; the knowledge of the Father they value as the dawn" (30.3–7). This is then

---

9. See 1.1.4 below.

reinforced by "Blessed is he who has opened the eyes of the blind." In Genesis 3:5 and 7 the eyes of Adam and Eve were opened by eating the fruit, so that they had knowledge and understanding, and Jesus in the Gospels opens the eyes of the blind. The Spirit "gave them the means of knowing the knowledge of the Father and the revelation of his Son."

> For when they had seen him and had heard him, he granted them to taste him and to smell him and to touch the beloved Son. When he had appeared instructing them about the Father, the incomprehensible one, when he had breathed into them what is in the mind, doing his will, when many had received the light, they turned to him. (30.27–31.1)

The opening of 1 John first leaps to mind, and then Jesus breathing the Spirit into the disciples at John 20:22. But the sequel suggests that the physical contact is metaphorical: for the "material ones were strangers and did not see his likeness," and he came "by means of fleshly appearance" (31.1–7).[10] So is the flesh mere appearance, taking Romans 8:3 "in the likeness of flesh" too literally?

What he brought was speech: "speaking new things, still speaking about what is in the heart of the Father, he brought forth the flawless word" (31.9–13). This is not the only place where we seem to have an echo of John 1:18: the Son is the secret in the Father's bosom, and his bosom is the Holy Spirit according to Gospel of Truth 24.9–10. Meanwhile, the passage under examination continues:

> Light spoke through his mouth, and his voice gave birth to life. He gave them thought and understanding and mercy and salvation and the powerful spirit from the infiniteness and the gentleness of the Father. He made punishments and tortures cease, for it was they which were leading astray from his face some who were in need of mercy, in error and in bonds; and with power he destroyed them and confounded them with knowledge. He became a way for those who were lost and knowledge for those who were ignorant, a discovery for those who were searching, and support for those who were wavering, immaculateness for those who were defiled. (31.13–35)

10. It is worth observing that Layton's translation apparently construes the Coptic somewhat differently. But it seems that, rather than implying a contrast between those who responded and those who only saw the fleshly appearance (i.e., ordinary Christians?), the gist is that the bonds of error and the material were confronted and overcome through the power of the word. Cf. the ensuing description of the rescue of those led astray, in bonds and in error, in the final quotation on this page.

So again we find echoes, this time of the Johannine prologue, the word of God spoken from the heart of Father, bringing light and life. That a reading of scripture lies at the root of all this is surely clear.

1.1.4. Names in the Book of the Living: Gospel of Truth 19.34–23.31 and 37.35–43.22

Speaking of the "little children, those to whom the knowledge of the Father belongs," we read in Gospel of Truth 19–20 that

> There was revealed in their heart the living book of the living—the one written in the thought and mind [of the] Father, and which from before the foundation of the all was within the incomprehensible (parts) of him—that (book) which no one was able to take since it is reserved for the one who will take it and will be slain. (19.34–20.6)

We are reminded of the vision in Revelation 5, where the only one worthy to take the book is the Lamb who was slain. There follows the passage reviewed earlier: before "he was nailed to a tree," we are told, "he put on that book." The passage as a whole now appears to identify the book written in the mind of the Father with Jesus nailed to a tree, locating it in the heart of the little children who have knowledge of the Father. Without the intervention of "that book," "no one could have appeared among those who believed in salvation." But

> those who are to receive teaching are the living who are inscribed in the book of the living. They receive teaching about themselves. They receive it from the Father, turning again to him . . . Then, if one has knowledge, he receives what are his own and draws them to himself . . . [H]e enrolled them in advance. (21.3–8, 11–14, 23)

Again the Johannine literature lurks in the background (e.g., John 12:32), while the notion of enrollment suggests "names": "Those whose name he knew in advance were called at the end, so that one who has knowledge is the one whose name the Father has uttered. For he whose name has not been spoken is ignorant. Indeed, how is one to hear if his name has not been called?" (21.25–34). Only with response to the call of one's name does one discover oneself to be from above, but if called, "he hears, he answers, and he turns to him who is calling him and ascends to him. . . . Each one's name comes to him" (22.4–7, 12–13). Surely scriptural motifs are echoed here—perhaps passages like

Romans 10:14–15. But in the Gospel of Truth it is all about recognizing that one belongs within the Father, rejecting error and returning, knowing where one comes from and where one is going.

So knowledge of the living book is what has been revealed. But the crucial point is that the book containing the names is identified with the Son who, we now learn, is the name of the Father:

> Now the end is receiving knowledge about the one who is hidden, and this is the Father . . . Now the name of the Father is the Son . . . He gave him his name which belonged to him . . . His is the name; his is the Son. It is possible for him to be seen. But the name is invisible because it alone is the mystery of the invisible which comes to ears that are completely filled with it. For indeed the Father's name is not spoken, but it is apparent through a Son. (37.37–38; 38.7, 11–12, 14–24)

It is important here to recall what was said in the previous chapter about the sanctity of God's name in Jewish tradition. In this text God is beyond conception, utterly transcendent, inexpressible and unnameable. It is the unspoken name of the Father that becomes apparent through the Son. "Who therefore will be able to utter a name for him, the great name, except him alone to whom the name belongs and the sons of the name in whom rested the name of the Father, (who) in turn themselves rested in his name?" (38.25–32). One is reminded of Revelation 19:12: "he has a name inscribed that no one knows but himself." The Father alone, we are told, can beget a name for himself, and no one else gave it to him. The name is "not from words" nor does it "consist of appellations," for "he is unnameable, indescribable, until the time when he who is perfect spoke of himself" (39.3–5, 15–19).

So we reach the climax, the reiteration of the coming of the Son "from the depth," to speak "about his secret things." The author, like Marcion, challenges the notion that the Father is "harsh" or "wrathful." One recalls the passage cited earlier that stated that "he made punishments and tortures cease" (31.20).[11] Those who "stretch out after the one above and the perfect one" do not "lack the Father's glory" (perhaps reminiscent of Romans 3:23); they do not "go down to Hades," but "rest in him who is at rest." The resurrection has apparently already happened within them.

> They themselves are the truth; and the Father is within them and they are in the Father, being perfect. (42.25–29)

11. See the end of 1.1.3 above.

The true brothers, those upon whom the love of the Father is poured out[12]
... exist in true and eternal life, and speak of the light which is perfect.
(43.5–7, 10–13)

The treatise then ends with these words: "The Spirit rejoices in it and glorifies the one in whom it existed because he is good. And his children are perfect and worthy of his name, for he is the Father: it is children of this kind that he loves" (43.14–24).

So, the final words of the Gospel of Truth again tantalize us with their scriptural resonances. Imagine hearing this homily in one of those school-like assemblies in second-century Rome. Why would one not accept it as the true meaning of the gospel? The Gospel of Truth is surely an attempt to uncover what scripture is really about—at least the true import of early Christian texts already in circulation and soon to be treated as canonical.

1.2. Behind and Beyond the Gospel of Truth

It is not always easy to follow the Gospel of Truth as it winds around the same repeated themes and eschews explanation; nor is it easy to know how much to read it against the reports of those gnostic "systems" found in Irenaeus's critique along with several of the other rediscovered gnostic texts. This section will set the Gospel of Truth in a broader context while avoiding, as not directly relevant here, the vexed historical questions about gnostic origins and the extent to which Gnosis was more than a Christian heresy. The focus will be on the doctrines seemingly presupposed by the text we have been studying.

1.2.1. The Gospel of Truth and the Valentinian System

Though this is far from explicit in the Gospel of Truth, Valentinus would appear to share with other so-called gnostics certain common teachings (i.e., doctrines):

1. an account of the origin of all things which involves a precosmic fall, so treating the material universe as the result of an accident or error—this despite the monistic assertion that all is contained in the ultimate unity;
2. a distinction between the Creator God (the demiurge) and the supreme Father;
3. the ultimate Father characterized by radically transcendent and apophatic language;

---

12. Perhaps an echo of Romans 5:5.

4. a message of salvation which offers reunion with the ultimate divine for the spiritual elite, who by receiving secret knowledge through revelation are already awakened from their drunken stupor.

Much gnostic teaching—and this has been confirmed by some of the gnostic texts now rediscovered—concerned itself with elaborate accounts of the precosmic process that produced the present unsatisfactory situation. These were easily represented as absurd myths and genealogical speculations, and this Irenaeus contrived to do in his rehearsal of the Valentinian system. The ultimate Forefather was a great *Bythos*, an abyss infinite and incomprehensible. There emerged alongside him Thought (known also as Grace) and Silence. Thought took Silence as consort and deposited a seed in her, and the pair produced another male-female pair: Mind (known also as the Only-begotten) and Truth. From these came Word and Life, Design and Wisdom (*Sophia*), the eight primal aeons constituting the Ogdoad. The Ogdoad gave rise to further aeons who made up the Decad and the Dodecad, a total of thirty aeons constituting the *plērōma* (Gk. fullness).

One key question in contemporary philosophy was how the Many related to the ultimate One, that is, how the one ground of all being could produce the complexity and multiplicity of things. The gnostic scheme was one kind of answer: spiritual multiplicity was produced by a process of emanation from the ultimate divine infinite—indeed the names of the aeons in many schemes reflected philosophical interests. But philosophical sophistication was married with implied sexual imagery of a distinctly mythological kind, each pair of apparent abstracts consisting of a masculine and feminine word in Greek. No doubt the male-female pairs reinforced the notion of fresh generation, though the overall effect would seem to be a fragmentation of the divine unity, a differentiation of aeons (eternal aspects) of the divine *plērōma*. None of this is spelled out as doctrine in the Gospel of Truth, but some of its more obscure passages might well be illuminated by it.

Having shown how the spiritual world is "furnished," the Valentinian myth went on to explain the material world. *Sophia* (Wisdom) was overtaken by passion, wanting to know the ultimate Forefather. The word "know" has double meaning, as the sexual imagery becomes both explicit and symbolic. In principle it was impossible to know one who was infinite and therefore incomprehensible, so her rash attempt led to an "abortion," a misconceived creature, Achamoth (a corruption of the Hebrew word ḥokmah "wisdom"). We might suggest that Sophia committed the primal act of *hybris*, that overreaching pride which always leads to tragic disaster (*nemesis*). Achamoth was expelled from the *plērōma*, and produced the demiurge, who being ignorant of the spiritual world created the material universe. Sophia wanted to save her offspring, who became fragmented and mixed up in this alien environment. Again, this "myth" makes sense of some key ideas in the Gospel of Truth, in particular the notions (1) that the all was searching for knowledge of the Father; and (2) that error and oblivion produced the material creation.

So were the Valentinians the first theologians, in other words, the first to construct a system of Christian philosophical *dogmata*, as Harnack suggested? Certainly they were asking philosophical questions about truth, about origins, and about good and evil, and they were offering answers. It is also true that some of the answers were not dissimilar to the basic approach of contemporary philosophy, whether Stoic or Middle Platonic. But surely gnostic doctrine was fundamentally revelatory rather than rational—it was after all the rational that failed. As Mark Edwards writes, "Notwithstanding the closeness of the Gnostics to Plotinus and some striking reverberations of Platonic myth in that of the Valentinians, there is less than half a truth in Harnack's dictum that the teachings are an 'acute Hellenization of Christianity.'"[13]

1.2.2. The Gospel of Truth and Scripture

So, to what extent was scripture the source of the gnostic revelation? In our reading of the Gospel of Truth we have seen much to confirm David Dawson's reading of Valentinus.[14] Using Valentinus's fragments and the Gospel of Truth as clues, Dawson showed how Valentinus "erases the line between text and commentary, as interpretation becomes new composition."[15] He talks in terms of an "Apocalypse of the Mind," and the implied comparison is apposite. Valentinus, we might say, imaginatively reconfigures texts such as Genesis, the Gospels, and the works of Paul in a manner not unlike the creative reminting of biblical language and images found in works such as the book of Revelation.[16] Here, however, the resultant cosmic myth does not concern what we might call the world-stage, beginning with divine creation and ending with an eschatological new creation. Rather the story of fall and redemption is recast in the interests of what Dawson calls "psychodrama." This "revisionary freedom"

---

13. Edwards, *Origen against Plato*, 32.
14. David Dawson, *Allegorical Readers and Cultural Revision in Ancient Alexandria* (Berkeley: University of California Press, 1992).
15. Dawson, *Allegorical Readers*, 128. See 130–31 for further quotations in this section.
16. See especially Austin Farrar, *A Rebirth of Images: The Making of St. John's Apocalypse* (Westminster: Dacre, 1949).

Dawson regards as "the authentically Gnostic spirit," but he draws attention to the fact that the new composition "gains much of its effectiveness precisely because the new story contains oblique, sometimes nearly subliminal, echoes of the old story."

In the Valentinian tradition, texts other than the scriptures were also reconfigured. Dawson notes that:

> In a sermon entitled *On Friends*, Valentinus claims that the wisdom common to both classical Greek literature ("things written in publicly available books") and Christian literature ("the writings of god's church"), whether conceived as speech ("utterances") or writing ("the written law"), is first available in the hearts of "the people of the beloved" (frag. G). One does not need to go to derivative sources, for the truth originally lies in the very interior of one's being.

Book learning was transcended. Dawson's point is that the gnostic sense of being in touch directly with the truth meant greater creative freedom with respect to existing texts, even though those texts were assumed to contain truth when read with the right gnostic spectacles. The crucial thing for the gnostic was the insight that discerned, through any and all ancient texts, truths that had actually been received from elsewhere. Valentinus was not alone in this stance. The Nag Hammadi library contains not just gnostic treatises emerging from a clearly Christian ambience, but also some that definitely do not, alongside a fragment of Plato (the ethical work known as the *Sentences of Sextus*), some Hermetic literature, and even one text claiming Zoroastrian heritage. Absorbing "world literature," we might say—especially religious and philosophical material but also magic and astrology—gnostics transmuted it all into a syncretistic amalgam within a new framework of understanding. As well as being revelatory rather than rational, gnostic doctrine was paratextual, we might say, rather than scriptural, and mystical rather than traditional. This is surely borne out by what we have seen in the Gospel of Truth.

It is undeniable, however, that the Hebrew scriptures and Christian texts had powerful influence on most of the forms of Gnosticism concerning which we have much information. Indeed, gnostic texts not only present themselves as Gospels, Acts, and Epistles, similar to the canonical texts thus designated, but also as Apocalypses. Furthermore, they share a remarkable number of features with Jewish and Christian apocalyptic literature, including common imagery and number symbolism; themes such as the contrast between light and darkness, life and death; and even similar motifs such as heavenly journeys and revelations. In the book of Baruch summarized by Hippolytus (*Haer.* 5.21), a gnostic scheme parallel to that of Valentinus appears in the dress of Jewish angels, whose Hebrew names often express attributes of the divine: Gabriel (Might of God), Phanuel (Face of God), Michael (Who is like God?), Raphael (God heals). The spiritual world of gnostic revelation in this guise seems not unrelated to the heavenly court of Jewish apocalyptic literature, as both perhaps presuppose the differentiation of the various divine attributes. Besides this, apocalyptic literature often includes "wisdom" elements in its revelations, while the Valentinian myth of Sophia surely owes something to the personified wisdom developed in the biblical wisdom literature from Proverbs through Ben Sira to the Wisdom of Solomon—indeed, as already noted, the name "Achamoth" points to the corruption of the Hebrew word for wisdom.

Crucially, however, the demiurge of gnostic revelation becomes the "god of this world,"[17] a lesser being more like the devil of the cosmic war found in apocalypses than the Creator God whose ultimate victory is promised. There is much to suggest alienation from the God of the Jewish scriptures was a big factor in the shaping of typical gnostic features, not least the way in which Genesis 2–3 is read "upside down." For the "jealous" God of Genesis, the Creator of the universe, becomes an inferior being, jealous of the spiritual world he is barely aware of, while the serpent is the "goody" in the story, the embodiment of the spiritual principle of wisdom who brings to humanity knowledge of good and evil, so enabling the divine spark in Adam to reach self-knowledge and escape from the clutches of the demiurge. Given that serpents were commonly seen as symbols of wisdom, knowledge, and skill (for example, the sign of Asclepius, the Greek god of medicine, or the magician's staff in Egypt), such a reading of Genesis was not by any means implausible.

Yet, for all that, the namelessness of the God of the Jews would seem to have influenced the radically apophatic characterization of the ultimate Father: the God of the scriptures has become divided against Godself, and the ultimate monism has turned into a dualism—which again is reminiscent of apocalyptic literature.

So is all this the radical Hellenization of Christianity proposed by Harnack? Surely it is, and yet it is not. Some aspects appear as distorted reflections of the philosophical schemata of Hellenistic philosophies; the radical rejection of matter as evil was too extreme for the Neoplatonist Plotinus.[18] But issues about being and becoming, the One and the Many, the fascination with cosmology and ori-

---

17. Cf. the ruler of this world in John 12:31; 2 Cor 4:4.
18. See Mark Edwards, "Gnostics and Valentinians in the Church Fathers," *JTS* 40 (1989):

gins, the association of nonbeing and matter were all live questions, as we saw in the last chapter, while the context of the Hellenistic world would explain both the syncretism and the allegory. Yet, one of the core influences would seem to come from the Jewish world, especially its apocalyptic literature, and in the end gnostic thought does not yield rational, philosophical doctrine. Its truth is revelatory and mystical with a deeply ambiguous sense of "knowledge"—it is more about self-knowledge, identity, and relationship than what we might call "doctrine." In its Christian form gnostic teaching makes sense of scripture by going beyond reading books, beyond any constraint on discerning the meaning sought. Scripture is exploited to bolster mystical insight and to produce new scriptures that take up the old into transmuted and potentially alien frameworks.

However, it would take the "fractionated" Roman church some time to recognize that what Valentinus taught was alien. After all, the Gospel of Truth has a spirituality that makes it seem like good devotional reading in the tradition of the Johannine material; it offers salvation through knowledge of truth. Unless alerted to what is implied by its teaching, what was the problem with gnostic groups functioning inside the Church and on its fringes? Their viewpoint was subtly attractive. Indeed, in the Valentinian scheme even the names of the aeons include words significant in Christian scripture: Grace, Only-begotten, Truth, Word, Life, even Church. The Ogdoad relates symbolically to the Sabbath, and the eighth day of resurrection. Sophia's myth was an exegesis of Proverbs 8 and the Wisdom of Solomon.[19] Surely these insights gave access to the deeper meaning of scripture?

2. THE CANON OF TRUTH

Knowledge of truth was also vital for the archcritic of Valentinus: Irenaeus of Lyons.[20] But for him truth was to be found in the apostolic tradition and scripture read according to the right *hypothesis*. Rather than turning immediately to the great work he directed specifically against "*gnosis* falsely so-called," we will trace through the argument of his smaller work, *The Demonstration of the Apostolic Preaching*, which focuses on the relationship between scripture and the doctrines or articles of faith, which he upholds. To begin with, we will simply set his position beside that of the Gospel of Truth.

37–38; this article is republished in his *Christians, Gnostics and Philosophers in Late Antiquity* (Farnham: Ashgate, 2012).

19. Cf. discussion in Edwards, *Origen against Plato*, 30 and 32.

20. E.g., Irenaeus, *Haer.* 1.9.5.

2.1. *Irenaeus's* Demonstration of the Apostolic Preaching and the Rule of Faith[21]

Prior to its discovery there was awareness of this work, since Eusebius makes reference to it, but little more was known about it until 1904 when an Armenian manuscript was found containing its text in translation alongside a version of the final two books of Irenaeus's *Against Heresies*. The survival of Irenaeus's originally Greek writings has depended on such Latin and Armenian translations.[22]

The *Demonstration of the Apostolic Preaching* (Gk. *Epideixis tou apostolikou kērygmatos*) describes itself as a "summary memorandum" assembled to aid understanding, to bear the fruit of salvation, and to confound false opinions. Many scholars treat it as intended for catechesis. From the outset Marcianus, to whom the work is addressed, is urged to "keep to the Rule of Faith" handed down from the apostles. This rule of faith (also known as the canon of truth) is paralleled in the writings of Origen and Tertullian. Summaries of apostolic teaching are rehearsed, a bit like creeds in that they are shaped in a similar way and utilize overlapping phrases, but unlike creeds in being flexible rather than exact formulae learned by rote word for word.[23] In detail they display considerable variety, yet, as the Greek word *kanōn* implies, all would appear to provide criteria for true faith. This is the summary given in the *Demonstration*:

> And this is the order of our faith, the foundation of the edifice and the support of our conduct: God, the Father, uncreated, uncontainable, invisible, one God, the Creator of all: this is the first article of our faith. And the second article: the Word of God, the Son of God, Christ Jesus our Lord, who was revealed by the prophets according to the character of their prophecy and according to the nature of the economies of the Father, by whom all things were made, and who, in the last times, to recapitulate all things, became a man amongst men, visible and palpable, in order to abolish death, to demon-

---

21. A version of this section appeared as "*The Demonstration of the Apostolic Preaching*: How Irenaeus Provides Clues to the Relationship between Creeds and Scripture," in *The Creed and the Scriptures*, ed. Markus Bockmuehl and Nathan Eubank, WUNT (Tübingen: Mohr Siebeck, forthcoming). Used with permission.

22. Translation in John Behr, ed., *On the Apostolic Preaching* (Crestwood, NY: St. Vladimir's Seminary Press, 1997). The fact that toward the end there is a cross-reference to *The Refutation and Overthrow of Knowledge Falsely So-Called* (Irenaeus's full title for *Adversus haereses*) may indicate it was written later, though Behr suggests the final chapters may be an addition.

23. Cf. Young, *Making of the Creeds*.

strate life, and to effect communion between God and man. And the third article: the Holy Spirit, through whom the prophets prophesied and the patriarchs learnt the things of God and the righteous were led in the paths of righteousness, and who, in the last times, was poured out in a new fashion upon the human race renewing man, throughout the world, to God. (*Epid.* 6)

The threefold shape evident here is common to the various versions of the canon of truth (besides the versions in Origen and Tertullian, Irenaeus himself provides more than one iteration across his own writings). All of these versions thus anticipate the shape of the creeds, and they also focus on certain common narrative elements often through catchphrases such as born of the Virgin, suffered, died, rose again, ascended to heaven, and will come again in glory. Similar catchphrases are found in the New Testament and other earlier Christian writings, so it would seem that in Christian groups a stereotyped "in-language" began forming from the beginning to encapsulate their basic teaching. All sources for this rule of faith come from a time when the canon of scripture was, roughly speaking, in place, and scriptural quotations, offered as prooftexts, sometimes expand the common outline. Thus, scripture provided proof of the rule of faith. But there was more than that to their relationship, as we shall see.

2.2. *Proof from Prophecy*

The *Demonstration* falls into two parts. The second part offers proof that the prior exposition is true, and prophecies, now demonstrably fulfilled, provide that proof. The argument here basically follows that of Justin Martyr, whose position we explored in the last chapter, as Irenaeus's introductory remarks show:

> That all those things would thus come to pass was foretold by the Spirit of God through the prophets, that the faith of those who truly worship God might be certain in these things, for whatever was impossible for our nature, and because of this would bring disbelief to mankind, these things God made known beforehand by the prophets, that, by foretelling them a long time beforehand, when they were fully accomplished in this way, just as they were foretold, we might know that it was God who previously proclaimed to us our salvation. (*Epid.* 42)

Irenaeus goes on to demonstrate that God has a Son, who assisted in the act of creation and then appeared to Abraham at Mamre, to Jacob in his dream of the ladder, and in the burning bush, and also is referenced in the prophecies of

David, Isaiah, and others, these being quoted along with other classic testimonies from the Psalms (*Epid.* 43–52). Other prophecies are then cited to prove the human birth of Jesus Christ, his messiahship and healings, his passion, and his resurrection and ascension (*Epid.* 53–85). Finally, Irenaeus shows how scripture predicted the apostles' witness, love's fulfillment of the law, the new covenant, the new people of God with a new Spirit in their hearts saved by Jesus Christ, who is now ascended to heaven (*Epid.* 86–97).

Toward the end Irenaeus briefly turns to errors in relation to God, such as thinking that beside the Creator there is another Father, together with errors in relation to the Son of God and the Spirit. Wariness is enjoined, but there is here no direct refutation:

> So, error, concerning the three heads of our seal, has caused much straying from the truth, for either they despise the Father, or do not accept the Son—they speak against the economy of his incarnation—or they do not accept the Holy Spirit, that is, they despise prophecy. And we must be wary of all such and flee from their thought, if we truly wish to be pleasing to God and to obtain, from him, salvation. (*Epid.* 100)

Overall the argument is that the basic elements of the rule of faith are guaranteed by scripture, especially "the three heads of our seal."

2.3. The Threefold Shape of the Rule of Faith / Canon of Truth

Irenaeus treats the rule's threefold shape as the essential basis of the faith received from the apostles. Early on in his exposition we can discern the reason for the threefoldness, for he indicates that this apostolic rule of faith

> exorts us to remember that we have received baptism for the remission of sins, in the name of God the Father, and in the name of Jesus Christ, the Son of God, [who was] incarnate, and died, and was raised, and in the Holy Spirit of God; and that this baptism is the seal of eternal life and rebirth unto God, that we may no longer be sons of mortal men, but of the eternal and everlasting God. (*Epid.* 3)

After further exposition, Irenaeus continues:

> For this reason the baptism of our regeneration takes place through these three articles, granting us regeneration unto God the Father through his

Son by the Holy Spirit: for those who bear the Spirit of God are led to the Word, that is to the Son, while the Son presents [them] to the Father, and the Father furnishes incorruptibility. Thus, without the Spirit it is not [possible] to see the Word of God, and without the Son one is not able to approach the Father; for the knowledge of the Father [is] the Son, and knowledge of the Son of God is through the Holy Spirit, while the Spirit, according to the good pleasure of the Father, the Son administers, to whom the Father wills and as He wills. (*Epid.* 7)

Now baptism "in the name of God, the Father and Lord of the universe, and of our Saviour Jesus Christ, and of the Holy Spirit" previously appears in Justin's *1 Apology* 61, and a generation or so later than Irenaeus we find in *The Apostolic Tradition* attributed to Hippolytus a description of the baptismal liturgy which indicates that candidates were asked three questions, with each affirmative response being followed by dipping in the water.[24] The questions making up this "Interrogatory Creed," as it is sometimes known, were as follows:

Do you believe in God, the Father Almighty?
   Do you believe in Christ Jesus, the Son of God, who was born of the Holy Spirit and Mary the virgin, and was crucified under Pontius Pilate, and was dead and buried, and rose on the third day alive from the dead and ascended in the heavens, and sits at the right hand of the Father and will come to judge the living and the dead?
   Do you believe in the Holy Spirit and the holy church and the resurrection of the flesh? (*Trad. ap.* 21)

The threefold shape of the rule of faith clearly reflects its link with baptism.

So, was it Matthew 28:19 that ensured the firm connection between baptism and the threefold name? Can we assume that emerging Christian scripture, by influencing the baptismal liturgy, also shaped the creeds? At first sight it might seem that way. We might recall, however, that studies of Gospel texts in

---

24. The text of *The Apostolic Tradition* from B. Botte, *La tradition apostolique de saint Hippolyte: Essai de reconstitution*, Liturgiewissenschaftliche Quellen und Forschungen 39 (Münster: Aschendorff, 1963). English translation in *On the Apostolic Tradition*, ed. and trans. Alistair Stewart-Sykes (Crestwood, NY: St. Vladimir's Seminary Press, 2001). For the different versions and sources see the introduction and commentary by Stewart-Sykes and also Paul F. Bradshaw, Maxwell E. Johnson, and L. Edward Phillips, *The Apostolic Tradition: A Commentary*, Hermeneia (Minneapolis: Fortress, 2002).

the second century tend to suggest that the final canonical forms took time to be fixed.[25] For example, as noted in the previous chapter, Marcion might well have possessed an earlier form of Luke than the version known to those who later accused him of expurgating that Gospel. In the case that now concerns us, we can state that neither Justin nor Irenaeus appear to quote or allude to Matthew 28:19 with reference to baptism in the threefold name, despite the fact that Irenaeus was certainly familiar with that Gospel and Justin quotes Jesus's sayings in their Matthaean form. So, was Matthew 28:19 not yet found in the versions of the Matthaean Gospel that they had available? We also know that a divergent baptismal practice appears in the book of Acts—there baptism is simply in the name of Jesus. Indeed, today Acts justifies the anti-Trinitarian "Jesus Only" stance of the Oneness Pentecostals.[26] So which came first, Gospel text or liturgical practice? It would seem that scriptural canon and liturgy emerged alongside one another in such a way that now it is hard to trace how there may have been influence one way or the other.

2.4. The Names

Getting the baptismal names right was clearly important: "names" might have magical powers—indeed, magic and exorcism were already exploiting the powerful name of Jesus. For Irenaeus the three names used in baptism carried "the seal of eternal life and rebirth unto God." For us they may be a significant clue to how the rule of faith related to scripture. The "home" of both canon of truth and canon of scripture is "the worship of the Christian community," writes Tomas Bokedal, and they cannot be understood apart, being "two sides of one and the same norm." Their "early mutual dependency" lies in identifying the "name" of God through narrative.[27]

For Bokedal the canon of scripture is not simply a list of books. Long before any lists, indeed well before Irenaeus, the manuscripts of Christian scripture were shaped in material ways distinct from the Jewish scriptures. Two very early and distinctive characteristics of Christian biblical manuscripts point both to this differentiation and also to the interdependence of the canon of truth and the biblical canon: these features are the use of codices rather

---

25. E.g., Parker, *Living Text of the Gospels*; and Lieu, *Marcion*, 209. Canonical Luke is the result of redactional development subsequent to the form known to Marcion; cf. our discussion in the previous chapter.

26. See above in chapter 1.

27. The key phrases just used come from Tomas Bokedal, *The Foundation and Significance of the Christian Biblical Canon* (London: Bloomsbury, 2014), 277, 282, 284–88, 308.

than scrolls and the *nomina sacra*. We have already noted the idiosyncratic preference for codices; here we need to explore further Bokedal's argument about names.

Consistently in both Old and New Testament manuscripts, keywords—*nomina sacra*—were highlighted by Christian scribes by using contracted forms with a stroke marking off the contraction. The second-century Epistle of Barnabas appears to know this convention, which is present even in the earliest surviving fragments of Gospel texts.[28] *Theos*, *Christos*, *Iēsous*, and *Kyrios* are the earliest found, these *nomina sacra* thus linking textually the names of God and Jesus and almost certainly reflecting early devotional practices. *Stauros*, *Pneuma*, and *Patēr* are sometimes given similar treatment, though less frequently. So Bokedal argues that the *nomina sacra* inscribed vocabulary typical of the rule of faith into the textual form of the scriptures.[29] As he writes, "The presence of these in an 'Old Testament' manuscript clearly sets it apart as of Christian provenance," and "[b]y this fusion of creedal-like elements and the biblical text, a distinct Christian sacred text was established for the faith communities."[30] Thus the *nomina sacra* are "an important link bridging the potential structural, theological and narrative gap between the Scriptures and the second century oral kerygma, the developing *regula fidei*."[31]

Obviously Bokedal's argument depends on an extraordinarily early dating for this distinctively Christian form of scripture. Is it consistent with the point made about the late emergence of the canonical forms of the Gospels, or indeed with Skarsaune's suggestion that full texts of the LXX were only indirectly available to Justin?[32] We need to acknowledge that the term "tunnel-period" has been used of the second century.[33] For, with respect to the transmission of

---

28. The origin of this scribal practice has often been associated with the Jewish practice of reverentially marking off the sacred divine name, though that does not offer a precise precedent. Note, for example, Larry Hurtado's theory regarding the *nomina sacra*: TIH with a bar above represents the numeral 318, which is mentioned in Gen 14:14; according to Barn. 9.7–8, IH equals 18, which represents Jesus, and T equals 300, which represents the cross; this gematria would explain the use of the supralinear stroke over the abbreviations, and the use of IH rather than IΣ for the abbreviation of Iησους, perhaps encouraged by the Hebrew word for "life." See chapter 3 of Larry W. Hurtado, *The Earliest Christian Artifacts: Manuscripts and Christian Origins* (Grand Rapids: Eerdmans, 2006).

29. Bokedal, *Biblical Canon*, 93.

30. Bokedal, *Biblical Canon*, 109 and 112 respectively.

31. Bokedal, *Biblical Canon*, 116.

32. See p. 49 n. 10 above.

33. A favorite term of my onetime text-critic colleague, Neville Birdsall.

the scriptures, much happened without leaving clear evidential traces. What we can say is that by the time of Irenaeus the fourfold Gospel, as well as corpora of apostolic and prophetic writings, were recognized as scriptural, their unity and order guaranteed by the apostolic rule of faith. What the *Demonstration* does is provide the clues to establishing the significance of the "names" as the connecting link between Christian reading of scripture and the canon of truth, a point perhaps already highlighted by the scribal practice of marking off the *nomina sacra*. As we explore Irenaeus's retelling of the biblical narrative in the *Demonstration* we shall find more clues to the significance of the names for our question concerning the relationship of scripture and creed. Meanwhile we take note of the fact that a kind of coinherence of scripture and the precursor to the creed is emerging out of early liturgical practice.

2.5. The Rule of Faith and Rule of Life

Baptism and initiation form the context of the rule of faith. Indeed, for Irenaeus "rebirth unto God" is what it is all about. Everything belongs to God, who is the Creator of all; the regeneration effected through baptism is the means of restoring communion between God and humanity. How this happens is expressed in the three articles of the canon of truth. However, according to *Demonstration* 1–2, besides the right way there are many wrong ways. The right way requires holiness of body and soul, which is reached by keeping to the rule of faith and performing the commandments. Rather than a set of doctrinal propositions the rule of faith is the way of salvation, setting out where we came from, where we are going, and how we can get there. The key motifs in Irenaeus's first brief exposition are creation, recapitulation, prophecy, renewal, and righteousness; and knowledge of God means relationship and transformation rather than abstract propositional truth claims.

Now relationship implies narrative—stories involving mutual interactions among participating characters. So an implied overarching narrative from the beginning to the end is captured in the character sketches outlined in those creed-like statements about God the Father, about the Word or Son of God, and about the Holy Spirit. Indeed, in *Demonstration* 3–10 we are given a sketch of the way things are through portraits of the three "names" into which each believer is baptized. The rule of faith is essentially confessional, doxological testimony, we might say, to God's actions and intentions, implicitly drawing on the biblical narrative. In no obvious sense a précis of the events and stories of the Bible, it is nevertheless the key to the overarching biblical narrative.

2.6. *The Rule of Faith as the Hypothesis of Scripture*

For Irenaeus the proper order and connection is vital for maintaining true likenesses of the "names" (*Epid.* 1). In his larger work, *Against Heresies*, the heretics are reprimanded for ignoring the proper order and connection of the scriptural books, so dismantling the true picture. His analogy there is of a mosaic—the work of a skillful artist, who had produced with gems a beautiful portrait of a king that was unpicked by heretics and rearranged to compose a dog or a fox (*Haer.* 1.8.1). Later Irenaeus would compare what they had done to a *cento*, a literary game where lines from the Homeric epics are effectively picked out and reordered to create a new narrative so that anyone might think they were reading Homer if they were not acquainted with the original (*Haer.* 1.9.4). The discernment of how the various discrete texts of scripture are connected and ordered is facilitated by the order and connection of the rule of faith. Thus, for Irenaeus the indispensable hermeneutical key is the rule of faith.

I have previously suggested that the rule of faith provided a "framework which is partly external to the text yet encapsulates the essential meaning of the text."[34] Back then, the claims of "canon criticism" seemed to alleviate the disintegration of scripture consequent upon the historico-critical method. But whence the canonical meaning? It seemed necessary to reassert scripture's dependence, for overall sensemaking, on the apostolic tradition captured in the rule of faith. After all, the very dispute in which Irenaeus was engaged proved that anyone could make any sense they liked of scripture if they read it without that rule. My approach has since been challenged: for example, in the prolegomena to his study of Irenaeus's Christology, Anthony Briggman has argued that *Against Heresies* 1.10.1 should be read as an outline of the *hypothesis* of scripture rather than as a version of the rule of truth.[35] The distinction between these two things, I suggest, is not in the end convincing, especially in the light of the *Demonstration*. Rather the notion that the rule of faith itself might be regarded as scripture's *hypothesis* is well worth consideration.

What, then, was the meaning of *hypothesis* in ancient literary theory? It referred to the overall intended meaning—in other words, the plot or argument, whether of the work as a whole or a particular passage, and that is certainly

---

34. Frances Young, *Virtuoso Theology: The Bible and Interpretation* (Cleveland: Pilgrim, 1993); originally published as *The Art of Performance: Towards a Theology of Holy Scripture* (London: Darton, Longman, and Todd, 1990), 53.

35. Anthony Briggman, *God and Christ in Irenaeus* (Oxford: Oxford University Press, 2019).

what we have in *Against Heresies* 1.10.1. Since *Against Heresies* 1.8 Irenaeus has been showing how the Valentinian scheme is one that neither the prophets announced nor the Lord taught nor the apostles delivered; the Valentinians, taking no account of the order and connection of the scriptures, "weave ropes of sand." Those analogies to a disordered mosaic or a Homeric *cento* appear right here. But Irenaeus then claims, "The church, though dispersed throughout the whole world, even to the ends of the earth, has received from the apostles and their disciples, this faith" (*Haer.* 1.10.1). "This faith" is then specified in what is apparently a distinctive version of the threefold confession of the rule of faith. It is distinctive in that the affirmation of Christ's birth from a virgin, death, resurrection, and ascension appears not in the clause concerning the Son of God but in the clause concerning the Holy Spirit, who proclaimed God's dispensations through the prophets (a point that mirrors, of course, Justin's apologetic use of prophecies to tell the gospel story).[36] Granted that this summary is not explicitly referred to as the rule of faith, it is nevertheless introduced as the faith received from the apostles, and just a few paragraphs earlier it is affirmed that anyone who adheres to the canon of truth received in baptism will recognize the names, parables, and so on taken from scripture, but not accept the dog or the fox, for such adherents are able to restore their proper order and fit them to the body of truth.

Surely, then, the *hypothesis* of scripture and the rule of faith must be regarded as identical, and this is exactly what the *Demonstration* articulates in detail. In the *Demonstration* and in *Against Heresies* 1.10.1 alike, the overarching story is captured—God's saving purposes played out providentially as recapitulation in Christ ensures "rebirth unto God" through the Spirit. Thus, the threefold rule of faith, or canon of truth, constitutes the *hypothesis* of scripture.

2.7. Irenaeus's Reading of Scripture in the Light of Scripture's Hypothesis

So let us now return to the *Demonstration* to consider how the *hypothesis* directs the way in which Irenaeus reads scripture. Significant are two features of Irenaeus's presentation of the biblical narrative:

1. His selection of biblical stories—his choices are clearly intended to illustrate the pattern of fall and redemption and to demonstrate the necessity of God's grace.

---

36. See 1.3 in chapter 3, above.

2. The subtle introduction, in the process of retelling the narratives, of the three "names" of the rule.

So, for example, *Demonstration* 11 tells of the creation of humankind: "fashioned with God's own Hands," indeed, "fashioned in the image of God," alive by the in-breathing of the "breath of life," so being "like God," and set to "rule over everything upon earth." Embedded in that account are the three "names." The true image of the Father is the Word, after whose image is fashioned the human, while the Spirit is the breath of life, and for Irenaeus the Word and the Spirit are the two "Hands" of God through whom God creates.

Irenaeus then moves on into the biblical story (*Epid.* 12). Set in paradise, this "lord of the earth," the image of God on earth, is to advance from infancy. The Word of God (the second of the "names") was always walking in paradise, talking with the man and prefiguring the future when he would dwell with him. There follows the naming of the animals and the creation of Eve from Adam's rib; Irenaeus comments that they were not ashamed, "kissing and embracing each other in holiness like children." Human immaturity, however, made them prey to being misled by the seducer. So Irenaeus recounts God's commandment and humankind's disobedience, deceived by the jealous angel hidden in the serpent, and their consequent banishment from paradise.

The recapitulation of that story in Christ has long been seen as the focal point of Irenaeus's theology of fall and redemption. Surprisingly he does not here jump to that solution. For what he now pursues is the playing out of fall and redemption time and again through the biblical saga, patterns and types foreshadowing, even instancing, the overarching sense of the whole narrative in a kind of providential *oikonomia*, and his choice of individual stories points us to this fundamental key to scripture. From Adam we move to Cain and Abel (*Epid.* 17), and then onto the expansion of wickedness until a fresh beginning with Noah, the one who remained righteous (*Epid.* 18–22). Along with other second-century Christian writers, such as Melito (*On Pascha*) and Theophilus of Antioch (*To Autolycus*), Irenaeus would seem to discern in Genesis explanatory tales of origins and other motifs familiar from Hesiod, such as descent from a Golden Age, thus building into the presentation of biblical material a sense of God's providential and saving purpose. The origins of ethnic difference, for example, he finds in the account of the cursing and blessing of Noah's sons: the cursing of Ham rests on Canaanites, Hittites, Arabs, Egyptians, and other ungodly peoples, while Abraham, Isaac, and Jacob receive the blessing of Shem, and the blessing of Japheth rests on the gentiles, called eventually to dwell in Shem's house through Christ. The covenant with

Noah ensures no future universal destruction, as well as a ban on taking the lifeblood of humans—the Genesis text justifies this by restating the point that humankind is made in God's image. Irenaeus, however, enlarges this by identifying God's image as the Son who in the last times would appear "to render the image like himself" (*Epid.* 22). Each of the biblical stories Irenaeus selects points forward through the discernment of God's purposes and the articulation of the Son's role.

So on goes the narrative, and as humankind proliferates we reach the Tower of Babel, through which humankind is scattered across the earth and its unity confounded (*Epid.* 23). The fulfillment of Shem's blessing comes with the story of Abraham, whose "lone, silent and failing" search for God was salvaged when God was revealed "through the Word, as through a ray of light" (*Epid.* 24). Abraham's departure from Mesopotamia, God's promises to him, his circumcision, and the birth of Isaac show how Shem's blessing passed through Abraham, Isaac, and Jacob to the twelve tribes of Israel. But four generations of slavery in Egypt now become the focus, Irenaeus shifting attention directly from Abraham to Moses and the exodus (*Epid.* 25). For "the God of the patriarchs, of Abraham, of Isaac and of Jacob" was the one who

> saved the sons of Israel from this [i.e. the slaughter of the firstborn], revealing in the mystery the Passion of Christ, by the slaughtering of a spotless Lamb and by its blood given to <be> smeared on the house of the Hebrews as a guard of invulnerability: the name of this mystery is the Pascha, source of liberation.

Thus the biblical narrative is refocused in light of Christ, the key second "name."

Next Irenaeus sketches the desert wanderings, telling how the Decalogue was received on tablets of stone written by God's finger—the finger he identifies as "the Holy Spirit who issued from the Father," so incorporating the third "name" (*Epid.* 26). There follows the establishment of the Aaronic priesthood to serve the "tabernacle of testimony," that is, as "a visible structure on earth of things which are spiritual and invisible in the heavens—and the figures of the form of the church, and the prophecy of things to come—in which [were] the vessels and the altars and the ark, in which he placed the tablets" (*Epid.* 26).

The prophetic import of the provisions is paramount. As the Israelites spy out the promised land, God reveals "the Name which alone [is] able to save those who believe in it," as Moses renames one of the envoys "Jesus" (the Greek form of Joshua) (*Epid.* 27). But doubt is sown among the people, the route diverted because of their unbelief, and that generation dies in the desert, and after forty years their children reach Jordan. There everything—God's great deeds and new legislation—is recapitulated by Moses in the book of Deuteronomy, "in which also are written many prophecies about our Lord Jesus Christ and about the people and about the calling of the Gentiles, and about the Kingdom" (*Epid*. 28). For Irenaeus the biblical narrative constantly points forward.

Now, however, Irenaeus's summary becomes much compressed (*Epid*. 29–30). Moses is succeeded by Jesus/Joshua, who leads entry into the land and its partition among the tribes, then immediately the reader is transported to Jerusalem with David and Solomon, "who built the temple to the name of God after the likeness of the Tabernacle, which was made according to the pattern of heavenly and spiritual things by Moses." There is cursory reference to the prophets sent from God—just enough is sketched to set within the overarching biblical story the great catalogue of prooftexts still to come. For, as we noted earlier, more than half of the *Demonstration* will utilize the prophets' words as evidence of predictions fulfilled, thus proving that it was all "according to the prophecies," the key claim of the rule of faith—indeed the fundamental claim lying at the core of the earliest confessions found in the New Testament. In fact, the prophets are given a double significance in Irenaeus's overarching narrative, for (1) their role in the perennial story of fall and return is clarified—they admonished the people and returned them to the God of the patriarchs; but (2) they also

> were made heralds of the revelation of our Lord Jesus Christ, the Son of God, announcing that his flesh would blossom from the seed of David, that he would be, according to the flesh, son of David, who was the son of Abraham, through a long succession, while, according to the Spirit, Son of God, being at first with the Father, born before all creation, and being revealed to all the world at the close of the age as man, "recapitulating all things" in Himself, the Word of God, "things in heaven and things on earth."

We have at last reached the point where Irenaeus is ready to remind us what scripture's grand narrative is all about, namely, the restoration of communion between God and the human creature (*Epid*. 31). That restoration, he says, "could not happen if it were not for his coming to us." All were implicated in the first formation of Adam, he explains, and we were bound to death through disobedience; so it was fitting

> by means of the obedience of the One, who on our account became man, to be loosed <from> death. Since death reigned over the flesh, it was necessary that, abolished through flesh, it released man from its oppression. So, "the

Word became flesh" that by means of the flesh which sin had mastered and seized and dominated, by this it might be abolished and no longer be in us. And for this reason our Lord received the same embodiment as the first formed, that he might fight for the fathers and vanquish in Adam that which had struck us in Adam.

As is well known, Irenaeus mapped out Christ's recapitulation of Adam in many parallels and/or reversals, and these are now presented (*Epid.* 32–34):

1. The virgin earth and the Virgin Mary produce like-embodiment, so that, as written in the beginning, he might become the man "according to the image and likeness of God."
2. The willing obedience of the Virgin Mary reverses the disobedience of the virgin Eve.
3. The transgression through the tree is undone by obedience on the tree that is the cross.

The cross, in its height, depth, length, and breadth, also captures visibly the invisible all-pervasiveness of the Word of God, so gathering the dispersed from all sides to the Father. The reversal of the consequences of Babel is surely implicit here—indeed, Irenaeus now ties together the plotlines that he has selected and underlined in recounting the biblical story, affirming that the promises to Abraham and to David were fulfilled (*Epid.* 35–36).

The climax engages again with "the economy of the Virgin" and its vital importance for death's undoing and the revitalization of humankind:

> He demonstrated the resurrection, becoming Himself the "firstborn from the dead," and raising in Himself fallen humanity, . . . as God had promised, by the prophets, saying, "I will raise up the fallen tabernacle of David."
>
> And, if one does not accept His birth from a Virgin, how can he accept His resurrection from the dead? . . . if He was not born, neither did He die; and if He did not die, neither was He raised from the dead; and if He was not raised from the dead, <death> is not conquered nor its kingdom destroyed; and if death [is] not conquered, how are we to ascend to life, having fallen under death from the beginning? (*Epid.* 38)

Thus, the narrative leads up to key confessions concerning the incarnation and resurrection: the one who is the firstborn of the Virgin but also Word of God summons humankind back to communion with God and that makes possible participation in incorruptibility (*Epid.* 40).

Finally, Irenaeus turns to the apostles, who are sent to turn people from idols, purify their souls and bodies by baptism, and dispense the Holy Spirit to believers, so establishing churches and making evident how the blessing of Japheth is realized in the calling of the gentiles, those who had been waiting to receive "'the dwelling in the house of Shem', according to the promise of God" (*Epid.* 42). So we are alerted once more to the *hypothesis* that has determined the selection of stories and the tracing of continuities across the entire biblical narrative. Thus the baptismal canon is filled out so as to render its sense and meaning; baptismal regeneration and the rule of faith are the foundations for Irenaeus's reading of the order and connection of the multiple scrolls or codices received as scripture.

Implicit, then, is mutual coinherence between the canon of truth and the canon of scripture. Never straightforwardly a summary sketch of the biblical narrative, the rule of faith was nevertheless meant to capture scripture's *hypothesis* (in the ancient usage of the term)—in other words, to point to what scripture is all about, its fundamental plot or argument, namely, the providential *oikonomia* of the one Creator God through whose Son and Spirit creation was effected and salvation granted. Indeed, this discussion surely invites us to consider again, alongside the coinherence of scripture and doctrine, the remarkably early appearance, via the threefold baptismal confession, of a Trinitarian reading of scripture.

3. So Was It Gnosticism That Provoked Definition of the Scriptural Canon and the Canon of Faith?

3.1. Irenaeus and the Gospel of Truth: Parallels and Contrasts

Before framing an answer to the above question it is worth pausing to consider the outcome of setting the Gospel of Truth beside Irenaeus's *Demonstration*. Some observations are classic; others may occasion a little surprise:

1. Unexpected, perhaps, is their common interest in "names," though what they signify is rather different, given the different context shaping each discussion. In each case identity is important, but in the Gospel of Truth the focus is on the revelation of secret identities and even of an identity in principle unnameable, whereas for the *Demonstration* identity is disclosed through narrative and action. The substance of the revelation is therefore almost incommensurable, despite the common language of Father, Son/Word, and Holy Spirit.

2. The coming of the savior is equally crucial for both texts, but the object and nature of that coming is not identical. Both are interested in where we have come from and where we are going to, and both understand it in terms of the union, relationship, or communion with God, but again the way to be taken is very different. Holiness of body and soul contrasts with knowledge. In the Gospel of Truth we find allusion to Revelation 3:7; in Irenaeus's response to gnostic teaching we also find reference to the book of the Father, which no one was able to open except the Lamb (*Haer.* 4.20.2). However, the context of the latter is the sovereignty of the one God over things in heaven and on earth that is "delivered" to the Son by the Father (Matt 11:27 is quoted), and this includes the fact that the Son is made Judge of the living and the dead. Irenaeus will later repudiate the idea found in the Gospel of Truth that "punishments and tortures . . . were leading astray . . . some who were in need of mercy" (*Haer.* 4.28.1). The one Creator God is for Irenaeus the all-seeing God to whom all are accountable, as we found in some of the earliest Christian texts.

3. Most obvious is the presence of biblical prophecy as a key element in the work of Irenaeus and its complete absence in the Gospel of Truth. The locus of revelation in the latter case appears to be a timeless reality, whereas in the former it is providential history. Both may read nonliterally, metaphorically, or symbolically, but one is in the interest of allegorical meaning, the other of prophetic discernment. This contrast is usually attributed to different evaluations of the material creation and its place within the divine purposes. However, a further way of looking at it would be to relate it to very different understandings of what might constitute scripture, and what might be the nature and function of books so designated.

4. To sum up these differences, one might make a contrast between rootlessness and rootedness. On the one hand, we observe the free association of language and ideas drawn from many sources, plucked out of context, and exploited as symbols to generate a self-identity without particular historical or cultural roots. On the other, an appeal to common traditions earthed in community liturgy and grounded in a grand narrative generated from a realistic reading of texts agreed to have scriptural authority by that community.

3.2. Did Gnosticism Provoke Canonical Definition?

In order to answer that key question we will take in turn Irenaeus's principal arguments against Gnosticism and assess how far his teaching can be regarded as freshly articulated in response to those rival doctrines.

3.2.1. On God and Creation

For Irenaeus the ultimate one God, Father of all, is to be identified with, not differentiated from, the Creator God. Given the material explored in our previous chapter this can hardly be regarded as novel. Rather, Irenaeus's thought is rooted in traditions, affirmed from 1 Clement on, which were firmly based in scripture and, by now, affirmed in the countercultural formulation "creation out of nothing." Need one say more? Yes—we do need to emphasize that in response to the threat, Irenaeus insists on three points:

(1) Paramount is the fundamental goodness of God's creation, the Word and the Spirit being God's hands crafting what the one God purposes. In each of his works we find favorite texts strung together to signify this:[37]

a. By the Word of the Lord were the heavens established and all the might of them by the Spirit (Ps 33:6).
b. All things were made by Him, and without Him was nothing made (John 1:3).
c. For he commanded and they were created; he spake and they were made (Ps 33:9).
d. But our God is in the heavens above, and in the earth; He hath made all things whatsoever he pleased (Ps 115:3).
e. One God, the Father, who is above all and through all and in all (Eph 4:6).

(2) Irenaeus also makes a point of underlining the way that humankind was formed after the likeness of God and molded by God's hands—that is, by the Son and the Holy Spirit, to whom God said, "Let us make man" (Gen 1:26).[38] He is absolutely clear that not just a part but the whole of a human being, made in God's likeness by the hands of the Father, is to be conformable to and modeled on the Son (*Haer.* 5.6.1). That means body as well as soul and spirit, he affirms, referring to 1 Thess 5:23: "Now the God of peace sanctify you perfect; and may your spirit, soul and body be preserved whole without complaint to the coming of the Lord Jesus Christ." In other words, the human creation is only fully realized eschatologically through the incarnation and the gift of the Spirit, though this did exist proleptically from the beginning as God's hands shaped what was to be. For it is the incarnate Word after whose image humankind was created: "For <I made> man <in> the image of God, and the image of God is the Son,

---

37. *Haer.* 1.22.1 links (a) and (b); *Haer.* 3.8.3 links (a), (c), and (d); *Epid.* 5 links (a) and (e). (The enumeration of the Psalms follows convention, not the numbers in the LXX.)

38. *Haer.* 4 Preface 4.

according to whose image man was made; and for this reason, He appeared in the last times, to render the image like himself" (*Epid.* 22). This somewhat cryptic statement is made plainer by reference to a passage in *Against Heresies*:

> This Word was manifested when the Word of God was made man, assimilating Himself to man, and man to Himself, so that by means of resemblance to the Son, man might become precious to the Father. For in times long past it was *said* that man was created after the image of God, but it was not *shown*; for the Word was as yet invisible, after whose image man was created. Wherefore also he lost the similitude easily. When, however, the Word of God became flesh, He confirmed both these: for he both showed forth the image truly, since He became what was His image; and he re-established the similitude after a sure manner, by assimilating man to the invisible Father by means of the visible Word. (*Haer.* 5.6.2; emphasis mine)

(3) Irenaeus also embraced the radical apophatic tradition—God, he agrees, cannot be measured and contains all things without being contained (*Haer.* 2.1.2; 4.4.2), as well as being beyond all sense perception, indeed indescribable, inconceivable and nameless. But God is not unknown (*Haer.* 4.4.2; 6.1–7.3; 20.1–9; *Epid.* 47)—rather, the one Father and Creator is known through the work of the Spirit and the Son, not least through the dispensations of God revealed to the prophets and fulfilled in the incarnation of the Word.

Such doctrines Irenaeus articulates against the gnostics, but they had their roots in scripture and had already been shaped during the second century, particularly by the apologists as we saw in the previous chapter. Justin, Theophilus, and others had tried to make sense of the gospel within the same cultural and intellectual context as Marcion and Valentinus, and Irenaeus capitalizes on their pioneering reaffirmation of biblical theology in terms relevant to that world.

3.2.2. On Recapitulation

There was a time when I would have argued that Irenaeus's doctrine of recapitulation was specifically developed to counter the gnostic reading of Genesis: determined to expose their "upside-down" reading of the text, he developed a scriptural doctrine of human fall and redemption, which would also undermine their claims to explain the disaster of the material creation by reference to a precosmic defect, error, or ignorance within the spiritual pleroma. But that approach devalues the significance of those precursors outlined in the Pauline Epistles (Rom 5:12–17; 1 Cor 15:45–49) and in Justin's *Dialogue*:

> Christ became man by the Virgin in order that the disobedience which proceeded from the serpent might receive its destruction in the same manner in which it derived its origin. For Eve, who was a virgin and undefiled, having conceived the word of the serpent, brought forth disobedience and death. But the Virgin Mary received faith and joy, when the angel Gabriel announced the good tidings to her that the Spirit of the Lord would come upon her, and the power of the Highest would overshadow her ... and she replied: "Be it unto me according to thy word." (*Dial.* 100)

Besides, the analysis of the *Demonstration* offered here now compels me to suggest that reaction to Gnosticism was not crucial for forming this doctrine, though it probably did contribute to Irenaeus's elaboration of it.

3.2.3. On the Scriptural Canon

It is surely clear that argument with Marcion and the gnostics did reinforce the need (1) to specify what books were scriptural and how they were to be interpreted; (2) to summarize exactly what doctrines lay behind the confession made in baptism; and (3) to specify the nature of the salvation brought by Jesus Christ. But again the above analysis of the *Demonstration* suggests that Irenaeus, as of course he himself claimed, was not so much innovating as articulating and clarifying traditions that he had inherited, and this was so whether he was identifying the books that constituted the old covenant and told of its fulfillment in the new, or rehearsing a rule of faith full of traditional phrases, deeply honed in liturgy and professed at baptism, which also provided the *hypothesis* or hermeneutical key for those scriptures.

4. Conclusion

Irenaeus's articulation of both canons—the biblical canon and the canon of truth—was vitally important for consolidating the future and, in thus affirming Irenaeus's rootedness in the apostolic tradition, I find myself nearer to Newman and Behr than I expected. And yet, surely the overall articulation of his understanding of biblical doctrine was only possible at the end of the second century, honed as it was through confrontation with rival readings.

All the protagonists in these debates were in their own way seeking understanding of what they had received in faith, and their differences were all within a specific historical, cultural, and intellectual context. To some extent, then, Harnack was right in attributing the definition of dogmas to "Hellenization," but the label is perhaps somewhat misleading in that it does not capture the reality on the ground, namely, that grasping and communicating the gospel necessitated acculturation to the rationality of those formed by the intellectual commonsense of the Greco-Roman world.

What the *Demonstration* as a whole has shown is that exposition of the rule of faith, vital for salvation, could only be offered through a retelling of the biblical story, which itself could only be grasped in proper order by using the rule of faith as hermeneutical key.[39] The three "names" constituted the meaning of the scriptural narrative. Creed-like confessions provided the key to the scriptures through characterizing the three "names" at work in the biblical story. Conversely the scriptures provided the prooftexts to confirm the truth enshrined in that rule—scripture canon and creedal canon proving to be coinherent, together guaranteeing the truth by which the baptized were to live.

As a result of the explorations in this and the previous chapter, I conclude that the definition both of the core canon of scripture and of the canon of faith—the precursor to the creeds—occurred at the same time and in mutual interaction. Also, such definition was rooted in liturgy and grounded in affirmation of the *monarchia* of the one and only supreme and transcendent God, the Creator of all to whom all are accountable and whose providential purposes will ultimately be fulfilled, above all through the Logos of God and the divine Spirit. Herein lay the beginning of Christian theology, both biblical and doctrinal.

---

39. Cf. Bokedal, *Biblical Canon*, 287, quoting Paul M. Blowers, "The *Regula Fidei* and the Narrative Character of Early Christian Faith," *Pro Ecclesia* 6 (1997): 212.

5

Divine Pedagogy

UNEARTHING THE INTENT OF THE HOLY SPIRIT

Aspects of Origen's career, context, and teaching activity have already claimed our attention.[1] Although Origen was retrospectively condemned as a heretic for certain problematic doctrines, Origen's influence meanwhile was deep and widespread. So what he meant by doctrine, and how the first great exegete of scripture understood its connection with scripture, must be of prime significance for this study. These topics will be the principal focus of this chapter, much else being left aside given the existing range of scholarship on his life and work.

1. Doctrine as Pedagogy

1.1. Different Levels and the Learning Journey

One of Origen's concerns was the nurturing of educated Christians capable of distinguishing between different philosophical or gnostic claims and committed to the truth enshrined in scripture. However, as we discovered earlier, he also saw Christianity as a universal philosophy capable of improving all kinds of human beings.

Another illuminating discovery on my part was Karen Jo Torjesen's reassessment of the supposed distinction Origen makes in his writings between different levels of Christian believer, apparently classifying people according to their capacity to read scripture literally, morally, or spiritually.[2] She sug-

---

1. See chapter 2.
2. Karen Jo Torjesen, "'Body,' 'Soul,' and 'Spirit' in Origen's Theory of Exegesis," *Anglican Theological Review* 67.1 (1985): 17–30.

gests that rather than categorizing persons (as gnostics seem to have done), Origen proposed that these three levels of meaning relate to three stages in an educational process, making it possible to move from one level to another, as none of the levels of meaning was exclusive of the others—indeed the higher levels were grounded in the letter of the text. Attractive as it seems, this view is probably not entirely sustainable in the end. Ron Heine has observed that the *Commentary on Matthew* clearly distinguishes between the crowds and the disciples—the latter pursuing deeper understanding while the former merely hear the stories.[3] Indeed, Origen's homilies demonstrate awareness of differing levels of understanding in his audience, and in response to Celsus's jibes he repeatedly celebrates the fact that Christianity could educate the lower classes, even slaves and women, to be good, unlike philosophy with its elitist character (*Cels.* 6.1).[4] But that is the point surely—no one is excluded from the reach of God's pedagogical purpose, which is adapted to the capacity of each. There are some who, like the apostles, are summoned into the house where they receive explanations of what the crowds hear in parables and progress to deeper insights.

So the multitude matters. Yet Origen also insists that Christianity appeared as "something worthy of serious attention, not only to people of the lower classes, as Celsus thinks, but also to many scholars among the Greeks" (3.12; cf. 3.49). He does not want the Christian assembly to consist only of the "stupid"; rather he seeks "the cleverer and sharper minds because they are able to understand the explanation of problems and of the hidden truths set forth in the law, the prophets and the gospels" (3.74). So,

> we do everything in our power to see that our gathering consists of intelligent people, and we do dare to bring forward in the common discourse at the time of our gathering our most noble and divine beliefs when we have an intelligent audience. But we conceal and pass over the more profound truths whenever we see that the meeting consists of simple-minded folk who are in need of teaching which is figuratively called milk. (*Cels.* 3.52)

This Origen goes on to justify on the basis of 1 Corinthians 3:2–3 and Hebrews 5:12–14: Paul had fed them milk not meat because they were not yet ready

---

3. See the introduction to *The Commentary of Origen on the Gospel of Matthew*, ed. Ron Heine, OECT (Oxford: Oxford University Press, 2018), 1:7–20, referring to Origen's discussion of Matt 13:36–43.

4. See also e.g., *Cels.* 1.9: simple faith can produce reformed characters; 3.49: the gospel calls the stupid to make them better. Cf. the discussion in chapter 2.

for more advanced food. But, Origen affirms, "we do want to educate all people with the Word of God, even if Celsus does not wish to believe it" (*Cels.* 3.53–54). For Moses, the prophets, and the one "who enlightened humankind"

> left no-one without some experience of his mysteries. On the contrary because of exceeding love towards humankind he was able to give the educated a conception of God which could raise their soul from earthly things, and nevertheless came down to the level even of the most defective capacities of ordinary men and simple women and slaves, and, in general, of people who have been helped by none but by Jesus alone to live a better life, so far as they can, and to accept doctrines about God such as they had the capacity to receive. (*Cels.* 7.41)

Surely these attitudes were the fruit of Origen's experience of teaching at a wide range of levels, during the years in Alexandria as well as in the course of his concurrent activities in Caesarea offering homilies in church as a presbyter, as well as teaching in school.[5]

Admitting Celsus's parallels between Christianity and Plato, Origen sees no problem with these agreements "if the doctrine is beneficial and its intention sound." In an extended discussion he not only affirms that "the writings of the Jews are proved to be earlier than those of the Greeks," but also insists that "the same doctrine expressed in the beauty of Greek style" should not be thought "superior to its expression in the poorer style and simpler language used by Jews and Christians" (7.59–60). Origen offers a parable: food prepared for the rich and luxurious is not necessarily good for poor and simple peasants, whereas their own habitual cooking brings better health for most of them. So, "will we prefer those who prepare food for the benefit of the learned, or those who cook for the multitude?" As Origen states, "it is obvious that humanity itself and the interest of humankind as a whole suggest that the physician who has cared for the health of the majority helps others more than the physician who has cared for the health of only a few" (7.59).[6]

Surely, "Plato and the wise philosophers of the Greeks" resemble "in their fine utterances" the physicians "who have cared only for those supposed to be the better classes, while they despised the multitude," whereas "the prophets

---

5. Cf. the discussion in chapter 2 above.
6. Note this frequent image: cf., e.g., 3.74: claiming to be a "philanthropic physician who seeks the sick that they may bring relief to them and strengthen them."

among the Jews and the disciples of Jesus" who renounced human wisdom and "the wisdom according to the flesh" are comparable to those who prepare "the same very wholesome quality of food by means of a literary style which gets across to the multitude" (7.60).

But Origen certainly did not rule out progress from one level to another for those capable of such advance:

> the divine nature, which cares not only for those supposed to have been educated in Greek learning but also for the rest of mankind, came down to the level of the ignorant multitude of hearers, that by using the style familiar to them it might encourage the mass of the common people to listen. After they have once been introduced to Christianity they are easily able to *aspire to grasp even deeper truths* which are concealed in the Bible. For it is obvious even to an ungifted person who reads them that many passages can possess a meaning deeper than that which appears at first sight, which becomes clear to those who devote themselves to Bible study, and which is clear in proportion to the time they spend on the Bible and their zeal in putting its teaching into practice. (*Cels.* 7.60 [emphasis mine])

So, despite the caveats noted earlier, it is worth returning to Torjesen's discussion. In *Hermeneutical Procedure and Theological Method in Origen's Exegesis* she traces out Origen's exegetical practice, demonstrating that for Origen the exegete's task was to enable the pedagogical work of scripture in assisting the journey of the soul.[7] Discernible in his homilies and commentaries, she suggests, is a progression corresponding with his conception of the three stages of that journey: purification, then knowledge of the Logos, and ultimately union with God. The redeeming and saving work of the Logos is thus educative, assisting the move from one step to the next. The process enables progressive transformation, the pastoral task of the church in the exegesis of scripture facilitating *paideia*. Each hearer is drawn into the text: the literal sense refers to its wording—what the words meant to psalmist or prophet; the spiritual sense is what it means for the one journeying in faith and participating in the history of salvation. This is effected by universalizing the text's import or by allegory.

---

7. Karen Jo Torjesen, *Hermeneutical Procedure and Theological Method in Origen's Exegesis* (Berlin: de Gruyter, 1985). The discussion here reflects my article "Paideia and the Myth of Static Dogma," in *The Making and Remaking of Christian Doctrine. Essays in Honour of Maurice Wiles*, ed. Sarah Coakley and David Pailin (Oxford: Clarendon, 1993), 265–83.

"The purpose of inspiration is paideia, the progressive perfection of the Christian through assimilation of the saving doctrines," states Torjesen.[8] Not all Christians are yet ready for every doctrine, so any given homily includes teachings geared for different levels—for the beginner, for those advancing, and for those perfect. Such doctrines effect salvation through scripture and its exegesis. There may be caveats as to whether this progression is really for every soul—indeed, as to whether Origen really intended to separate classes of Christians.[9] But Origen clearly does expect people to engage in a learning process that transforms life, the diversity of scriptural teachings providing a perfect instrument for the gradual revelation of the Logos.

Building on this approach, Peter Martens explores the way Origen traces "the contours of the exegetical life." He writes, "For [Origen] the ideal scriptural interpreter was someone who embarked not simply on a scholarly journey but, more ambitiously, upon a way of life, indeed a way of salvation, that culminated in the vision of God."[10] Scripture was written "for the cure of the soul," as Origen remarks in his *Commentary on John*; it was meant to be "'useful or 'beneficial,' serving as an instrument in the divine plan of salvation for those who read and heard it well."[11] It was its divine authorship that gave study of scripture this paramount position in Christian life.

For Origen, then, the Logos communicates himself to the soul through scriptural teaching. Progressive disclosure enables deepening apprehension of the Logos as the soul advances on its journey. For the catechumenate at the beginning stage what is needed is purification from sin, healing from the soul's physician. Then, through moral and mystical pedagogy, sanctification and redemption ensues as the soul is prepared for perfection. Scriptural history becomes universal, for the journey of the soul constitutes the allegorical meaning of, for example, Israel's wanderings, the text being taken to refer to spiritual realities. As the word of God, scripture is doctrine—divine pedagogy.

1.2. The Intent of the Divine Author

Repeatedly Origen affirms that the biblical authors were assisted by the Holy Spirit and looks to discern the Spirit's authorial aim (*skopos*) or intent

---

8. Torjesen, *Hermeneutical Procedure*, 42.
9. Torjesen, "Origen's Theory of Exegesis."
10. Peter W. Martens, *Origen and Scripture: The Contours of the Exegetical Life*, Oxford Early Christian Studies (Oxford: Oxford University Press, 2012), 6.
11. Martens, *Origen and Scripture*, 193, citing *Comm. Jo.* 10.174.

(*boulēma*).[12] In his most systematic survey of how scripture is to be read and understood, book 4 of his *First Principles*, Origen couples affirmation of the Spirit's enlightening of the prophets and apostles with the intent to reveal "unspeakable Mysteries, so that anyone capable of being taught through application to spiritual meanings" might "become partaker of all the doctrines of the Spirit's counsel." For Origen souls could not reach perfection without "the rich and wise truth about God," and this involved "the doctrines concerning God and His only-begotten Son," along with explanations of evil and so forth (*Princ.* 4.2.7).[13]

But the Spirit also had another aim, "pursued for the sake of those unable to endure the burden of investigating" such important matters. This was to conceal such doctrine in a narrative about the visible creation that, nevertheless, was capable of improving the majority insofar as they would receive it (*Princ.* 4.2.8). This concealment, however, would be cracked open by those capable of doing so, for in order to alert them to meanings beyond the obvious, "the Word of God arranged for certain stumblingblocks, as it were, and hindrances and impossibilities to be inserted in the midst of the law and the history." Such impossibilities are there "for the sake of the more skilful and inquiring readers," who "by giving themselves to the toil of examining what is written" will discover the necessity of seeking "a meaning worthy of God" (4.2.8).

Origen had already stated that "certain mystical revelations made known through the scriptures" are not understood, and the prophecies "are filled with riddles" (4.2.2–3). He did not merely prefer spiritual meanings, but notoriously asserted that some passages have no literal sense at all (4.2.5). Now we find that concealment of true doctrine was the *intention* of the earthly narrative from creation through history (4.2.8; 3.11), and that *aporiai* (stumbling blocks, puzzles, hindrances, even impossibilities) were purposely inserted into the law and biblical history to circumvent failure to move beyond the letter to learn more of the divine (4.2.9). It was necessary to "search the scriptures" (John 5:39) to investigate its prophecies and mysteries; discovery of the hidden "treasures of wisdom and knowledge" (Col 2:3) required the help of God (4.3.5; 3.11). This paradoxical idea that God's revelatory word was indirect was, however, culturally apt, as we can see by paralleling Plutarch's discussion of oracles with

---

12. E.g., *Hom. Sam.* 5.4; *Comm. Matt.* 16.12; *Comm. Jo.* 1.15, cited by Martens, *Origen and Scripture*, 195.

13. Text in P. Koetschau, ed., *De Principiis*, Origenes Werke 5, GCS 22 (Leipzig: Hinrichs, 1913); English translation: G. W. Butterworth, *On First Principles* (London: SPCK, 1936; repr., Gloucester, MA: Smith, 1973).

Origen's hermeneutical principles.[14] Origen, like Justin before him, absorbed contemporary cultural norms, not least in treating the scriptures as a collection of oracles to be deciphered.

As observed in chapter 3, among his *Moralia* Plutarch has essays raising two questions: "Why are there fewer oracular shrines active than there were in the past?" and "Why do oracles now come in prose not verse?"[15] We noted that Plutarch's defense of oracles turned on the idea that one providence orders the universe and everything in it, so predictions through oracles are not at all unexpected.[16] He also wrote that whereas oracular riddles usually responded to inquiries or offered solutions to the problems of life, on occasion the god would also pose problems, thus creating a craving for knowledge. Philosophy begins with inquiry, and inquiry begins in wonder and uncertainty (*E Delph.* 384). So naturally most things concerning the god are concealed in riddles, which constitute a tantalizing invitation to investigate. Dissolving ambiguities is at the core, for logical reasoning is promoted by ambiguous oracles (*E Delph.* 385–86). Older oracles, then, made use of myths, proverbs, circumlocutions, vagueness, metaphors, riddles, and statements with double meanings. Some people, Plutarch suggests, are nostalgic for such old riddles, allegories, and metaphors (*E Delph.* 406). For the mind is steered toward things divine through sacred symbols—some obscure, others clearer (*Is. Os.* 378)—and so to avoid superstition or atheism philosophical reasoning needs to be adopted as guide to these mysteries. The *ainigma* of the divine is enshrined in all kinds of odd rites, sacred animals, holy names, numbers, and signs, all to be treated as mirroring the one uncontaminated, unpolluted, pure, transcendent Being (*Is. Os.* 382).

Origen's position parallels this perspective on the divine as both hidden and revealed, as inadequately mediated through what is other than the divine, the import of which is properly the subject of inquiry. His predecessor, Clement, had already argued that discourse concerning the divine is hidden in mysteries and necessarily symbolic, the transcendent God being "without form or name" (*Strom.* 5.12).[17] Indeed Clement had generalized the point: "All then, in a word, who have spoken of divine things, both Barbarians and Greeks, have veiled the first principles of things, and delivered the truth in enigmas, and symbols, and allegories, and metaphors, and such like tropes" (*Strom.* 5.4). The motif

---

14. The following reflects my paper, "Riddles and Puzzles."
15. See Plutarch, *Pyth. orac.* and *Def. orac.*
16. Cf. chapter 3 above.
17. Text of *Stromateis* in O. Stählin, *Clemens Alexandrinus II: Stromata I–VI*, GCS 15 (Leipzig: Hinrichs, 1906); English translation in *ANF* 2.

of revelatory concealment Clement finds not only in Greek oracles but also Pythagorean symbols, Platonic myths, and Egyptian hieroglyphs. Among all these, he includes a discussion of the hidden meanings of the Jerusalem temple, its veiled Holy of Holies, and the unutterable name of God (*Strom.* 5.5–9). As both poets and philosophers speak of hidden mysteries, so "it is proper that the Barbarian philosophy [= the Jewish scriptures] should prophesy also obscurely and by symbols" (*Strom.* 5.8).

On this sort of basis Origen chides Celsus for his assumption that the Bible is not susceptible to allegorical interpretation: "Are the Greeks alone allowed to find philosophical truths in hidden form, and the Egyptians too, and all barbarians whose pride is in mysteries and in the truth they contain?" (*Cels.* 4.38). Can Celsus really think that "the Jews alone, and their lawgiver, and the authors of their literature" had no share in this viewpoint, despite the fact they had been taught "to ascend to the uncreated nature of God and look upon God alone," basing their "hopes only on God." Origen acknowledges readers who "could find Plato's meaning by examining philosophically what he expresses in the form of myth," and then "would admire the way in which he was able to hide the great doctrines as he saw them in a myth on account of the multitude, and yet to say what was necessary for those who know how to discover from myths the true significance intended by their author" (4.39). But, he claims, "it is not quite clear whether Plato happened to hit on these matters by chance, or whether, as some think, on his visit to Egypt he met even with those who interpret the Jews' traditions philosophically, and learnt some ideas from them."

Origen, then, recognized that the indirectness of God's word fitted the culture, even claiming priority for Jews and Christians, and the associated notion that difficulties in interpretation were put there to stimulate inquiry he understood as the specific authorial intent of the Holy Spirit. Divine pedagogy involved setting challenges not only with respect to ethics and way of life but also in terms of grasping transcendent truths. The challenge was to discern the spiritual meaning of scripture hidden in the letter.

1.3. Paideia *and* Dogma[18]

Paideia, then, implies a process of development through education and advancing understanding, moving beyond literal meaning to the spiritual. For even if the literal is beneficial to start with (*Princ.* 4.2.6), it can lead to mis-

---

18. Parts of this section reflect material from my essay, "Paideia and the Myth of Static

leading interpretations—Origen not only criticized Jews and heretics for their literal reading (a somewhat odd charge to which we will return), but he also challenged those simple, uninquiring believers who took God's promises to mean resurrection to a luxurious life of eating, drinking, and enjoying the fulfillment of bodily desires or who thought God harsh and unjust.[19] Constantly Origen invited his hearers to deepen their grasp of the truth. But was that sought-after truth enshrined in *dogmata*, teachings that constituted Origen's "doctrine"? And was the source of that teaching more Plato than the scriptures? Indeed, was Origen's hermeneutic a way of reading philosophical doctrine into, or out of, scripture? There have always been some who have taken that view, and not just Origen's critics in the Origenist controversies of the fourth and sixth centuries.

In the Bampton lectures of 1866, published as *The Christian Platonists of Alexandria*, Charles Bigg still assumed that the *First Principles* could be treated as a source for Origen's doctrine.[20] In his view Origen did accept a role, though somewhat limited, for "tradition which handed down certain facts, certain usages, which were to be received without dispute." Tradition, however, provided no clues as to "the why or the whence," so leaving room for "the office of the sanctified reason to define, to articulate, to co-ordinate, even to expand, and generally to adapt to human needs the faith once delivered to the Church."[21] Bigg took for granted that Origen presented the result of his inquiries as his established doctrines, whether of God, the Logos, the Trinity, the soul, or other matters. For Bigg, Origen's viewpoint on such classic doctrinal affirmations could simply be expounded by treating *First Principles* as a theological system to which Platonism had substantially contributed.

A century later Henri Crouzel offered a very different perspective.[22] Origen belonged to a time when discussion, debate and hypothesis was still permissible, he suggested. Indeed, like any other intellectual Origen could consider alternative theses—after all, his pupil at Caesarea tells us he offered his students

---

Dogma," in *The Making and Remaking of Christian Doctrine: Essays in Honour of Maurice Wiles*, ed. Sarah Coakley and David Pailin (Oxford: Clarendon, 1993), 265–83.

19. Regarding the former, see *Princ.* 2.11.2; cf. *Cels.* 4.57; 5.18–20; 7.32–34; 8.49–50, where Origen tries to counter Celsus's literalist assumptions about Christian faith in future resurrection. Regarding the latter, see *Princ.* 4.2.1; cf. discussion on p. 123 below.

20. Charles Bigg, *The Christian Platonists of Alexandria* (Oxford: Oxford University Pres, 1886).

21. Bigg, *Platonists*, 191.

22. Henri Crouzel, *Origène* (Paris: Aubier, 1962); English translation of Crouzel is *Origen*, trans. A. S. Worrall (Edinburgh: T&T Clark, 1980).

all the different opinions for consideration and he was often hard to pin down. Origen was not systematic, and that is why we have problems deciding whether or not he taught controversial doctrines such as *metempsychosis* (transmigration of souls).[23] It was later Origenist controversies that began attributing doctrines to him, for that was a different era and Origen's orthodoxy was the issue. Crouzel acknowledges that Origen had "great admiration for Plato," but insists that he "retains independence of him and is able to criticize him." Origen may note common moral ideals, but the philosopher, unlike the Christian, "does not relate his actions to God by thanksgiving." Both heretic and philosopher are engaged in "an idolatrous project" in that both "worship what their minds construct."[24] In evaluating Origen's thought as a whole, Crouzel preferred to direct attention to Origen's exegesis of scripture as his priority—it was, after all, the predominant aspect of his life's work.

Debate has continued around Origen's Platonism. Trigg's 1982 biography of Origen rowed back from "the tendency to downplay Origen's Platonism" both in Crouzel and, before him, Daniélou.[25] Crouzel, Trigg states, "took Origen's manifestly critical comments about philosophy in many of his works as proof that Origen could not himself have been a Platonist."[26] Yet, in Trigg's view:

> Platonism, besides agreeing with Christianity on the goodness, if limitedness, of the created world and on the compatibility of God's providence with human freewill, provided Origen with what Christianity manifestly lacked, a rational understanding of God's purpose in which all of these seemingly disparate and contradictory doctrines formed a coherent whole.[27]

For Trigg it is clear that for Origen philosophy is "a preparatory discipline," answering to the "needs of Christian theology in its battle with the Gnostics." For him "false doctrine was bad philosophy," "true doctrine is good philosophy," and "good philosophy is Platonism," writes Trigg.[28] Hence "the extraordinary power of Platonism over Origen's thought."

By contrast in 2002 Mark Edwards underlined the profound disparities between Origen's teaching and the Platonism then current, with precise chrono-

---

23. Crouzel, *Origen*, 166.
24. Crouzel, *Origen*, 157–60.
25. Jean Daniélou, *Origène* (Paris: La Table Ronde, 1948); English translation of Daniélou in *Origen*, trans. Walter Mitchell (New York: Sheed and Ward, 1955).
26. Trigg, *Origen*, 284.
27. Trigg, *Origen*, 73.
28. Trigg, *Origen*, 74.

logical and philosophical points providing evidence, and a focus on both the pioneering and essentially Judeo-Christian spirit of Origen's intellectualism.[29] A few telling sentences:

> Unlike the God of Origen, the One can make no choices: it causes without creating, presides without governing, superabounds without love.[30]

> Of the Platonists it is almost true to say that the higher their notion of the First Principle the less inclined they were to worship it . . . Origen's theology, unlike that of the Platonists, requires that a deity should have a cult.[31]

> Origen's is an autonomous philosophy, designed to answer, not to flatter, the teaching of the schools. No doubt he has turned his pen to many questions that would never have occurred to him had he been ignorant of Plato, the Stoics or Aristotle, just as it might not occur to apologists of our own day to reflect on the laws of nature, or institutional poverty or on the origins of consciousness had they never heard of Einstein, Marx or Freud.[32]

And that surely is the point. The philosophy into which Origen had been encultured through his education was the essential handmaid for clarification of the truth within then current rational frameworks. Deserved or not, and whether offered in disparagement or admiration, the label "Platonist" does capture the way in which Origen was engaged with the intellectual issues of the day, recognized the commonalities between Platonism and Christianity, and had the educational equipment to demonstrate how the distinct Christian philosophy produced the best answers. It was philosophy that helped shape what he calls in *First Principles* "a single body of doctrine"; but it was scripture that enshrined that doctrine and that enabled true progress in the moral and spiritual life—proper Christian *paideia*, the fundamental aim of his scholarship and teaching activity.

So inquiry into the implications of scripture, including questions about the meaning intended by the Holy Spirit, could be pursued using all the intellectual tools available.[33] As earlier observed,[34] in a letter to a pupil, Gregory, preserved in the *Philocalia*, Origen recommends those parts of Greek philoso-

29. Mark Julian Edwards, *Origen against Plato* (Farnham: Ashgate, 2002).
30. Edwards, *Origen against Plato*, 61.
31. Edwards, *Origen against Plato*, 72.
32. Edwards, *Origen against Plato*, 161.
33. See further the discussion in Martens, chapter 4 passim.
34. Cf. 4.2 in chapter 2 above.

phy that are fit should serve as preparatory studies for Christianity, along with other studies, such as geometry and astronomy, insofar as they are helpful for the interpretation of scripture. For geometry, music, grammar, rhetoric, and astronomy are generally regarded as ancillary to philosophy, and by analogy one may speak of philosophy as ancillary to Christianity. Scripture itself enigmatically points to this as the Israelites plunder the goods of the Egyptians and recycle them for the worship of the true God (Exod 12:35–36; 31:1–11). After all, God the Creator of all is ultimately the source of all wisdom and rationality: "all rational beings are partakers of the Word of God, that is, of Reason, and so have implanted within them some seeds, as it were, of Wisdom and Righteousness" (*Princ.* 1.3.6). Elsewhere Origen states that "the same God has implanted in the souls of all the truths which He taught through the prophets and the Saviour" (*Cels.* 1.4). According to Origen, if Celsus

> had been a philosopher with any sense of obligation to others, he ought to have avoided destroying with Christianity the helpful beliefs which are commonly held among people, and should have given his support, if he could, to the fine doctrines which Christianity has in common with the rest of humankind. (*Cels.* 4.83)

What, then, was Origen's concept of doctrine? Surely it was the divine teaching enshrined in scripture, and especially the maieutic and pedagogical process whereby the ethical virtues and transcendent truths to be found therein delivered wisdom and perfection to the aspiring student. So, to assess Origen's Christology, for example, simply according to the categories supplied by the typical "History of Doctrine" approach loses its real dynamic. To speak of humanity and divinity and the relationship between them makes sense only in the context of the overall pedagogical accommodation of the Logos to the level of those who need healing and sanctification.

> For Christians see that with Jesus human and divine nature began to be woven together, so that by fellowship with divinity human nature might become divine, not only in Jesus, but also in all those who believe and go on to undertake the life which Jesus taught, the life which leads everyone who lives according to Jesus' commandments to friendship with God and fellowship with Jesus. (*Cels.* 3.28)

Understanding the Gospels requires the penetration that discerns the divinity beneath or within the particularities of the earthly presence. There is a profound continuity between the two, a kind of sacramental relationship. The transformative and progressive response to the teaching of the Logos envisaged by Origen belongs, it seems, to an entirely different realm of discourse from what we might call "correct doctrine."

Yet we already observed how Origen described "the rich and wise truth about God" in terms of "the doctrines concerning God and His only-begotten Son."[35] This passage goes on to list other doctrines:

> of what nature the Son is, and in what manner he can be the Son of God, and what are the causes of his descending to the level of human flesh and completely assuming humanity; and what, also, is the nature of his activity, and towards whom and at what time it is exercised. It was necessary, too, that the doctrines concerning beings akin to man and the rest of the rational creatures, both those that are nearer the divine and those that have fallen from blessedness, and the causes of the fall of these latter, should be included in the accounts of the divine teaching; and the question of the differences between souls and how these differences arose, and what the world is and why it exists, and further how evil is so widespread and so terrible on earth. (*Princ.* 4.2.7)

So could it be said that, despite the pedagogical and maieutic flavor of his approach to teaching, Origen actually intended to define a body of doctrinal truth?

2. Right Doctrine, Right Reading

It would not be surprising if Origen did intend to define a body of doctrine; for that is what philosophers did and, notoriously, different philosophical traditions offered different options (*haireseis*) when it came to teaching the truth about the way things are and the way to live life. Furthermore, they uncovered those truths through the exegesis of ancient books, interpreting Homer and Plato for example, in the light of their doctrines.[36]

One of the most significant aspects of Peter Martens's study *Origen and Scripture* is his proposal that, for all the scholarship concerning his exegetical techniques and his allegorical method, it was doctrine, right or wrong,

---

35. See p. 115 above, citing *Princ.* 4.2.7.
36. See, e.g., Robert Lamberton, *Homer the Theologian* (Berkeley: University of California Press, 1986).

which Origen recognized as determinative of right or wrong reading. Origen repeatedly accuses Jews and heretics of wrong interpretation—indeed, of interpreting the text literally instead of probing it for deeper spiritual meanings. Martens notes how this has surprised and puzzled those who know anything about the Jewish exegesis or gnostic hermeneutics of the period and, mining the range of Origen's extant works for examples, he shows that in both cases it is basically not an argument about philological method but about doctrine or practice.[37] Origen's fundamental objection to Marcion, Valentinus, and Basilides, often listed together as a trio, is that they believed

> in two Gods: the God of the Law and Prophets on the one hand, and the God of Jesus on the other . . . [W]here Origen censured a literal exegesis in Gnostic circles, a wider examination of the literary context shows that he had a *specific* literal interpretation in mind: tearing asunder the unity of God, and thus, also, the law from the gospel.[38]

Much the same principle is found with reference to Origen's critique of Jewish literalism. It is "best read not simply or even primarily as a disapproval of philological procedures, but rather as a critique of a particular set of literal interpretations supportive of troubling liturgical and doctrinal commitments."[39] It was "the interpretation that endorsed the continued adherence to the Jewish law, in particular, its liturgical and ceremonial customs, such as circumcision, keeping the Passover, Sabbath regulations, dietary customs, and the distinctions between pure and impure" that "drew Origen's repeated censure."[40] In *Against Celsus*, Origen asserts that "the reason why we do not live like the Jews is that we think the literal interpretation of the laws does not contain the meaning of the legislation" (*Cels.* 5.60). Jews also failed to identify who fulfilled the messianic prophecies because they read the prophecies too literally and did not understand them intelligibly or spiritually rather than visibly.[41]

So which came first, the right hermeneutic or the right set of dogmatic statements? According to Martens it was emphatically the latter. The right reading, according to Origen, went back to Jesus and Paul:

---

37. Martens, *Origen and Scripture*, 114–18 and 138–40.
38. Martens, *Origen and Scripture*, 115, 117.
39. Martens, *Origen and Scripture*, 134.
40. Martens, *Origen and Scripture*, 141.
41. *Cels.* 3.1ff.; cf. 2.38. Martens, *Origen and Scripture*, 143–45.

in his response to Celsus' charge that Jesus was profane when he challenged the literal observance of the Mosaic law, Origen offers a sweeping reply: "Was it profane to abandon physical circumcision, and a literal Sabbath and literal feasts, literal new moons, and clean and unclean things, and rather to turn the mind to the true and spiritual law, worthy of God?" Jesus' ministry offered a lens for assessing the law correctly.[42]

As for Paul, "throughout his entire career, Origen repeatedly invoked Paul's name as the practitioner and guide par excellence to the allegorical interpretation of Israel's scriptures."[43] Ultimately what delivered the right reading, for scholars as for simple believers, was "a commitment to Christianity from which they gathered a spectrum of loyalties, guidelines, dispositions, relationships, and doctrines that tangibly shaped how they practiced and thought about their biblical scholarship."[44]

In this section we shall test this out by inquiring how far Origen, throughout his career, basically inherited and essentially affirmed the doctrinal position established by the end of the second century.[45] How far would Origen recognize the summary we offered in the conclusion to the previous chapter: namely, that the rule of faith and the core canon of scripture established the *monarchia* of the one and only supreme and transcendent God, to whom all are accountable and whose providential purposes will ultimately be fulfilled above all through the Logos of God and the divine Spirit? We shall do this by surveying his late apologetic work, *Against Celsus*, before returning to the earlier *First Principles*, notorious as the source of doctrines subsequently contested. In this way, we may find retrospective light cast on the latter by Origen's later defense of Christian belief.

2.1. Against Celsus—*Replaying the Second-Century Arguments*

According to Eusebius (*Hist. eccl.* 4.36.2), Origen was over sixty when he wrote eight books in reply to *The True Doctrine*, a work produced some seventy years earlier by one Celsus. Though regarded by both Origen and Eusebius as a cer-

---

42. Martens, *Origen and Scripture*, 157, quoting *Cels.* 2.7, with cross-reference to *Cels.* 2.1–3.

43. Martens, *Origen and Scripture*, 158, with a raft of references in a long footnote listed there by biblical reference, including the following passages from *Against Celsus*: *Cels.* 2.2, citing Heb 8:5; 10:1; Col 2:16; *Cels.* 4.43, citing 1 Cor 10:11; *Cels.* 4.44, citing Gal 4:21–24, 26; *Cels.* 4.49, citing 1 Cor 9:9–10; 10:1–2, 3–4; Eph 5:31–32.

44. Martens, *Origen and Scripture*, 6.

45. For Origen's debt to the second century, see further Hal Koch, *Pronoia und Paideusis* (Berlin: de Gruyter, 1932).

tain Celsus the Epicurean, in the many quotations embedded in Origen's reply the author offers a critique of Christianity that seems to be based on a more Platonic standpoint. According to Origen's Preface, it was Ambrose, his long-standing patron, who requested such a response, even though Origen himself is sceptical about the capacity of "written arguments in books to restore and confirm [anyone] in his faith if it has been shaken by the accusations brought by Celsus against the Christians."

My rereading of *Against Celsus* has delivered the latest of those illuminating experiences to which I have referred from time to time. What is so striking in the present context is how much the questions aired in our previous two chapters are addressed within the to-and-fro of debate between Origen and Celsus, and how much Origen replays responses to them that we have found in Clement of Rome, Justin, and Irenaeus. The issues to which I refer include:

1. the fulfillment of prophecy, which is taken to prove both the truth contained in scripture and the claims made about Jesus Christ;
2. the Creator being identified as the supreme God, who is the providential overseer of all and everything, including inner thoughts, and the ultimate judge to whom all are accountable;
3. the unknowability of that same God, the one who is transcendent and unnameable, and whose self has been made known through the Word and the Spirit;
4. defense of the unity of scripture and of the one God against the critique brought by Marcion and others.

It is worth surveying various passages to illustrate these points.

2.1.1. Oracles and Prophecies

The issue of prophecy and its fulfillment appears upfront and recurs throughout. Origen counters Celsus's dismissal of Christianity as "originally barbarian" with this:

> the gospel has a proof which is peculiar to itself, and which is more divine than Greek proof based on dialectical argument. This more divine demonstration the apostle calls 'a demonstration of the spirit and of power'—of spirit because of the prophecies and especially those which refer to Christ, which are capable of convincing anyone who reads them. (*Cels.* 1.2)[46]

---

46. Quoting 1 Cor 2:4.

Later, after an argument about the virgin birth and the narrative of Jesus's baptism, Origen accuses Celsus of intentionally evading "the strongest argument confirming Jesus's authority, that he was prophesied by the prophets of the Jews, Moses and those after him and even before him" (1.49).

There follow a number of examples to prove the point. Again, in book 3, Origen states: "we prove clearly that he was the one prophesied by quoting both from the prophecies about him (and there are many of them), and from the Gospels and the utterances of the apostles, which are carefully explained by those who are able to understand them intelligently" (3.15; cf. 4.21). Later in book 6 we find: "it is true that we make use of *the sayings of the prophets* to prove that Jesus is the Christ proclaimed by them beforehand, and to show from the prophecies that the events recorded of Jesus in the Gospels fulfilled them" (6.35).[47]

In book 7 Origen tackles Celsus's critique of "the assertion that the history of Christ Jesus was prophesied by the prophets among the Jews" (7.2–7). Celsus chides Christians for regarding as "of no account" the predictions of the Delphic Oracle and other such prophets, while regarding as "wonderful and unalterable" those coming from people in foreign places like Judea.[48] Origen reckons the claims of those oracles cited by Celsus are easily overthrown by Aristotle's arguments, not to mention the statements of Epicurus, but if they are genuine, they are more likely caused by evil daemons taking possession of the priestess' consciousness. Origen is sure that someone in communion with the deity "ought to possess the clearest vision," and on these grounds he defends the Jewish prophets. They had "clear mental vision and became more radiant in their soul" because of "the touch, so to speak, of what is called the Holy Spirit upon their soul." By contrast "the Pythian priestess is out of her senses and has not control of her faculties when she prophesies"; he likens the spirit in her to one "of the race of daemons which many Christians drive out of people who suffer from them"—exorcizing them not by magic but by prayer. Origen expands upon his point:

> Of the Jewish prophets some were wise before they received the gift of prophecy and divine inspiration, while others became wise after they had been

---

47. Italics indicate quotations from Celsus's original; cf. 3.1–2.

48. Cf. *Cels.* 4.95, where the contrast between Jewish prophecies and others is discussed, though there the argument is about supposed intelligence beyond the human race—birds and animals providing auguries and signs of the future.

illuminated in mind by the actual gift of prophecy itself. They were chosen by providence to be entrusted with the divine Spirit and with the utterances that the Spirit inspired on account of the quality of their lives, which was of unexampled courage and freedom; for in the face of death they were entirely without terror. And reason demands that the prophets of the supreme God should be such people.[49] ... They always looked upon God and the invisible things which are not seen with the eyes of the senses, and on that account are eternal. (7.7)

Origen points to the Bible where the life of each prophet is to be found, providing a series of examples.

> These and countless others prophesied unto God and foretold the story of Jesus Christ. That is the reason why we reckon of no account the predictions uttered by the Pythian priestess ... or by countless other alleged prophets; whereas we admire those of the prophets in Judaea, seeing that their strong, courageous, and holy life was worthy of God's Spirit, whose prophecy was imparted in a new way which had nothing in common with the divination inspired by daemons. (7.7)

The clincher, as it had been for Justin, lay in future events proving the truth of the predictions:

> the prophets' contemporaries wrote down their prophecies and saw to it that when posterity read them they should admire them as the words of God, and be benefited not only by the words of rebuke and exhortation but also by the predictions, being convinced by the resulting events that it was a divine Spirit that foretold them, and might continue in the practice of religion according to the teaching of the Word, being persuaded by the law and the prophets. (7.10)

That double aim—moral benefit plus future proof—affected the form in which they spoke:

> The prophets, according to the will of God, said without any obscurity whatever could be at once understood as beneficial to their hearers and helpful towards attaining moral reformation. But all the more mysterious

49. Here Origen quotes Heb 11:37–38 to demonstrate their courage.

and esoteric truths, which contained ideas beyond the understanding of everyone, they expressed in riddles and allegories and what are called dark sayings, and by what are called parables or proverbs. (7.10)

That, of course, is why study is required to find their meaning. For Origen the starting point of allegorical interpretation is unpacking oracular riddles, and as much as it was for his predecessors, the argument from fulfilled prophecy was fundamental to his defense of Christianity.

2.1.2. God's Knowledge of Us: Judgment, Providence, and Creation

Near the end of his final book, Origen states that Celsus "ought to have considered the common Father and Creator of all, who sees everything and hears everything, and judges the purpose of each individual who seeks him" (8.53). If he had, he "would not have poured abuse in this way on Moses and the prophets and on Jesus and his apostles." Like Clement of Rome and earlier Christian writers, Origen clarifies that the one God is the providential overseer to whom ultimately all will be accountable.

This is no afterthought. Tackling Celsus's opening remarks near the start of book 1, Origen says: "There is therefore nothing amazing about it if the same God has implanted in the souls of all the truths taught through the prophets and the Saviour; God did this that everyone might be without excuse at the divine judgment, having the requirements of the law written in the heart" (1.4). Later, defending Christian books from Celsus's charge that they deserve "pity and hatred," Origen "challenges anyone to dare to assert" that believing in "the God of the universe," and doing "every action with the object of pleasing God, whatever it may be," is not "the source and origin of every benefit," for "not only words and works but even thoughts will be open to God's judgement." Indeed, "what other teaching would be more effective in converting humankind to live a good life than the belief or conviction that the supreme God sees everything that we say and do, and even what we think?" (4.53).

Judgment is, indeed, a persistent theme, but it is part of the divine pedagogical or medicinal purpose:

> when, to speak loosely, we understand as evils the pains inflicted on those who are being educated by fathers and teachers and schoolmasters, or by doctors on those who undergo operations or cauterizations in order to cure them, we say that the father does evil to his sons or that the schoolmasters or teachers or doctors do so, and yet do not regard those who inflict the

beating or perform the operation as doing anything reprehensible; so also if Scripture says that God inflicts pains of this nature in order to convert and heal those who are in need of such punishment, there can be no ground for objection to what the Bible says. (6.56)

Earlier Origen had suggested that Celsus's ridicule of certain passages in the Bible revealed his failure to understand them. He mocked these texts for speaking of God as though God were subject to human passions—passages in which "*angry utterances* are spoken against the impious and *threats against* people who have sinned" (4.71). Origen here already made the analogy with speaking to little children so as to correct them; the "threats" were simply ways of saying what will happen to those who are bad. Origen adds here the analogy of a physician cutting or applying cauterizing irons, concluding: "Therefore we do not attribute human passions to God, nor do we hold impious opinions about God" (4.72). God's wrath is not an "emotional reaction"—persons bring it on themselves by their sins, and Origen cites biblical passages to show this.[50] Since scripture teaches us not to be angry (e.g., Ps 36:8; Col 3:8), it is inappropriate to attribute to Godself the emotion that God wants us to abandon altogether, he suggests.

Judgment, therefore, belongs to God's providence. Previously Origen had argued that apart from divine providence "no benefit comes to humankind." It is by divine providence that a physician is able to heal bodies, so

> how much more must that be true of him who cured, converted, and improved the souls of many, and attached them to the supreme God, and taught them to refer every action to the standard of God's pleasure, and to avoid anything that is displeasing to God down to the most insignificant of words or deeds or even of casual thoughts? (1.9)

The proof of Christianity is that multitudes have renounced evil; surely "a doctrine so beneficial to mankind could not have come to human life apart from divine providence." As we have already noted, Celsus's comparisons between Plato and scripture Origen accepts as "true doctrines" meant to help as many as possible. Indeed, Origen does not want "to wrestle . . . against the opinions [Celsus] expresses which are derived from philosophy, as some might

---

50. Cf. *Cels*. 5.16 on "fire and punishments"—it all depends on whether one is "pure in doctrine, morals, and mind."

suppose."[51] But compared to the disciples of Jesus, Plato is elitist and "the wise philosophers and scholars among the Greeks were in error about God in their religious practices": "God chose the foolish things of the world (1 Cor 1:27–29) to put the wise to shame." What Plato said was true, but "it did not help his readers towards a pure religion at all." With batteries of biblical quotations he invites the reader to "see the difference between Plato's fine utterance about the highest good and what the prophets said about the light of the blessed."

For Origen, as for Justin and Irenaeus, it could only be the one supreme God, Creator of all, who could exercise this providential oversight in goodness and love, drawing all toward communion with the divine. Celsus, of course, scorns the idea of one God (1.23). But Christians name God "the Creator of the universe, the Maker of heaven and earth, who sent down to the human race such and such wise prophets" (1.25). Celsus prefers "expert physicians," by which he means philosophers, whereas "we [Christians] deliver those who believe us from serious wounds caused by the doctrines of so-called philosophers.... And lead them to the pious doctrine which teaches them to devote themselves to the Creator" (2.75).

Like Paul the apostle, Origen chides those who "worship irrational animals, or images, or created things, when they ought to be moved by their beauty to admire and worship their Maker." Celsus had called Christians and Jews "worms and ants," but Origen identifies as "human" those who "following their reason" have "ascended from the beautiful things in the world to the Maker of the universe and have entrusted themselves to the Creator" (4.26). Celsus cannot accept that things like "plants, trees, grass and thorns" were made for humankind, but "We Christians, however, who are devoted to the only God who created these things, acknowledge our gratitude for them to their Creator, because God has prepared such a home for us and, with a view to our benefit, for the animals which serve us" (4.75). Here Origen directly links Celsus's critique of the one God, along with his rejection of a "designing reason which caused them to exist" or "a Mind surpassing all admiration," to his refusal to acknowledge providence.

Thus, creation is celebrated and affirmed time and again, as it had been through the second century; it is fundamental to Origen's understanding of the supreme God and God's providential *philanthrōpia*. Yet Origen does not directly engage with the doctrine of creation as such in this work, treating it as not required "for the treatise we have in hand" (6.52). He notes Celsus's dismissive words, "Besides, the cosmology too is very silly" (6.49).[52] He claims that if Celsus had produced some plausible arguments, he would have addressed

---

51. Further quotations in this paragraph are from *Cels.* 6.1–5.
52. With response through 6.49–52.

them, even though whole treatises would be needed to explain the Mosaic account of the creation of the world; he refers readers to his studies in Genesis (of which only fragments survive). Focusing rather on Celsus's charges that "the Spirit of the supreme God came among people on earth as to strangers," and "some things were devised by another Creator, different from the great God," Origen makes it quite clear that Celsus has misunderstood some heresy or other, indeed, that Celsus even directs against Marcion the very objections Origen himself would make (6.53). Celsus, he says, "jumps to the conclusion that from our affirmation that even this world is the work of the supreme God it follows that we believe God to be the maker of what is evil." That point, of course, leads Origen back to the pedagogical, indeed providential, purpose of "physical and external evils" (6.54–56).

Thus, judgment, providence, and creation are closely connected in Origen's mind, and there can be little doubt that behind this debate lie those issues we explored in the second century, the legacy of which surfaces as Origen endeavors to justify Christianity to its critic. The *monarchia* of God, such a crucial second-century conclusion, remains fundamental.

2.1.3. Our Knowledge of God: Knowing and Worshipping the One Unknowable Creator of All

Divine providence Origen recognizes as a doctrine held also by other philosophical *haireseis*, Stoics in particular (1.21). Of course, they got it wrong in thinking of God as "a material substance," therefore "capable of change and complete alteration and transformation," and therefore "liable to corruption." But luckily there is nothing able to corrupt God. Jews and Christians, of course, preserve "the unchangeable and unalterable nature of God."

Celsus himself falls into the opposite trap. Rather than involving God in materiality and change, he separates everything from God while affirming that "all things are derived from God" (6.65). Behind this apparent contradiction is the kind of philosophical dilemma explored in an earlier chapter: the distinction that seemed necessary between the Supreme Being, the unknown One beyond everything, and some lesser being, who was the demiurge or creator of the material world. Earlier Origen had tackled Celsus's view that God made nothing mortal; the works of God are immortal beings, souls not bodies (4.52). Origen, like his Christian predecessors, identifies the Creator of all, matter included, with the radically unknowable source of everything, the God known only because of the divine will to make Godself known through the Logos and the Spirit, through creation and scripture.

Celsus, however, regards Plato as "a more effective teacher of the problems of theology" (7.42).[53] Origen tells us that he quotes from the *Timaeus* the famous tag, "Now to find the Maker and Father of the universe is difficult, and after finding him it is impossible to declare him to all." To this Celsus adds, "You see how the way of truth is sought by seers and philosophers, and how Plato knew that it is impossible for all to travel it." He then refers to the way "we might get some conception of the nameless First Being which manifests it either by synthesis with other things, or by analytical distinction from them, or by analogy," stating that thus he "would like to teach about that which is otherwise indescribable," though he doubts whether Christians would be able to follow. We may recognize here the three ways by which God is known commonly appealed to by Platonists.[54]

Origen admits, "Plato's statement which he quotes is noble and impressive." Plato may say it is difficult to find the Maker and Father of this universe, but that implies it is not impossible. If Plato had really found God, he would not have "reverenced anything else and called it God and worshipped it."

> But we affirm that human nature is not sufficient in any way to seek for God and to find God in the pure nature of the divine, unless it is helped by the God who is the object of the search. And God is found by those who, after doing what they can, admit that they need God, and God shows the divine self to those whom God judges it right to appear, so far as it is possible for God to be known to humankind and for the human soul which is still in the body to know God.

Origen thus radicalizes God's transcendence, going beyond the Platonic or philosophical concept of God: God is only known if and when God reveals the divine self. Furthermore, even though Plato recognizes "that it is impossible for one who has found the Maker and Father of the universe to declare that being to all," Plato does not use the terms "indescribable and nameless"—he implies that being can be described, though declared only to a few. Scripture quotations substantiate a more radical view whereby God is "unspeakable" yet seen by "the pure in heart," and the one "who has seen me, has seen the Father" (2 Cor 12:4; Matt 5:8; John 14:9).

Celsus may appeal to the standard ways of synthesis, analysis, and analogy; but the Logos of God says that "No one has known the Father except the Son, and the

---

53. The following quotations all come from discussion in *Cels.* 7.42–44.
54. See 2.2 in chapter 3 above.

one to whom the Son may reveal God," and that means that God is only known "by a certain divine grace," by "God's action" in the soul, by "a sort of inspiration."

> Moreover, it is probable that the knowledge of God is beyond the capacity of human nature (that is why there are such great errors about God among people), but that by God's kindness and love to humankind and by a miraculous divine grace the knowledge of God extends to those who by God's foreknowledge have been previously determined, because they would live lives worthy of God after God was made known to them. . . . I believe that because God saw the arrogance or the disdainful attitude towards others of people who pride themselves on having known God and learnt the divine truths from philosophy, and yet like the most vulgar keep on with the images and their temples and the mysteries which are a matter of common gossip, God chose the foolish things of the world, the simplest of the Christians, who live lives more moderate and pure than many philosophers, that God might put to shame the wise, who are not ashamed to talk to lifeless things as if they were gods or images of gods.

Ultimately the crucial thing for Origen is right worship—worshipping the Supreme God, source of everything. He writes, "even an uneducated Christian is convinced that every place in the world is part of the whole, since the whole world is a temple of God; and he or she prays in any place, and by shutting the eyes of sense and raising those of the soul ascends beyond the entire world."

In an earlier section on cosmology Origen had contested anthropomorphic views of God attributed by Celsus to Christians, not least the idea that God needed to rest on the seventh day (6.64). Origen is clear that the Creator God is the utterly transcendent One: invisible by nature, unmoved, incorporeal, the one participated in rather than participating in anything, even being. Here too he affirms that God is not attainable by reason, that God cannot be named, that none of the descriptions by words or expressions can show the attributes of God. But the Logos of God "has led the mind of anyone who wants to be saved to the uncreated and supreme God."

> Therefore, no Christian would reply to Celsus or to any other critic of the divine Word, by saying *How can I know God?* Each of them, in accordance with their capacity, has known God. And no one says: *How can I learn the way to him?* For he has heard the one who says, "I am the way, the truth, and the life," and by travelling along the way has experienced the benefit that the journey brings.

The outcome of the second-century debates Origen reaffirms, both the incomprehensibility of the one God and the identity of that one God with the God of creation and revelation.

2.1.4. Scripture: Wrong Doctrine, Wrong Reading

Celsus has picked up that there are sects or *haireseis* among Christians.[55] Interestingly Origen regards this as perfectly to be expected. He acknowledges that Marcionites and Valentinians "altered the gospel," but "those who alter the Gospels and introduce heresies foreign to the meaning of Jesus' teaching do not give ground for any criticism of genuine Christianity" (2.27). More than once he asserts that philosophy is just the same, with "disagreement not just about small and trivial matters but about the most important subjects" (5.61). Medicine, too, could be criticized "because of the sects within it." Origen admits there are "some among us who do not say that God is the same God as that of the Jews." He also admits there are others—he thinks Celsus refers to the Valentinians—who "call some natural and others spiritual." But all this has nothing to do with "us who belong to the Church," who find fault with both those positions. Epicureans may call themselves philosophers, but those who abolish providence cannot really be philosophers, "nor can those be Christians who introduce strange new ideas which do not harmonize with the traditional doctrines received from Jesus." Elsewhere he asserts: "we do know what the deceivers teach, yet we deny it as alien to us and blasphemous and not in agreement with the doctrines of genuine Christians which we confess to the point of death" (6.32). At an earlier stage Origen had reported that Celsus "reproaches us for the sects within Christianity" (3.12–13). His response was that "any teaching which has a serious origin, and is beneficial to life, has caused different sects," citing medicine again along with philosophy. Indeed, Paul had suggested that "there must also be heresies among you" (1 Cor 11:19), their purpose being to show by contrast what is genuine. He adds that there is another factor here: the variety of interpretations of the writings of Moses and the sayings of the prophets. As Christianity seemed "worthy of serious attention, not only to people of the lower classes as Celsus thinks, but also to many scholars among the Greeks, sects inevitably came to exist," simply because different people sought to understand the doctrines of Christianity, and "interpreted differently the scriptures universally thought to be divine,

---

55. *Cels.* 6.61–65, and elsewhere.

and sects arose named after those who . . . were impelled by certain reasons which convinced them to disagree with one another." The existence of heresies is no reason to despise "the sacred books of Moses and the prophets." In the case of medicine one just chooses the best, and in the case of philosophy "the doctrine which has convinced," so anyone who "looks carefully into the sects of Judaism and Christianity becomes a very wise Christian." Interestingly he appears to suggest that, just as studying different philosophies enables intellectual advance, so too knowing rival versions of Christianity gives one the wisdom to identify the truth—heresies show by contrast what is genuine, enabling conviction.

This implies, as we saw Martens arguing above, that Origen recognized the importance of the right doctrinal commitments for unveiling the truth hidden in scripture. As scripture itself cannot settle the issue of truth, given the variety of interpretations, more fundamental are "the traditional doctrines received from Jesus" (5.61). Certainly wrong doctrine produces wrong reading: Marcion and Valentinus have "altered the gospel" and Marcion's wrong reading is why Origen has to insist on one God, who is Creator of all but not the creator of evils (6.52–53; 4.65–66).

True, nowhere does Origen set out the rule of faith in this debate with an outside critic. He does, however, say:

> we preserve both the doctrines of the Church of Christ and the greatness of God's promise, establishing that it is a possibility not by mere assertion but by argument. For we know that even if heaven and earth and the things in them pass away, yet the words about each doctrine, being like parts in a whole or forms in a species, . . . will in no wise pass away. (5.22)

Furthermore, he defends, on the one hand, the doctrines set forth in the rule of faith—those about God and creation, as we have seen, but also the virgin birth (1.32–35; 6.73), the incarnation (4.2–7; 5.2–5 and elsewhere), the sufferings of Christ (1.54–55; 2.34–38), and the resurrection (even of the same body, though admittedly transformed and incorruptible) (2.55–66; 4.57; 5.18–22; 6.32). On the other hand he also defends the provenance of these doctrines: the apostles "taught Christianity and succeeded in bringing many to obey the Word of God by divine power"—after all they were uneducated and had no capability to give an "ordered narrative by the standards of Greek dialectical and rhetorical arts" (1.62). Behind the apostles is Jesus, "who by the power within him introduced a system and doctrines which benefited the life of humankind and converted people from the flood of sins" (2.8) and ultimately the doctrines Origen defends "were uttered by the Logos who was the divine Logos with God in the beginning."[56]

2.1.5. Conclusion

In debate with Hellenistic philosophy Origen stands firmly in the apostolic tradition, differentiating the true Christian position on key points from that of Marcion and the gnostics. For all his acknowledged affinities with Plato and the philosophers, at the end of his life Origen not only explicitly defends Christianity from Celsus's elitist contempt, justifying its appeal to and inclusion of the simpleminded, the stupid, the ordinary, the every man, even the every woman and slave, but he also stands firmly within the framework of what was becoming orthodox Christian doctrine. This doctrine was at one level grounded in scripture and deduced from it through a range of philological and exegetical techniques. But these techniques, shared by the various Christian *haireseis* as well as the philosophical and literary thinkers of the time, were capable of delivering outcomes different from the accepted apostolic tradition. Right reading therefore required the right framework. To what extent is this perspective already present in the *First Principles*?

2.2. First Principles: *Toward a "Single Body of Doctrine"*

When Origen wrote his treatise *First Principles*, he produced what is in effect the first attempt to articulate a theological system or, as he put it, a "single body of doctrine."[57] What he was aiming to do in his own context has been much debated: Was he providing a typical philosophical textbook from a Christian perspective? Or was he mainly concerned to tease out the principles of scriptural interpretation? Maybe the title (*Peri archōn*) was cleverly ambiguous, implying Christian engagement with the topics of "physics," that is, the search for the first principles (*archai*) of the universe, alongside an exposition of the basic elements of scriptural interpretation, namely, the premises (*archai*) of the faith.[58] Origen's preface might seem to support this conclusion, though it

---

56. *Cels.* 5.22, reinserting the words omitted in the above quotation. Note the allusion to John 1:1.

57. *Princ.* 1.pref.10. English translation, unless otherwise noted, from Butterworth, *On First Principles*.

58. Joseph W. Trigg, *Origen: The Bible and Philosophy in the Third-Century Church* (London: SCM, 1985), 91–92.

is difficult to be sure exactly how and where the word *archē* is used since the original Greek has not survived. Certainly Origen appears to be setting out his teaching, like philosophers before him, as the true and right doctrine—the outcome of his rigorous inquiry. But suppose we allow our study of *Against Celsus* to cast backlight on the question. Might it not be the case that Origen is seeking to specify the right doctrine to shape the right reading of scripture? After all, it is only in book 4, after setting out right doctrine, that Origen turns to demonstrating the right methods for discerning scripture's meaning. Jews and heretics, he was sure, misread scripture. By what criteria could rival readings be assessed? Origen shows awareness of this issue right at the beginning of *First Principles*, and it is surely one good reason for his doctrinal project: to differentiate right doctrine for right reading of scripture.

It is not my intention to provide yet another account of this treatise. Suffice it to say that the work belongs to Origen's time in Alexandria, was probably completed when he was between thirty-five and forty years of age, and most of it is only extant in the Latin translation made by Rufinus during the first Origenist controversy towards the end of the fourth century. It should therefore represent reasonably well-established teaching if we trust the translation, but at crucial points we probably cannot. I also do not intend to survey further the scholarship purporting to set out Origen's doctrine or scriptural hermeneutic on the basis of this work—there are plenty of such accounts in the scholarly literature. Rather I propose to draw out certain features of his argument that bear on either his perception of the relationship between doctrine and scripture or on his position with respect to the doctrinal position established by the end of the second century.

2.2.1. The Rule of Faith

First Principles opens with the statement that believers "derive the knowledge which calls people to lead a good and blessed life from the very words and teaching of Christ," with the further explanation that these include Moses and the prophets, for they were filled with the spirit of Christ and prophesied about him.[59] But the very next paragraph notes that many who profess to believe have conflicting opinions about substantial matters, not just trivia. So "a definite line and unmistakable rule" is needed, and Origen finds that canon in the tradition "handed down in unbroken succession from the apostles."

---

59. This and the next paragraph summarize and quote from the Preface to book 1 of *First Principles*.

True, he then asserts that the grounds for what the apostles taught were left to be investigated by those who have the gifts of the Spirit—particularly the graces of language, wisdom, and knowledge—and also that other doctrines were just stated without any clarification of the how and why, so as to supply those who would prove diligent "lovers of wisdom" with an exercise to display their skill. The silences left by the tradition are appreciated as intellectual challenges, as will be scripture's *aporiai*.

Still, the apostles' teachings "in plain terms" remain fundamental, and they are immediately rehearsed in what is a recognizable version of the rule of faith, though with further indication that some things not spelled out there need investigation. For "the contents of scripture are the outward forms of certain mysteries and the images of divine things," he claims. Origen furthermore states that the church accepts this, though the inspired meaning is recognized only by those gifted with the grace of the Holy Spirit in the word of wisdom and knowledge. The climax of this Preface is the unambiguous statement that anyone wanting to construct a connected body of doctrine "must use points like these as elementary and foundation principles," and then "by clear and cogent arguments discover the truth about each particular point," so producing "a single body of doctrine."

As we move into the body of the treatise it becomes clear that the three "names" that proved so significant for Irenaeus constitute a pattern to which Origen recurs, first in the overarching perspective set out in book 1 and again in book 2 as he develops the relationship of the Triad with the world.[60] This pattern picks up the initial statements of his version of the apostolic rule.[61]

1. The first is that God is one; that this one God caused the universe to be when nothing existed; that this God was the God of all the righteous, the twelve patriarchs, Moses, and the prophets; that this God sent Jesus Christ, according to previous announcements made by the prophets, to call Israel and then the gentiles; and that this God is both just and good, the Father of Jesus Christ and the one who gave the Law, the Prophets, and the Gospels, the God of the apostles and of both the Old and New Testaments.
2. The second concerns Christ Jesus, who came to earth; who was begotten of the Father before every created thing and served the Father in creating everything; who remained God even as he took a body; was born of a

---

60. Admittedly this is less evident in book 2. However, *Princ.* 2.1–5 deals with God's relationship with the world, referring sometimes to the Triad, but generally to the One Creator God, while 2.6 turns to the incarnation, and 2.7 to the Holy Spirit.
61. *Princ.* 1.pref.4–8.

virgin and the Holy Spirit; and truly was born and suffered, not merely in appearance, truly died our common death, and truly rose from the dead.
3. The third concerns the Holy Spirit—Origen acknowledges much is not clearly known and needs to be investigated, but the Spirit inspired both prophets and apostles, and there was not one Spirit in the former and another in the latter.

What seems to distinguish Origen's rule from that of Irenaeus, however, is that he does not stop at these three clauses. "Next after this," he says, "the apostles taught that the soul will be rewarded according to its deserts." He speaks of resurrection, of free will and choice, of the devil and his angels, of the world beginning at a definite time and destined to end, of the scriptures and their hidden meaning. Behind all this, however, are those basic affirmations we found established in the second century:

1. God as Creator and overseer, the judge of all: the praise and blame of judgment presuppose free will, after all;
2. creation out of nothing implying an eschaton;
3. the true meaning of scripture lying hidden until the prophecies were fulfilled.

It is precisely these basic affirmations that shape Origen's approach to spelling out his "single body of doctrine." It is all about the pedagogical purposes of God to be uncovered through reading God's word in scripture according to this overarching, unitive framework. Prior commitment to the apostolic tradition, rather than any particular hermeneutical method, was what enabled Origen to distinguish the right meaning and truth in scripture, as we found argued by Martens and also discerned through our study of *Against Celsus*. Only right doctrine could make sense of scripture.

2.2.2. Inquiries into Meaning and Truth

As noted, in Origen's view inquiries had to be made about things not plainly stated or explained by the apostles. What he meant by this is subsequently given a striking scriptural basis by allusion to Pauline texts:

Let us endeavour to "leave behind the doctrine of the first principles of Christ," that is, of the elements, and "press on to perfection," that the wisdom which is spoken to the perfect may be spoken also to us. For he who had acquired this wisdom promises that he speaks it to the perfect, and that it is a wisdom different from the "wisdom of this world, and the wisdom of the rulers of this world, which is coming to naught." And this wisdom will be distinctly stamped upon us "according to the revelation of the mystery which hath been kept in silence through times eternal, but now is manifested both through the scriptures" and "through the appearing of our Lord and Saviour Jesus Christ"; to whom be glory for ever and ever. Amen. (*Princ.* 4.1.7)[62]

Origen engages in such inquiries, however, with a certain hesitancy and willingness to defer to other inquirers. "We have previously pointed out what are the subjects on which clear doctrinal statements must be made," he says at one point and continues, "Now, however, we are dealing, as well as we can, with subjects that call for discussion rather than for definition" (1.6.1). Later, having outlined three opinions about the end of all things, he says that each reader must judge for him or herself whether one of them might be approved and adopted (2.3.7). On another occasion he invites his readers to work things out for themselves, as "we must not be supposed to put these forward as settled doctrines" (2.8.4). Again, after spelling out his thoughts on "such very difficult subjects as the incarnation and deity of Christ," he adds: "If there be anyone who can discover something better and prove what he says by clear statements out of the Holy Scriptures, let his opinion be accepted in preference to mine" (2.6.7). Origen knew that debate was inevitable. After all, scripture did not always provide clear statements. Furthermore, what constituted scripture was a collection of sacred books susceptible to multiple interpretations. Indeed, it was for him a positive advantage that any one passage could convey multiple meanings—literal, moral, or spiritual—for, given the divine pedagogical purpose, it could through its multiple senses meet the needs of multiple minds at multiple levels of understanding and multiple stages of development. Origen's approach to exegesis could embrace all that, while also challenging rival readings he took to be false.[63] So what was the relationship between these multiple meanings and the truth embraced in that "single body of doctrine"? In order to tease out the interaction between doctrine and scripture as Origen undertakes his inquiries we will observe how he plays the one with, or against, the other, by working through some examples.

---

62. Translation of the Greek version, citing Heb 6:1; 1 Cor 2:6; Rom 16:25–27; 2 Tim 1:10.
63. As book 4 of *First Principles* indicates, as well as remarks in *Against Celsus* and elsewhere.

2.2.3. From Scripture to Doctrine: The Holy Spirit

Outlining the rule of faith, Origen acknowledged that in regard to the Holy Spirit much was not yet clearly known and investigation was needed. The doctrine comes from the apostles, and it is "certainly taught with the utmost clearness in the Church, that this Spirit inspired each one of the saints, both the prophets and the apostles" (1.pref.4). However, whereas God's providence and Son were ideas held in common with others, it is only "by means of those scriptures which were inspired by the Holy Spirit" that "the higher and divine teaching about the Son of God" is brought to human knowledge (1.3.1), and indeed the very existence of the Holy Spirit is known only to "those familiar with the law and prophets, or those who profess their belief in Christ." Maybe this is a clue to why Origen thought the Holy Spirit needed particular investigation—it appeared to be unique to the Christian philosophy.

Scripture, then, is the basis for developing teaching about the Holy Spirit (1.3.2). Origen quotes Psalm 51:13 and Daniel 4:9, refers to the baptism of Jesus and to John 20:22 and Luke 1:35, and then cites Paul's teaching in 1 Corinthians 12:3 and Acts 8:18:

> From all of which we learn that the person of the Holy Spirit is of so great authority and dignity that saving baptism is not complete except when performed with the authority of the most excellent Trinity, that is, by the naming of Father, Son and Holy Spirit; and that the name of the Holy Spirit must be joined to that of the unbegotten God the Father and his only-begotten Son. (1.3.2)[64]

Origen thus aligns himself with the perspective we found in Irenaeus: baptismal liturgy shapes doctrine, and scripture testifies to the saving power of the three names.

Origen next makes it clear that there is "no substance which has not received its existence from God." Throughout scripture there are declarations that prove this (1.3.3) and scripture "refutes and dismisses" the "false doctrines" of both preexistent matter and immortal souls. And also "up to the present," Origen appears to assert, "we have been able to find no passage in the holy scriptures which would warrant us in saying that the Holy Spirit was a being made or created." Reference to the spirit moving upon the waters at

---

64. Alluding to Matt 28:19.

creation might also seem to include the Holy Spirit with the creative activity of Father and Son. However, we will eventually need to confront a problem. Origen was later condemned for suggesting that both the Logos and Spirit were created beings, and a Greek fragment inserted at this point insists that everything is created apart from the Father and God of the universe. Did the Latin translator, Rufinus, smooth over a difficulty here? Whatever the answer to that question, the important thing is to observe the extent to which scripture is mined by Origen for clear statements about the Holy Spirit, and how the whole approach so far is shaped by the liturgy of the church, together with established doctrines, such as creation out of nothing, which Origen takes to be apostolic tradition.[65]

Next Origen embarks on a different inquiry (1.3.4): Should we understand the Holy Spirit every time the word "spirit" occurs in scripture? He agrees with predecessors who have said we should in the case of the New Testament, quoting Galatians 5:22 on the fruit of the Spirit. "We, however, think that this peculiar use may be observed in the Old Testament also," he writes, citing a straightforward example, Isaiah 42:5. He then offers a case that can only be considered symbolic and speculative: the two six-winged seraphim of Isaiah 6, which he identifies as the Son and the Holy Spirit, cross-referencing Habakkuk 3:2 (LXX): "in the midst of the two living creatures thou shalt be known." Needless to say, this was bound to contribute to those later controversies about the nature of the Son and the Spirit; the cross-reference could imply that Origen meant that they were creatures. But what Origen actually focuses on here is the way knowledge of the Father is revealed by the Son and "made known to us through the Holy Spirit," and this is substantiated by reference to Matthew 11:27, 1 Corinthians 2:10, and the Paraclete passages from John's Gospel alongside John 3:8.

From scripture Origen now argues that the Holy Spirit did not gain knowledge of the Father, as we do, through the Son's revelation—you cannot imagine the Holy Spirit was ignorant or only became Holy Spirit after gaining knowledge, otherwise the Holy Spirit would never have been included in the Trinity, and, in any case, such ideas imply an inappropriate temporality. Again, is this the result of Rufinus's editing? A Greek fragment inserted here suggests a definite hierarchy: the Son is less than the Father, and the Holy Spirit still lesser

---

65. See further note 66 below; also the discussion in volume 2, chapter 2. Origen's logic led him to argue that God was eternally Father and Creator, so both Son and all created rational beings were eternally generated/created; it may well be the case that he never made the clear differentiation between generation and creation that emerged in later debate.

than the two; but, though "the power of the Holy Spirit" is less than that of the Father and Son, it nevertheless "exceeds that of every other holy being." The sources of such fragments were usually antagonistic towards Origen so their authenticity may be questionable, and in any case it was the editor's choice to insert it at this point.[66] Moreover, it is noticeable that this fragment does elevate the Holy Spirit above all other holy beings. Furthermore, amazement at the Spirit's "tremendous majesty" was already stimulated earlier in Origen's discussion (1.3.2) by reference to the fact that, despite the possibility of forgiveness for speaking a word against the Son of Man, there is no forgiveness for blasphemy against the Holy Spirit (Matt 12:32).

Hierarchy or not, the activites of each of the three are certainly different. As Origen teases this out he again interweaves scriptural texts and argument. He makes a crucial distinction: "the working of the power of God the Father and God the Son is spread indiscriminately over all created beings, but a share in the Holy Spirit is possessed, we find, by the saints alone" (1.3.7). This is "the peculiar grace and work of the Holy Spirit." His climax begins thus:

> God the Father bestows on all the gift of existence; and a participation in Christ, in virtue of his being word or reason, makes them rational. From this it follows that they are worthy of praise or blame, because they are capable alike of virtue and wickedness. Accordingly there is also available the grace of the Holy Spirit, that these beings who are not holy in essence may be made holy by participating in this grace. (1.3.8)

This process of growth in holiness enables one to become the person the God who made them wished them to be and to receive the power "to endure to eternity." It is "the work of wisdom to instruct and train them, and lead them on to perfection, by the strengthening and unceasing sanctification of the Holy Spirit, through which alone they can receive God." This is the way to "the holy and blessed life." Origen builds upon this essentially pedagogical activity of the

---

66. The editor of the GCS text, Koetschau, had a policy of attempting to insert fragments culled from other sources to make up for omissions that Rufinus acknowledged he had made in his translation. Butterworth's English translation follows Koetschau's Greek text in this regard. Both earlier in *Princ.* 1.3.3 and here, the fragments inserted derive from Justinian's *Letter to Menna*—in other words citations made at the height of the Origenist controversy. Recent scholarship has become suspicious of these fragments: see further John Behr, ed., *Origen: On First Principles*, 2 vols. (Oxford: Oxford University Press, 2019), esp. appendix 2, which is a comprehensive list and discussion of Koetschau's attempt to "restore the original text."

Holy Spirit, consistently placing it within the "ceaseless work on our behalf of the Father, the Son and the Holy Spirit," to whose unity he bears testimony, affirming no separation despite diversities of workings.

To sum up what we have found in book 1: Origen's whole discussion of the Holy Spirit is grounded in clear statements of scripture. Of some sixty biblical quotations or allusions, only the one made to Isaiah's vision in the temple is in any sense symbolic or allegorical. In Origen's view the very idea of the Holy Spirit is only found in scripture and is clearly stated there, and the work of the Holy Spirit is the making of saints.

When Origen returns to the Holy Spirit in book 2 of *First Principles,* however, rather than just the saints receiving the Holy Spirit, he is more inclined to think that "any rational creature receives without any difference a share in the Holy Spirit just as in the wisdom of God and the word of God" (2.7.2). Is this a contradiction? I suggest not directly. The overall context is quite different, namely, a debate with Marcionite and Valentinian attempts to divide God into two by differentiating the Testaments. Origen asserts that just as it is the very same God and the very same Christ, so also it is the very same Holy Spirit who was in the prophets and the apostles, that is, "both in those who believed in God before the coming of Christ and in those who have taken refuge in God through Christ" (2.7.1). He then appeals to Acts 2:16–17, the fulfillment of Joel's prophecy, "I will pour out my spirit on all flesh," reinforcing this with Psalm 82:11, "all nations shall serve me." Implicitly, then, he directs attention to the dispensational relationship of the Testaments: "after the coming of the Saviour" and "through the grace of the Holy Spirit," there is a shift. Before, only a few understood the Law and the Prophets and hardly anyone could get beyond the literal meaning; now "innumerable multitudes of believers" reject literal understanding of circumcision, Sabbath rest, and sacrifices, even though they are "unable to explain logically and clearly the process of their spiritual perception." As in *Against Celsus,* Origen celebrates that Christianity benefits even the simpleminded, who are led to a more spiritual understanding of what scripture requires of them. This discernment Origen attributes to the power of the Holy Spirit. It is important to recognize here again the combination of scriptural prooftexts with the legacy of those second-century debates.

The rest of this chapter in book 2 turns to the then contemporary controversy about the Holy Spirit, and once again brings us into the realm of the Holy Spirit's role in the divine pedagogy. The gifts of the Spirit are various, depending on a person's need. Alluding to 1 Corinthians 12:8–9, Origen develops this point against some unnamed disturbers of the church (surely, those we know as Montanists), who have latched onto the name Paraclete, "likened him to some common spirits or other," and taught the kind of asceticism condemned in 1 Timothy 4:1–3, phrases of which Origen quotes (2.7.3). He explains that "the Paraclete is the Holy Spirit, who teaches truths greater than can be uttered by the voice, truths which are, if I may say so, 'unspeakable.'" The Paraclete is so named because of his work of consolation, "for anyone who has been deemed worthy to partake of the Holy Spirit, when he has learnt his unspeakable mysteries, undoubtedly obtains consolation and gladness of heart." Noting that Jesus Christ is called "paraclete" in the Johannine Epistle (1 John 2:1), Origen suggests that "this title 'paraclete' means one thing when applied to the Saviour and another when applied to the Holy Spirit." The Greek word, he explains, can mean both "comforter" and "intercessor." So in the case of the Savior it means "intercessor": "when used of the Holy Spirit, however, the word 'paraclete' ought to be understood as 'comforter', because he provides comfort for the souls to whom he opens and reveals a consciousness of spiritual knowledge." The discussion here alludes to John 16:12–14 and 14:26–27.

Once again Origen largely relies on clear statements of scripture, not mystical or allegorical meanings, both to condemn opponents and to open up discernment of the nature and role of the Holy Spirit within the overarching providence of God. He moves from scripture to doctrine, yet his moves are informed by what has emerged as apostolic tradition in the debates of the second century. Prior to this whole discussion we find what is in the rule of faith: "the doctrine that the scriptures were composed through the Spirit of God," who is "united in honour and dignity with the Father and the Son" (1.pref.8).

2.2.4. From Doctrine to Scripture: God

By way of contrast let us go back to Origen's opening discussion of God. The startling thing here is that he begins with an axiomatic position that, he admits, is not scriptural. It would seem to be a deliberate tactic, for it illustrates the important point that scripture uses other ways of expressing concepts many hold in common. That this is how Origen presents it perhaps gives it a rather different spin from the easy assumption that he is reading Platonic perspectives into scripture.

The final clause of Origen's rule of faith states that

> the scriptures were composed through the Spirit of God and that they have not only that meaning which is obvious, but also another which is hidden

from the majority of readers. For the contents of scripture are the outward forms of certain mysteries and the images of divine things. (1.pref.8)

Almost immediately he picks up the term "incorporeal," which is "unknown not only to the majority of Christians but also to the Scriptures." He dismisses a potential example in a book called *The Teaching of Peter* on the grounds, first, that it is not canonical and he can prove it was not written by Peter or anyone inspired by the Spirit of God, and, second, that the word there has a different meaning. "Nevertheless," he continues:

> we shall enquire whether the actual thing which Greek philosophers call *asōmaton* or incorporeal is found in the Holy Scriptures under another name. We must also seek to discover how God is to be conceived, whether as corporeal and fashioned in some shape, or as being of a different nature from bodies, a point which is not clearly set forth in the teaching. (1.pref.9)

Thus heralded as an issue, incorporeality almost inevitably dominates his discussion of the nature of God, not to mention Christ, the Holy Spirit, every soul and every rational nature also.

Embarking then on his exposition of the first clause of the rule, that concerning God the Father, Origen challenges

> some who will try to maintain that even according to our scriptures God is a body, since they find it written in the books of Moses, 'Our God is a consuming fire', and in the Gospel according to John, 'God is spirit, and they who worship him must worship in spirit and in truth.' Now these will have it that fire and spirit are body and nothing else. (1.1.1)[67]

He turns the discussion around by reference to 1 John 1:5: God is light. The sense of that must be that God enlightens the understanding of those who are capable of receiving truth, he writes, cross-referencing "By light shall we see light" (Ps 35:10 LXX). This light is taken to constitute "thy word and thy wisdom, which is thy Son, in him shall we see thee, the Father." This cannot have anything to do with the light of our sun, nor can one suppose that "from that material light the grounds of knowledge could be derived and the meaning of truth discerned." Light, therefore, does not suggest that God is a body, and by similar reasoning the appeal to "consuming fire" is dismissed: "what God

---

67. Quoting Heb 12:29 and John 4:24.

consumes are evil thoughts of the mind, shameful deeds and longings after sin." Further argument proves that spirit is not some kind of body:

> It is a custom of Holy Scripture when it wishes to point to something of an opposite nature to this dense and solid body, to call it spirit, as in the saying, 'the letter killeth, but the spirit giveth life.' Here undoubtedly the letter means that which is bodily, and the spirit that which is intellectual, or as we also call it, spiritual. (1.1.2)

Thus "spirit" points to the intellectual realm, to spiritual knowledge, and with respect to the other text in question, John 4:24, worship not in material places but in truth (1.1.2, 4). Later he will essentially reproduce this discussion in *Against Celsus*, focusing on interpretation of the same scriptural texts and demonstrating that, though Christians share with the Stoics the doctrine of providence, they do not agree that the first principle is corporeal (*Cels*. 6.70).

Origen now feels free to explore further the transcendence of this immaterial divine Being.

> Having then refuted, to the best of our ability, every interpretation which suggests that we should attribute to God any material characteristics, we assert that in truth God is incomprehensible and immeasurable. For whatever may be the knowledge which we have been able to obtain about God, whether by perception or by reflection, we must of necessity believe God is far and away better than our thoughts about him. (*Princ*. 1.1.5)[68]

Next, arguments and analogies are deployed to suggest how far God is beyond the capacity of the human mind. Our eyes cannot bear to look at the sun itself, but we can infer its greatness from its rays.

> So, too, the works of divine providence and the plan of this universe are as it were rays of God's nature in contrast to God's real substance and being, and because our mind is of itself unable to behold God as God is, it understands the parent of the universe from the beauty of God's works and the comeliness of God's creatures. God therefore must not be thought to be any kind of body, nor to exist in the body, but to be a simple intellectual existence, admitting of no addition whatever . . . but is Unity, or if I may say

---

68. Origen does not mention Isa 55:8–9, but it is plausible that he had it in mind.

so, Oneness throughout, and the mind and fount from which originates all intellectual existence or mind. (1.1.6)

It may be tempting to comment that Origen has all along been taking the Platonist view and contesting the materialism of the Stoics, as we saw him doing in *Against Celsus*. But while his argument about the One suggests Platonist philosophy, this analogy recalls Paul's argument in Romans 1 that God's invisible nature is evident in the things God created. What is implicit in this association is a profound sense that the one God, the Creator, is utterly other than anything created. Origen is again in line with the conclusions of second-century argumentation.

True, Origen now uses as an analogy the capacity of our minds to transcend our bodies, to act or move without needing space or volume, to engage in intellectual pursuits, to reason and argue, and to contemplate the invisible. Thus he claims in a rather Platonic manner a certain affinity between the mind and God, "of whom the mind is an intellectual image" (1.1.7). The point, however, is to justify from our own experience the existence of incorporeal realities. It also prepares the way for Origen to return to scripture, recognizing that scripture will be more authoritative for those who seek instruction or proof from that source. Citing Colossians 1:15 and John 1:18 to establish God's invisibility, he states that it is in the very nature of God impossible for God to be seen. For, "to see and to be seen is a property of bodies, to know and to be known is an attribute of intellectual existence" (1.1.8). Matthew 11:27 speaks of knowing not seeing, simply because "'to see' and 'to be seen' cannot suitably be applied to incorporeal and invisible existence." This is then clinched by reference to Matthew 5:8: "Blessed are the pure in heart; for they shall see God"—"for what else is 'to see God in the heart' but to understand and know him with the mind?" The "divine sense" of which Solomon speaks (Prov 2:5) is "not of the eyes but of a pure heart" (1.1.9).

Thus, scripture is found to teach God's incorporeality "under another name." Indeed, Origen has had to probe scripture, using one scripture text to illuminate another, in order to elucidate the true meaning. What he produces is neither straightforwardly literal nor allegorical, but rather a subtle "stretching" of language so as to apply it to this unnameable subject, that is, God. At first sight it might seem that a particular philosophical view shaped a doctrine which is then imposed on scripture. Implicit, however, are assumptions deriving from the apostolic tradition received via the debates of the second century. What we have witnessed in *Against Celsus* is already in play: God is the one and only God, the incomprehensible, transcendent one, yet the Creator, the source of everything; it is through God's providence and the beauty of God's creation that God is indirectly perceived by the pure in heart.

2.2.5. Beyond Doctrine and Scripture

In the preface to book 1 of *First Principles* Origen states:

> The church teaching also includes the doctrine that this world was made and began to exist at a definite time and that by reason of its corruptible nature it must suffer dissolution. But what existed before this world, or what will exist after it, has not yet been made known openly to the many, for no clear statement on the point is set forth in the Church teaching. (1.pref.7)

Given this vacuum it is scarcely surprising that Origen sought to fill it. Notoriously he mapped out a precosmic rational creation, a fall that occasioned the material creation and a restoration of all things in the end. The similarities between these Origenist speculations and both Neoplatonist and gnostic schemes have often been highlighted. However my rereading of *First Principles* in the light of what we have discovered so far has been another illuminating experience: to a significant extent it was from scripture and the apostolic tradition which he had received that Origen drew the principles that led to his conclusions.

For Origen free will was fundamental. True, in book 3 of *First Principles* he struggles with some passages in scripture that seemed to challenge this, but basically he deduced it from the long-standing early Christian view of God as overseer and judge of everything, even one's thoughts and motivations. The implication of this is praise and blame, and praise and blame imply the possibility of choice and responsibility for one's actions or failures. From this follows the notion of fall and redemption, which Origen shares with all the various Christian *haireseis*, not least the one that was emerging as the church's agreed orthodoxy.

But why did Origen project the fall back before the creation of the world? It is absolutely clear from *First Principles* that he adopted these speculations as a way of making the case for God being both just and good—crucial given the debates of the second century. He is desperate to provide an explanation of the unfairness of present realities (*Princ.* 2.9.3–6): some are born barbarians, some Greek; some have excellent laws, others follow savage customs; some are born humble, in subjection, or slavery, others are brought up with more freedom and opportunity; some have healthy bodies, others are invalids; some are defective in sight, others in hearing or speech. There is a problem with the world's variety if it was made by God, "the God whom we call good and righteous and absolutely fair," and it is raised by "those who come from the schools of Marcion, Valentinus and Basileides." They assert that souls are diverse by nature, and the world cannot have been made by God nor be ruled by providence—so "no judgement of God on everyone's deeds is to be looked for." In the face of this, Origen endeavors "to search out and discover how the great variety and diversity of the world is consistent with the whole principle of righteousness." His answer is that this diversity is the result of God placing "everyone in a position proportionate to one's merit"—it is not due to chance, nor to diversity of natures, nor to different creators.

> As . . . without any doubt it will happen in the day of judgement that the good will be separated from the evil and the righteous from the unrighteous and every individual soul will by the judgement of God be allotted to that place of which his merits have rendered him worthy, . . . so also in the past some such process, I think, has taken place. For we must believe that God rules and arranges the universe by judgement at all times. (2.9.8)

Origen reads back the eschaton to the beginning: "impartial retribution," according as each one deserves, is the principle on which God has arranged the universe, and this means "it is possible for us to understand that even before this life there were rational vessels" and "each vessel received, according to the measure of its purity or impurity, its place or region or condition in which to be born" (2.9.8).[69] Thus, belief in God's judgment and providence together requires both free will and preexistence; they are also the prerequisite for Origen's pedagogical understanding of God's purposes.

There is, furthermore, another way in which doctrine already established enters Origen's logic. "Creation out of nothing" implies change from not being to existing, so creatures are of necessity subject to change and alteration. Any goodness they have is not inherent in their nature, but a gift from the Creator. Free will was granted so that they could make their own "the good that was in them." Unfortunately, sloth and weariness, plus disregard and neglect of better things, meant their withdrawal from the good (2.9.2). Again, Origen's precosmic fall is derived from already established elements in the second-century understanding of the apostolic tradition.

The precosmic fall, along with the emphasis on the incorporeality of the spiritual creation, almost inevitably seems to align Origen with an entirely pes-

69. Cf. *Princ.* 1.5.3; 3.3.5.

simistic view of matter and bodies. What is surprising is that that proves to be far from the case. True, bodies are sometimes treated as punishment (e.g., 1.8.1) or as prisons—he refers to Romans 8:21 to point to "deliverance from bondage" when "God shall be all in all" (1 Cor 15:28), describing "the end and consummation of the world" as release from "bars and prisons" (1.7.5) or as an obstacle to union with God. He wonders how likeness to the incorporeal God can be in a body (3.6.1). Nevertheless, elsewhere we find Origen state that "the saints will receive back the very bodies in which they have lived in holiness and purity during their stay in this life, but bright and glorious as a result of the resurrection" (2.10.8). Indeed, Origen often picks up Paul's language of "spiritual body,"[70] and asserts that at the consummation the "bodily nature will assume that supreme condition to which nothing can ever be added" (3.6.9; cf. 2.2.2). Such reasoning we found also in his defense of resurrection in *Against Celsus*.

Time and again Origen associates "body" with change and transformation (*Princ.* 2.1.4; 4.4.6), but that means there can be coarser and finer versions of body. Indeed, Origen appears to doubt whether rational creatures can lead a life without a body (4.4.8), and occasionally seems to suggest that life without a body is found in the Trinity alone (2.2.2; cf. 1.6.4), though some editing on the part of Rufinus is suspected. Doubtless there was a certain ambivalence in Origen's thinking—a Greek fragment, again preserved by opponents of Origen, insists that "the nature of bodies is not primary," that rational beings "came to need bodies" because of "certain falls," and that "when their restoration is perfectly accomplished, these bodies are dissolved into nothing."[71] Yet the goodness of the Creator never lets him treat matter as evil: he is absolutely clear that matter is not uncreated or eternal, but brought into being by God for God's providential purpose.

Origen states that he has so far not found anywhere where the term "matter" is "used in canonical scripture to denote that substance which is said to underlie bodies." The word means something different in Isaiah 10:17, and though it appears in the book of Wisdom not everyone accepts that book as scripture (*Princ.* 4.4.6). Yet matter

> is so great and wonderful as to be sufficient for all the bodies in the world, which God willed to exist, and to be at the call and service of the Creator in all things for the fashioning of whatever forms and species God wished, receiving into itself the qualities which God had willed to bestow upon it. (2.1.4)

70. E.g., *Princ.* 2.2.2; 2.10.1–3; 3.6.4, 6–7.
71. *Princ.* 4.4.8. The source is again Justinian; see p. 143 n. 66 above.

Origen's inquiries beyond the rule of faith never lead him into denying the goodness of the Creator, nor the fundamental pedagogical purpose of the temporal world in which we find ourselves. To that extent he truly was heir to the doctrinal conclusions of the second century and read scripture in this light.

It need hardly be added that scripture encourages hope in eschatological restoration. Second-century debates had established that creation at a point in time—a beginning—meant there would be an end; Origen repeatedly affirms in *First Principles* that the end is always like the beginning and reads back into the precosmic realm the postcosmic vision of God as "all in all" (1 Cor 15:28).[72] Again he is developing existing doctrine.

Finally, it is noticeable that what Origen has projected onto the heavens is his understanding of what it means to be a human living this life on earth. The whole purpose of God is to lead each and every one to perfection, through participation in Christ and sanctification in the Holy Spirit.[73]

> Holiness is in every created being an accidental quality and what is accidental may also be lost.... Consequently it lies with us and with our own actions whether we are to be blessed and holy, or whether through sloth and negligence we are to turn away from blessedness into wickedness and loss. (1.5.5)

3. Retrospect and Prospect

I have deliberately not provided in this chapter yet another overall account of Origen's approach to scriptural exegesis, nor of his hermeneutical principles, nor of his theological system. Allegory has barely been mentioned, and little has indicated why his work became controversial in subsequent centuries. Rather I have focused on aspects particularly relevant to the interrelationship of doctrine and scripture, and the context in which they became essential to the identity of Christianity. What now remains is to focus the key findings from this somewhat unusual account of Origen and assess their importance for this study overall.

3.1. Doctrine and Scripture

Was Origen interpreting scripture through Platonist doctrine? No—it is not as simple as that. But Origen did think doctrine was needed to interpret scripture

---

72. *Princ.* 1.6.2; cf. 1.1.1, 3; 3.5.4; 3.6.3, 8.
73. See, e.g., *Princ.* 1.3.8.

correctly. In his view it is because the meaning of scripture is not always self-evident that doctrine becomes fundamental. Erroneous interpretations by Jews and rival versions of Christianity were abundant and just taking the text at face value often seemed easily to support those rival readings. These arose, according to Origen, from a failure to probe scripture for its deeper meaning, the meaning unveiled by the apostolic tradition. In any case, discerning how events had fulfilled enigmatic prophecies showed how God's Word was veiled until clarified by the coming of Jesus. Yet read in the light of the apostolic tradition, scripture could often quite straightforwardly fill out that basic summary.

So doctrine based on the traditions stemming from Jesus's disciples alone ensures right reading. The rule of faith, remarkably promulgated by those simple, uneducated apostles—all the more convincing for that as sophistry is unlikely (*Cels*. 1.62)—provides the basic framework within which the problems of scripture may be elucidated. This canon does not, however, cover everything, and even what it does state clearly lacks reasonable explanation. So probing scripture to uncover its mysteries is the vital task of the scholar, but to do this involves the gifts of the Spirit—language, wisdom, and knowledge. It also means assimilating and probing further those doctrinal conclusions already mapped in response to the questions and challenges that the church has already faced—specifications concerning the sense of the rule of faith, such as the notion of God's *monarchia* and *creatio ex nihilo*.

Reviewing how in practice Origen deployed doctrine in reading scripture and scripture in exploring doctrine, we may trace a model for their interrelationship applicable more widely in early Christian argument.

1. The apostolic tradition, or rule of faith, provides a framework and indeed, as Irenaeus seemed to suggest, the overall hypothesis of scripture.
2. Questions about the interpretation of scripture are brought into relationship with this framework, and deductions from scripture are tested by their conformity with it.
3. Questions arising from the contemporary intellectual context to which the apostolic framework gives no answer are addressed by recourse to scripture, seeking answers either by assembling relevant texts and attempting to interpret scripture by scripture, or by searching the deeper meanings in scripture—a process that may involve the identification of fundamental but nonscriptural terms, like *asōmaton*, as important for capturing truths inherent in the biblical material.

As we move into those crucial doctrinal debates about the Trinity and Christology in volume 2, we shall find all these strategies employed as scripture is exploited to refine dogmatic definition, and nonscriptural terms, such as *homoousios*, become fundamental. I suggest, again, that neither the Newman/Behr position nor that of Harnack captures the complexity of this process. In some ways they complement each other, but we need to take account both of dogmatic continuities and of adaptations as the sense of scripture and the meaning of the apostolic faith were thrashed out within that particular intellectual context.

3.2. Divine Pedagogy

The idea of God's pedagogical purpose shapes the whole of Origen's thinking. Life is a school; the church's teaching (i.e., doctrine) and its textbooks (i.e., scripture) together constitute the means whereby sinners are turned into saints. The whole point of philosophical teaching in the ancient world was to foster a moral way of life; the persistent proof of Christianity's superiority to other philosophies, offered repeatedly to Celsus, is the fact that it makes people virtuous and brings an end to wickedness. Its power to do this, even for slaves and women and not just the educated and sophisticated, must ultimately come from its divine source. Indeed the whole point of God's providence is to train people in goodness through teaching appropriate to their level.

Furthermore an important point, to which Martens draws attention, is that Origen's eschatology envisages this schooling as ever ongoing.[74] Drawing on the *Commentary on John*, Martens quotes: "Scripture has not contained some of the more lordly or more divine aspects of the mysteries of God . . . all of the Scriptures even when perceived very accurately, are only very elementary rudiments of and very brief introductions to all knowledge." Then Martens notes how in *First Principles* Origen reminds us that Paul was unable to reach the end of searching the "depth of the divine wisdom and knowledge."[75] So the future life would be "a school room where minds found increasing enlightenment."[76] As Origen himself put it:

> even though someone may have departed out of this life insufficiently instructed . . . he can be instructed in that Jerusalem, the city of the saints, that is, he can be taught and informed and fashioned into a "living stone," a "stone precious and elect," because he has borne with courage and endurance the trials of life and the struggles after piety. There, too, he will come

---

74. Martens, *Origen and Scripture*, 234–42, quoting *Comm. Jo.* 13.27, 30.
75. *Princ.* 4.3.14, quoting Rom 11:33.
76. Martens, *Origen and Scripture*, 236–37.

to a truer and clearer knowledge of the saying, already uttered here, that "Humankind does not live by bread alone but by every word that proceeds out of the mouth of God." (*Princ.* 2.11.3)[77]

There follows (*Princ.* 2.11.5–6) a description of progress through "paradise"—"this will be a place of instruction and, so to speak, a lecture room or school for souls, in which they may be taught about all they have seen on earth"; then to the heavenly places where God will show to them "the causes of things and the perfection of his creation"; and so, "increasing in mind and intelligence," to the attainment of perfect knowledge, gazing "face to face," beginning to "see God," that is to understand God through "purity of heart" (2.11.7).

Meanwhile, God's providence is at work in creating a suitable educational environment to set all on the path to this ultimate goal. Life is a school. What the church teaches is the philosophy with the best doctrine, some of which is held in common with others, especially Plato.

However, in school questions and answers may foster open inquiry or, more often, particularly at elementary levels, rote learning.[78] Increasingly *haireseis* became considered not, as we have found them in Origen's view, as alternatives to be explored so that the true and genuine might be revealed by way of contrast, but rather as false deceits against which warning was necessary. Open inquiry gradually gave way to strict formulae to be memorized, while the key elements of Christian orthodoxy came to be specified in creedal statements thought to summarize the true meaning of scripture. This trend we will observe in the next chapter, while volume 2 will trace the process whereby controversy over the relationship between Father and Son, as well as over the divinity and humanity of Christ, produced precisely articulated dogmas justified by reference to scripture.

---

77. Alluding to 1 Pet 2:4–6.
78. As noted in discussion in chapter 2.

6

Creeds

FROM CONFESSION TO DOGMA

It is generally supposed that the classic creeds, which are now regularly recited in traditional liturgies, sum up Christian doctrine. Creedal formulae as such emerged by the fourth century. It was supposed that creeds, like the rule of faith (explored above in chapter 4), covered in their threefold pattern the import of the overarching scriptural narrative while also affirming such traditional clauses as Christ's birth from the Virgin Mary and the resurrection of the flesh. The creed would be taught to catechumens, memorized, and recited publicly as a confession of faith before baptism. Variant creedal forms emerged in different localities, but from Nicaea through the evolving so-called Arian controversies, agreeing upon a creed became the way of arriving at consensus as to true doctrine, and until the reaffirmation of the Nicene Creed at Constantinople, church councils kept trying to enshrine their doctrine in fresh yet formally traditional creedal statements.[1] Where the rule of faith had once been a criterion for exposing gnostic heresy, creeds now became "tests of orthodoxy." Liturgical confessions of faith were becoming dogmatic statements, and lists of dogmas were being assembled—indeed, tradition suggested that as many as ten "holy dogmas" were to be found in the fourth *Catechetical Homily* of Cyril of Jerusalem.[2]

We will end this chapter with Epiphanius, his work offering a striking example of how the Christian faith could be understood as constituted by correct

---

1. The relationship between the creeds of Nicaea and Constantinople is complex; one is certainly not an edited version of the other, as often supposed. The classic treatment is J. N. D. Kelly, *Early Christian Creeds* (London: Longman, 1960).
2. This comes from the heading in certain manuscripts, and the reference given in Theodoret's *Eranistes* (Florilegium 2.7): "from the fourth catechetical address concerning the ten dogmas." Greek text in Gerard H. Ettlinger, ed., *Eranistes* (Oxford: Clarendon, 1975).

dogmatic statements, along with reaction against allegorical interpretation of scripture—is there a connection between the two? First, however, we will explore Cyril's mid-fourth-century catechesis. His catechetical homilies may confidently be treated as giving us insight into the basic *dogmata* taught to aspiring church members. The fact that catechumens were instructed in this way signifies that churches still looked like schools—indeed, as the Roman world was being Christianized, regular homilies based on scripture reading still made this new religion unusual in that regard. Cyril's catechesis demonstrates how basic Christian teaching persisted as a steady undercurrent even as storms and disputes raged overhead. Cyril avoids explicit reference to contemporary controversies, though occasional comments betray awareness of them. Undoubtedly the disputes reinforced the subtle shift from confession to doctrine, the increasingly propositional approach to cataloguing dogmas, and the trend toward fixed formulae to be learned by rote, but Cyril's *Catechetical Homilies* surely show that this was already underway.

The bulk of this chapter, then, will probe the classic creedal affirmations, considering Cyril's treatment of each, then in some cases using it as a launch pad for wider exploration of the dogma in question, especially if it is not treated elsewhere in these volumes. We shall observe fundamental continuities between these later formulations and the second-century resolution of those early questions about scripture's makeup and meaning. We shall look, too, for the interconnections between these doctrines and for their coherence both with their scriptural roots and with one another, for Cyril certainly regarded the discrete dogmas as the building blocks of a single coherent doctrinal scheme (*Procat.* 11). What we shall trace is the overall "ecology" within which sit the key doctrines of the Trinity and Christology, those core dogmas whose precise articulation through controversy we still have not explored, as they were already so related to other themes as to create a theological whole based on a coherent reading of scripture.[3] We begin, therefore, with Cyril's own presentation of the coinherence of creed and scripture.

1. Cyril of Jerusalem: Scripture Digested for Catechesis

In Cyril's *Catechetical Homilies* we find some explicit statements on the relationship between creeds and scripture:[4]

---

3. See further in volume 2.
4. *Cat. orat.* 4.17; 5.12. Greek text in W. K. Reischl and J. Rupp, eds., *S. Patris Nostri Cyrilli*

158   CHAPTER 6

1. Where the divine and holy mysteries of the creed are concerned, one must not teach even minor points without reference to the sacred scriptures.
2. For the creed is guaranteed by scriptural proof and not clever argument.
3. The creed is firmly based on the whole of scripture.
4. It is a summary of the whole teaching of the faith in a few lines, since not everyone has the time or capacity to read the whole of scripture.
5. The articles of the creed are the most important doctrines collected from the whole of scripture to make up a single exposition of the faith.

Such statements cry out for examination. Cyril may seem to present the kind of view already found in Irenaeus, but it is by no means evident that he had the same sense that the creed represented the *hypothesis* of scripture.[5] How was it, then, that he understood the creed as a summary or précis of scripture? How did he imagine that those highly selective articles of the creed could be representative of scripture *as a whole*—or indeed his associated proofs from scripture in the form of isolated sentences or phrases abstracted from context and relying on prophetic and symbolic interpretations? Lastly, it is not by any means obvious how the implied mutual relationship with creeds could be inherent in the scriptural texts, for Cyril himself warns that heretics teach other dogmas and offer other readings of scripture.

1.1. What Did Cyril Mean by "Summary"?

If we turn to Cyril's *Procatechesis* (his introductory homily of welcome and warning), we can get a sense of what Cyril expects his hearers to receive from this catechetical course of homilies. He plays on their designation as catechumens: previously they have been those hearing from outside. They have heard mysteries without understanding; they have heard the scriptures without recognizing their depth. Now they will understand things they did not know (*Procat.* 6). Catechesis is to be thought of as a house fitted together with stones of knowledge: he will explain them point by point and later their mutual connections, for failure to join them together will leave an unsound structure (*Procat.* 11).

Those stones of knowledge or "holy dogmas" are specified in the fourth of the catechetical homilies, each to be developed further in subsequent homilies (*Cat. orat.* 4.2). It is not easy to identify "the ten dogmas" of the fourth homily;

Hiersolymorum Archiepiscopi Opera quae supersunt Omnia (Munich: Libraris Lentneriana, 1848–1860); English translation in *NPNF* 7 unless otherwise noted.

5. See chapter 4 above.

although (as previously noted) that title is attested as early as Theodoret. The manuscripts vary in terms of the stated number of dogmas and their subheadings, suggesting the perplexity surrounding their division is very ancient. But such attempts to enumerate these "dogmas" confirm the impression of the text itself that what a dogma or teaching was meant to be was a proposition about the truth, the implied pedagogy being rote learning rather than encouragement to any kind of searching or questioning. The list of holy dogmas moves through the basic creedal propositions concerning God, Christ, the virgin birth, the cross, the burial and resurrection, the ascension, future judgment, and the Holy Spirit, and then on to statements about humankind, soul and body, saints and sinners, with lifestyle injunctions reinforced by the promise or threat of resurrection to eternal bliss or damnation. Dogma, then, goes beyond creedal propositions. It includes teaching about the right way of life—saving knowledge. Indeed, for Cyril, holding to such propositions is inseparable from good works: "What use is it to have a fine knowledge of the dogmas about God and to be a shameless fornicator? Conversely, what use is the most admirable self-control, if one is an impious blasphemer?" (*Cat. orat.* 4.2).

In the following homily (5.10–12) Cyril makes clear that faith is not just assenting to and memorizing those truths, but receiving gifts of the Spirit that transcend human powers. These two senses of faith belong together in that reception of such powers results from being enlightened by the doctrines of faith forming the image of God in the soul by directing attention toward the God known through the holy dogmas. It is here that he proceeds to insist that the creed is based on the whole of scripture, must be memorized, and should be kept as food for the journey through every moment of life.

So what does this suggest about Cyril's understanding of a "summary"? His implicit understanding is surely shaped by the way philosophy was taught in the surrounding culture. Philosophers provided various options (*haireseis*), each setting out his teachings (*dogmata*), perhaps grounding them in ancient traditions stemming from the past as the Pythagoreans did, or perhaps in ancient texts such as Plato, or even Homer. The meaning of those texts lay not on the surface but in the truths within them, whether overt or hidden. True, meaning was often uncovered by allegory, but, although Cyril is not a prime allegorist, it is still the underlying meaning of the whole of scripture that he wishes to capture in his list of dogmas or teachings. At roughly the same date, Athanasius was arguing that even though *homoousios* does not appear in scripture, it captures its *dianoia* (mind),[6] while earlier Origen had sought the unitive *skopos* (the aim or intent) of the whole. Setting out the fundamental teachings to which

---

6. See further volume 2, chapter 2.

the initiated were expected to subscribe—teachings about life, the universe, and especially God—provided for Christians as for others the context for wise teaching about the soul and its destiny and also for the ethical or lifestyle prescriptions that were the prime interest of philosophical teachers of the era.

The interesting point here, however, is the way in which, by the fourth century, there seems to have been a shift in understanding about how scripture and doctrine relate. Irenaeus, I suggested, understood the rule of faith as the *hypothesis* of scripture; this was perhaps a more literary—or in terms of that era, rhetorical—rather than philosophical approach. The gnostics, by failing to discern the true *hypothesis* and misplacing the stones that make up the mosaic, produced a portrait of a fox rather than a king. What Irenaeus sought to draw out in his "summary memorandum" was not a list of key dogmas, but portraits of the "three names" into which his hearers had been, or perhaps would be, baptized: the "names" whose identity is revealed in the scriptural narrative. This baptismal context was shared by Cyril and Irenaeus along with their joint insistence that the way of life is inseparable from assent to the truths taught by the church, those truths being distinct from other "options" or *haireseis*. Irenaeus, however, is perhaps closer to understanding how the rule of faith captures the narrative identity of the divine character(s) into whose story the baptized are invited. Even though the rule of faith lacked reference to the major narratives of scripture—the patriarchs, the exodus, the exile, and the healing and teaching mission of Jesus—there is less of a disjunction of genres.

Cyril can still unquestioningly assert that the creed is a summary of scripture. But, along with many in the fourth century, has he lost scripture's flow in the process of listing dogmatic propositions?

1.2. Cyril's Scriptural Proofs and Quotations

It is immediately apparent that, with a high rate of allusion, Cyril's discourse is steeped in scriptural phraseology and example. But the question is how does Cyril use scripture to prove doctrine? Though no allegorist, he looks for the true teaching of scripture underlying the wording, just like everyone else at the time. As for Irenaeus so for Cyril, primary proofs lie in the fulfillment in the events of the New Testament of the prophecies and "types" found in what by now is designated the Old Testament. This is particularly true in his homilies dealing with the virgin birth and the cross, not least because Cyril is determined to show his hearers how to meet the objections of the Jews (*Cat. orat.* 12–13). Signs, types, and symbols come into play as piecemeal correlations are made between details of the passion and Old Testament passages.

However, looking more closely we find that Cyril's argumentation for each of his "holy dogmas" does tend to give rise to wider engagement with the biblical narrative. A potentially abstract outline of God's oneness and otherness (*Cat. orat.* 6) is brought down to earth by Abraham's confession, "I am earth and ashes" (Gen 18:27; *Cat. orat.* 3); by Job's wonder at creation (*Cat. orat.* 4); by Ben Sira's exhortation not to inquire into what is too deep for you (*Cat. orat.* 4); and by repeated quotations from the Psalms and elsewhere enjoining praise (*Cat. orat.* 3–5). In an exposition of the one Son of God (*Cat. orat.* 10):

1. Gospel quotations are used to show how Father and Son have to be confessed together.
2. The creedal affirmation of oneness prevents the many names in scripture from suggesting more than one divine Son—it is simply the case that the one Savior provides for multiple needs.
3. Key words and stories from the Old Testament, their usage long traditional, demonstrate the presence of the one Son with the Father all along.

By the time we get to discussion of the virgin birth in homily 12, Cyril is ready to set the reason for the incarnation in the broad context of creation and fall, referring not just to paradise but also to Cain and Abel, Noah, Moses, and the prophets, and quoting texts to document not just humankind's grievous wounds but also how salvation was foretold. Traditional prooftexts that might seem arbitrary and contextless are woven into an overall account of God's gracious and redeeming purpose. And in the thirteenth homily, which expounds the crucifixion and burial, that overarching narrative of fall and redemption is even more effectively drawn out, with key quotations reinforcing the glory of the cross within that larger biblical narrative.

So what often seem piecemeal and typological quotations of scripture provide for Cyril a way of confirming his bigger picture and substantiating the fact that his "holy dogmas" not only comprise the key to discerning all the connections running through scripture, but also constitute scripture's fundamental meaning.

1.3. So What about Alternative Readings?

Cyril has virtually acknowledged that the "holy dogmas" enshrined in the creed are the hermeneutical key to a right understanding of scripture, even as those "holy dogmas" are both sourced from and guaranteed by scripture: creed and scripture are coinherent. But, if that is the case, why should there be false interpretations of scripture and impious doctrines that can lead astray, against which Cyril is arming his hearers? If creed and scripture are so mutually reinforcing, why are there other readings and other (false) dogmas derived from scripture?

Cyril, of course, resorts to blaming the devil for distortions of the truth, but he is also suspicious of "curious inquiry" into "what is not in scripture." Heretics are too clever by half. It was perhaps the fourth century context of dogmatic controversy that threw him back on basic long-standing Christian affirmations earthed in scripture and enshrined in creedal form. Not for Cyril any further speculation! This kind of attitude we will find still expressed in the christological controversies of the fifth century. As we know, Cyril's attempts to avoid these controversies neither kept him out of trouble nor ensured an unambiguous reputation, but the ups and downs of his episcopal career need not detain us here. This brief exploration of how he understood the relationship between creed and scripture has confirmed, perhaps, that he may be read as representative of many traditionally minded Christian leaders disturbed by the doctrinal controversies of the time. Scripture and doctrine were not only taken to be coinherent, but also to be the framework within which the Christian life of proper morality and perfect devotion was to be lived.

However, this has maybe also shown that, in his understanding of what kind of truth was to be distilled from the biblical material, he shared a general shift from Irenaeus's way of identifying God, Christ, and the Holy Spirit through the overarching biblical story to identifying them through dogmatic propositions about the divine nature, these to be enlarged at a later stage through reference to scripture's narratives. Doubtless this can be attributed to the bitter fourth-century conflicts over orthodoxy occurring at the very time when it had become politically vital for the church to show a united front. But it is surely more than a subtle shift in the implied meaning of dogma or doctrine. It implies an end to inquiry or questioning and a pedagogy that offered standard answers.[7] This change would retrospectively impact one of the greatest Christian teachers of those early centuries: Origen. By the end of the fourth century the first Origenist controversy had called distinctive features of his teaching into question. One may also ask whether Arius[8] was a victim of this "dogmatizing" tendency or its catalyst, but the irony is that Cyril himself was caught out by the repercussions.

---

7. See 1.1 in chapter 3 above.

8. Rowan Williams, *Arius: Heresy and Tradition* (London: Darton, Longman and Todd, 1987).

As we have seen, alternative readings of scripture continued to generate controversy, a process that seems to have no end! Yet the mainstream tradition of Christianity accepted Cyril's basic instinct, namely, that the essential meaning of scripture is summed up for Christians in the creeds inherited from this period in the church's history.

2. "Holy Dogmas": Scriptural Roots, Doctrinal Legacies

Already we have noted Cyril's listed dogmas in homily 4, starting with God and then Christ before adding the virgin birth, the cross, the burial, resurrection, and ascension, then future judgment and the Holy Spirit, then followed up by the soul and body, food and clothing, resurrection of the body, baptism, and the scriptures. We have observed how hard it is to see how all these make up ten dogmas, but also how in Cyril's view they make up a single coherent structure and also how the range, which embraces not just beliefs but ethics and lifestyle, reminds us that *dogma* meant "teaching" in general. We will now consider each dogma in turn, beginning in each case with Cyril's brief introduction to each topic in homily 4 then pursuing his larger development in later homilies; in the case of some discussions, however, we will also draw on other texts to highlight continuities or varying emphases in early Christian approaches to the particular dogma in question. The aim is to present an overall picture of classical Christian doctrine and its scriptural basis prior to exploring the specific debates on the Trinity and Christology in the second volume.

2.1. God

What Cyril says about God is a prime example of continuity with the doctrinal decisions of the second century. The introductory summary offered in his fourth homily (*Cat. orat.* 4.4–6) insists on:

1. God's oneness: "unique, unbegotten, without beginning or change or alteration."
2. the fact that the one God is both just and good, with warning against those who divide God into two—we recall Marcion;[9]
3. the fact that the one God is the Creator of everything, heaven and earth, angels and archangels, and the Father of one, namely, our Lord Jesus Christ.

---

9. See chapter 3, above.

Cyril adopts the Irenaean description of God as not circumscribed—rather God is "in everything and outside everything." God foresees the future, knows everything, and is not subject "to the succession of things, or to generation or chance or fate" but complete and perfect, always the same. His final points note (1) that God has prepared punishment for sinners and rewards for the righteous—again a matter at issue in the second century; and (2) that deification of the sun, moon, or indeed love, is idolatry to be avoided, as is heresy.

Homilies 6 through 9 develop this summary further, homily 6 addressing God's *monarchia*. Interestingly Cyril's initial move is to quote 2 Corinthians 1:3, stating that the thought of God the Father must involve the Son, and glory is to be ascribed to both as indivisible—the Father does not have one glory and the Son another. This highly Johannine comment anticipates the emphasis of homily 7, which focuses on God's divine Fatherhood. This Fatherhood implies a Son equal in dignity, and this is what Jews failed to recognize. God may be called the Father of many, but only *katachrestikōs* in a derived or metaphorical sense (*Cat. orat.* 7.5), whereas "by nature and in truth" God is Father "of one only, the only-Begotten Son, our Lord Jesus Christ." Cyril then insists on the fact that this was not a matter of change or passion, citing James 1:17, and piles up more texts to show that the perfect Father begat a perfect Son, the Father delivering everything to the Son and the Son honoring the Father. Thus their worship is inseparable. Indeed, the notion that Christ is merely "equal in honour to righteous persons" (7.7) is confronted with a further raft of scriptural texts, and a series of exegetical points distinguish between different usages of the term "father": Paul is father of the Corinthians, the devil father of those who consent to him, and believers may become children of God by adoption, which comes from God's lovingkindness (7.9–10). However, the one God, the Father, the unsearchable and ineffable is only seen and declared by the Only-begotten (John 1:18). Relying on biblical material, and without reference to then current controversies, Cyril's teaching surely articulates the basic instinct reacting against the Arian claim that the Logos/Son was a creature, even if the first and greatest of the creatures. Christ's Sonship was to be treated with the utmost seriousness because it guaranteed the Fatherhood of the Father. Opening homily 8, Cyril differentiates Christianity, not only from the polytheism of the Greeks, but also, as implied already in homily 7, from the Jewish doctrine that fails to acknowledge the Son of God (8.1–2).

Back in homily 6, Cyril also spends time on the problem of putting things into words—we cannot say enough about God, but only as much as human nature can grasp (6.2–4). We cannot explain what God is; admitting ignorance is the height of knowledge. So he urges his hearers to "magnify the Lord with me" (Ps 33:4 LXX), and his presentation now picks up the resonances of biblical praise. The great Abraham before God admits he is "earth and ashes" (Gen 18:27); how can earth and ashes sing a hymn worthy of the God "who holds together the circle of the earth and views its inhabitants as locusts" (Isa 20:22 LXX) and numbers stars and raindrops (Ps 146 LXX; Job 36:27)? Cyril exploits such texts and others to indicate how inadequate are our faculties to grasp the Creator, yet we can still praise and glorify our Maker. So whereas the language of his summary in homily 4 might suggest an apophaticism that bespeaks "Hellenization," his fuller exposition grounds that reserve in worship and in a biblical respect for the unnameable God. Indeed, Cyril surely confirms the thesis I advanced years ago: that scripture and the Jewish tradition of never pronouncing God's name actually radicalized Christian expression of God's transcendence beyond anything found in Greek philosophy—it was not simply a matter of Hellenization.[10]

In homily 6 Cyril now points out that not even angels see God—or at least they do merely according to their capacity. Only the Holy Spirit, together with the Son, can see adequately, he says, quoting 1 Corinthians 2:10 and Matthew 11:27: "For [the Son] sees God as he needs to see him and reveals him through the Spirit according to each one's receptivity; for the Only-begotten Son shares in the Father's godhead together with the Holy Spirit. The Begotten knows his Begetter, and the Begetter knows the one he has begotten" (*Cat. orat.* 6.6).[11] Again scripture seems to be pushing Cyril toward Trinitarianism, despite his tendency to identify the one God with the Father. We might say his theology is basically traditional and pre-Arian.

The rest of Homily 6 insists on the divine oneness: different descriptions such as good and just, almighty, and Sabaoth do not make God diverse or various. Nor do scriptural images imply God actually has wings or seven eyes (Ps 17:8; Matt 23:37; Zech 4:10). God is perfect (Matt 5:48) as he writes: "perfect in sight, perfect in power, perfect in greatness, perfect in justice, perfect in lovingkindness: not circumscribed in any space, but the Creator of all space" (*Cat. orat.* 6.8). God's power reaches not just to earth but also under the earth. More biblical quotations rub home God's wisdom and greatness, while the polytheism of the Greeks and the error of heretics are attributed to the devil.

It now becomes clear that the dualism Cyril consistently had in the back of his mind had its contemporary manifestation in Manichaeism, though like other

---

10. Young, "God of the Greeks."
11. Translation here by Edward Yarnold, SJ, *Cyril of Jerusalem* (London: Routledge, 2000), 117.

heresiologists he attributes its origin to Simon Magus and now traces it through Marcion and the gnostics (6.12–36). So, as anticipated, what he actually says about the one God is in direct continuity with the theological position mapped out through the answers given to those second-century challenges. It similarly derives from interpreting the complexities and potential contradictions of the Bible within the intellectual frameworks of the time. The same can be said of his treatment of "Almighty" and "Maker of heaven and earth," the subjects of Homilies 8 and 9. The brief reflection on "Almighty" insists that God's sovereignty reaches earth and not just heaven, focusing mainly on God's patience. God has power over all, including heretics, idolaters, and even the devil, but the "all-wise providence" uses what is wrong to enable victory and salvation for the faithful. The story of Joseph and his brothers substantiates this (8.4). Lurking here are those old issues about theodicy and the tendency to make God relate only to spiritual realities and not matter. Needless to say, homily 9 presupposes the fact that the one God and the Creator are identical, and indeed makes explicit the identity of the Creator and the Father of our Lord Jesus Christ.

The initial theme of homily 9 concerns the impossibility of seeing God with the eyes of the flesh. John 1:18 establishes this, Ezekiel 1:28 indicates that only the "likeness" of God's glory was seen by the prophet, and Exodus 33:20 clinches the point. Further biblical texts reinforce the dangers of seeing God's face. This reflection prepares for the main point: it is the works of the divine that give us some conception of God's power. Wisdom 3:5 indicates that by the greatness and beauty of creatures their Maker is seen, and that the heart is lifted up "proportionately" from their greatness to a greater conception of God. Daniel and Ezekiel are deployed for descriptions of God's throne, and if we cannot understand that, how can we comprehend the one who sits on it? But it is possible for us "to send up praises of God's glory from the works that we see" (9.3).

Cyril now spends much of the rest of the homily waxing lyrical about nature, from the starry heavens above to the waters below, the sun and moon, the seasons, the rain watering the earth for its harvests and flowers, cattle and minerals, not to mention the sea and its fish, the air and its birds, the earth and its wild animals—it is from all this that one understands the Creator's power. Along the way is a remarkable reflection on Isaiah 45:7, the affirmation that God creates darkness as well as light. Cyril treats it as ridiculous to attribute darkness to some other Creator and draws out the benefits of night—servants get respite from their masters, and we all get rest and a chance for prayer, singing psalms, reading scripture, and remembering our sins (9.7). His rhetoric is adorned with scriptural quotes and allusions, and its climax reflects on our own human nature, the remarkable framing of the human body, its capacity to reproduce, the constant beating of the heart, the wonderful contrivance of the eyes, and the breath of life given by the Creator. And all this has left out ten thousand other things, he says (9.15–16). So the response is Psalm 104:24: "How wonderful are your works, O Lord; in wisdom have you made them all." As Cyril writes, "For to you belong honour and glory and majesty, both now and throughout all ages. Amen" (9.16).

Three things are striking:

1. the continuing insistence on God as Creator of everything—the fundamental doctrine that the second-century challenges had firmly established;
2. the biblically grounded shift to praise of the Creator through the divine works on display in nature;
3. the deep appreciation of the created, natural order and the implication that our inadequate understanding of these wonders is as nothing to our inadequate grasp of God.

In chapter 3 we noticed how profoundly countercultural was that early Christian insistence, already adopted in the second century, that the one God was the Creator of the material world. This remained true in the fourth century when Neoplatonism provided a powerfully attractive version of that ambivalence about matter, together with a strongly apophatic account of the Ultimate One. For the Christian tradition, however, the essentially biblical approach to the issue in terms of identifying the transcendent one God as the Creator of everything—matter, soul, angels and all—was the foundation of a discourse new to antiquity and, as I have argued elsewhere, the catalyst that would eventually shape Christianity's most fundamental doctrines.[12] Rereading texts one may notice things that have not really registered before, not least because meanwhile they have grown in significance. The delight of rereading Cyril has been to notice how his teaching about God shifts so firmly to doxology, to a rhetoric of wonder and praise for creation. People seeking baptism were invited into a new perspective, a celebration of the cosmos and of their own creatureliness within it, grounded in an essentially Pauline appeal to the works of the Creator as revelatory of the One who made them (cf. Rom 1:19–20).

It would hardly be possible to do justice to the topic if we were to attempt here to use Cyril as a launch pad to explore this across other early Christian literature. Elsewhere I have shown how the doctrine of creation significantly modified the

12. See Young, "Creation: A Catalyst."

anthropological thinking of Gregory of Nyssa and Augustine, both of whom had a tendency to work within Neoplatonic intellectual frameworks.[13] Yet they both recognized human being, body and soul, as utterly creaturely, the body as fearfully and wonderfully made, eventually to be re-created and reenlivened with its own soul at the resurrection. Elsewhere I have also noted how Basil of Caesarea, in his nine homilies on the six days of creation in Genesis 1 known as the *Hexaemeron*, began by insisting that the visible world points beyond itself, finite "bodies" offering some conception of the infinite divine Being, though this was precisely what philosophers missed by their inherent atheism. Addressing various cosmological issues and drawing upon then current scientific thinking about the natural world, Basil endeavors at greater length than Cyril to conjure up worship not of the creature but the Creator. Like Cyril he refuses to identify darkness with evil, dwelling on the harmony of the cosmos. Again, elsewhere I have observed how time and again Augustine would endeavor to interpret Genesis so as to counter Manichaeism and give an intelligible account of the fact of creation by God: "The obscure mysteries of the natural order, which we perceive to have been made by God, the almighty craftsman, should rather be discussed by asking questions than by making affirmations" (*Gen. imp.* 1.1).[14] Augustine confesses he has not the slightest idea why mice, frogs, or worms were created, but affirms God saw all things together were good, setting everything within God's providence (*Gen. Man.* 1.6, 26).[15] Given these previous explorations, here for comparison with Cyril we will observe how Gregory of Nazianzus treated God as Creator in his *Theological Orations*.

Gregory's five *Theological Orations* were, of course, directed against followers of Eunomius, the latter-day Arians, and they will demand attention on that score in the next volume.[16] Here we concentrate simply on how Gregory

13. For the following points, see my previous publications: "Creation and Human Being: The Forging of a Distinct Christian Discourse," StPatr 44 (2010): 335–48; and "Naked or Clothed? Eschatology and the Doctrine of Creation," in *The Church, the Afterlife and the Fate of the Soul: Papers Read at the 2007 Summer Meeting and the 2008 Winter Meeting of the Ecclesiastical History Society*, ed. Peter D. Clarke and Tony Caldon (Woodbridge: Ecclesiastical History Society, 2009); both republished in *Exegesis and Theology*. See also my "From Cosmology to Doxology: Reading Genesis alongside Plato and Darwin," in *God's Presence: A Contemporary Recapitulation of Early Christianity* (Cambridge: Cambridge University Press, 2013), 44–92.

14. English translation of Augustine's unfinished *On the Literal Interpretation of Genesis* from *On Genesis*, trans. Edmund Hill, ed. John E. Rotelle, The Works of Saint Augustine 1/13 (Hyde Park: New City, 2002), 114–51.

15. Translation of *On Genesis against the Manichaeans* from Hill, *On Genesis*.

16. Text and translation in Frederick W. Norris with Lionel Wickham and Frederick

develops the themes just set out in Cyril's catechesis. The first oration addresses the heretics with supreme irony, implicitly making the point that theological questions are not to be undertaken lightly or spoken about without regard to our creaturely limitations: Job was stunned into silence when confronted with God. This is a prelude to opening up the mystery of the transcendent God in the second oration. Gregory presents himself as eager yet afraid to enter the cloud and speak with God, identifying himself with Moses (*Orat.* 28.2): "I ascended the mount. I penetrated the cloud, became enclosed in it, detached from matter and material things and concentrated, so far as I might be, in myself" (28.3). But when he looked he could only see God's back parts (Exod 33:23), traces of God "like shadowy reflections of the sun in water," and this was true both for Moses and Paul, even when caught up to the third heaven. Plato's famous dictum is cited: it is difficult to conceive God and to define God in words is impossible, for it is not just the peace of God which passes all understanding (28.4–5).

Gregory now quotes Psalm 8:3: "I consider the heavens, the work of your fingers, the moon and the stars." But far beyond these, he says, is the nature that is above them, the incomprehensible, the infinite. Gregory distinguishes between knowing something exists and knowing what it is, then develops a parable: anyone who sees or hears a beautifully made lute thinks of the lute maker or lute player; similarly we think of the incomprehensible one who made, moves, and preserves all created things (*Orat.* 28.6). This Creator Gregory describes as infinite, limitless, without body, yet pervading all things, a point backed up by Jeremiah 23:24 and Wisdom 2:7 (*Orat.* 28.8). So being incorporeal, God is also without beginning, unbegotten, unoriginate, unchanging, incorruptible. But just saying what God is not does not indicate what God is (28.9). This apophaticism merely points to a Being beyond the universe, self-existent, utterly transcendent, Gregory argues. The point is that the divine cannot be apprehended by human reason—the mind faints when it tries to go beyond corporeal things. Gregory uses various things like Spirit, Fire, Light, Love, Wisdom, and Righteousness to show how we are confined to the created environment and cannot look at Deity absolutely (28.13). As a result some have turned created things like the sun or the moon into gods, a point developed at some length. In the end, however, reason "implanted in us from the beginning" leads up to God, but what God is in nature and essence remains beyond us (28.16).

Williams, *Faith Gives Fullness to Reasoning: The Five Theological Orations of St. Gregory Nazianzen*, VCSup 13 (Leiden: Brill, 1991).

A series of biblical examples are now reviewed—Enoch, Noah, Abraham, Jacob, and Elijah. These figures may have met God, but they never could boast that they "had taken in the nature, the total vision, of God" (28.18). To these are added Peter, as well as Isaiah and Ezekiel, not to mention Paul. Paul tried to arrive not at the nature of God—he knew that was impossible—but rather at God's judgments (Rom 11:33), yet ended up in astonishment at their riches and depth, confessing them unsearchable (28.21). Gregory parallels the words of David (Ps 36:7) and then adds Psalm 139:6, which leads him into reflection on our own amazing makeup, on nourishment, on parenthood, on multiple species created with different characteristics, on voices and ears, eyes, the mind, on the variety of animals, fish, birds, insects, bees, grasshoppers, plants—on and on he goes detailing the marvels of the natural world and the way nature sets before us a banquet of both necessities and luxuries.[17] This at least means you can know God by these benefits, while the height of mountains and clefts in coastlines surely offer proof of God's majestic workings. The natural philosophers, or scientists of the time, have scarcely offered explanations of many other phenomena—Gregory rhetorically presents the ocean, the air, weather patterns, the sun, and the seasons. You hardly know what lies at your feet, Gregory suggests, ending with a picture of heavenly praise to the Creator of all things. His initial point is that "even the nature of beings on the second level is too much for our minds" so how much more that which is above all! The main point, however, is that the works of the Creator give us an inkling of this unknowable Being.

But, as Cyril stressed, this transcendent Creator is Father—Father in relation to the Son, the Only-begotten—so on to the second clause of the creed.

2.2. Lord Jesus Christ, Son of God

A quarter of a century before Cyril delivered his catechetical homilies the key word *homoousios* (of one substance) had been introduced into the creed agreed upon at Nicaea—a nonscriptural term deployed against Arius, who was apparently happy to sign any statement couched entirely in scriptural terms, though many sensed he was promulgating heretical views. How Trinitarian and christological doctrines were deduced from scripture through argument and controversy will be the subject of volume 2. Here we simply observe how Cyril, avoiding actual engagement with contemporary disputes, presented to his catechumens an essentially scriptural account of Christ, his divinity and

---

17. These sentences summarize Gregory of Nazianzus, *Orat.* 22–31.

relationship with the Father, as well as his incarnation. It would appear that ordinary congregations, led by people like Cyril, really did not need *homoousios* in order to embrace the right doctrinal reading of scripture.

Homily 4 introduces the topic (*Cat. orat.* 4.7–8). The prime focus is that the one and only Son of God is God begotten by God: life begotten by life, light begotten by light, "he did not begin to be in time, but was begotten by the Father before all ages, eternally and inconceivably." Thus Cyril naturally uses terms recalling the Johannine Prologue, and then picks up further New Testament hints: he is substantially God's Wisdom and Power and Righteousness, and has been seated at God's right hand before all ages. Cyril is clear that this was not a status received after the passion, but the royal dignity was always his—indeed, he was the Creator of all things "for the Father's sake." Begotten and Begetter have mutual knowledge of one another—for "no one knows the Son except the Father, and no one knows the Father except the Son" (Matt 11:27; cf. John 10:15). Son and Father are to be neither separated nor conflated into a Son-Father. Finally, Christ is identified as God the Word, though Cyril finds this needs explanation, which he promises to provide later. In this summary we can identify the significant points he will develop at greater length in homilies 10 and 11.

(1) In the second century the apologists had found it conceptually helpful to take up the idea (already present in the Johannine Prologue) that God's Logos/Word was incarnate in Jesus. Cyril worried that this risked making him like an "uttered word" that is "dispersed in air" without substantial existence, like something out of nothing, he perhaps implies. In homily 11 he will explain further that the begetting is not like the mind begetting speech—speech once uttered is scattered in the air and expires (*Cat. orat.* 11.10). Christ was begotten as substantial living Word, indeed the Creator of rational beings. It is clear, then, that Cyril prefers to develop the equally Johannine concept of the Father-Son relationship, the truly divine Son being necessary for God to be Father. In this preference he may well reflect a shift in focus in this period, a reaction against Logos-theology perhaps reinforced by reaction against Arius's deployment of it.[18]

(2) Implicitly Cyril rejects certain Arian positions: there was no time when he was not, and he always sat at God's right hand, as scripture indi-

---

18. Such a shift in focus from "Logos" to "Son" was canvassed by Peter Widdicombe, *The Fatherhood of God from Origen to Athanasius* (Oxford: Oxford University Press, 2000); Ron Heine, however, referring to his own article, "Origen on the Christological Significance of Psalm 45," *Consensus* 23.1 (1997): 21–37, noted in a private communication that Origen had already objected to applying christologically the words of Ps 45:1: "My heart has brought forth a good word," on the same grounds as Cyril offers here.

cates. His status did not involve adoption, advancement, or promotion.[19] The only-begotten Son is Lord of all things—"the Father's obedient Son who did not usurp his Lordship but received it by nature from one who gave freely," a statement backed up by quoting Luke 10:22: "All things have been handed over to me by my Father" (*Cat. orat.* 10.9). New Testament texts are assembled to confirm his Lordship: the song of the angels at his birth (Luke 2:10–11), the angels serving him at the temptation (Matt 4:11, backed up with Col 1:16 and other references to angels as his servants), and he is proclaimed as "Lord of all" in Acts 10:36 (*Cat. orat.* 10.10). Cyril adopts the traditional reading of passages in the Old Testament attesting to the presence of Christ the Lord alongside the Lord God. The classic was Genesis 1:26–27 where God proclaims the words, "Let us make man in our image" (*Cat. orat.* 10.6). But in homily 10 Cyril also appeals to Exodus 33:19, which reads "I shall pass before you [i.e., Moses] in my glory, and in your presence I shall call upon the name of the Lord"—this suggests one Lord calling to another, as does Exodus 34:4–7 where the Lord passes by and again calls on the name of the Lord (*Cat. orat.* 10.7–8). Psalm 110:1, "The Lord says to my Lord," already deployed in the New Testament, confirms that one Lord converses with another (*Cat. orat.* 10.9).[20] Along with countless other early Christian exegetes, then, Cyril understands that the Lord seen by Moses was the preexistent Christ, "for the Lord is gracious and always adapts to our weaknesses" (*Cat. orat.* 10.6), a point confirmed by quoting 1 Corinthians 10:4. According to Exodus 33:20, "No one shall see my face and live." This, explains Cyril, is why he assumed a human face, so that we might see it and live; he revealed only a little of his majesty at the transfiguration and the disciples fell to the ground in terror (*Cat. orat.* 10.7). Overall Cyril reflects a deep instinct rooted in the scriptures and certainly one that would resist Arius's tack of reducing God's Son to a creature, even if the first and greatest of the creatures. The incarnate one was Creator and not creature, and on this rests his royal sovereignty: "he rules over his own handiwork by his Father's decree" (*Cat. orat.* 10.5).

(3) Cyril is determined to convey to his hearers the oneness, indeed, the uniqueness of Christ. His Sonship is real; others are sons by adoption (e.g., *Cat. orat.* 11.4). Nor can his many titles be taken to signify a multiplicity of sons. The creed gives a precise formulation to prevent that: "one Lord Jesus Christ" (10.3–5). The one Savior, he explains, provides for our many different needs, as he picks up titles from scripture: vine, door, mediator, high priest,

---

19. See, e.g., *Cat. orat.* 10.5; 11.2.
20. See further discussion in volume 2.

sheep, stone—he becomes all things for all people (1 Cor 9:12) while remaining what he is by nature: "he adapts to our weaknesses like a skilled doctor or a sympathetic teacher" (*Cat. orat.* 10.50). Cyril rather painstakingly explains that these titles are not to be taken literally. Spiritually Christ is the door to the Father (*Cat. orat.*10.3) and already he had stated that if you deny the revealer you remain in ignorance, if you slight the Son, the Father becomes angry, and if you want to show reverence for God, you need to adore the Son or the Father will not accept your worship (*Cat. orat.* 10.1–2). Again we are drawn back to the Father-Son relationship: Cyril's text for homily 10 is 1 Corinthians 8:5: "for us there is one God, the Father, from whom all things exist and for whom we exist, and one Lord Jesus Christ, through whom all things exist." In his opening words he explains that those who believe in one God ought also to believe in his only-begotten Son, for you cannot deny the Son and have the Father, repeating this point again later: "besides knowing there is one God you need to know that he has an Only-begotten Son" (*Cat. orat.* 10.1, 2). And homily 11 reinforces this. Jesus Christ is not one of many "anointed" ones—he was not promoted to priesthood from among human beings but possessed it from his Father from all eternity. So we believe in "one Lord Jesus Christ, the Only-begotten Son of God." As Son he was not adopted, as Only-begotten he has no brother (11.1–2). This truth he had to show his disciples, and Cyril elaborates on the story of Peter's confession at Caesarea Philippi (11.3). Again Cyril rubs home the truth that he was truly Son, Son by nature, without beginning and not promoted from slave to son but "eternally begotten as Son by an inscrutable and incomprehensible birth." Where earlier he had trawled scripture for usages of the word "father" here he does the same for the word "son." Some received adoption as sons, but Christ was "Son from the beginning, Son of the Father in every way like his Begetter, light begotten from light, truth from truth, wisdom from wisdom, king from king, God from God, power from power" (11.4). The genealogies in the Gospels you must understand as referring to his humanity. He was Son of God before all ages, but at the end of the ages he became Son of David, a title he assumed as something not previously possessed, whereas Son of God he possessed eternally. Cyril is not embarrassed to state that Christ had two fathers: David according to the flesh and God the Father according to his divinity, reinforcing this with reference and allusion to scripture (11.5).

(4) Cyril is most concerned to correct any misconceptions about the begetting: it must not be thought of in bodily terms, nor should the Son be less than perfect once begotten, weak or ignorant like a child (11.7). It was not like Abraham begetting Isaac, for God was not originally childless—the Father

always had the Son. Nor is it like a teacher begetting pupils: Cyril quotes Paul's claim to have begotten the Corinthians (1 Cor 4:15). Nor is it like the adoption the catechumens will receive at baptism: the voice at Jesus's baptism affirmed he was already God's Son (11.8–9). It is here he adds that the begetting was not like the mind begetting speech. In fact the begetting of the Son by the Father was not in a way a human being can comprehend, but in a way known to God alone, indeed unknown to every created nature, the earth, the sun, and the heavens. Cyril finds scriptural texts to substantiate these instances and confound those who embark on speculations concerning the Creator (11.10–12). He tells his hearers not to be afraid to admit ignorance—after all, they share ignorance with the angels. Only the Begotten and the Begetter know each other, and scripture bears witness that the Begotten is God. The Johannine texts bear this out: as the Father has life in himself, so the Son (John 5:26) and all are to honor the Son as they honor the Father (John 5:23) (*Cat. orat.* 11.13). Spelling it out yet again Cyril insists there is one only-begotten Son of the one and only Father. The begetting is outside time: God did not lead the Son from nonbeing to being or bring a nonexistent being to adoption. There are not two first principles (*archai*): the Father is the *archē* (head) of the Son, one *monarchia* and Emmanuel is "God with us" (11.14). As we explore in volume 2 the various controversies that led to the honing of the doctrine of the Trinity, these points will become more significant, along with Cyril's appeal to Baruch 3:36–38: "He is our God. There is none beside him. . . . After this he was seen on earth and consorted with humankind" (*Cat. orat.* 11.15). Cyril's thought is aligned with response to the third-century Monarchians and the fourth-century rejection of Arianism as he appeals to biblical testimonies to the true divinity of Christ. He draws attention to the fact that God the Son, with God the Father within him, did not say, "I am the Father," but "the Father in me and I in the Father," and furthermore "I and the Father are one," to prevent us separating them or constructing a compound Son-Father. The dignity of the Godhead, the kingship—these are respects in which Father and Son are one, and they are one because there is no disharmony or disagreement between them. Their wishes are the same, their creations are not distinct, but a single act of creation of all things (11.16).

(5) Much of Cyril's presentation focuses on scriptural testimony to Christ: the priestly and royal prerogatives of the one Jesus Christ who was to come were signified by Moses's choice of Jesus (Greek for Joshua) and Aaron (10.11). Cyril points out many ways in which the first Jesus (i.e., Joshua) prefigured the later Jesus: he appointed twelve; he saved the harlot Rahab because she believed; he even brought down the walls of Jericho, Cyril here quoting the gospel prediction (Mark 13:2) that "stone would not be left on stone." If such parallels seem

a bit far-fetched, it is important to accept that Cyril is following traditional patterns of prophetic reading. His testimonies note the way Jesus's Hebrew name means Savior, though the Greek form he suggests means "healer" (*Cat. orat.* 10.3). Gospel stories of physical and spiritual healing are now assembled. Then, developing the theme of his priesthood, he turns to Psalm 110:4, already quoted in Hebrews 7:17, to establish the eternity of Christ's appointment by God to the priesthood according to the order of Melchizedek (*Cat. orat.* 10.14). When Christ came, Cyril states, the Jews denied him but the demons knew him; the high priest did not know him but the Samaritan woman did, and so too the prophets and apostles (10.15–17). The climax of homily 10 is a litany of "many true testimonies concerning Christ" (10.19) drawn from the gospel narratives: the Father bears witness, the Holy Spirit does also, and so do the angel Gabriel, the Virgin Mother of God, the manger, Egypt, Simeon, Anna, John the Baptist, the river Jordan, the sea of Tiberias, the blind, the lame, the dead restored, the demons, the winds Christ muzzled, the five loaves multiplied for the five thousand, the holy wood of the cross, Gethsemane, Golgotha, the Holy Sepulchre, the sun that was eclipsed at the moment of the saving passion, and the darkness from the sixth to the ninth hour.

(6) Cyril is anxious to warn his catechumens against pitfalls, and as he brings homily 11 to a close these are gathered together (11.17–21). Though he never names heretics, both the Arians and the Monarchians lie behind his warnings, and he tries to steer between left and right as he repeats points made earlier. To be avoided are:

1. any idea that the Father became human or suffered;
2. any suggestion that there was a time when the Son was not;
3. any notion of a Son-Father, or that the Father was at one time Father and at another time Son;
4. any view that the Son is honored by being proclaimed Father or the Father honored by suspecting the Son is numbered among created things;
5. any suggestion that the begetting involved diminution or change, or was within time rather than timeless;
6. any idea that God is Father of the Son and of creatures in the same sense;
7. any heresy that introduced different creators of the universe.

These warnings are counterbalanced with positive affirmations reinforcing what has already been said and bolstered by his many scripture quotations and allusions. For Cyril certainly believes that what he presents is the truth taught by scripture—scripture's own doctrine.

On the whole, then, Cyril's teaching about Christ avoids emerging terminology, such as *homoousios*, preferring the language and narratives of scripture, and eschews propositional definitions apart from his concern to get an appropriate meaning for the divine begetting. It also contests novel deductions, especially anything that threatens the eternity of the Son and his unity with the Father, remaining deeply traditional in its reading of scripture and its prophetic or christological meaning. Despite the upheavals of the fourth century, Cyril allows us access to the reality of the ongoing, steady teaching of the church, with its deeply traditional doctrines about God and Christ almost entirely drawn from scriptural testimony.

2.3. Born of the Virgin Mary

Earlier we noted how Theodoret introduces one of the quotations he gathered in the *Eranistes*: "Cyril of Jerusalem: from the fourth Catechetical Lecture concerning the ten dogmas. Concerning the birth from the Virgin." The paragraph quoted then speaks of the only-begotten Son coming down from heaven to earth because of our sins, assuming this same humanity as ours and being subject to the same passions as ours, being born of the holy Virgin and the Holy Spirit, the incarnation not being in semblance or show but in truth, not passing through the Virgin as through a pipe but truly made flesh from her, truly eating, truly drinking, truly nourished by milk.[21] It then suggests that if his incarnation had been a phantom, so would our salvation be a phantom, adding that the Christ is twofold: man in what is seen, God with respect to the unseen, man as eating like us, God as feeding the five thousand, and so on—a catalogue of such contrasts proving the double nature of Christ (which, as far as Theodoret was concerned, was the whole point).

That Cyril regarded birth from the Virgin as one of the "holy dogmas" is surely clear. Yet, surprisingly, reconstruction of the creed that Cyril would get his catechumens to memorize does not include this specific point—the language is closer to the somewhat barer creed adopted at Nicaea in 325, which simply speaks of Christ being made flesh and becoming man without specifying, as would the later creed of Constantinople (381), that his enfleshment was "from the Holy Spirit and Mary the Virgin." Nevertheless, the matter was firmly part of the tradition, invariably included in the rule of faith, and more often than not appears in creeds, including the one known in the West as the Apostles' Creed. True to this wider consensus, in the twelfth homily Cyril develops much further that initial statement in his fourth.

---

21. The teaching of Valentinus, according to Irenaeus, *Haer.* 1.7.2.

The twelfth lecture is headed, "On the words 'incarnate and made man'" and takes as its text Isaiah 7:10–14. The opening address, however, is to those "nurtured on purity and instructed in chastity," who are invited to raise a hymn to the "Virgin-born God" with "lips of purity." The conclusion of the homily also invites virgins and solitaries to acknowledge the glory of chastity, including men alongside women—indeed, "let us all by God's grace run the race of chastity," for "virgins share the lot of Mary the Virgin." Virginity, of course, had been a Christian ideal since the second century: Peter Brown quotes Galen as saying of Christians that "their contempt for death is patent to us every day, and likewise their restraint from intercourse," and also comments that Justin "presented Christianity . . . as a religion distinguished from all others by the stringency of the sexual codes observed by its married believers."[22] Athenagoras, defending Christians from the charge of "godless banquets and sexual unions" refers to the Christian belief that "to remain a virgin and abstain from sexual intercourse brings us closer to God."[23] By the fourth and fifth centuries, with the burgeoning monastic movement, the ascetic ideal of chastity was being further fostered by the virginity of Mary, while conversely emphasis on Mary's virginity was being reinforced by that ethical ideal.[24] This was a significant element in emerging Mariology alongside the controversy around Theotokos.[25] How much does this doctrine owe to those trends, trends that were subsequently questioned particularly at the Reformation?

Cyril's treatment of the subject rather suggests that the established place of the Virgin among the "holy dogmas" had more to do with being true to scripture and tradition than to anything else. Indeed, much of the twelfth lecture is devoted to proving that the scriptural promises had clearly been fulfilled by the coming of Jesus Christ, establishing the correct location of his birth from Micah 5:2, determining the exact timing from Daniel 2:44 together with elaborate chronological calculations (*Cat. orat.* 12.17–26),[26] and answering Jewish objections to the Christian reading of Isaiah 7:14, namely, that the Hebrew word meant not virgin but "young woman" and the reference was to

---

22. Peter Brown, *The Body and Society: Men, Women and Sexual Renunciation in Early Christianity* (London: Faber & Faber, 1989), 33–34.

23. Athenagoras, *Leg.* 33; Greek text and English translation by William R. Schoedel, ed. and trans., *Legatio and De Resurrectione*, OECT (Oxford: Clarendon, 1972).

24. See, e.g., Verna Harrison, "Gender, Generation and Virginity in Cappadocian Theology," *JTS* 47 (1996): 38–68.

25. Both virginity and Mariology have been topics much alive in recent scholarship. For my own take on these matters see chapter 7 of my book *God's Presence*.

26. Cyril assembles and discusses classic scriptural passages, such as Gen 49:8–11; Zech 9:9; Ps 2:7, 9, etc.

Hezekiah (12.21–22). In making such exegetical points Cyril was anticipated by both Justin and Origen.[27]

The heading of this homily, however, indicates that the overall subject is the incarnation. Clearly Cyril aimed to equip the catechumens to defend the doctrine against sceptics and heretics. Early on he identifies three questions to deal with: Why the incarnation? Can God's nature permit incarnation? Is it possible for a virgin to bear a child without a man? (12.4). Here we will focus on that final question, using it as springboard to trace more widely early Christian discourse on the subject of Christ's birth from a virgin.

On whether such a birth is possible, Cyril differentiates between the response needed for Greeks and for Jews (12.27). In both cases his prime purpose seems to have been to make the claim plausible. As far as the Jews are concerned, he appeals to multiple biblical miracles, not least other miraculous births: surely it would be harder for an aged, barren woman like Sarah to conceive than a virgin in the prime of youth? But his list is by no means confined to births—Moses's wooden staff was turned into a serpent, a living creature; Eve was brought forth from Adam's side; Adam himself was made from dust rather than a body. It is worth noting that these examples evoke creative rather than generative acts, a point we shall find pertinent more than once. Indeed, with respect to Moses's staff, Cyril explicitly notes that the Creator was not limited by the nature of trees (12.28–29).

Cyril adopts a parallel tactic with respect to the Greeks: to make birth from a virgin plausible Cyril suggests stopping their mouths with their own fables (12.27). Alluding to various myths, he asks how, given such claims as that Dionysus was born from the thigh of Zeus, they could say that it was impossible for a son to be born from a virgin's womb. At first sight this seems a surprising move. The apologists had expended much energy condemning Greek myths.[28] Justin has his Jew, Trypho, suggest that he, Justin, ought to be ashamed making such foolish assertions as do Greeks who claim that Perseus was begotten of the virgin, Danae, Zeus having descended upon her in the form of a golden shower (*Dial.* 67). Origen certainly saw the danger of drawing parallels with such pagan myths, for that is exactly what Celsus had done, introducing a Jew "as disputing with Jesus and pouring ridicule on the pretence,

---

27. Justin, *Dial.* 43 and 67; Origen, *Cels.* 1.34.

28. See e.g., Athenagoras, *Leg.* 13–30: "What reason is there to believe some stories and not to believe others . . . ?" (*Leg.* 30.5). Also Theophilus, *Autol.* 1.9ff.; 2.2–8; 3.2–8: his third discourse seems geared overall to show that the Bible is true by contrast with Greek literature. Greek text and English translation in R. M. Grant, ed., *Theophilus of Antioch: Ad Autolycum*, OECT (Oxford: Clarendon, 1970).

as he thinks, of his birth from a virgin, and as quoting the Greek myths about *Danae* and *Melanippe* and *Auge* and *Antiope*" (*Cels.* 1.37).[29] It was all too easy with ill intent to place the gospel birth narratives alongside myths about divine impregnation. Yet, like Cyril, both Justin and Origen had themselves used parallel cases to enhance the story's plausibility.

In his *1 Apology* Justin suggests that there was nothing new in the Christian claim that the Word was born without sexual union, was crucified, died, rose, and ascended (*1 Apol.* 21). He spells out stories of "the sons of Zeus," Hermes, Asclepius, Dionysus, Heracles, and others, referring also to Zeus's many liaisons with women he seduced. True, he here slips to critique, attributing these acts to wicked daemons for "we have been taught that only those who live close to God in holiness and virtue attain to immortality" (*1 Apol.* 21).[30] But Justin still pursues his parallels with claims in Greek literature: he suggests that there is nothing odd in "God's Son, who is called Jesus," being called Son of God, given his wisdom, "for all authors call God father of men and gods." Furthermore, "When we say . . . that he was begotten by God as the Word of God in a unique manner beyond ordinary birth, this should be no strange thing for you who speak of Hermes as the announcing word from God" (*1 Apol.* 22). Even his crucifixion is comparable to what happened to the sons of Zeus; their sufferings, Justin admits, were different, but that means "his unique passion" is not worse, rather his intention is to show it was better. And despite the critique Justin attributes to Trypho, here in his *Apology* Justin continues:

> If we declare that he was born of a virgin, you should consider this something in common with Perseus. When we say that he healed the lame, the paralytic, and those born blind, and raised the dead, we seem to be talking about things like those said to have been done by Asclepius. (*1 Apol.* 22)

With these analogies, then, Justin tries to give plausibility to the story of Jesus.

However, Justin also indicates that he intended to provide evidence that, by contrast with the poets who rehearsed "myths they had invented," the things Christians say "are the only truths and older than all the writers who have ever lived" (*1 Apol.* 23). It eventually turns out that the evidence promised rests entirely on the fulfillment of prophecy. Turning in due course to Isaiah

---

29. Each of the women named became pregnant by Zeus or by other mythical persons such as Heracles.

30. Note again the implicit association of holiness with virginity.

7:14, Justin spells out the point that God had indicated in advance "through the prophetic Spirit" that incredible things would happen, so that "when this occurred it should not be disbelieved, but received with faith because it had been predicted" (*1 Apol.* 33). He now repudiates the suggestion that the birth from a virgin is just like what the poets say about Zeus coming on women for sexual pleasure. For "if she had had intercourse with any one whatever, she would no longer be a virgin: but the power of God having come upon the virgin, overshadowed her, and caused her while yet a virgin to conceive" (*1 Apol.* 33). One wonders whether, in using the word "overshadowed," Justin implicitly notes Luke's implied reference to Genesis—the Holy Spirit once overshadowing chaos now creatively overshadows the Virgin's womb. Is new creation the hidden yet most significant point? Be that as it may, Justin differentiates to avoid misleading implications yet does not hesitate to employ analogies for the sake of plausibility.

Origen, it is true, avoids obvious myths for Celsus, as noted already, had anticipated the potential analogy. But Origen too wanted to make birth from a virgin plausible. In *Against Celsus* 1.37 he cites as a natural analogy the then widespread belief that vultures preserved the continuation of the species without copulation—if the Creator made it possible in one case why not others? Once more it is noteworthy that the analogy offered is a creative rather than a generative act. However, the immediate point is that Origen could insist that Greeks should have no difficulty with the idea of birth from a virgin, citing the view that the first human beings "must have come into existence without sexual intercourse, but from the earth instead," generative principles existing in the earth itself. Origen also thought it "not out of place" to quote Greek stories—we are not the only ones to make this kind of claim, he suggests, mentioning the suggestion that the god Apollo impregnated the mother of Plato. But "these stories are really myths," he insists. People were led "to invent such a tale about a man because they regarded him as having superior wisdom and power to the multitude, and as having received the original composition of his body from better and more divine seed, thinking this was appropriate for men with superhuman powers" (*Cels.* 1.37; cf. 6.8). To put that remark in context we need to understand how it reflects the ancient assumption that human procreation was analogous to the planting of a seed. Just as the whole oak tree was potentially in the acorn, which simply received nourishment to grow and develop from the earth, so the potential human being was in the seed planted in the womb by the male. It is scarcely surprising that, as noted above, Cyril had to contest the idea that Mary's womb was only a kind of pipe or channel, or that Irenaeus had had to challenge those who suggested Christ had taken nothing from the Virgin, insisting at length that he had received his flesh from her, that it was real flesh, and that he was truly made what we are through being born of a woman (*Haer.* 3.22).

At this point it is worth scrolling back to see what initiated Origen's discussion. Celsus had put into the mouth of his Jew a rumor that the mother of Jesus had been turned out by the carpenter to whom she was betrothed for adultery with a soldier named Panthera. Origen notes that this was concocted to get rid of the miraculous conception by the Holy Spirit, but shrewdly points out that this meant unintentionally admitting that Jesus was not born of an ordinary marriage. He suggests that a shameful birth outside legitimate marriage is implausible for someone with Jesus's mission to do great deeds, teach, and convert so many from evil ways, advancing the hypothesis (which he attributes to Pythagoras, Plato, and Empedocles, philosophers apparently much quoted by Celsus) that "there are certain secret principles by which each soul that enters a body does so in accordance with its merits and former character." He pursues the idea, asking, "Why then should there not be a certain soul that takes a body which is entirely miraculous, which has something in common with humans in order to be able to live with them, but which also has something out of the ordinary, in order that the soul may remain uncontaminated with sin?" Implicit, surely, is the virginity of Mary; we note again virginity's deep-seated association with holiness and closeness to God.

Yet, as for Justin, so too for Origen, far more important is the fulfillment of Isaiah's prophecy, something that Celsus had not even noticed—Origen almost chides him for not making his Jew "ingeniously explain away" the Christian prophetic interpretation. He embarks on a discussion of the Hebrew word and its controversial Greek translation, *parthenos* (*Cels.* 1.34). Like Justin before and Cyril after, Origen was well aware of those Jewish objections to Christian exploitation of that text. He cross-references other biblical texts to prove that "virgin" rather than "young woman" is the meaning, as Cyril would later. For both, the most fundamental argument for the birth of Jesus Christ from a virgin lay in the fulfillment of that prophecy.

Yet the biblical roots of this "holy dogma" went far beyond the argument from fulfillment. Returning to Cyril, we find that his response to the first question regarding the incarnation produced an overarching summary of the biblical story of fall and redemption somewhat similar to that which Irenaeus had offered in his (also probably catechetical) work, *The Demonstration of the Apostolic Preaching*.[31] Cyril likewise runs through Adam, Cain and Abel, Noah, the chosen

---

31. See chapter 4 above.

people and their idolatry at Sinai, the sending of the prophets for the healing of the wounds of humankind, and then the sending of the Son (*Cat. orat.* 12.5–8). With plenty of references to the signs that showed the fulfillment of prophecies, Cyril indicated how Christ came down for our salvation, to sanctify baptism (12.10–15), and also to recapitulate the fall: "Through Eve still virgin came death; through a virgin, or rather from a virgin, must life appear: that as the serpent beguiled the one, so to the other Gabriel might bring good tidings" (12.15). The type/antitype between the serpent and Gabriel, death and life, is already found in Justin (*Dial.* 100), while Irenaeus saw the creation of humankind from the virgin earth recapitulated in one born of a virgin (*Epid.* 32). Cyril is aligned with scripture and a long tradition of its reading. The virginity of Mary was core to the story of re-creation and the restoration of God's image and likeness.

Implicit in these responses is an appeal to the power of the Creator at work in that restoration; explicit is the reality of the human flesh taken from Mary. For time and again we find slippage from "born of the Virgin Mary" to eating and drinking, suffering and dying, for example, in Cyril's statement of this holy dogma in the fourth homily and in Justin's much earlier discussion. The reality of the incarnation is what is at stake. So how did Cyril answer that other question: Can God's nature permit incarnation? His answer seems to be that it must be so because this prophecy, along with many others, was actually fulfilled:

> Did Christ become human in vain? Are our teachings mere speculations and human inventions? Aren't the sacred Scriptures our salvation? And the prophet's predictions? So keep this deposit unshaken and let no one disturb you. Trust God made man. That it was possible for him to be made man has been proved. (*Cat. orat.* 12.16)

He goes on to cite Abraham entertaining the Lord, Jacob saying he saw God face-to-face, then Moses in the cleft of the rock on Sinai, and also Elijah, each standing beside the Lord (Exod 33:22; 1 Kgs 19:9), and later with the Lord on Mount Tabor at the transfiguration. The God of the Bible, he implies, can certainly consort with human beings. Indeed, scripture, and in particular the fulfillment of its prophecies, is his ultimate court of appeal, as it had been for Justin and Origen before him.

In volume 2 we shall find how these matters figured in the christological controversies. Following the traditions we have traced, Nestorius affirmed that

> without male seed, he fashioned from the Virgin a nature like Adam's (who was himself formed without male seed) and through a human being

brought about the revival of the human race. "Since," Paul says, "death came through a human being, through a human being also came the resurrection of the dead." (1 Cor 15:21)[32]

The virgin birth had long been associated with the true humanity of the Christ. By the fifth century, however, other issues had come to the fore: That which was formed in the womb could not, surely, be God? Could a second birth really be attributed to the one previously begotten by the Father? Is it even plausible that God could have a mother? Was it not his flesh, the body he took as a temple, which Mary bore? Surely, then, Mary is really *anthrōpotokos* rather than *theotokos*? So it was not the feasibility of miraculous birth from a virgin that figured in this discussion—it was rather the nature of that to which she gave birth. All accepted Irenaeus's point that it was the flesh which Christ took from Mary, and it was real flesh; what was more difficult was the whole notion that God could be born at all. This was a fresh challenge—a new question to be hammered out. Yet it did not fundamentally change the status of belief in birth from the Virgin.

For "born of the Virgin Mary" was deeply entrenched in the tradition that produced the creeds. It fitted into perceptions of the overarching biblical story of fall and redemption, Mary recapitulating Eve as Christ did Adam and as Gabriel did the serpent. For Christian doctrine this statement also significantly allied itself with assertions resisting docetism and reinforcing true incarnation as well as the re-creative power of the Creator. But above all it proved the fulfillment of prophecy; it was enshrined in the gospel narratives, and therefore was a scriptural truth to be taught as true and holy dogma.

2.4. Crucified under Pontius Pilate, Was Dead and Buried

It might seem that the passion of Christ was highly problematic for the theologians of early Christianity. In pre-Nicene days it had been possible for Tertullian to employ the presumption of divine impassibility to counter the Monarchians—they "put to flight the Paraclete and crucified the Father!" His notorious taunt was to the point—it was only the "economy" that allowed the invisible and impassible God to become visible and passible. Then, post-

---

32. See further volume 2, chapter 5. Quote from Nestorius, *First Homily against Theotokos*. Latin text (and Greek fragments) in Friedrich Loofs, ed., *Nestoriana: Die Fragmente des Nestorius* (Halle: Niemeyer, 1905), 249–64; English translation in R. A. Norris, ed., *The Christological Controversy* (Philadelphia: Fortress, 1980), 123–31.

Nicaea, with the Son *homoousios* with the Father, the so-called Antiochenes and Alexandrians tied themselves and each other in knots trying to reconcile the passion narrative with the impassibility of the divine Son who became incarnate. All this will become clearer in volume 2.

Against that backdrop it is instructive to turn to Cyril of Jerusalem as he addresses his catechumens on the subject of the cross, for the divine *apatheia* is not even a side issue. As was affirmed in scripture and confessed in the rule of faith and the creeds, the passion was "for us and our salvation." For Cyril the catechist, then, the priorities were (1) the reality of the cross—for if a sham, salvation would be a sham; and (2) the glory of the cross—it was nothing to be ashamed of, but rather something to die for, martyrdom being still within living memory. Despite that, however, according to the general viewpoint of modern scholarship, the early church never formulated a doctrine of salvation or a theory of atonement. Let us again use Cyril's lectures as a springboard to interrogate that widespread perspective and explore this "dogma." It is true that salvation was understood in many and various ways, was never defined in creedal or conciliar statements, and was associated with the incarnation or with the resurrection as much as with the cross. Yet, according to the creeds, it is the cross which is "for us and our salvation."

Homily 13 picks up two of the "holy dogmas" outlined in the fourth lecture. Cyril in homily 4.10 insisted that "truly he was crucified for our sins." Denial of this is impossible given that his congregation's meeting place is Golgotha (as Cyril was teaching in the Church of the Holy Sepulchre in Jerusalem), and "the whole world has since been filled with the wood of the cross, piece by piece," this doubtless being an allusion to the supposed discovery of the cross a generation earlier when Constantine ordered the excavation of the site and construction of the church. The concrete reality of the crucifixion is paramount. Cyril also emphasizes here that it was not "for his own sins that he was crucified, but that we might be freed from our sins." Despised and beaten as a human being, he was "acknowledged as God by the whole of creation," a point confirmed by the eclipse of the sun "because it could not bear the sight" of "its Master dishonoured." Homily 4.11 also begins by emphasizing that "truly he was placed in the rock tomb as man," then notes "the rocks in terror were split asunder." Cyril states that Christ went down to the underworld to rescue the just, naming Isaiah, David, Samuel, and all the prophets, including John the Baptist: "Wouldn't you want Jesus to go down to rescue such as these?" Thus the summary of these dogmas highlights the factuality of the narratives while hinting at their significance.

Now to the fuller treatment in the thirteenth homily. The scripture reading is taken from Isaiah 53. Cyril begins by indicating that "the boast of all boasts is the cross." He details a series of marvels: the healing of the man born blind, the raising of Lazarus, the feeding of the multitude—but what good was that, he asks, for other blind people, for people killed by sin or starved of knowledge? "The crown of the cross brought light to those blinded by ignorance, freed all those constrained by sin, and redeemed the whole of humankind" (13.1). Here Cyril aligns himself with the in-language of generations of believers, from the New Testament writers through the apologists, Irenaeus, Origen, and Athanasius. The human predicament is characterized in terms of sin and ignorance along with their consequence, death. Salvation is expressed in multifarious images—healing, rescue, redemption—and the passion is the act of grace that has this effect.

But how? Cyril here tackles the issue of universal redemption (13.2). It happens because "the one who gave his life was no ordinary man, but the Only-begotten Son of God." Paraphrasing Romans he speaks of the sin of one man, Adam, having the power to bring death to the world. So, if one man's sin gave death dominion over the world, why should life not receive dominion through the righteousness of one man? This gives him entry to the recapitulation themes long since developed by Irenaeus and by now deeply traditional.[33] Adam and Eve were expelled from paradise because of the fruit of a tree, and surely it is now easier for believers to enter paradise through the tree of Jesus—the tree, of course, being the cross (the Greek *xylon* referring to anything wooden, from a stave to a gibbet, from a tree to a pole). The cross is real but also symbol. If death came through the first man God created, surely the one who created him can introduce eternal life, since he is life itself. The overarching biblical narrative of fall and redemption undergirds Cyril's approach.

Now alluding to 1 Corinthians 1:18 and 25 Cyril reverts to affirming that the cross is nothing to be ashamed of—rather we should make it "our boast" (13.3). It may be a scandal to Jews and folly to gentiles, but to us it is God's power, for the one who gave his life for us was no ordinary man but the Son of God. Cyril refers to the Passover lamb and how, in Moses's time, it averted the destroying angel: surely "the lamb of God who takes away the sin of the world" (John 1:29) is much more able to save. Cyril describes demons cowering before the sign of the cross, attributing this to the fact that the crucified one was sinless, and he assembles a list of Old and New Testament witnesses to confirm this.[34] Others died for their own sins, but he died for the sins of others. Later on (13.5) Cyril would specify that Christ died for the sake of sins he did not share: not avarice, for he was a teacher of poverty; not lust, and here Cyril quotes Matthew 5:28; not violence, for he turned the other cheek, and so on. It was not for sins of

---

33. See above in chapter 4.
34. Including 1 Pet 2:22; Isa 53:9; Luke 23:14; Matt 17:24; and Luke 23:41.

word or deed or thought, nor sins against his will that he died. Cyril again quotes 1 Peter 2:22–23 and Isaiah 53:9 with Matthew 16:22–23, adding texts to show how he prophesied his death (*Cat. orat.* 13.6).

A long-standing association of two fundamental typologies surely lies behind Cyril's assurance that Christ died for our sins, reinforced, of course, by specific biblical statements to that effect.[35] The rediscovered *On Pascha* attributed to Melito of Sardis provides the clues. This second-century text was gradually reconstructed during the 1930s from various papyrus leaves, fragments, and versions; then a complete copy turned up in one of the Bodmer papyri and was published in 1960.[36] Often referred to as a homily, it has been convincingly argued that it was a Christian Passover haggadah—a liturgy for Passover night to be used by Christians on the fourteenth of Nisan.[37] (That Melito was a Quartodeciman is attested by Eusebius.[38])

What this text makes clear is the way in which the cross was understood in terms of Passover and Exodus, this type being construed through the Adam-Christ typology.[39] Thus it begins by referring to the reading from Exodus, then draws out the fulfillment of Passover in the Passion (*paschein* meaning to suffer, and Passover in Greek being *Pascha*—a false etymology, but widely found in early Christianity). The story is dramatically reenacted as the claim is made that the blood of the Passover lamb averted the angel of death because he saw "the mystery of the Lord in the sheep, the life of the Lord in the slaughter of the sheep, the type of the lamb in the death of the sheep" (*Pasch.* 32). This is now explained by developing a parallel narrative, beginning in Eden as "sin set his sign on everyone and those on whom he etched his mark were doomed to death" (*Pasch.* 54). So the Lord prepares for his suffering with prophetic predictions and prefigurations, and the climax is his suffering for the mystery of the *Pascha* is Christ; he is the one led like a lamb and slaughtered like a sheep (*Pasch.* 64), ransoming us from the land of Egypt:

35. The following reflects my much fuller discussion in *Construing the Cross: Type, Sign, Symbol, Word, Action* (Eugene: Cascade, 2015).

36. Text and English translation in Stuart George Hall, ed. and trans., *On Pascha and Fragments*, OECT (Oxford: Clarendon, 1979). See also the English translation in *On Pascha*, ed. Alistair Stewart-Sykes (Crestwood, NY: St. Vladimir's Seminary Press, 2001).

37. Alistair Stewart-Sykes, *The Lamb's High Feast: Melito, Peri Pascha and the Quartodeciman Paschal Liturgy at Sardis* (Leiden: Brill, 1998).

38. Eusebius, *Hist. eccl.* 5.24. The term comes from the Latin for fourteenth. In the late second century the bishop of Rome challenged Asian bishops who kept the fourteenth of Nisan (i.e., Jewish Passover) as the beginning of the Paschal festival and did not follow the Roman practice of remembering the resurrection on the first day of the week, Sunday.

39. See further in chapter 1 of my book *Construing the Cross*.

> This is the one who clad death in shame,
> and, as Moses did to Pharaoh,
> made the devil grieve . . .
> This is the one who delivered us from slavery to freedom,
> from darkness into light,
> from death into life,
> from tyranny into an eternal Kingdom,
> and made us a new priesthood,
> and a people everlasting for himself. (*Pasch*. 68)

So Melito spelled out hints in the New Testament that had not previously been articulated so explicitly.[40] Indeed, modern commentators have struggled to explain why the forgiveness of sins came to be attributed to the Passover lamb, but the reading of the Passover typology in terms of the Adam-Christ typology clarifies this novel association. Furthermore, Melito provides us with the dominant way in which the passion of Christ was read in those early centuries: it was about God's act of rescue from slavery to sin, death, and the devil, and God's call into the people of the new covenant sealed by Christ's blood. Cyril, though not fully rehearsing here this profound overarching grasp of the biblical narrative, nevertheless presupposes it in his emphasis on Christ dying as the Passover lamb to save us from our sins.

Returning to Cyril's discussion we find him insisting again on the reality of Christ's suffering—if it was just a pretense then our redemption would be a pretense (*Cat. orat.* 13.4). His passion was real, Christ really was crucified and we are not ashamed of the fact, Cyril states. In fact, we boast of it, he claims, though he does briefly admit that he would not have affirmed the cross if it had not been for the resurrection. His emphasis, however, is on the willingness with which Christ went to his passion (13.5–6): he set his face to go to Jerusalem (Luke 9:51), knowing what was in store. For Jesus the cross is glory: "the hour has come for the Son of Man to be glorified" (John 12:23). This Jesus said at the very moment when Judas was plotting against him, Cyril notes, adding John 13:31, a restatement as Judas left to do the deed: "Now is the Son of Man glorified." Cyril hastens to assure his catechumens that, of course, Christ always had glory—"glorified with the glory he possessed from the foundation

---

40. Cf. 1 Cor 5:7 and the lamb slain in Revelation; the Passover associations of the Last Supper and the eucharist; Hebrews' use of Psalm 95; and especially passages from the Gospel of John (e.g., 18:28; 19:14, 31, 36) that indicate the rather literal fulfillment of the Baptist's words in 1:29, 36.

of the world" (cf. John 17:5)—but now he was glorified for his endeavor. He was not killed by force or constraint but by choice, delighted at the salvation of humankind, not ashamed of the cross. He had the power to lay down his life and take it again (John 10:18). "It was not a common man who suffered," Cyril reaffirms, "but God made man."

Cyril, acknowledging now that Jews raise objections, speaks of Jeremiah's Lamentations showing how the message would shift to gentiles (*Cat. orat.* 13.7). This provides the occasion for putting forward "testimonies concerning the Passion." Everything about Christ, he states, is included in scripture, "inscribed not on tablets of stone, but on the prophetic monuments, written unmistakably by the Holy Spirit" (13.8). This homily is easily the longest, as more than half of it retells the passion story through prophetic predictions, biblical types, Gospel fulfillments, and interpretative comments from the Epistles. The scriptures certainly were for Cyril the foundation of this "holy dogma." We will sample a selection, beginning with the crown of thorns. Just like any other king (Solomon, for example, in Song 3:11) Jesus was crowned by soldiers, and "the crown itself was a mystery; for it was a remission of sins, a release from the curse" (13.17). The ground was cursed because of Adam; Jesus "assumes the thorns that he may cancel the sentence" and was "buried in the earth, that the earth which had been cursed might receive the blessing instead of the curse" (13.18). Cyril amplifies this, perhaps rather obliquely, with reference to the fig leaves and the cursing of the fig tree, then goes on to trace "the truth of the types" associated with paradise, confessing himself astonished. That he will shortly switch to the "harmless lamb led to be slaughtered," together with reference to John the Baptist's greeting and the Passover timing, surely seems all the more significant in light of the association already traced. Meanwhile, however, the prime item is the tree: from the tree came sin, which lasted until the tree (13.19). He does not need to identify this *xylon* as the cross since it is so traditional. Later he will also speak of the tree of life being planted in the earth so that the earth which had been cursed might enjoy blessing and the dead might be released (13.35), as well as return to the Pauline theme that as by one man came death so by one man came life (13.28).

Meanwhile, Deuteronomy 28:66 (somewhat implausibly) confirms that "your life hangs before your eyes." Cyril then picks up the association already made in John's Gospel between the cross and the brazen serpent that healed the Israelites from snakebite in the wilderness (Num 21:9; John 3:14). They only had to look on the serpent fixed to a cross to be saved by believing. Life comes by means of wood, he suggests, noting Noah's wooden ark and the rod whereby Moses parted the Red Sea (13.20). The potential multiple senses of *xylon* enables this further play with scriptural associations.

Thus with many prooftexts Cyril takes his catechumens through the story, emphasizing how the Savior endured all these things. He quotes Colossians 1:20 and explains how Christ brings peace: "we were enemies of God through sin, and God had appointed the sinner to die." So one of two things had to happen: either God, being true, should destroy everyone, or, being loving, should cancel the sentence. Instead, being wise, God managed to keep both the truth of the sentence and divine lovingkindness. Quoting 1 Peter 2:24, Cyril affirms that the transgression of sinners was not so great as the righteousness of the one who died for them, laying down his life willingly. This observation closely parallels the account Athanasius offers in *On the Incarnation*. The situation has been fittingly described as "the divine dilemma."[41] God's decree meant that the human race was perishing, for God's word could not be made void; on the other hand, it was not worthy of God's goodness that the Creator's handiwork should come to nothing (*Inc.* 6). Repentance would not have saved God's honor or dealt with the corruption now imprisoning humankind. The only possibility was for the Word of the Father to re-create everything, suffer on behalf of all, and advocate for all before the Father. For both Cyril and Athanasius the cross was the saving act of dying the death deserved by sinners so as to release them from the penalty and enable new life, as indeed it would be for Nestorius, who recognized that God "did not dissolve the debt by an order, lest mercy violate justice" but rather Christ "paid the debt back as a son of Adam."[42]

Cyril's final paragraphs reaffirm the need to not be afraid of acknowledging the crucified, but to make the sign of the cross as a seal on the forehead and over every daily action, including eating, drinking, coming in and going out, before sleeping, or going on journeys, for the cross is powerful protection. His catechumens are to resist Jews, Greeks and heretics and take the cross as "an indestructible foundation on which to build the rest of the faith" (*Cat. orat.* 13.38). This insistence on the cross as something to take a pride in continues to the end, and it is perhaps a reminder, along with his emphasis on the sinlessness and innocence of Christ, that still Christians were subject to mockery for worshipping a condemned criminal. Even without philosophical anxieties about the possibility of the divine being subjected to suffering, the cross was an awkward "dogma," and what is striking is the way its justification drew less on theoretical arguments about atoning transactions and more on

---

41. A heading used in the English translation of *The Incarnation of the Word of God: De Incarnatione Verbi Dei*, trans. A Religious of C. S. M. V., 2nd ed. (London: Mowbray, 1953).

42. From Nestorius's first homily on the *theotokos*. Text in Loofs, *Nestoriana*; translation by Norris. See further volume 2, chapter 5, 1.1.

a vivid range of biblical images, all ultimately feeding into a reading of the overarching biblical narrative of fall and redemption. The cross would return with Christ, Cyril stated: not only is it the king's crown but his standard, to which all nations, including the Jews, will eventually submit.

What we have found in Cyril is typical: a multiplicity of ways of characterizing salvation, drawing from biblical material and amplifying scriptural images. Ideas about propitiation, mediation, sacrifice, ransom, and atonement figure among this multitudinous mix of metaphors and images drawn from scripture—we will also observe them figuring in arguments between Theodoret and Cyril of Alexandria, as well as in the exegesis of Theodore and Chrysostom.[43] It is indeed true that salvation was understood in many and various ways and was often associated more with incarnation or resurrection than with the cross.[44] This is well exemplified by the range of titles Origen uses to expound the name of Christ in the first book of his *Commentary on John*, all of which express aspects of his saving and healing work: Wisdom, Word, Life, Truth, Son of God, Righteousness, Savior, Propitiation, Light of the World, Firstborn of the Dead, the (Good) Shepherd, Physician, Healer, Redemption, Resurrection and Life, Way, Truth, and Life, Door, Messiah, Christ, Lord, King, Vine, Bread of Life, First, Last, the Living one, Alpha and Omega, and First and Last. And all of these are drawn from the scriptures. There is a richness of imagery here that feeds into a sense of the Savior uniting in himself the multiplicity of creation and the unity of God. Athanasius, too, could list all that the Savior is for us: absolute Wisdom, very Word, the Father's own Power, absolute Light, absolute Truth, absolute Justice, absolute Virtue, absolute Holiness, absolute Life, Door, Shepherd, Way, King, Guide, Life giver, universal Providence (*C. Gent.* 46–47). Christ's absoluteness enables particulars to participate in what he is, so coming to share in his Sonship by adoption. Irenaeus, too, could name various ways in which the Savior brought salvation: "The Lord through his passion destroyed death, brought error to an end, abolished corruption, banished ignorance, manifested life, declared truth, and bestowed incorruption" (*Haer.* 5.20.2). But it was Irenaeus, of course, who had brought it all together in the notion of recapitulation: "the sin of the first-created was amended by the chastisement of the first-begotten.... Therefore he renews all things in himself, uniting humanity with the Spirit" (*Haer.* 5.19–21).

That Irenaeus's model of fall and redemption through recapitulation became the most widespread way both of understanding salvation and of reading

---

43. See further volume 2, chapter 5, especially 1.4, for Cyril and Theodoret, and chapter 4, 4.2, for Chrysostom's exegesis.

44. See further chapter 5 of my book *God's Presence*, esp. 235–42.

the scriptures is borne out by what we have seen in the *Catechetical Homilies* of Cyril of Jerusalem and could be demonstrated through many other texts, as I have shown more fully elsewhere.[45] Here I just note that Cyril of Alexandria would affirm that

> The common element of humanity is summed up in [Christ's] person, which is also why he was called the last Adam: he enriched our common nature with everything conducive to joy and glory, just as the first Adam impoverished it with everything bringing gloom and corruption. (*Comm. Jo.* 1.9)[46]

True, this statement is easily characterized as salvation through incarnation and *theopoiēsis*—indeed we may surmise that the Alexandrian Cyril did not grasp what Nestorius and the Antiochenes were saying about atonement through the cross.[47] But from Irenaeus to Ephrem the Syrian, the cross was incorporated into the recapitulation pattern, a pattern perceived to have its roots in scripture:

> In the month of Nisan our Lord repaid
> The debts of that first Adam:
> He gave his sweat in Nisan in exchange for Adam's sweat,
> The Cross, in exchange for Adam's Tree.
> (Ephrem, *Hymn. eccl.* 51.8)[48]

2.5. Resurrection and Ascension

As for the cross, so too the reality of the resurrection was paramount for Cyril of Jerusalem, whether he was addressing the event of Jesus's resurrection or the resurrection hope of believers. To convince his hearers of each of those resurrection dogmas, however, he adopted very different strategies. Here we focus on the former, moving as ever from his introduction in homily 4 to his exposition in later homilies and using his approach again as a springboard for wider consideration of this matter.

"Jesus, who was buried, truly rose on the third day" (*Cat. orat.* 4.12). If bothered by Jews, says Cyril, Christians should ask them whether Jonah emerged from the whale on the third day: if so, why not Christ? Referencing a dead man

---

45. E.g., *God's Presence*, chapter 5; and *Construing the Cross*.
46. English translation by Norman Russell, *Cyril of Alexandria* (London: Routledge, 2000).
47. See further volume 2, chapter 5, especially 1.4.5.
48. Quoted from Sebastian Brock, *The Luminous Eye: The Spiritual World Vision of Saint Ephrem the Syrian* (Collegeville, MN: Cistercian, 1992), 33.

being raised by the touch of Elisha's bones, he implies it is even easier for the Creator of humankind to be raised by the power of the Father. He calls on the disciples as witnesses, and their willingness to accept "torture and death for the truth of the resurrection." Scripture only requires two witnesses, he states, and here are twelve: Why should Jews still be incredulous? Thus far runs the summary in homily 4, anticipating the more fully developed case in homily 14.

In homily 14 the opening move celebrates the shift from grief and lamentation to joy and gladness. But the overriding argument consists in a catalogue of testimonies—prophecies from scripture and witnesses to the fact of Jesus's resurrection. The initial verses of 1 Corinthians 15 provide the text. The apostle here, says Cyril, directs us to the scriptures: it is "according to the scriptures" that he was buried and raised on the third day. So Cyril searches for scriptural testimonies to the burial, then to the location and timing of the resurrection as well as confirmation of the story of the women and the empty tomb. To expound the full range of his testimonies would surely be more than we need here. Suffice it to say that he mentions classics, such as

- Psalm 16:10: "You will not leave my soul in Hades, nor let your Holy One suffer corruption"
- Psalm 30:1–3: "I will exalt you, O Lord, for you lifted me out of the depths, and did not let my enemies rejoice over me . . . you brought up my soul from the grave, you spared me from going down into the pit"
- And also Psalm 88, another expression of being numbered among the dead, while the words of verse 13, "in the morning my prayer comes before you," confirms the timing of the resurrection.

But Cyril also produces some surprising suggestions, an example being Genesis 49:9, which testifies to his burial with the words, "He lay down and crouched like a lion . . . who shall raise him up?" Perhaps most surprising is the repeated appeal to the Song of Songs. First, phrases from the Song are exploited to confirm that it was in a garden he was crucified and buried (*Cat. orat.* 14.5), the place now obscured by Constantine's magnificent structure over the tomb (14.9): "a garden enclosed . . . a spring sealed," "a cave in a rock" (Song 4:12; 6:11; 2:10–14). Then the Song indicates the season: "The winter is past, the rain is past and gone, the flowers appear on the earth and the time of pruning is come" (Song 2:12). Fall and restoration happened, then, in springtime, the time of Passover and the time of creation. The true vine sprang up in place of thorns and thistles, fulfilling Psalm 85:11 (*Cat. orat.* 14.10–11). The Song of Songs (5:1) tells of myrrh and spices: the women came with spices

(Luke 24:1) and Nicodemus with myrrh (John 19:39). "I did eat my bread with my honey" (also Song 5:1) points to the bitterness of the passion and sweetness after the resurrection: in Luke 24:41 (according to Cyril's variant reading) the risen Christ ate fish with honeycomb when he appeared to the disciples (*Cat. orat.* 14.11). The women who came in the dark (John 20:1) seeking Jesus and not finding him are also traced in the Song (3:1): "By night on my bed I sought him whom my soul loved and I found him not." In the Gospel of John, Mary says, "They have taken away my Lord and I know not where they have laid him." In her person, then, the Song said to the angels: "Have you seen him whom my soul loves? Scarcely had I passed them [the two angels], when I found him whom my soul loves, I held him, and would not let him go."[49] Thus Cyril tells the story of Jesus appearing to Mary and of his instruction not to hold him, then he weaves together more gospel texts and prophetic words.

What really concerns Cyril is proof against the Jews' refusal to believe. So he now develops those key points already sketched in homily 4: Elijah and Elisha raising the dead, Jonah's three days in the whale—all stories in the Hebrew scriptures (*Cat. orat.* 14.15–20). To believe in the latter is surely harder than believing Christ was raised. Such texts, in any case, were types of Christ's resurrection, he explains, and moves on to New Testament texts affirming the resurrection. The witnesses to the resurrection event are called in: the twelve; Jesus's brother James, "the first bishop of this diocese"; Paul; and even the night; the full moon; the rock of the sepulchre; the stone that was rolled away; the angels; the apostles Peter, John, Thomas; his hands and feet with the print of the nails; the women; the soldiers; and also Tabitha, raised by his name; the miraculous draught of fishes; and the very place of resurrection where Cyril and his hearers were meeting together (14.21–23). Throughout it is scripture that testifies to the truth of the resurrection, which is scripture's teaching—its doctrine, its dogma.

With all this Cyril couples brief treatment of the ascension, hoping that he need not enlarge on the topic as providentially the previous day's lectionary had led him to fuller exposition the day before (*Cat. orat.* 14.24). Homily 4 had treated this topic as the culmination of Christ's "course of patient endurance," the proof being that the crucified is worshipped by the whole world, and that the sign of the cross has such power over the devils so that his catechumens should make the sign of the cross at every point in their everyday life—eating, drinking, sitting, lying, standing, speaking, walking—you name it! Once again Cyril insists that there is no reason to be ashamed of the cross, for Christ is

---

49. *Cat. orat.* 14.12, quoting Song 3:3–4.

now ascended and sits at God's right hand (4.13). His preoccupation with the cross at this point is intriguing, though here in homily 4 it leads him naturally into the next dogma, namely the judgment to come.

In homily 14 his principal concern continues to be scriptural testimonies. He quotes, for example, Psalm 47:5, "God has gone up with a shout," alludes to Psalm 24, and mentions scriptural examples of ascent, including Habbakuk, Enoch, Elijah, and even the apostles, such as Paul's ascent to the third heaven and Peter with the keys to heaven. His other concern is to ensure that the catechumens do not think that Christ's sitting at God's right hand is the result of "advancement." Implicitly he confronts the Arian position, insisting on his being always begotten, that he was seen by Isaiah in his temple vision, and quoting Psalm 110: "the Lord said to my Lord." He came down and then ascended, and now is present, overseeing even our innermost thoughts (14.24–30).

Christ's sovereignty, then, is the paramount issue. In neither homily 4 nor homily 14 does Cyril open up christological questions—issues that would exercise people a generation later, such as whether the flesh was taken up into the Trinity. The discussion of Christ's resurrection and ascension remains at the level of confirming these dogmas from scriptural testimony and the evidence of Christ's power at work in the world, notably through the effectiveness of the sign of the cross in dispelling evil. Cyril's approach is fundamentally in line with the apologetic tradition. In *1 Apology* Justin had appealed to Psalms 24 and 110 to prove that "God the Father of all would bring Christ to heaven after he had raised him from the dead," until he had "subdued his enemies, the devils" (*1 Apol.* 45 and 51). Justin's *Dialogue with Trypho* works through Psalm 22 line by line to show how it predicted his birth and death, then finally his resurrection, this then being backed up by reference to the sign of Jonah (*Dial.* 98–107). Origen challenges Celsus's Jew with those stories about Elijah and Elisha—Greek stories of heroes descending to Hades and coming back are fantasy, but not so these scriptural narratives, and the resurrection of Jesus predicted by the prophets was even more remarkable (*Cels.* 2.55–58). Cyril offers his catechumens proofs and examples long rehearsed in the tradition and deeply rooted in scripture.

What is perhaps surprising is that here Cyril does not make any explicit connection between Christ's resurrection and that of believers, apart from mentioning the faith and hope into which his catechumens will be initiated through baptism. This contrasts with, for example, Augustine's treatment of the risen Christ as "the pledge of coming resurrection for his members,"[50] not

---

50. See Gerald O'Collins, SJ, *Saint Augustine on the Resurrection of Christ: Teaching, Rhetoric, and Reception* (Oxford: Oxford University Press, 2017).

to mention the Easter sermon of Gregory of Nazianzus, which suggests that the one who rose from the dead "today" might "renew me also by his Spirit." Gregory speaks of being clothed in the new humanity, and graphically identifies with the Passover story, "Yesterday the lamb was slain.... Today we have clean escaped from Egypt." Then, with biblical allusions, he enters into the death and resurrection of Christ:

> Yesterday I was crucified with him; today I am glorified with him; yesterday I died with him; today I am enlivened with him; yesterday I was buried with him, today I rise with him.... Let us become like Christ, since Christ became like us ... he became poor that we through his poverty might be rich; he took the form of a servant that we might receive back our liberty; he came down that we might be exalted; he was tempted that we might conquer; he was dishonoured that he might glorify us, he died that he might save us; he ascended that he might draw to himself us who were lying low in the fall of sin. (Gregory of Nanzianus, *Orat.* 1.4)[51]

Does Cyril make more of this kind of connection when dealing with the resurrection of believers? If anything, he makes the opposite move, quoting Paul: if the dead do not rise, then Christ is not raised (1 Cor 15:16) (*Cat. orat.* 18.17). As we shall see, for him to prove general resurrection is to confirm the saving death and resurrection of Christ.

2.6. Judgment

Christ's return as judge is the climax of his treatment of the christological clause of the creed, both in the summary featured in homily 4.15 and in the fuller treatment of homily 15. His principal focus is on distinguishing from the rise of antichrists the return of the true Christ, who will come from heaven this time, not from earth, to be the judge of all and to establish his eternal kingdom.

That eternity is significant: Cyril is anxious to contest those who suggest on the basis of 1 Corinthians 15:25 that Christ's kingdom will have an end—doubtless he has Marcellus of Ancyra in mind. This point he elaborates in homily 15.27–33 with a battery of prooftexts and exegesis of the contested verse: the Son's "subjection" does not mean his absorption into the Father, nor will it be forced, as his obedience comes from free choice and natural love. Comparing Romans 5:14 and 2 Corinthians 3:14–15 he argues that "until" does not imply simply "up to that

---

51. Greek text in PG 35; English translation in *NPNF* 7.

time." His kingdom is an everlasting kingdom and Cyril has many more scriptural testimonies to prove it, if it were not getting so late in the day, he says.

Meanwhile homily 15 surveys the biblical teaching on Christ's two advents (15.1–4). Graphically compared and contrasted, they are given justification by appeal to the twofold generation of the Son, of God before the ages and of the Virgin at the end of the ages, as well as on the basis of various scriptural testimonies. The Son comes with glory at the end of the world, for as creation had a beginning so it has an end, and the world is to be re-created afresh. Borrowing phrases from Hosea 4:2, Cyril shows how "theft and adultery" and all sorts of sin "have been poured over the earth," then speaks of this world passing way so that a better world can appear. This is backed up by Isaiah 34:4 and verses from Matthew 24 as well as other testimonies. Notions of world reformation occur elsewhere in patristic literature, notably in association with the resurrection, but also as the consequence of the world having a beginning and so necessarily having an end; for example, Gregory of Nyssa in his work on the *Making of Humankind* indicates this is interconnected with the doctrine of *creatio ex nihilo* (*De hom.* 23–24). Cyril's catechetical teaching demonstrates its perceived rootedness in biblical doctrine.

Cyril now draws on New Testament texts to affirm our ignorance of the end and the necessity of knowing the signs so as not to be deceived by Antichrist (citing Acts 1:7 and more verses from Matthew 24) (*Cat. orat.* 15.4–9). Heretics mislead and there are wars and rumors of wars, so we must keep watch. In the face of internal church wrangling among bishops Cyril seeks to reassure his converts, pointing them to what has been written—in other words the scriptures: the hearer can become better than the teacher, the last be first, and there was treachery even among the apostles. Further reference to Matthew 24, together with the quotation of the bulk of 2 Thessalonians 2, presses home the point: there are heretics in disguise and the devil is always trying to deceive. Eventually Cyril underlines that these teachings are not "our own invention" but have been learned from the scriptures that are used by the church (*Cat. orat.* 15.13), turning now to Daniel and back again to Paul and Matthew 24. This lengthy exposition finally returns to the second coming not from earth but on the clouds of heaven and with the sign of the cross, a terror to Christ's foes but joy to those who believe in him (15.22).

So Cyril turns to the judgment, reassuring his hearers that the judge is no respecter of persons and will not overlook the poor, the slave, the woman, the sick, for he himself took the form of a servant. Nothing is unrecorded: every prayer, every Psalm, every good deed, every act of fasting, but also every adulterous act, every covetous deed, every false oath, every blasphemy from now on, as former deeds are blotted out by baptism (15.23). In what follows Cyril assumes that post-baptismal sin comes under judgment. Christ comes to judge every human race, Romans, barbarians, a great multitude; God the Father is present with Jesus Christ seated alongside him and the Holy Spirit with them as an angel's trumpet summons us. Cyril urges his hearers to dread being condemned and to anticipate the divine judge's knowledge of the truth, as each rises clad in their own sins or their own righteous deeds. Again he assembles a huge range of biblical prooftexts as he contrasts the kingdom with the eternal fire and uses Matthew's parable of the sheep and the goats to show how to escape the latter by good deeds (15.24–26). Such teaching could be paralleled right across the spectrum of patristic literature. It figured so large precisely because preachers took it that God's judgment and justice lay at the heart of biblical teaching.

2.7. Sin

In his *Procatechesis*, the opening address both welcoming and warning those seeking baptism, Cyril insists they should immediately cease from evil deeds. His message is that we are not allowed to receive baptism twice or three times, so if you fail once you cannot put matters right (*Procat.* 7). This is backed up with the quotation of Ephesians 4:5: "there is one Lord, one faith, one baptism." This reminds us that at times the early church had taken Hebrews 6:4–6 to signify that repentance for sin after baptism was excluded. Indeed, still in this period it was the case that on such grounds baptism was often put off until one's deathbed (Constantine being an example), or only received at the point of leaving the world to undertake the monastic life. This perspective had already provoked the formation of incipient systems of penance to enable a return to communion, particularly in the aftermath of the Decian persecution when the readmission of the lapsed, who had technically committed apostasy, became a serous issue. It is clear that Cyril too understood it to be the teaching of scripture that baptism is a crucial turning point. God requires nothing but good intention, he says, and sins are blotted out by willing and believing, but God, the one who judges, knows even the heart, so lip service is not enough (*Procat.* 8).

This notion that all hearts are open to God and everyone will be accountable to God at the time of judgment is deep-seated within the Christian tradition. It is a consistent theme in the early texts known as the Apostolic Fathers, as the following examples show:[52]

---

52. Earlier we also briefly observed its connection with creation in 1 Clement. See section 2 in chapter 3 above.

- Let us observe how close God is, and that none of our thoughts, none of the inner debates we have, escape God's attention.... For God is a searcher of thoughts and desires (1 Clem. 21.3, 8–9)
- Nothing escapes the Lord's notice—indeed, even our hidden secrets are present to God. So let us act in everything we do as if he were dwelling within us, so that we may be God's temples and he may be our God within us (Ign. *Eph.* 15.3)

The deep and lasting impact of texts such as Psalm 139 and the interiority of Jesus's teaching is clear: that is, sayings such as those in the Sermon on the Mount which suggest that anger is as bad as murder, lust as adultery (Matt 5:21–22, 27–28), or the saying in Mark (7:14–23) that it is not what goes into a person which defiles but what comes out. This is as much a core element of the church's teaching as its dogmatic propositions and equally claimed as scriptural.

Sin as such receives no treatment as a specific dogma in homily 4. The first three homilies demonstrate the biblical perspective that is the context for these dogmas, and it is here that we find teaching relevant to the subject. Homily 1 is about the possibility of new birth in Christ, of freedom from bondage to sin, of the pre-baptismal process of exorcism, and of forsaking worldly desires and attitudes. Homily 2 is an account of the nature of sin, an explanation of the predicament in which humankind finds itself: the basic story of the creature of a good Creator bringing evil on itself through free will. Homily 3 is about baptism, about dying to sin so as to rise in righteousness. What, then, is Cyril's doctrine of sin?

Cyril is sure that sin is not something living, nor an angel or demon, nor an invasive enemy, but an evil that grows out of oneself—it arises whenever God is forgotten (*Cat. orat.* 2.2). True, there is a prompter, the devil's suggestions, however these affect only those who consent. Too easily, however, those suggestions get a foothold and take root, so the seed must be torn out. Cyril then explains how the devil is a fallen angel, the first author of sin, backing this up with scriptural quotations from Old and New Testaments and indicating that through the devil "our forefather Adam" was cast out of paradise (2.4). But Cyril's hearers are not to despair—there is hope of repentance, and God is loving and merciful, points backed up by Psalm 31:19 and 32:5 (*Cat. orat.* 2.5–6). Cyril then embarks on a quick journey through pertinent stories in the Bible: from Adam through Cain and Abel, Noah, Rahab, the golden calf, David and Nathan, Ahab, and more. In many ways, though, the focus is specifically on the repentance theme, which parallels Irenaeus's *Demonstration of the Apostolic Preaching*, possibly itself a catechetical work.[53] On the basis of so many examples Cyril's catechumens are exhorted to make confession and receive forgiveness. Sin and salvation, fall and redemption—this reading of the biblical story from the beginning to the end is the fundamental framework of the dogmatic propositions confessed in the creed, and so functions as core teaching even though not articulated as distinct dogmatic propositions.

It is noticeable that Cyril's account rests so fundamentally on free will, an approach with a strong pedigree in Origen's teaching but never a matter of controversy in the East as other aspects of Origenism became. This is perhaps a bit surprising: the Adam-Christ typology and the notion of recapitulation were deeply embedded, as we have noted, and that surely implies solidarity in sin and solidarity in salvation, as indeed does the account offered in Athanasius's *Against the Pagans* and *On the Incarnation*.[54] Free will, however, remained the presupposition required for moral exhortation, the call to repentance, and teaching on the justice and judgment of God—one only has to consider the homilies of Chrysostom to grasp the force of this. Even so, in the West free will did become contentious: if one could be saved through making the right choices and exercising moral will power, what need of grace, mercy, and forgiveness? The matter came to a head, of course, in the controversy between Augustine and the Pelagians.

Excursus: Original Sin

To explore that controversy adequately would necessarily involve a massive digression, and here is not the place for yet another account to add to the many available. Let a telling summary of the issues suffice as a brief introduction:

> [Augustine and Pelagius] agreed on far more than that on which they disagreed. Both saw humanity as baked into a corporately sinful social tradition. Pelagius insisted that sin is not physically hereditary, and therefore by free choice we can escape. God (he said) had given

---

53. See above in chapter 4.
54. See further my article "Adam and Christ: Human Solidarity before God," in *The Christian Doctrine of Humanity*, ed. Oliver D. Crisp and Fred Sanders (Grand Rapids: Zondervan Academic, 2018), 144–64. Text and translation in Robert W. Thomson, ed. and trans., *Contra Gentes and De Incarnatione*, OECT (Oxford: Clarendon, 1971).

moral law for the conscience, free will, remission of sins in baptism and penance to rebuild resolve, above all, grace to help wherever there was truly good will.[55]

That summary of Pelagius's position maps easily on to what we have noted in Cyril's catechetical teaching, and both would seem to reflect the general implications of scripture. How and why, then, did Augustine disagree?

We may first respond with a few preliminary observations:

1. The practice of infant baptism was certainly an issue in the debates, for after all how could an innocent babe have committed sins which required baptismal washing away?
2. Augustine's anxieties about sexual acts undoubtedly played into the view that through procreation sin passed from one generation to the next—as it has been graphically put, "human sinfulness is a sexually transmitted disease."[56]
3. The Latin translation of Romans 5:12 had a role in encouraging the idea that all had sinned "in" Adam, which prompts the observation that previous scholarship has pointed to Augustine's reading of Paul as a major factor in shifting his perspective.[57] He had, after all, previously embraced free will as a crucial step away from Manichaeism.
4. More than anything else, Augustine's argumentation was driven by his appreciation of the creative work of providence and the grace of God—like Paul he understood that we are saved by faith, not by our own efforts.

What concerns us here, however, is the role of scripture in forming the characteristically Western doctrine of original sin.

More than once in his lifetime controversy forced Augustine to follow logic into a rather extreme position, and here is no exception. With this in mind, rather than specifically working through the controversial literature, we will engage with one major work, namely, *The*

---

55. Henry Chadwick, *Augustine* (Oxford: Oxford University Press, 1986), 109.
56. Stephen Greenblatt, *The Rise and Fall of Adam and Eve* (London: The Bodley Head, 2017), 108.
57. Paula Fredriksen, "Beyond the Body/Soul Dichotomy: Augustine's Answer to Mani, Plotinus, and Julian," in *Paul and the Legacies of Paul*, ed. William S. Babcock (Dallas: Southern Methodist University Press, 1990), 227–51.

City of God.⁵⁸ This allows us to grasp how the doctrine of original sin has its roots in scripture and tradition. For surely it is an outworking, or deepening, of the old Adam-Christ typology, an expression of human solidarity whether in sin or salvation. Furthermore, there are ways in which *The City of God* (at least from book 9 on and especially books 15–18) bears comparison with conspectuses of biblical history such as Irenaeus's *Demonstration of the Apostolic Preaching*, or indeed Cyril's catechetical overview.⁵⁹ While concentrating largely on what is apposite to the doctrine of sin, we will endeavor to keep the overall argument of this massive work in view.

The first ten books of *The City of God* are devoted to refuting those who blamed Christianity for the recent sack of Rome by Alaric and his invading Goths, claiming it was all because the old gods who made Rome great had been abandoned. Roman history, religion, astrology, and philosophy are all subjected to lengthy and trenchant criticism so as to introduce the true worship of God and the universal way of salvation. In the course of these ten books we find occasional anticipatory contrasts drawn out:

1. between true and false worship (*Civ.* 10 and passim);
2. between those old gods and the true God who made everything, including souls. Emphasis is placed on divine direction and providence, with a sketch of how we were not abandoned when overwhelmed by sins—for the Word/Son was sent to purify us by his sacrifice and act as mediator (*Civ.* 7.29–31; 9.15);
3. between the philosophical treatment of passions as inducing sin and the scriptural subjection of the passions to God's discipline (*Civ.* 9.5).

Such points prepare the reader for the fundamental contrast between the two cities—the one based on love of God, the other on love of self. The city of God is "vouched for by the scriptures" and "is manifestly due to the guiding power of God's supreme providence," states Augustine as book 11 opens. He characterizes his task as to discuss the rise, development, and desired ends of the two cities, the earthly and the heavenly,

---

58. Latin text in Bernard Dombart and Alphonse Kalb, eds., *De Civitate Dei libri viginti et duo*, 2 vols. (Leipzig: Teubner, 1928–1929); English translation: Henry Bettenson, trans., *City of God*, ed. David Knowles (Harmondsworth: Penguin, 1972).

59. See chapter 4 above and section 2.7 in this chapter.

"currently interwoven, as it were, in this present transitory world, and mingled with one another" (11.1). Never will Augustine simply identify the church as the heavenly city and the state as earthly; the distinction proves to be far more nuanced than that.[60] Scripture, together with the doctrine of creation, provides the perspective within which the discussion proceeds.

Ever the intellectual, Augustine begins by affirming that God communicates "by the direct impact of the truth" to anyone "capable of hearing with the mind," for humankind is made in God's image and nearness to God is found in that part of human nature which rises above what is shared with "the brute creation." Already, however, there is indication that something is inherently lacking. Augustine observes how

> the natural seat of human reason and understanding is itself weakened by long-standing faults which darken it. It is too weak to cleave to that changeless light and to enjoy it; it is too weak even to endure that light. It must first be renewed and healed day by day so as to become capable of such felicity. (*Civ.* 11.2)

The mind has to be trained and purified by faith for its journey to the truth, and here the incarnation comes in. Christ Jesus is the mediator between God and humankind: he spoke through the prophets and then his own mouth, constituting the scriptures in which Christians put their trust.

So Augustine starts to engage with scripture, beginning with creation and its implications for time, the soul, God, angels, and the blessings of paradise. Soon, however, his preoccupation becomes the fall of the devil and his offending angels. He roundly rejects Manichaean teaching: it is not the case that the devil "has evil as an essential principle of his being" (*Civ.* 11.13).[61] John 8:44 is interpreted to mean that the devil was once without sin, this being backed up by Isaiah 14:12 and other prophetic material. Indeed the devil was "the Lord's handiwork"—there is nothing that did not have its being from God (11.14–15). Everything is fundamentally good, indeed the choice of evil—turning away from God—would not be a fault if it were not the case that goodness—adhering to God—

---

60. See R. A. Markus, *Saeculum: History and Society in the Theology of St. Augustine* (Cambridge: Cambridge University Press, 1970).

61. *Civ.* 11.13; cf. 19.13: perversion makes the devil evil.

were natural (11.17).⁶² Furthermore God's goodness "turns evil choices to good use," and, though experienced as harmful when used without restraint and in improper ways, much that heretics seize on to deny the goodness of creation in fact has benefits (11.17, 22). At this point Augustine asserts that there is no such thing as evil: evil is merely the name for the privation of good, a notorious and much debated definition. Yet it fits well with his account of sin as the choice to turn away from God, depriving oneself of the true light and embracing darkness.

Thus free will definitely figures in Augustine's account of the origins of evil, at this point identified in the precosmic defection of the devil. This is the backdrop to Augustine's eventual account of sin in humanity. Meanwhile, as he himself admits (11.34), many questions distract him from his purpose; fascinating though they are, they need not further detain us. However, we might be inclined to think that scripture can seem a bit submerged by all these distracting questions. That is hardly a fair comment, however: the creation story of Genesis is not only implied but aspects of it are probed exegetically with many cross-references, and texts are found to substantiate what is said about the devil and his fall, by now a universally accepted story, despite the fact that there is no sign of it in Genesis.⁶³ The essential goodness of God's creation is the main burden of all the argumentation in book 11, and it is presented as the doctrine of scripture. Augustine even reproaches Origen for assigning a purpose for the material creation that is incompatible with scripture's insistence on "the purpose of God's goodness in the creation of good." The whole universe is good, even with its sinners (*Civ.* 11.23).

Through his account of good and bad angels, Augustine has established certain principles, which he restates as book 12 opens:

1. Every nature created by God is by nature good.
2. Created nature is changeable—the only unchanging good is God.
3. Failure to adhere to God is a perversion.
4. This fault or perversion is contrary to nature and so is proof that

---

62. *Civ.* 11.17; cf. 22.1: there would have been no evil if that nature which was capable of change had not produced evil for itself by sinning. That sin "is itself the evidence that proves the nature was created good." If not good, then "this apostasy from God" could not have been their evil.

63. This might be substantiated not only by reference to Cyril's *Catechetical Orations*, but by assumptions met throughout our discussion of Christology, salvation, etc.

"God created their nature so good that it is harmful for it to be separated from God" (12.1).

Now Augustine redefines the terms: goodness is correlated with existence. God said to Moses: "I am the one who is," and this supreme existence gave existence to creatures made out of nothing. No existing nature is contrary to God—the only contrary nature is the nonexistent (12.2). Evil is by implication associated with nonexistence, and thus understandably could be treated as the privation or perversion of good. So Augustine's account puts *creatio ex nihilo* at the heart of the issue, as Athanasius had done in his *On the Incarnation*. For Athanasius Adam's disobedience meant loss of the Logos—the life and rationality with which he had been endowed, and so death—and the drift back to the nothingness from which humankind had been created (*Inc.* 5). Gregory of Nyssa had traced mutability to the change whereby created beings were brought into existence from the nonexistent (*De hom.* 16.12). For Augustine changeability is the main factor in the perversion of good, for it made defection a possibility; in his view, the choice for perversion was not merely harmful but worthy of punishment (*Civ.* 12.3). His basic approach is not out of line with other early Christian accounts of the factors contributing to human frailty: the correlation of goodness with existence is Augustine's philosophical way of articulating this.

This does mean, however, that Augustine is now distracted into defending the Creator from blame for the transience and defects of earthly things and reaffirming "God's providential design" (12.4–5). But he is soon back pulling together his ideas on sin and evil and raising the question of what caused the angels to defect (12.6). Pride is his answer; there is no "efficient cause" of an evil act except evil choice, which comes from an evil will. Again Augustine insists that anything that exists is good not evil, so an evil will is a perversion, possible because it was created from nothing and so changeable. At the start of this section he still focuses on the angels, their bliss being adherence to the one who supremely is and their misery their turning away toward themselves. It ends, however, with the example of two men, both tempted by the body of a beautiful woman, one turning to unlawful enjoyment and the other to chastity. The theoretical position applies to both angels and humans.

So far choice figures large, implying the exercise of free will, and Augustine underlines the point that one should not look for an efficient cause for a wrong choice: it is not a matter of efficiency but deficiency, "the evil will itself is not effective but defective." To seek the cause of defection is like "trying to see darkness or hear silence"; awareness of either is "not by perception but by absence of perception" (12.7). The failure, however, "is voluntary, not necessary, and the punishment that follows is just" (12.8). Nor can God be held responsible—a point that leads Augustine once more into many by-ways where we need not follow. He is primarily anxious to prove that God's purposes have not been subject to change and to resist cyclical views of history or of creation's eternity.

Creation, then, remains the context of Augustine's explorations, and finally he reaches the creation of humankind. He has already asserted that "the whole human race took its beginning from the one man whom God first created," scripture being his authority for this statement (12.9). He has also argued against the view that the human race always existed (12.10) as well as against the recent creation of humanity (12.13), and indeed the idea that God's creation of the human race involved a change of mind (12.15). So now (12.22) he states that humankind was not an innovation in God's design, but was intended as "a kind of mean between angels and beasts." Obedience to the Creator would mean fellowship with the angels; disobedience would mean living with the beasts "under sentence of death" and "a slave to desires."[64] One individual was created, but God's intention was that the unity of human society and the bonds of human sympathy would be consolidated by kinship—the creation of woman from Adam is used to confirm this.

Augustine next insists on God's foreknowledge of human sin, commenting on the lack of peace among humans compared with other species, despite the fact that human derivation from a single ancestor was meant to foster harmony. But God also foresaw that through divine grace some would merit adoption as God's sons. Augustine's description here echoes a number of scriptural texts as well as suggests that these would benefit from the truth that the human race was started from one man to show how pleasing to God is unity in plurality (12.23). The two cities are thus foreseen from the beginning, as Augustine will point out at the end of the book (12.28). Meanwhile he states that God made humankind in God's own image, insisting that God breathed the soul into Adam and that it was God, not the angels, who created humankind, expounding the scriptural narrative of human creation and repudiating

---

64. Here Augustine takes much the same view as Gregory of Nyssa in his *De opificio hominis*.

rival Platonist claims. But the significant point for our exploration of original sin is the way Augustine's reading of the Genesis narrative puts human solidarity at the core of God's creative purpose.

So on to book 13 and the story of the fall. It seems remarkable that we have gotten so far before reaching this narrative; indeed, the fundamental contrast between love of God and love of self is already established, that deep distinction between the two cities whose intertwined history Augustine will soon be telling. So sin has essentially been defined long before we get to what has been judged crucial to Augustine's doctrine, and free will has remained a core element in his account. Very quickly, however, we see how Adam's fall changes the situation. Mortality being the consequence of the fall, Augustine provides a preliminary discussion of death and what it means for body and soul. But his purpose is to show how the punishment inevitably passed from Adam and Eve to "whatever sprang from their stock," since anything born from them could not be different from what they had been (13.3). Contrasting the creation of Adam from dust and the procreation of Adam's descendents, he indicates that "the whole human race was in the first man," and "it was what the race became after his sin and punishment" that was passed on. For Adam's sin meant that human nature itself was vitiated and altered, and

> he produced offspring in the same condition to which his fault and its punishment had reduced him, that is, liable to sin and death. But if infants are released from the bonds of this sin through the grace of Christ the Mediator, they can only suffer the death which separates soul from body; they do not pass on to that second death of unending punishment, since they have been freed from the entanglement of sin. (*Civ.* 13.3)

Now we may discern what Augustine's doctrine is about: free choice is no longer operative because human beings are no longer free—they are constrained by a nature twisted and bound up in sin and death from which they need to be rescued before they can exercise free choice for themselves. Scripture is quoted to substantiate this: "Humankind was in a place of honor, but did not realize it: they have been brought to the level of the animals without understanding and been made like them" (Ps 49:12, 20).

Augustine's focus, however, remains on death. The punishment of death has been turned to good use, he suggests, as the penalty for the offense is turned into an instrument of virtue, the punishment of the sinner becoming the merit of the righteous, pointing to the martyrs. God's grace has turned death into the means by which humans may pass into life (13.4). That does not mean death is a good thing. Augustine now refers to the ambiguous role of the law in the Pauline Epistles. It is not an evil thing though it certainly increases the evil desire of the sinner: "the law is good, because it is the prohibition of sin, while death is evil, because it is the reward of sin," writes Augustine. Yet unrighteousness can put anything and everything to a bad use; conversely, righteousness can put good and evil alike to a good use (13.5).

Pursuing questions about death preoccupies Augustine for a long time. Eventually, however, he returns to the story in Genesis, reflecting on the recognition of nakedness and recourse to fig leaves. There was no change to the organs except that sense of shame: "thus, they felt a novel disturbance in their disobedient flesh, as a punishment which answered their own disobedience." Augustine explains that the soul had rejoiced in its freedom to act perversely, disdaining to be God's servant, so it was deprived of the obedient service that the body had at first rendered, the flesh beginning to "lust in opposition to the spirit" (Gal 5:17), a "conflict that attends us from our birth" (13.13). Thus humankind was willingly perverted and condemned, begetting perverted and condemned offspring. We were all in that one man, Augustine reaffirms—we did not yet possess individual forms. And of course, when that "seminal nature" was vitiated by sin, a human could not be born from a human in any other condition. Hence "the misuse of freewill" started "a chain of disasters," and only those "set free through God's grace escape from this calamitous sequence" (13.14). The doctrine of original sin is thus deduced from the Genesis narrative read with Pauline eyes.

Augustine returns to the issues around death: whether it really is penal, whether bodies can become immortal, and what a "spiritual body" might be, tackling both Plato and the exegesis of scripture. Pauline texts become prominent as he teases out the Adam-Christ typology. Deduction from scripture is paramount as he reaches the climax of book 13, expounding the distinction between those who, with spiritual bodies, will share citizenship with the holy angels, and those who face the "second death" at the final judgment—a notion derived from the book of Revelation (Rev 2:11; 20:6, 14; 21:8). Dead they may be, but certainly alive enough to suffer eternal torment in the fires of Gehenna. Summarizing where we have got to at the start of book 14, Augustine reaffirms the point that God chose to make the starting point of humankind a single person so that kinship would reinforce the unity of the human race, linked together by the bond of peace, but disobedience changed human nature for the worse—"bondage to sin and inevitable death was the legacy handed on to their posterity" (14.1). Some, however, have been rescued by the grace of God.

Augustine thus introduces the two fundamental divisions in human society, far more significant, he suggests, than all the diversity of peoples, customs, languages, and cultures. Scripture justifies referring to them as two cities, he writes, probably alluding to Ephesians 2:19 and Philippians 3:20, both of which speak of our citizenship in heaven. One city consists of those who choose to live by "the standard of the flesh," the other those who choose to live by "the standard of the spirit." Choice remains core to Augustine's thinking, but the ability to make the choice for the heavenly city must surely now depend on responding to and receiving the saving grace of God. The rest of book 14 engages with scripture, on the one hand, and classical literature, on the other, to refute the notion that sin is simply the fault of the body; to explore the passions and the will and their relationship; to distinguish between scripture's understanding of love and the lust and shame associated with procreation; to speculate on what might have been the human condition prior to the fall, or if the fall had not happened; and yet again to uphold the justice of the punishment and the providence of God. All this prepares the way for Augustine's grand conspectus of history, using the Bible to trace the two cities in two lines of descent, pursuing either human glory and human wisdom or divine wisdom and true worship. Like Irenaeus and Cyril before him, but with far greater attention to detail, Augustine works his way through Cain and Abel, Noah, Abraham, and on through the prophets to Christ and the church (books 15–18). The final books (19–22) then discuss our ultimate destiny, resurrection, the last judgment, and the vision of God.

This huge work has enabled us to set the doctrine of original sin in its wider context, especially its roots in scripture and tradition. The focus has been on providence, with a vision of God turning even evil into good. There is no sign of arbitrary condemnation, but rather emphasis is placed on the perversion of what is inherently good. If Augustine had known about viruses, they would have provided him with the analogy he needed: all humanity is affected by this pandemic of sin having inherited a defective immune system, and the incarnation provides the vaccine that enables the renewal of our freedom to choose healthy living. Most important for our purposes, however, is the observation that the doctrine of original sin is a way of capturing the import of the Adam-Christ typology and providing the foundation for the overarching story of fall and redemption that Christian doctrine discerned as the fundamental meaning of the Bible.

2.8. Final Clauses: The Church, the Resurrection of the Body, and the Last Things

Homily 18 is Cyril's final word before his catechumens go for baptism. Sticking closely to the underlying creedal pattern, it principally focuses on the resurrection of the flesh and eternal life, though mentioning also one baptism of repentance for the remission of sins and one holy catholic church. By contrast, these creedal statements are ignored in the list of holy dogmas in homily 4 as Cyril ranged over other items—soul and body, food and clothing, the scriptures. But in homily 18, referring back to his treatment of baptism in the earliest homilies, he does offer some comment on the clause about the church, sandwiched between his discussion of bodily resurrection and his treatment of eternal life. To the former we will return after consideration of the latter.

2.8.1. Bodily Resurrection and Eternal Life

As mentioned above, Cyril's proofs and arguments for the reality of general resurrection are quite different from those to which he appeals in the case of Christ's resurrection. They illustrate a different approach to confirming scripture's teaching, for prooftexts and prophecies play a much smaller role. Yet once again the arguments are drawn from a long-standing apologetic tradition.

Resurrection had been rooted in the doctrine of creation since the second century. Homily 4 briefly sets out this argument: "A hundred years or so ago where were you?" asks Cyril. Surely the one who brought the nonexistent into being can raise up what already exists but has decayed. This is followed, first, by natural analogies—corn which dies and rises year by year, trees which spring back to life after the winter—and then by a creative miracle from scripture—Moses's rod transformed into a serpent. Now come specific scriptural testimonies, Isaiah 26:19 and Daniel 12, both asserting resurrection and eternal life, the latter indicating a difference between the rising of the just to join choirs of angels and that of the unjust to endure torment for their sins (*Cat. orat.* 4.30–31). Such points will be filled out in the eighteenth and final pre-baptismal address, for which the scriptural reading is Ezekiel 37.

The initial focus for Cyril in this later homily is the connection between the resurrection hope and the morally good life: "the expectation of recompense nerves the soul to good works," while disbelief lets a person abandon themselves to perdition. Indeed, those believing that their bodies will rise again will make sure the body is not defiled (18.1). On the subject of resurrection he feels the need to arm his catechumens against the objections of Greeks and Samaritans who will argue that the dead body moulders and is turned into worms, that the shipwrecked have been eaten by fish which are themselves then eaten, that fighting with wild beasts can mean bones ground to powder or being consumed by bears or lions, while vultures and ravens feed on unburied corpses and fly scattered in every direction. So, how is the body to be collected together again? Well, India may be far from the land of the Goths and Spain far from Persia, but the whole world is held in the palm of God's hand (Isa 40:12), so surely God can sort out what is held in that palm and restore each fragment to its own (18.2–3).

These arguments recall the second-century treatise on the resurrection by Athenagoras. He had challenged similar opposition to the idea of resurrection with the connection between resurrection and creation: they must either deny that the creation of human beings has a cause, or they need to demonstrate that God, despite being Creator, either cannot or will not restore dead bodies so as to reconstitute the human beings they were before (*Res.* 2.2–3). Whatever the objections raised, such as what happens to those eaten by wild animals or turned into food for fish after drowning, Athenagoras trumped them with the power and wisdom of the Creator. Nor would he allow that raising up and reconstituting a decomposed body was unworthy of God: if making a corruptible and passible body is not unworthy of God, how much more so is the greater work of making an incorruptible and impassible body. The resurrection then "is possible for, willed by and worthy of the Creator" (10.6). Like other second-century apologists Athenagoras insisted that human nature is constituted by an immortal soul and a body, the two united at its creation (15.2), so reconstitution of that union is necessary for the permanence of humanity as such—that this permanence was God's will and purpose he had already shown. All arguments so far, Athenagoras stated, arise from the same principle: namely, creation. Resurrection is the logical outcome (18.1).

This tradition is what Cyril follows. He has already argued that the body is God's work, that it is not the cause of sin but the garment of the soul and can become a temple of the Holy Spirit (*Cat. orat.* 4.22–23), and that it is to be cared for as it is destined for resurrection (4.30). What is striking is that this doctrine could not only qualify antiquity's general assumption of the soul's immortality—Tatian, for example, insisting that the soul is mortal—but also substantially modified the Platonism of such theologians as Gregory of Nyssa and Augustine.[65] The immortality of the soul Gregory dismissed as pagan nonsense: body and soul were brought into being together, and this wholeness would be restored in the resurrection.[66] Facing those same old objections, Gregory not only dismisses such questioning as unworthy of God's power and authority, but even draws a picture of how the dissolved particles of the body are imprinted with an identity and reconstituted by the soul's knowledge of them—a parallel with modern notions of the persistence of DNA has been drawn![67] However, as for Athenagoras and Cyril of Jerusalem, so for Gregory the most fundamental point is that not just the body but the soul owes its very existence to the Creator, and the reconstitution of human nature is less problematic than the initial creation from nothing. For Augustine, too, creation is the most powerful testimony for belief in Christ's physical resurrection as well as future resurrection to the new age of humankind. Nothing is beyond the resources of the Creator, so the classic problem cases are irrelevant: the Creator simply reuses the original substance of the person as an artist reuses material.[68] From his early instinct to argue in Platonic fashion for "the indestructibility of the soul as a philosophically evident truth,"[69] Augustine's view had shifted by the time of writing *The City of God* to the integration of soul and body as the reality to be realized at the resurrection through the transforming power of the Creator God.

Thus the dogma of the resurrection of the body, or indeed of the flesh, was established and promulgated—surely against the odds. It may seem based largely on logic, but the process of reasoning had the biblical doctrine of creation as its basis. Furthermore, it was invariably finessed by reference to 1 Corinthians 15: the body was not simply to be reconstituted but transformed in

---

65. See further my article "Naked or Clothed?"

66. Gregory of Nyssa, *De hom.* 25–26; cf. *De anima et resurrectione*.

67. Vasiliki Limberis, "Resurrected Body and Immortal Flesh in Gregory of Nyssa," in *Jesus Christ in St Gregory of Nyssa's Theology: Minutes of the Ninth International Conference on Gregory of Nyssa (Athens 7–12 September 2000)*, ed. Eliad D. Moutsoulas (Athens: University Press, 2005), 515–28.

68. Augustine, *Civ.* 22.1–3, 12–14, 19–20, for example. Cf. O'Collins, *St. Augustine and the Resurrection*, 37–41.

69. Brian E. Daley, *The Hope of the Early Church* (Cambridge: Cambridge University Press, 1991), 142.

ways barely conceivable—it would be a spiritual body, incorruptible and immortal, not the rotten flesh and blood that could not inherit God's kingdom (1 Cor 15:50). Clearly this doctrine, by now enshrined in the creeds, was profoundly countercultural, and its authority derived from scripture. As previously observed Christ's resurrection is generally not cited as a precedent guaranteeing general resurrection; rather the biblical doctrine of creation undergirds all resurrection claims and hopes. But there is a further biblical perspective that Cyril and others brought into play—namely, the judgment to come.

Indeed, in homily 18, no sooner has Cyril capped the objections with God's universal creative power than he appeals to the principle of justice (*Cat. orat.* 18.4–5). He raises the issue of murderers who die in their beds: without judgment and retribution after death God must be charged with unrighteousness! For Athenagoras too the consideration of the reward and punishment due to each person in accordance with just judgment provides an important argument for resurrection, but it is secondary to that from creation (*Res.* 18.2). He suggests that judgment had been used as the primary argument; in his view, however, this is false, for all arise but all who arise are not judged, his example being infants and very young children, so "the resurrection does not take place primarily because of the judgement but because of the will of the Creator and the nature of those created" (*Res.* 14.6). After dealing with his argument from creation, Athenagoras turns to providence: the Creator provides for all created things according to their needs, and humankind being needy requires food, being mortal requires a succession of offspring, and being rational requires justice. Now, just judgment requites the composite creature for its deeds, and that clearly does not take place in this life. At length Athenagoras points out the unfairness of judging the soul or the body on its own: virtue and vice are not applicable to the soul as a separate entity, and some commandments do not apply directly to the soul, notably, "You shall not commit adultery." But it is not only just judgment that requires the reconstitution of the composite creature—it is the realization of that creature's proper end and happiness. So ultimately it is the Creator's purpose for humankind that constitutes the basic argument for resurrection.

Cyril also does not dwell on the judgment as an argument for resurrection—the final judgment has already figured in his sequence of homilies on the creed. Rather, he moves quickly in homily 18 to develop the themes outlined in homily 4, both the natural analogies and the scriptural testimonies (*Cat. orat.* 18.6–18). Fundamentally he seems to think belief in resurrection is instinctive because it is natural. Why, he wonders, do grave robbers receive condemnation? It is because there is an instinct for resurrection. Trees blossom again after being cut down, as do vines after pruning or transplantation: why not humans? Wheat rots in the ground, and then springs up. Flies and bees drown in water then revive, and dormice hibernate. His biology may be primitive, and the potential analogies may climax with the mythical phoenix, but the point fundamentally rests in the doctrine of creation. Cyril's final argument against the Greeks is the waxing and waning of the moon (18.10).

Next Cyril turns to the Samaritans: since they receive only the law, they would not allow the prophecy of Ezekiel, which had been read to the catechumens before this homily. To Moses God identifies the divine self as the God of Abraham, Isaac, and Jacob, notes Cyril, but if these patriarchs had come to an end, then God would be God of those with no existence (18.11). Next he draws on further scriptural testimonies to God's power to restore or transform: Aaron's rod, for example, and the creation narrative, from dust to flesh (18.12–13). Prophets, Psalms, and Job are valid for those who believe, and so further prooftexts appear (18.14–16). Yet it remains true that whereas the principal argument for Christ's resurrection lay in such scriptural testimonies, Cyril almost entirely argues to the dogma of general resurrection on the basis of the doctrine of creation, as the tradition had been doing since the second century.

What we have been observing in this section on resurrection is the reasoned articulation of what scripture teaches, together with the generation and justification of dogmatic propositions through that process. After the second century's struggle with the antimaterialist positions of sects like the gnostics, it was not controversy but the apologetic tradition that shaped the dogmatic discourse concerning resurrection; for, of all creedal propositions, resurrection of the body—whether of Christ or of believers—was perhaps the most countercultural and thus the most exclusively grounded, less in rational argument and more in scripture—indeed, in scripture's overarching picture of God as the Creator who re-creates a world gone wrong.

2.8.2. The Church

Regarding the catholicity of the church, Cyril first explains that it extends from one end of the earth to the other (*Cat. orat.* 18.23). But the church is also "catholic" because:

1. It teaches universally and completely all necessary doctrines about things visible and invisible, heavenly and earthly.
2. It subjects to godliness the whole race of humankind, rulers and ruled, learned and unlearned.

3. It universally treats and heals every kind of sin, whether committed by soul or body, and possesses in itself every kind of virtue—deeds, words, spiritual gifts.

The word *ekklēsia* is now justified with a collection of scriptural references: Leviticus 8:3, Deuteronomy 4:20 and 9:20, and various Psalm texts (*Cat. orat.* 18.24). Cyril recognizes that these texts refer to the assembly of Israel, but suggests that after the Jews plotted against the Savior, he built a second holy *ekklēsia* of the gentiles, the church of the Christians. Further biblical texts predict this, confirming that the "Judean church" was cast off while the church of Christ was increasing all over the world (18.25–26). Cyril thus reflects the supersessionist view generally found in the early church.

Now, however, he recognizes that the word *ekklēsia* is applicable to many other assemblies—gatherings of evil doers, Marcionites, and Manichees, among others. This explains those vital epithets: one, holy, catholic. Such is the *ekklēsia* the catechumens need to seek out, the one that is the spouse of the Lord Jesus Christ, the "type of Jerusalem above" and "mother of us all" (Gal 4:26). Cyril elaborates this with further Pauline texts and confesses his discourse would need many hours to cover this topic (18.25–27).

Indeed, for us too, to broaden the discussion into a conspectus of early Christian ecclesiology would take far too many pages, material being scattered across epistolary, homiletic, exegetical, and controversial literature. We will content ourselves first with a brief look at images of the church that derive from scripture, dipping into the *Apostolic Constitutions* and some other early and Eastern material. Then we will turn to the West to review a work focused on the nature of the church, namely, Cyprian's *The Unity of the Catholic Church*, before briefly considering the issues at the heart of the Donatist schism. This will surely be enough to confirm the essentially scriptural character of thinking about the church, moving as it did within certain contours mapped by Old Testament typology and New Testament images.

2.8.2.1. Images of the Church Deriving from Scripture

The so-called *Apostolic Constitutions* comes from the late fourth century, but is a compendium that incorporates various earlier texts, such as the *Didache*, the *Apostolic Tradition* attributed to Hippolytus, and *The Teaching of the Apostles*.[70] In other words it edits together collections of regulations concerning the

---

70. Text in Marcel Metzger, ed., *Les constitutions apostoliques*, 3 vols., SC 320, 329, 336 (Paris: Cerf, 1985–1987); English translation in *ANF* 7.

church and how it is to be ordered—its ministers and its liturgy. The opening subject (book 1) covers the church in general, speaking of God's vineyard, of being heirs of God's kingdom and fellow heirs with Christ. The scriptural provenance of the language is obvious. In book 8 intercession for the church incorporates New Testament phrases: that this people will be made a "royal priesthood and a holy nation" (1 Pet 2:9); that God will look down on "this flock" and keep them steady and blameless "that they may be holy in body and spirit, not having spot or wrinkle" (1 Tim 6:14). The flock with its shepherd—the bishop—is a recurring image, with quotations from Ezekiel and elsewhere warning against bad shepherds and "scabbed sheep." As God's people—indeed, a "bride adorned for the Lord God"—the church consists of escapees from the ten plagues who have received the ten commandments, learned the law, kept the faith, and believed in Jesus. Now they are to offer tithes and sacrifices, their bishop being the high priest, presbyters being their priests, and deacons being their Levites, a typology found as early as 1 Clement (40–44). The high priest, Christ, is above them all, and they are a people who at one time were not a people (1 Pet 2:10)—hence the use of the biblical image of the vineyard, once applied to Israel by the prophets. The church is God's plantation.

As for Cyril so for this compendium and the majority of texts dealing with the church, it is assumed that the fulfillment of prophecy means the old Israel is reconstituted in the new *ekklēsia*—supersessionism runs deep. But this perspective also ensures that teaching about the nature of the church was profoundly scriptural rather than encapsulated in dogmatic propositions. The New Testament hints about the church being the "mother of us all" (Gal 5:32) and the bride or spouse of Christ (Eph 5:32) are repeatedly enlarged upon, the latter providing opportunity, from Origen to Gregory of Nyssa, to develop a mystical reading of the Song of Songs. Methodius is one who specifically develops Paul's words in Ephesians 5:28–32 on the mystery of Christ and the church.[71] He reads it back to Genesis 2:23–24, explaining how Paul could insist that a man who loves his wife loves himself, and so how Christ loves the church: "for we are members of Christ's body, of His flesh and His bones." Thus the image of the church as the bride of Christ is neatly associated with Paul's image of the church as Christ's body.

What is perhaps surprising is that this image of the church as Christ's body is absent from the *Apostolic Constitutions* and, as we shall see, also from Cyprian's work on the church. Needless to say it is found elsewhere and developed in various ways but, it has been argued, not always associated with the church as

---

71. Methodius, *Sym.* 3; Greek text in PG 18; English translation in *ANF* 6.

such, reflection occurring in arguments about Christology or soteriology.[72] In particular, it was suggested that incorporation into Christ's "mystical body" is associated with deification, with becoming part of redeemed humanity, which transcends the church. Such ideas may be attributed not just to Origen, but to Athanasius, the Cappadocians, and Cyril of Alexandria. Still the church as Christ's body is found earlier in Ignatius: "he calls you, who are part of His own Body, to Himself. A Head cannot come into being alone, without any limbs; for the promise that we have from God is the promise of unity, which is the essence of Himself" (Ign. *Trall.* 11.2). Elsewhere Ignatius speaks of the church being inseparably one with Jesus Christ, as Jesus Christ is with the Father (Ign. *Eph.* 5.1). Irenaeus speaks of God judging those who split "the great and glorious body of Christ" (*Haer.* 4.7). Origen tells Celsus that the whole church of God is the body of Christ, the Son of God being the soul: as the soul gives life and movement to the body, so the Logos "moves the Church and each limb of the members of the Church who do nothing apart from the Logos" (*Cels.* 6.48). Later Origen again states that "Christ is the head of the Church, so that Christ and the Church are one body" (6.79). Eusebius, at the climax of his *Church History*, speaks of the "unification of the members of Christ's body," bone conjoining with bone and joint with joint, as prophesied in Ezekiel 37:7 (*Hist. eccl.* 10.3).

The two most prominent images in the *Apostolic Constitutions* are the household and the ship. The household image we will also find developed in Cyprian and it is clearly grounded in the Pastoral Epistles. In the *Apostolic Constitutions* it undergirds the ethical perspectives that pervade the work. The ship image is more intriguing and repays a little further investigation. Book 2 provides a description of a church gathering: the bishop is the commander of a great ship, we are told. The building should be long and face east, with the bishop's throne placed in the middle, the presbytery on either side of him, and the deacons on hand, for they are like the mariners and managers of the ship. The laity are set in their proper places, men and women apart, while the doorkeepers and deaconesses watch over men and women respectively like sailors. In book 8 we find prayers that God will preserve the church unshaken and free from the waves of this life until the end of the world, and God is addressed as their protector, helper, provider, and guardian, their strong way of defense, their bulwark and security. The implication seems to be that, though anchored in God, the church needs divine assistance to sail through the storms of earthly existence.

---

72. J. N. D. Kelly, *Early Christian Doctrines* (London: Black, 1960), 403–6.

Indeed, this picture was clearly commonplace: similar motifs are frequently found in the correspondence of Basil of Caesarea, for example. There the context of heresy and schism is explicit, and the church needs "a great helmsman because of the continued storms and floods which rise against the Church" (*Ep.* 81).[73] "No one in his right mind," he suggests, "would board a boat without a pilot, or entrust himself to a Church in which those who sit at the helm are themselves causing the billows and tossing" (*Ep.* 210). Basil worries about shipwreck, storms, and fierce tempests. In his work on the Holy Spirit the present condition of the church is compared to a naval battle, rival fleets rushing to the attack (*De Spir.* 30.76). One cannot help deducing that the gospel story of the stilling of the storm played a role in encouraging such discourse, not to mention the fact that often the church is compared to Noah's ark.

2.8.2.2. Cyprian: *The Unity of the Catholic Church* and Beyond

For Cyprian the unity of the church was a major concern, faced as he was by schisms caused by the aftermath of the Decian persecution. His treatise *The Unity of the Catholic Church* opens with warnings that heresies and schisms are the new wiles of the devil, worse indeed than the persecution itself.[74] There is predictable appeal to remain steadfast, founded securely on the rock in opposition to the tempests and hurricanes of the world: Matthew 7:24 is quoted and other biblical material enhances the rhetoric. The Matthaean commission to Peter is reinforced by John 21:15–17, and John 20:21 shows how the other apostles were invested with the same authority. The oneness of the church is indicated by Song of Songs 6:9, "My dove, my perfect one is the only one," and Ephesians 4:4, "there is one body and one Spirit, one hope of your calling, one Lord, one faith, one baptism, one God and Father of all."[75]

These scriptural pointers are supported with natural analogies: many rays but one light, many branches but one tree, many rivers but one source. Such images might be said to have some biblical precedent though this is not explicit. Definitely biblical, however, is the notion of the church as the spouse of Christ (Eph 5:23), already implicit in the quotation from the Song of Songs. This is

---

73. Greek text and English translation in R. J. Deferrari, ed., *Saint Basil: The Letters*, 4 vols., LCL (Cambridge: Harvard University Press, 1926–1934).

74. Latin text and English translation in Maurice Bévenot, ed., *Cyprian: De Lapsis and De Ecclesiae Catholicae Unitate* (Oxford: Clarendon, 1971).

75. This paragraph draws from Cyprian, *Unit. eccl.* 1–4; 4 appears to include interpolations concerning the primacy of Peter, and some of the texts referenced are found in those contested passages.

now developed in terms of one house and one couch, a contrast being drawn with an adulteress: both Hosea and Proverbs are likely to have influenced these images. Galatians 5:32 denotes the church as "mother of us all," and it is here we find the famous dictum, "he can no longer have God for his Father who does not have the Church for his mother," and an ironic parallel is drawn with Noah's Ark—if anyone survived outside it, then those outside the church might have some hope. "Whoever is not with me is against me" (Matt 12:30), "I and the Father are one" (John 10:30), "And these three are one" (1 John 5:7): these texts are quoted to press home the requirement of unity, now symbolized by the robe of Christ for which lots were cast to avoid dividing or cutting it (John 19:23, 24). This is contrasted with the prophet rending his garment as the twelve tribes were divided into the two kingdoms of Judah and Israel (1 Kgs 11:31). Christ's robe is undivided, and this is a sign of the church's unity.[76]

Cyprian now turns to other biblical images. The first is the flock and the shepherd, quoting John 10:16. The second is the home or household. Cyprian gives two examples: Rahab prefigures the church in being urged to gather her kinsfolk into one house (Josh 2:19); and as the Passover lamb is to be eaten in one house (Exod 12:46), so the sacrament cannot be sent out from the one house of believers, the church. Along the way other texts, such as 1 Corinthians 1:10 and Ephesians 4:2–3, indicate the peace and unanimity that should be found within the church. The Holy Spirit, states Cyprian, came as a dove, and he rhetorically develops the contrast between the gentleness and simplicity of the dove, not to mention lambs and sheep, compared to the fierceness of wolves, dogs, and serpents—just as well that the latter leave the church rather than spread their contagion. These images again have obvious scriptural precedents, as does the idea that the wind may carry off the chaff but not the wheat, nor topple the solidly rooted tree—only the weak and feeble are carried off by the whirlwind. The Holy Spirit forewarns of heresies through the apostle (1 Cor 11:19)—heresies help to separate wheat and chaff, and prophetic words warn about false prophets, Cyprian suggests, quoting Jeremiah.[77]

Cyprian's treatise, then, is packed with scriptural language, allusion, and quotation; this is clear from surveying just one third of it! His fundamental point is clear: the sheer breaking up of the peace given by Christ—the refusal to be in agreement, to be in the bonds of love and charity—means those claiming the name of Christ but not in communion with the church have no right to quote scripture or to pray, given the injunction to forgiveness attached to

---

76. This paragraph, including quotes, draws from *Unit. eccl.* 5–7.
77. This paragraph draws from *Unit. eccl.* 8–11.

the Lord's Prayer. Nor can they assume that martyrdom can expiate the stain of discord (*Unit. eccl.* 12–14). On and on he goes with his battery of scripture references, proving that love is superior to prophecy and exorcism, and citing further warnings from both the Old and New Testaments. In a similar vein he meets with scripture the counterclaims made by those he treats as heretics and schismatics. But we have seen enough to realize that in Cyprian's ecclesiology, scripture is paramount, noting his biblical images: the rock in the storm, the spouse of Christ, the mother, the household, the flock, the harvest. This kind of picture, deriving from prophecies, parables, and sayings, will prove to be characteristic of early Christian reflection on the church.

Meanwhile, however, we attend briefly to one major controversy about the nature of the church, in which both sides appealed to Cyprian. If the Decian persecution lay behind the problems of unity in Cyprian's day, the aftermath of Diocletian's major onslaught was a long-term split in the North African church. Somewhat similar issues were at stake—namely the status of those who had compromised with the requirements of the state and failed in their loyalty to Christ. If the church was pure and holy, without spot or wrinkle (Eph 5:27), how could apostates be readmitted? This was Cyprian's issue. The issue between Donatists and catholics was whether clergy who had handed over the scriptures could continue to administer valid sacraments. The tension between the empirical church and the eschatological church raised practical matters to be settled on the ground: Was the church a school for sinners or a community of saints? The Donatists demanded a holiness they saw compromised by the catholics.[78] The catholics claimed a catholicity that no mere local schism could match, being out of communion with churches outside North Africa.

Peter Brown offers an illuminating comment on the underlying instincts at work in the North African context, a comment that suggests a deeper sense of scripture's import beyond mere appeal to specific texts.[79] He characterizes the Donatist idea of purity as "the purity of a group in relation to God," God being alienated from the church by "any breach in a narrow and clearly defined order of ritual behaviour." The prophets tell how "God closed His ears to His Chosen People because of their sins." Brown suggests that "anyone who reads a Donatist pamphlet, or, indeed, a work of S. Cyprian will be struck by the idea of ritual purity that stemmed straight from the Old Testament: the fear of a sudden loss of spiritual potency through contact with an 'unclean' thing." Hence the urgent need for both separation from contamination and destruc-

---

78. The classic study is by W. H. C. Frend, *The Donatist Church* (Oxford: Clarendon, 1952).
79. Peter Brown, *Augustine of Hippo: A Biography* (London: Faber & Faber, 1967), 218–19.

tion of anything deemed unclean. It was not a matter of individual personal purity, but of the church's holiness as a corporate, ritual entity, and this could easily be contaminated by contagion. Their favorite scriptural images for the church, as Markus notes, denoted separation: a sanctuary from contamination by the world, the "garden enclosed, a sealed fountain" (Song 4:12), the ark of Noah "caulked with pitch both inside and out (Gen 6:14) in order to prevent, as they preached, leaks either from or into it."[80]

We will eschew any attempt to trace the course of the conflict that clouded much of Augustine's episcopacy—other accounts are available—nor will we review here the controversial literature for its appeal to scripture. Suffice it to note (1) that from Cyprian's time appeal had been made to the parable of the wheat and tares, and now it justified the idea that the church would be "mixed" until the final judgment, so the church on earth had to be acknowledged as a *corpus permixtum*;[81] and (2) that (notoriously) Augustine quoted the parable of the wedding feast to justify the State's crackdown on Donatism: "Compel them to come in" (Luke 14:23).[82] The Noah's ark typology had long since permitted the observation that clean and unclean animals were alike taken on board.[83] Though, as noted already, the Donatists preferred to use it in terms of keeping out the dirty flood waters of the world.[84]

To sum up this subsection, there was substantial reflection on the nature of the church largely moving within contours mapped by Old Testament typology and New Testament images and principally deployed in circumstances of real or potential conflict with splinter groups, heresies, and schisms. The creedal affirmation of one, holy, catholic church faced challenges time and again, but encapsulated an ideal with essentially scriptural roots. The problem was how to reconcile the eschatological vision with empirical realities.

2.9. Conclusion

Introducing this chapter was the suggestion that we might discover through Cyril's *Catechetical Homilies* how those core Trinitarian and christological doctrines, whose precise articulation through controversy we would later trace, were so related to other themes as to create a theological whole based on a coherent reading of scripture. Cyril himself clearly understood the creed to be

---

80. Markus, *Saeculum*, 112.
81. E.g., Augustine, *Doctr. chr.* 3.45.
82. W. H. C. Frend, *The Early Church* (London: Hodder and Stoughton, 1965), 216, referring to *Ep.* 93 and 173; see further the discussion in chapter 6 of Markus, *Saeculum*.
83. Cf. Kelly, *Early Christian Doctrines*, 201, citing Hippolytus, *Haer.* 9.12.22ff.
84. Cf. Peter Brown, *Augustine of Hippo*, 221.

a summary of scripture and also regarded the discrete dogmas as the building blocks of a single coherent doctrinal scheme:

> Think of catechesis as if it were a house. If we don't use clamps in the right order to hold the structure together and to prevent gaps appearing so that the building becomes unsound, even our earlier efforts will be wasted. Stone must follow stone and corner fit corner in the right order. We must smooth away irregularities if the building is to rise. In the same way we bring you, so to speak, stones of knowledge . . . first I must explain them point by point, and only later their mutual connections. (Cyril, *Procat.* 1)

Reviewing our survey of each point the striking thing is how insistence on the goodness of the material creation integrates doctrines into a kind of ecological interdependence, doctrines such as the affirmation of the incarnation through the virgin birth, the reality of Christ's suffering under Pontius Pilate, and the notion of resurrection. A deeply countercultural yet profoundly biblical emphasis on positive evaluation of the bodily and the material cosmos, as created by God and as the sphere of God's saving providence, is what joins the whole together, including contentious issues around Christology. Yes, the overarching biblical story tells of sin and judgment, but this too is within the saving providence of the one God, Creator of all. Cyril's pedagogy may list key dogmas to be learned by rote in creedal form, but for him one meaning of "catholic" is that together they embrace the whole of the faith. Surely taken together they both encapsulate the old rule of faith and provide the key to understanding the scriptures, as had that rule for Irenaeus and earlier exponents of the faith.

3. Christian Teaching as Dogmatic Truth Grounded in a Plain Reading of Scripture

That Cyril's pedagogical approach reflected his era and had consequences can be most clearly seen by considering the contribution of Epiphanius of Salamis. Best known for his much-referenced compendium of heretical doctrines, his own doctrinal position repays a little attention as does his notorious involvement in the first Origenist controversy. Besides this, he also anticipated the reaction against allegorical reading of scripture, a point that the so-called Antiochenes would emphasize alongside their anti-Alexandrian Christology.[85]

---

85. See further in volume 2.

3.1. Epiphanius: Creedal Dogma and Scripture

Besides the *Panarion*—antidotes for the poison of heresy—Epiphanius wrote a small work entitled the *Well-Anchored One* (*Ancoratus*).[86] Here he affirmed that bad belief (*kakopistia*) was worse than lack of belief (*apistia*) (*Anc.* 9). There are things about which inquiry should not be made, he stated (*Anc.* 18). The true faith he established through formulaic confessions rather than by argument—then current ecclesiastical jargon, one might say. Indeed, Epiphanius not only quotes creeds but his very style and phraseology is comparable to creedal confessions as he piles up his participles: "the holy Word himself . . . becoming man in truth and being God in truth, not changing his nature, not altering his Godhead, begotten in flesh, the enfleshed Word, the Word become flesh" (*Anc.* 19). And so it goes on and on. Christ is "the only-begotten, the perfect, the uncreated, the immutable, the unchangeable, the unknowable, the unseen, become man among us . . . the one who though rich became poor for us . . . one Lord, King, Christ, Son of God, seated in heaven on the right hand of the Father" (*Anc.* 81). But resisting error is the most important guarantee of true faith, and Epiphanius's compendium of false "options" is anticipated in this little treatise, with its eighty heresies and their "mothers" traced back to the early breakdown of humankind's unity and common language as depicted in scripture.

Epiphanius is clear in this little work that scripture is the source of truth, and heresy is false because it does not receive the Spirit according to the traditions of the holy catholic church: "Search the scriptures . . . and the Spirit itself . . . will reveal to you the knowledge of the word of the Son of God, so that you may not wander from the truth and lose your own soul" (*Anc.* 19). In the *Panarion* it is clearly scripture that structures his great divisions of humanity—barbarism, Scythianism, Hellenism, Judaism (Gal 3:28; 6:15; Col 3:11)—and it is the scriptural reference to the eighty concubines in Song of Songs 6:7 that requires him to find eighty heresies. It is the threat to a straightforward reading of scripture that drove his fierce opposition to Origen, already evident in the *Ancoratus*.

Here is not the place to embark on a study of the Origenist controversy, but it is worth noting the grounds on which Epiphanius criticized Origen's legacy.[87] His first charge is that Origen influenced Arius and his followers. Then he ob-

---

86. Greek text of *Ancoratus* and *Panarion* in *Ancoratus und Panarion*, ed. Karl Holl et al., rev. ed., GCS 31, 37; GCSNF 10.1 (Berlin: de Gruyter/Akademie Verlag, 1980, 1985, 2013). Cf. my article, "Did Epiphanius Know What He Meant by Heresy?," StPatr 17 (1982): 199–205.

87. *Ancoratus* 13, 63; 56–58; 86–87; et al. and *Pan.* 64. See further Elizabeth A. Clark, *The Origenist Controversy: The Cultural Construction of an Early Christian Debate* (Princeton: Princeton University Press, 1992), esp. 86–104.

jects to the preexistence of souls and their imprisonment in bodies as a punishment for sin, especially Origen's interpretation of certain scriptural prooftexts to support this, for example, the claim that Adam lost God's image and that his being clothed in tunics of skin refers to the body. Origen's understanding of the resurrection is defective, Epiphanius states, adding that he allegorizes paradise, its waters, and the waters above the earth and below it. Origen's homilies on morals and various other things are fine, but his treatment of doctrines and theology is absurd nonsense. The nub of Epiphanius's objections concerns bodiliness and the material reality of humankind's original creation and eschatological being—these are not to be allegorized or explained away.

Epiphanius has the same pedagogical mindset as we have seen in Cyril, indeed in many ways a more extreme version of it. Dogmas, which are derived from the plain sense of scripture, are to be learned, adhered to, and not questioned for fear of distorting or abandoning the true faith received from the fathers of the holy catholic church.

3.2. Dogma and the Reaction against Allegory

More than once in the past I have addressed the question what lay behind the Antiochene reaction against allegory. I would now argue that the underlying reason was dogmatic rather than methodological.

There was a time when scholars assumed that it was the Antiochene concern with history which drove both their Christology and their exegesis. This was surely a flawed back-projection due to modern interest in the historical Jesus and the historical meaning of scripture. Yes, the Antiochenes were opposed to docetism and campaigned against Origenist allegory, but we need to avoid anachronism and probe deeper to understand their mindset.

My first essays on the subject did focus on methodological issues, suggesting that the Antiochenes followed the philological practices of the rhetorical schools rather than appropriating the tendency of philosophers to read off their doctrines from classics such as Homer by allegorizing.[88] There is surely

---

88. Cf. "The Rhetorical Schools and Their Influence on Patristic Exegesis," in *The Making of Orthodoxy: Essays in Honour of Henry Chadwick*, ed. Rowan Williams (Cambridge: Cambridge University Press, 1989), 182–99; "Typology," in *Crossing the Bondaries: Essays in Biblical Interpretation in Honour of Michael D. Goulder*, ed. Stanley E. Porter, Paul Joyce, and David E. Orton (Leiden: Brill, 1994), 29–48; *Biblical Exegesis and the Formation of Christian Culture* (Cambridge: Cambridge University Press, 1997); also "Re-Thinking the Alexandrian-Antiochene Hermeneutical Antithesis," in *The Oxford Handbook of Origen*, ed. Ronald E. Heine and Karen Jo Torjesen (Oxford: Oxford University Press, 2022), 175–91.

some truth in that perception, but those philological techniques were equally employed by Origen, Didymus, and the allegorists—indeed, they often provided the groundwork for justifying the move from analysis of the "letter" to discerning the "spirit" of the text. All alike recognized that literary devices such as metaphor, parable, and enigma needed interpretation. Furthermore, the critics of allegory also read doctrine out of scripture. It was my attention to the earliest work criticizing Origen that offered a moment of illumination.[89]

Eustathius, bishop of Antioch, wrote a treatise *On the Witch of Endor and against Origen*.[90] At first sight this is an astonishing work in that it criticizes Origen for his literalism! The point is that Origen took the witch's raising up of Samuel as a proof of resurrection, taking no notice of context, narrative flow, or the very term used for the witch (Gk. *engastrimythos*) which means "one who conjures up myths in her innards." The narrative sequence requires the conclusion that Samuel did not come up from Hades, argues Eustathius, but that the witch made it seem so. This triggers disgust at the way Origen here sticks to the letter while allegorizing creation, paradise, and many other things, including Gospel narratives. In other words, he anticipates Epiphanius's objections to Origen by about half a century and provides precedent for Diodore, Theodore, and the later Antiochenes.

As I have argued elsewhere, everyone in antiquity looked for deeper meanings, for moral benefit in reading literature, or for truth about the way things are, and the Antiochenes were no exception.[91] However, they rejected word by word allegory for a more "iconic" approach, whereby the narrative as a whole was to be taken as mirroring underlying truths. Diodore was just as bothered as Origen by a talking, scheming serpent, and acknowledged that it points "by an enigma" to the devil.[92] But such unpacking of riddles must not be allowed to undermine the integrity or reality of the story. Theodore suggests that the allegorists behave "as if the entire *historia* of divine scripture differed in no way from dreams in the night," and continues: "When they start expounding

---

89. See Frances Young, "The Fourth Century Reaction against Allegory," StPatr 30 (1997): 120–25.

90. Greek text in *Eustathii Antiocheni, Patris Nicaeni, opera quae supersunt omnia*, ed. J. H. Declerk, CCSG 31 (Turnhout: Brepols, 2002); see further Rowan A. Greer and Margaret M. Mitchell, *The 'Belly-Myther' of Endor: Interpretations of 1 Kings 28 in the Early Church* (Atlanta: SBL Press, 2007).

91. See Young, *Biblical Exegesis*, esp. 161ff.

92. Diodore, *Prologue to Psalm 118*. Text in Louis Mariès, ed, "Extraits du commentaire de Diodore de Tarse sur les Psaumes: Préface du commentaire—Prologue du Psaume CXVIII," *Recherches de Science religieuse* 9 (1919): 79–101; English translation by Karlfried Froehlich, *Biblical Interpretation in the Early Church* (Philadelphia: Fortress, 1984), 90.

divine scripture 'spiritually'—spiritual interpretation is the name they like to give to their folly—they claim that Adam is not Adam, paradise is not paradise, the serpent not the serpent."[93] In other words, and this is the key point, the Antiochenes objected to a hermeneutic that sat lightly to the overarching biblical narrative at the heart of the rule of faith.[94]

So, *the hermeneutic of scripture was to be determined by doctrine, especially the doctrines concerning creation, fall, paradise, and eschatological renewal.*

3.3. Conclusion

That very point, of course, goes right back to Irenaeus. Whether in creedal form or looser summaries like the rule of faith, *doctrine provided the key to correct scriptural interpretation.* Yet that doctrine was itself distilled from scripture in a process of making sense of it, turning its narratives and prophecy, psalms and wisdom into propositions that articulated the truth revealed. Doctrine or dogma was by now a set of truths to be taught and learned by rote. Definitions had been refined through argument, but the core elements were there from the beginning and the power of dogma lay in the perception that it was the correct understanding of what scripture taught, as agreed and approved by the tradition of the holy catholic church. I find myself nearer to Newman and Behr than I might have expected[95]—the basics of Christian doctrine were there in scripture from the beginning. Yet I would insist that the actual articulation of that underlying doctrine only took place through the clarification of scripture's discourse and the process of argument that we are tracing. Doctrine was increasingly defined and the open-ended intellectual explorations of one such as Origen were curtailed. Yet this did not in the end constrain either an intellectual spirituality or an exegetical imagination—rather it offered an engaging journey into a transcendent Being ever beyond the capacity of creaturely understanding, as we shall discover more fully in volume 2.

---

93. Theodore on Gal 4:24. Text in H. B. Swete, *Theodore on the Minor Epistles of St. Paul* (Cambridge: Cambridge University Press, 1880), 74–75; English translation in Froehlich, *Biblical Interpretation*, 97.

94. See further Frances Young, "Fourth Century Reaction" and "Alexandrian-Antiochene Hermeneutical Antithesis."

95. Cf. chapter 1.

7

Scripture, the Genesis of Doctrine

CONCLUSIONS AND CONSEQUENCES

It was perhaps inevitable that scripture should generate doctrine. Newman was right that scripture is both basic and problematical—"it cannot, as it were, be mapped, or its contents catalogued."[1] The dilemmas posed by the collection of disparate books at the heart of Christianity were perhaps even more obvious when they were not contained in a single volume, but were a multiple book collection whose boundaries took time to determine. A map was needed precisely to communicate what it was all about—what its fundamental teaching was and how to make sense of it. This was an issue to which Augustine, the great theologian of the West, was particularly sensitive. So, as part of the process of attempting to draw some overall conclusions to the present volume, this chapter will engage with his *Teaching Christianity*.[2] In many ways this work proves to be the culmination of the pedagogical traditions we have been tracing, and it can provide a foil for considering the results of our inquiries and their implications. Thus it can shape a review of what we have discovered about the relationship of doctrine and scripture in early Christianity, while also enabling us to look forward to the issues of the second volume, not to mention potential consequences for Christian theology in the postmodern world.

1. See in chapter 1 above.
2. Latin text and translation in *De Doctrina Christiana*, ed. and trans. R. P. H. Green, OECT (Oxford: Clarendon, 1995). References will be given by the book and paragraph numbers adopted by Green from the Latin text provided in CSEL 80. The translation quoted will be that of Edmund Hill (cf. note 3 below). For that reason the older numbering as used there will be added in brackets.

1. Augustine's *Teaching Christianity*: Context and Purpose

Translations of *De doctrina christiana* do not generally use the word "doctrine," for this is by no means a work listing dogmas or creedal statements. The Latin word *doctrina* might convey either the activity of teaching or its content, so we find *On Christian Teaching* or *Teaching Christianity* as translations of the title.[3] Some, however, have implicitly canvassed *On Christian Culture*, for culture in the Roman world was carried by the classics of Greek and Latin literature, the canon on which education was based, and what this work of Augustine is about is interpreting and communicating the substitute canon of classics at the core of the Christian subculture, namely scripture.[4] In part its implicit purpose would seem to be a demonstration that scripture has a powerful rhetoric of its own, despite the reaction to these strange barbarian books from cultured despisers, including at one time Augustine himself. This very discussion of Augustine's title bears out what this first volume has been about—Christianity's shaping of religion to be more "school-like" with dogmas and books conveying teaching about the truth placed absolutely central to its activities. There was no perceived gap between doctrine and scripture in early Christianity.

And maybe that discussion also opens the way to a solution of the much-discussed question: Why and for whom did Augustine write this? It was certainly not intended for catechumens—if anything it would be for their teachers, and a case has been made for that.[5] But perhaps it was undertaken to clarify Augustine's own mind. It seems that Augustine began to compose this work around the time of his consecration as bishop of Hippo. He had spent half his life pursuing a career as a rhetor—that was why he left Carthage for Rome, which resulted in him obtaining a teaching post in Milan, where Ambrose convinced him that Christian scripture was worth a second look. Now he was assuming teaching responsibilities in the church, promoting the Christian way of life on the basis of a different body of literature, and it is perhaps telling

---

3. For the former title see, e.g., *On Christian Teaching*, ed. and trans. R. P. H. Green (Oxford: Oxford University Press, 1997). Appropriate translation of the title is discussed in the introduction to his OECT edition; see the previous note. For the latter title see, e.g., *Teaching Christianity: De Doctrina Christiana*, ed. John E. Rotelle, trans. Edmund Hill, The Works of Saint Augustine 1/11 (Hyde Park: New City, 1996).

4. E.g., Peter Brown, *Augustine of Hippo: A Biography* (London: Faber & Faber, 1967), 263–64, following H.-I. Marrou, *Saint Augustin et la fin de la culture antique* (Paris: de Boccard, 1938). Cf. my *Biblical Exegesis*, especially chapter 3.

5. See the Translator's Note in Hill, *Teaching Christianity*, 95–97.

how *Teaching Christianity* is illuminated by noting parallels with the curriculum offered by the rhetor. As Kannengiesser put it: "His own rhetorical culture needed to be transferred from its former status, private and secular, to a new episcopal status, public and ecclesiastical."[6] The standard exegetical methods of *grammaticus* and *rhetor* clearly underlie Augustine's discussion. These I have mapped more than once in previous publications.[7] In brief, comments on texts would first analyze syntax and vocabulary, identifying figures of speech and generally attending to the wording of the text (*methodikē*), then would provide background information and other explanatory notes concerning the persons, characters, gods, stories, myths, and locations referred or alluded to in the text (*historikē*). Preparation for this involved a wide curriculum of studies, the kind of thing we discovered when considering Origen's teaching activities in chapter 2. Augustine similarly points to the necessity of a broad-ranging curriculum for discerning the reference of unfamiliar terms in scripture: languages (Hebrew and Greek, not just Latin), natural history, numbers, music, medicine, history, topography, astronomy, agriculture, navigation, logic, syllogisms and deduction, mathematics, rhetoric, philosophy—examples of how all of these can be useful appear in book 2 of the work. Augustine even uses the same scriptural justification as Origen had—the plundering of the Egyptians by the departing Israelites (Exod 3:21–22; 12:35–36).[8] Pagan learning is to be exploited, as long as superstition and idolatry are avoided—particularly astrology!

However, especially for the *rhetor*, the discernment (*inventio* or *heuresis*) of the subject matter, as distinct from the style or wording, was fundamental. The idea was to observe the suitability of the style and wording for the topic or argument in hand, for literature was to provide models for the budding orator to imitate. Augustine distinguishes between "things" (Lat. *res*, perhaps "realities") and "signs." Signs, unfamiliar and ambiguous, will be the subject of books 2 and 3 in which examples of scripture's difficulties will be analysed, while book 4 will tackle issues of rhetoric and style. Meanwhile book 1 identifies the realities signified by the sign language used in these biblical books. Thus the work essentially begins with *inventio*—the articulation of what scripture is all about. Doctrine thus provides the fundamental criterion for right reading of scripture, as we have seen before in the work of Irenaeus and Origen.

In his review of all his writings, the *Retractations*, Augustine tells us that he

6. Charles Kannengiesser, "The Interrupted *De doctrina christiana*," in *De Doctrina Christiana: A Classic of Western Culture*, ed. Duane W. H. Arnold and Pamela Bright (Notre Dame: University of Notre Dame Press, 1995), 4.
    7. First in "Rhetorical Schools"; see also *Biblical Exegesis*.
    8. *Doctr. chr.* 2.144–45 [2.40.60]; cf. chapter 2 above.

stopped writing in the midst of book 3 and did not take it up again for some thirty years.[9] Why he broke off he never tells us, but it seems likely that the first two books had already been in circulation—Augustine quotes book 2 in other writings and the early Leningrad Codex transmits books 1 and 2 without books 3 and 4 as *Liber de doctrina christiana*.[10] Quite probably the work was overtaken by the *Confessions*, each of these writings in their own way being a kind of justification of his position as a bishop and, *a propos Teaching Christianity*, a kind of Christian *rhetor* expounding books that once had been strange and foreign to him. Reading and interpreting scripture was not an easy task, and Augustine's prime purpose was to set out rules for tackling this and getting it right.

His Preface shows concern about critics of the project: people who will fail to understand the rules he sets out, people who may try to follow the rules but will fail to get any illumination as a result, but above all, people who reckon they need no rules—a special gift of God is enough for the elucidation of the difficulties of these texts. Augustine dismisses such an attitude: learning the alphabet requires human help—indeed learning language requires hearing it from childhood—so Christians should be willing to learn from human teachers, and teachers should be willing to pass on what they have learned. Paul, though cast to the ground and enlightened by a heavenly voice, still through human agency received baptism and was joined to the church, Augustine writes, adding further biblical examples. With a touch of irony, Augustine tells anyone who boasts of understanding by virtue of a divine gift to refrain from promulgating what they have learned, simply refering others to God's inner teaching. In book 4 Augustine will add reference to the Pastoral Epistles as essential for anyone in a position of teacher in the church. Paul there instructs Timothy and Titus on what and how to teach others:

> So what are we to think? Not, surely, that the apostle is taking up a position against himself, when after saying that teachers are made by the working of the Holy Spirit, he goes on himself to instruct them about what and how to teach? Or is it to be understood that even with the Holy Spirit giving bountifully to teachers in the things they have to teach, their functions as men are not cancelled out; and yet all the same *neither the one who plants is anything nor the one who waters, but the one who gives growth, which is God* (1 Cor 3:7)? (*Doct. chr.* 4.93 [4.16.33])

9. *Retract.* 2.4; English translation in Hill, *Teaching Christianity*, 98, where this extract is quoted.
10. Kannengiesser, "Interrupted," 5; cf. Kenneth B. Steinhauser, "Codex Leningradensis Q.v.I.3: Some Unresolved Problems," in Arnold and Bright, *Classic of Western Culture*, 33–43.

It is hardly surprising, then, that what Augustine offers generally parallels the methods he picked up from his own rhetorical training while addressing the particular problems posed by this alternative canon of literature. Furthermore, it is the moral dimensions of this literature that often attract his attention, as it would have done when he was a *rhetor* attending to the classics, for attention to literature was about formation of character and an ethical way of life. *Doctrina* in general was about a comprehensive cultural tradition being passed on through the reading and interpretation of authoritative books, and Augustine's unparalleled work essentially laid out such a program for Christians, thus confirming the school-like picture of early Christianity that has been advanced in this volume.

1.1. From Augustine's Inventio to Canon Criticism

So the work essentially begins with *inventio*—identifying the subject matter, the "realities" signified by the sign language used in these biblical books. It is sometimes suggested that book 1 presented "the content of Christian doctrine," even "laid out in the pattern of the baptismal creed."[11] However, this is not so obvious. Augustine certainly does not present the rule of faith or a creedal form as scripture's hypothesis in the way Irenaeus had. Rather Augustine begins by arguing his way like a philosopher to what is truly valued—one suspects he has those cultured despisers in mind, those like he once was. Distinguishing things to be enjoyed and things to be used, he outlines the Trinity as the one and only thing truly to be enjoyed for its own sake. In the end he identifies the dominical commandments to love God and love your neighbour as the subject matter of scripture and the criterion whereby any exegesis of any scriptural text is to be assessed—interpretation is misguided if it does not accord with that teaching. This does not seem to present the usual kind of summary of scripture's overarching narrative, or the usual set of doctrines comprised in that rule of faith.

Yet it is worth taking a closer look. For this seems to be Augustine communicating his fundamental theological take on the meaning of scripture, laying out in his own way his *inventio*, putting into his own framework of meaning the traditional rule of faith. As for Rowan Williams so perhaps for Augustine, "the loyal and uncritical repetition of formulae is seen to be inadequate as a

---

11. James J. O'Donnell, "*De Doctrina Christiana*," in *Augustine through the Ages: An Encyclopedia*, ed. Allan D. Fitzgerald, OSA (Grand Rapids: Eerdmans, 1999), 279.

means of securing continuity at anything more than a formal level."[12] Augustine needed to reexpress the realities he sought to communicate, especially if he had those cultured despisers in view.

So having set out the primary distinction between "things" and "signs," Augustine focuses on "things," adds the distinction between "enjoying" and "using," and tells a parable. Suppose we are travelers longing to return and enjoy our homeland: the distraction of enjoyable things along the way would hinder our ultimate goal; for, "delighted with the pleasures of the journey" and "enjoying what we ought to have been using," we would be reluctant "to finish the journey quickly" and so be estranged from the homeland "where alone we could find real happiness." So in this mortal life we are like travellers "away from the Lord" (2 Cor 5:6), and to return to our homeland "we have to use this world, not enjoy it," using it to discern *"the invisible things of God, brought to our knowledge through the things that have been made"* (Rom 1:20)—in other words "proceed from temporal and bodily things to grasp those that are eternal and spiritual" (*Doctr. chr.* 1.8–9 [1.4.4]). Just as for Irenaeus, Cyril of Jerusalem, and others, so for Augustine the material world is good and points to its Creator, though he is all too aware of its distractions.

This God is now characterized as Trinity—Father, Son, and Holy Spirit—and a thumbnail sketch of this doctrine is provided. By now, of course, this is the accepted way to articulate the relationship of the three names in the baptismal creed. Reflection on the sense of God as the most excellent and transcendent thing to be valued above all things, a view that Augustine is sure he holds in common with others, leads him into the perversion by which we are blown away from our homeland, our need for purification, and how "God the Trinity, author and maker of the universe, provides for all the things he has made" (1.22 [1.10.10]), wisdom itself deigning "to adapt herself even to such infirmity as ours," giving us "an example of how to live in no other mode than the human one" (1.23 [1.11.11]). Thus "the foolishness of God is wiser than men" (1 Cor 1:25)—a point now demonstrated through a collage of quotations from Paul and from the Johannine Gospel, which culminates in John 1:14 and a brief explanation of how just as a word in our minds can be spoken while our thought remains intact, "the Word of God was not changed in the least, and yet became flesh, in order to dwell amongst us" (1.26 [1.13.12]).

Wisdom, like a doctor, adapts to our wounds so as to bring healing. Augustine now explains that human beings fell through pride, so wisdom used human nature to bring restoration; deceived by "the wisdom of the serpent" we

---

12. Williams, *Arius*, 236.

were freed by "the foolishness of God." A catalogue of contrasts and similarities suggest not only the principle of homeopathic remedies but also features of Irenaeus's recapitulation doctrine (1.27–30 [1.14.13]). Thus Augustine's *inventio* does come up with the incarnation as the centerpiece of the overarching biblical story of fall and redemption. Belief in resurrection and ascension, future judgment, the church as the body of Christ (with allusions to the New Testament Epistles), and the forgiveness of sin now parallel the creedal pattern (1.31–38 [1.15.14–21.19]). Augustine's *inventio* is surely a fresh expression of the rule of faith, and as we have shown throughout this volume, there was in early Christianity a general assumption—indeed, a deep confidence—that the rule of faith or the creed was coinherent with scripture.

This, as we observed in chapter 1, is the very thing that became problematic in the era of modernist biblical criticism with its overriding interest in historical and literary questions. The single volume Bible was fragmented into its components, the differences between texts deriving from different authors and different centuries was highlighted. The composite nature of many of the texts was noted, analyzed, and split into sources so that the coherence of scripture was challenged, and the gap between Christian doctrine and these fundamental texts was exacerbated. Historical criticism could not establish the unity of the biblical witness. With postmodernism, however, the reaction began in the form of "canon criticism." Brevard S. Childs, in his *Introduction to the Old Testament as Scripture*, argued that the final canonical form of the text should be the focus and all scripture should be read as canon, that is, its genre.[13] Subsequent discussion highlighted the difficulties:[14] Which canon—Catholic, Protestant, Jewish? Can the canon as a whole be interpreted without identifying a key or a canon-within-the-canon, the classic example being the Lutheran insistence on justification by faith as such a key with the somewhat unsatisfactory result that James was judged a "right strawy epistle"? In any case, is it possible to identify the canonical sense without discerning earlier meanings through historical criticism? And what about the history of exegesis and multiple readings of texts?

My own critique of canon criticism arose from Irenaeus's appeal to the rule of faith in the face of gnostic alternative readings: "Irenaeus sensed that immediate context was not enough and that overall context would be unclear

---

13. Brevard S. Childs, *Introduction to the Old Testament as Scripture* (Philadelphia: Fortress, 1979).
14. See further my discussion in *Virtuoso Theology*, 15–17, where I briefly survey the various objections that had been raised.

to an undirected reader put in a library with a pile of codices.... Interpreters needed the guidance of an overall framework, and that overall framework was provided by a community which understood the unitive story."[15] Setting out the difficulties in treating the rule of faith as a summary of scripture, I suggested that the framework for discerning "the unity and harmony of scripture" was "partly external to the text" and suggested that this "framework of interpretation demanded the development of a systematic theology, related to the contents of scripture but not confined to them."[16] In other words canonical reading, I suggested, depends on things beyond the canon, for the gnostics proved that other deductions, other *hypotheses* or results of *inventio* based on this disparate collection of texts, were perfectly possible.

Now, however, in light of our investigations in this volume, I would like to modify somewhat the suggestion that the rule of faith was "partly external to the text," and reinforce the point that it "encapsulates the essential meaning of the text," that "the kernel of scripture ... is enshrined in the plan of salvation," which, as Irenaeus affirmed, was "handed down to us by the will of God in the scriptures" by "those through whom the Gospel came to us."[17] The canon of scripture itself owes its very existence to the network of schools that used these books in their instruction (*doctrina*), which they believed enunciated the truth. Indeed, as we saw in chapter 4, scriptural canon and canon (rule) of faith emerged concurrently and were both received as elements in the apostolic testimony. Furthermore, we have observed both Irenaeus and Origen attesting to the belief that the rule of faith came from the apostles. Surely their instinct that scripture and doctrine were coinherent reflected what in practice was the case: doctrine was derived from reading scripture according to the apostolic testimony, and scripture's proper interpretation was ensured by doctrinal criteria. As we shall see in the next volume, controversy over doctrine arose from different readings of scripture, while appeal to scripture provided proof of the truth of the doctrine in question. In early Christianity doctrine and scripture were treated as coherent with one another, and any proposed doctrine deemed unproven from scripture was treated as heresy, in other words, as another "option"—not the right way of thinking.

So a Christian reading of scripture requires the doctrinal framework that scripture itself generated as interpreters sought to articulate what scripture was all about—that is, Christian identity over time involves accepting the

---

15. Young, *Virtuoso Theology*, 47–48.
16. Young, *Virtuoso Theology*, 53 and 57–58.
17. Young, *Virtuoso Theology*, 53, quoting Irenaeus, *Haer.* 3.1.1.

coinherence of scripture and doctrine and interpreting each in relation to the other. Yet Rowan Williams's statement and Augustine's example also point to the need for fresh expression in different cultural and intellectual contexts. Though perhaps less ready for such open-ended inquiry as Origen, Augustine would hardly seem to endorse the kind of rigid dogmatic tendencies we found in Cyril and Epiphanius, and the words of Rowan Williams quoted earlier continue thus:

> The loyal and uncritical repetition of formulae is seen to be inadequate as a means of securing continuity at anything more than a formal level. Scripture and tradition require to be read in a way that brings out their strangeness, their non-obvious and non-contemporary qualities, in order that they may be read freshly and truthfully from one generation to another.[18]

Only acknowledgment of this "strangeness" can ensure countercultural challenge alongside the inevitable sensemaking through accommodation to current sociocultural and intellectual norms. Searching must accompany certainty, while certainty about the core "realities" must provide criteria for shaping the search for fresh expression and the answers to fresh questions. In volume 2 we will explore the way in which Trinitarian dogma facilitated a questing spirituality. Augustine perhaps might show how a measure of Origen's intellectual inquiry might accompany the firm dogmas of a bishop like Cyril of Jerusalem.

1.2. From Augustine's "Signs" to Scriptural Language and Doctrinal Concepts

"Things" are learned through "signs," states Augustine, introducing his basic distinction. "Things" do not always signify, but sometimes they do, and he instances the log whereby Moses removed the bitter taste of the waters (Exod 15:25), the stone that Jacob placed under his head (Gen 22:13), and the ram Abraham sacrificed in place of his son (Gen 22:13)—all are "signs" of other "things" (*Doct. chr.* 1.4 [1.2.2]). Words, on the other hand, are only used to signify something—though they are also things, otherwise they would not exist (1.5 [1.2.2]).

Turning to "signs" in book 2, Augustine indicates that it is not their existence that matters but rather the fact that they signify: "a sign . . . is a thing, which besides the impression it conveys to the senses, also has the effect of making something else come to mind." A footprint, smoke, a voice, a trumpet:

---

18. Williams, *Arius*, 236.

each indicates something other than itself (2.1 [2.1.1]). Some signs are natural, like the smoke that indicates fire, others given, particularly by one human to another, and "even the signs given by God, which are contained in the holy scriptures have been indicated to us through the human beings who wrote them down" (2.3 [2.2.3]). Augustine is as aware as modern historical critics are that the scriptures are human artifacts.

He now explores a range of signs used for communication—hand signals, flags, musical sounds, even finding examples from scripture such as the smell of the ointment with which Jesus's feet were anointed (John 12:3–7) or the healing of the woman who touched the hem of his garment (Matt 9:20–22; Mark 5:25–29; Luke 8:43–44). But words predominate and, fleeting though they are, the invention of letters means there are signs of words. Unfortunately, however, Babel meant the same signs could not be shared among all nations, and so even divine scripture ended up in the various languages of translators.

This disparity of signs implies a certain relativity in Augustine's thought, and indeed he exploits differing human conventions in more than one way. In book 2 he notes how the letter X, which denotes ten in Latin, has another value in Greek, its meaning not being by nature but reflecting some kind of agreement about what it should signify. Similarly *lege* is understood in one way by a Greek speaker and another by a Latin speaker. People in each language group "have not agreed about their meanings because they already had in themselves any signifying value," but because of convention (2.93 [2.24.37]). In book 3 he notes that social conventions vary, so "we have to pay careful attention to what befits places and times and persons" (3.45 [3.12.19]) and not hastily judge customs in dress or marriage, such as the polygamy of the patriarchs (3.47–49, 60–61 [3.12.20; 18.26–27]). However, Augustine is quick to insist that justice is not mutable or nonexistent (3.52 [3.14.22]), and soon he is pursuing the kind of moral criticism practiced in the rhetorical schools—the stories of King David are not examples to be followed, rather the figurative meaning is to be sought, though the recording of the sins of great men should be a warning and so the literal meaning has its use (3.67–74 [3.21.30–23.33]). Augustine may recognize a certain moral relativism and indeed the social location of language, but the signs have meaning because of the "realities" to which they point, that is, the reference to which a person intends to point by using those signs.

Still, some, such as Umberto Eco, have found an anticipation of postmodern semiotics in Augustine's sign theory:[19] "Textual semiotics and contemporary hermeneutics still move along the main lines set down by Augustine,

---

19. See my discussion in "Augustine's Hermeneutics and Postmodern Criticism," *Interpretation* 58.1 (2004): 42–55.

even when they are secularised semiotics or hermeneutics, even when they do not recognise their origin, and even when they look upon a worldly poetic text as sacred and a repository of infinite wisdom."[20] Augustine certainly did understand like postmodern theorists that there is no natural connection between a word and that to which it refers, and that metaphor and figures of speech render language even less direct. However, in his view it is *res* (realities) that are signified, precisely the point that postmodernism has called into question. He did not anticipate such radical relativism. Augustine "stipulates in advance what the terminus of the scriptural signs is and thus establishes the control in the light of which we are to interpret those signs. Augustine's is not, then, a neutral or disinterested concern with signs and signification. Once we know what scripture signifies, we can discern whether its locutions are figurative or not in any given case."[21] Yet to get from the signs to the realities is by no means straightforward. Readers aim somehow to find out "the thoughts and will of the authors it was written by" (*Doct. chr.* 2.9 [2.5.6]). Augustine might appear to share the notion of authorial intention with modern historical critics. However, his interests are not the same, as is evident in his emphasis on discovering thereby the will of God, not to mention the way in which he accounts for problems, ambiguities, and indeed the use of imagery. Like Origen, Augustine thinks these were intended by the Holy Spirit to counter pride, stimulate inquiry and effort, and prevent boredom.[22]

> What is not in dispute . . . is both that one gets to know things more enjoyably through such comparisons, and also that discovering things is much more gratifying if there has been some difficulty in the search for them. . . . Magnificent and salutary, therefore, is the way the Holy Spirit has so adjusted the holy scriptures, that they ward off starvation with the clearer passages, while driving away boredom with the obscure ones. There is almost nothing, in fact, that can be extracted from their obscurities, which cannot be found very plainly said somewhere else. (*Doct. chr.* 11.13–15 [2.6.8])

Augustine clearly accepts the principle of interpreting scripture by scripture, but probing the sense and reference of the signs is still no easy task. So books 2

---

20. Umberto Eco, quoted by Luigi Alici in the Introduction to Hill, *Teaching Christianity*, 50 n. 72.
21. Quotes from W. S. Babcock, "Caritas and Signification," in Arnold and Bright, *Classic of Western Culture*, 147 and 155.
22. Cf. 1.2 in chapter 5 above.

and 3 work through the problems of unfamiliar and ambiguous signs, literal and figurative language, scripture's various tropes and their significance, the meaning constantly being referred back to the will of God, which is love of God and love of neighbor.

The language of scripture thus points beyond itself, may carry multiple meanings, and keys are needed to unlock its hidden meanings. Augustine is in line with most exegetes of early Christianity, pursuing prophetic and christological meanings and engaging in a constructive critique of Tyconius's *Rules* to show how each rule results "in one being understood for another," this being "the peculiarity of figurative speech" (3.133 [3.37.56]). So, for example, "when things are said about Solomon which exceed his limitations," they "become luminously clear when referred to Christ or the church, of which Solomon is a part" (3.108 [3.34.47]). We need not pursue the details, as Augustine engages in discussion of many examples, except to note how Augustine incorporates into his sign-system the long-standing distinction between Jewish practices, which carry out "literally" all the prescriptions in the Law—circumcision, sacrifices, etc.—and Christian treatment of such legislation as fulfilled and rendered obsolete by Christ. Augustine indicates that "our freedom" consists in no longer being "burdened with the heavy duty of carrying out even those signs whose meaning we now understand." Rather from the Lord and from the apostles "just a few signs" have been "handed down to us"

> so easy to perform, and so awesome to understand, and so pure and chaste to celebrate, such as the sacrament of baptism, and the celebration of the Lord's body and blood. When people receive these, they have been so instructed that they can recognize to what sublime realities they are to be referred, and so they venerate them in a spirit not of carnal slavery, but rather of spiritual freedom. (*Doct. chr.* 3.30–32 [3.9.13])

So what about the language of doctrinal propositions? Is this different from the language of scripture? How do such statements signify? What kind of relationship is there between them and the realities to which they point? Let us take a closer look at Augustine's outline of the Trinity in book 1.10–12 (1.5.5):

1. The Trinity is "one supreme thing," or perhaps "the cause of all things; if indeed it is a cause." Already Augustine confesses that "to find any name that will really fit such transcendent Majesty" is not easy.
2. In fact it is better to say that "this Trinity is the one God *from whom are all things, through whom all things, in whom all things*" (Rom 11:36).

3. "Thus Father and Son and Holy Spirit are both each one of them singly God and all together one God; and each one of them simply is the complete divine substance, and altogether are one substance."
4. So "the Father is neither the Son nor the Holy Spirit; the Son is neither the Father nor the Holy Spirit; the Holy Spirit is neither the Father nor the Son"; each is simply itself, in other words, though "the three possess the same eternity, the same unchangeableness, the same greatness, the same power."
5. Finally, Augustine lodges their unity in the Father, their equality in the Son, and their harmony of unity and equality in the Holy Spirit.

Augustine seems to know what he is talking about, but he immediately confesses that his solemn utterance is "not worthy of God" (1.13 [1.6.6]). He has simply wished to say something, but failed to say what he wished to say. That is because God is inexpressible, yet in calling God inexpressible he has made God expressible—there is "Heaven knows what kind of battle of words," and "this battle of words should be avoided by keeping silent, rather than resolved by the use of speech." Yet, even though "nothing really worthy of God can be said about him, he has accepted the homage of human voices"—God wants to be praised with our words. Just hearing the syllables of the word "God" (*Deus* in Latin, so two syllables) evokes reflection on "some most exalted and immortal nature," and "our thoughts strive to attain to something than which there is nothing better or more sublime" (1.14 [1.7.7]). Augustine is convinced of the reality of the Trinity, but also of the inadequacy of the signs used to evoke the "thingness" to which they refer. So both scripture and doctrine point beyond themselves.

Augustine thus adopts the apophatic theology of so many early Christian thinkers, though his expression of it is again adapted to the particular discussion in which he is engaged. He does not produce a string of negatives—invisible, incorporeal, infinite, ineffable, incomprehensible, etc.—but rather anticipates Anselm.[23] God is that "than which there is nothing better or more sublime," and verbal signs are inadequate to convey such a reality.

Two issues arise: (1) how is it that apparently precise doctrinal propositions could sit alongside the adoption of abstract philosophical apophaticism? And (2) is apophaticism, as so many in the twentieth century thought, a mark of Hellenization—the loss of the personal God of the Bible in the abstractions of Greek philosophy?

---

23. Cf. Hill, *Teaching Christianity*, 126 n. 8. Did this suggest to Anselm his "quasi-definition of God as that than which nothing greater can be thought of"?

The first of these questions will prove particularly telling in volume 2, where we will trace the arguments that led to what some might call the "definition" of Trinitarianism. The fact is that it was the rejection of claims to define the Being of God which ultimately shaped the doctrine of the Trinity. And for Augustine here in *Teaching Christianity*, it is the very paradox of the one-in-three, the three distinct names in scripture and creed, each and all together being the one God, which means silence alone is possible, though God does wish us "to rejoice in praising him." Implicit is that deep sense of the radical difference between creatures and Creator, a profoundly scriptural viewpoint that we have seen shaping doctrinal debates throughout. Apophatic theology sat alongside and complemented doctrinal propositions for good reason.

As for the second question, I have long since argued that the traffic went the other way, and made the point again in chapter 3 above: it was the scriptures that radicalized the apophaticism of Platonism.[24] On the one hand, Platonism was always confident that through synthesis, analysis, and analogy one could speak about the divine and that, through its likeness to the divine, once the mind was sufficiently purified it would know God. Also it never took a positive view of infinity, which was associated with nonbeing, so its sense of God's incomprehensibility was never absolute. By contrast, Hellenistic Judaism was already more radically apophatic: even in the New Testament God is described as unapproachable, untraceable, inscrutable, and incomprehensible.[25] It was in the Judeo-Christian tradition that infinity came to be seen in positive terms, the Creator God containing all things without being contained.[26] The Jewish tradition of never pronouncing the name of God, along with certain key biblical texts such as "my thoughts are not your thoughts nor my ways your ways" (Isa 55:8) underlined the difference between creature and Creator, not to mention the inherent limitations of creaturely intelligence: "no one can see God and live" (Exod 33:20). It is hardly surprising that Origen could argue that God's incorporeality was expressed in scripture by means other than the use of that term.[27] Nor is it astonishing that biblical anthropomorphisms were interpreted allegorically in the same way as the philosophers treated Greek myths. In the ambient intellectual context it was inevitable that Platonist conceptions of God would be read into the scriptures, but there was more congruence than has often been recognized.

24. Cf. chapters 3.2.2 and 6.2.1 above. For fuller argument, see my article "God of the Greeks."
25. 1 Tim 6:16; Rom 11:33; Eph 3:8; cf. LXX, Philo, and Josephus.
26. Irenaeus, *Haer.* 3.1.2.
27. Cf. 2.2.4 in chapter 5 above.

What we have traced in this volume is the way in which a form of discourse was formulated from the "signs" of scripture, with all their multiplicity and complexity, which was comprehensible within the prevailing intellectual mindset and could represent the truth, however inadequately. Its language and concepts would, of course, be "Hellenistic," but that need not imply a betrayal of the realities to which scripture points. The next volume will explore the way in which proposed concepts were tested against scripture and refined through exegetical argument. Making sense of scripture is what generated doctrine.

1.3. From Augustine's Pedagogy to the Twenty-First-Century Renaissance in Theological Interpretation of Scripture

As we have seen, Augustine believed in the human transmission of teaching and his pedagogy was intended to change lives. Book 4 moves from questions about content to issues of style, that is, of effective communication. What is required on the part of the teacher is both wisdom and eloquence. It is not surprising that we can trace the *rhetor*'s experience here, despite Augustine disdaining to offer a standard rhetorical textbook. Such training can be had elsewhere, he says (*Doct. chr.* 4.3 [4.1.2]), and it is worth noting that Augustine's Christian pedagogy was never exercised in a school like that of Origen—it was integrated into the life and liturgy of the church through the reading of scripture and the delivery of sermons. Through much of book 4 Augustine will give examples of how the authors of scripture actually deploy rhetorical tropes and do so naturally, for like the acquisition of language itself such tropes can be learned simply by listening to good speakers. Such material, however, need not detain us here. The significant point is surely his emphasis on generating action on the part of the hearers, for, properly communicated, scripture presents God's word and God's will: response is required.

Ancient rhetorical theory identified three poles needed for conviction (*pistis*): (1) the speaker/author needed to have the right reputation, character, and lifestyle (*ethos*); (2) the content (*logos*) needed to be convincing; and (3) the hearers/readers needed to be swayed to respond (*pathos*).[28] Augustine's dis-

---

28. See James L. Kinneavy, *Greek Rhetorical Origins of Christian Faith* (Oxford: Oxford University Press, 1987). This triangle I have previously developed in several places: *The Theology of the Pastoral Letters* (Cambridge: Cambridge University Press, 1994); "Proverbs 8 in Interpretation (2): Wisdom Personified," in *Reading Texts, Seeking Wisdom*, ed. David F. Ford and Graham Stanton (London: SCM, 2003), 102–15 (republished in Young, *Exegesis and Theology*); "Ways of Reading the Bible: Can We Relativize the Historico-Critical Method

cussion presupposes this triangle: (1) *Ethos* is fundamental. "Whatever the grandeur of the speaker's utterances, his manner of life carries more weight," Augustine says. Yes, to speak "wisely and eloquently" can provide instruction, even "while living a worthless life," and "things that are right and true may be preached by a twisted and deceitful heart," so such preachers may "benefit many people by saying what they do not do, but they would benefit far more by doing what they say" (4.151–153 [4.27.59–60]). (2) Fundamental too is *pathos*—generating response is vital: "if the listeners are to be moved rather than instructed, so as not to become sluggish in acting upon what they know, and so as to give a real assent to things they admit are true, more forceful kinds of speaking are called for. Here what is necessary is words that implore, that rebuke, that stir, that check" (*Doct. chr.* 4.15 [4.4.6]). So, when "trying to persuade the people about something that has to be done," it is important "not only to teach, in order to instruct them; not only to delight, in order to hold them; but also to sway, in order to conquer and win them" (4.79 [4.13.29]). (3) Nor is the need neglected for the content (*logos*) to be understandable and true (4.150 [4.26.58]). The speaker intends "that by his words the truth should become clear to his hearers, that the truth should please them, that the truth should move them" (4.157 [4.28.61]). In Augustine's pedagogy, then, the three poles properly interact to produce not just conviction but action, and *Teaching Christianity* implies that the reading and interpretation of scripture involves that same interaction.

It could be said that during my scholarly career attention has shifted from each one of those poles to another. The author (the *ethos* pole, one might say) held sway as the historico-critical method focused on the original author's intent in the original context and sought objectively "to think the author's thoughts after him." Then came a reaction: Roland Barthes's famous article, "The Death of the Author."[29] It was recognized that the author has no control over the text once it is published. Structuralism attended to the meaning inherent in the text itself (the *logos*), and it was recognized that texts are not confined to the authorial meaning but may have unforeseen futures. Then came reader-response theory—a text is only realized when a reader turns the

---

and Rediscover a Biblical Spirituality?," in *Reading Scripture for Living the Christian Life*, ed. Bernard Treacy with Frances Young, J. Cecil McCullough, and Thomas Brodie (Dublin: Dominican, 2009), 7–25; republished as chapter 1 of Young, *Ways of Reading Scripture*, 9–24.

29. English translation in *Modern Criticism and Theory: A Reader*, ed. David Lodge (Harlow: Longman, 1988), 167–72.

black and white marks on the page into some kind of sense and reacts (*pathos*, so to speak); a text may be read differently on different occasions even by the same reader, while reading communities can establish traditions of reading. After these swings of the interpretative pendulum surely we need a return to that triangle, to acknowledging the interaction of author, text, and reader or, as Augustine explores it, of speaker, content, and hearer. It is these moves beyond the historico-critical straitjacket that have allowed the now fashionable reclamation of theological reading of scripture, and I suggest could potentially permit a return to seeing doctrine and scripture as coinherent, closing that gap we described in the opening chapter. Maybe this can only be tested out properly at the end of volume 2, when we have explored the way in which scripture was the genesis of Christology and the distinctive Christian doctrine of God as Trinity.

It is worth noting Augustine's emphasis was on more than instruction; it was also on the need to sway, to move readers and listeners into response and action. This is what the objectivity of the historico-critical method could so easily bracket out—indeed, the reason why it was perceived to generate no hermeneutic and why it exacerbated that gap. The move to "theological reading" does not seem to be so much an attempt to justify classic doctrines all over again, but rather an opening up to letting the prophets and apostles judge and challenge scripture's readers, a call to respond in discipleship to God in Christ, as distinct from the tendency of the historico-critic to make judgments, whether about the text's authenticity or its meaning.[30]

Augustine would certainly endorse this. In book 2 he had long since set out stages in response to scripture (*Doct. chr.* 2.16–24 [2.7.9–11]):

1. The first stage is being "converted by the fear of God to wishing to know his will."
2. Then comes growing "modest with piety"—not contradicting scripture as if we "could have better ideas and make better rules ourselves."
3. The third stage is that of knowledge: "that God is to be loved on God's account, and one's neighbour on God's account."
4. Then comes fortitude as "one extricates oneself from all deadly delight in passing things . . . turning instead to love eternal things."
5. Then comes counsel and mercy, as "you purge your restless . . . soul" and "drill yourself diligently in love of your neighbour."

---

30. See, e.g., David F. Ford, *The Gospel of John: A Theological Commentary* (Grand Rapids: Baker Academic, 2021).

6. Then "those eyes with which God can be seen" are purged by dying to the world, to become "single-minded and pure in heart."
7. Finally, such holy people can climb to wisdom.

It has been noted that the seven stages are basically the gifts of the Spirit found in Isaiah 11:2–3, interwoven with the Beatitudes and listed in reverse order because Psalm 111:10 states that the fear of the Lord is the beginning of wisdom.[31] Be that as it may, for Augustine scripture is God's word and conveys God's will: it is meant to teach love of God and love of neighbor and to generate a response of fear, amendment, and love.

Maybe the current renaissance of theological reading of scripture enables a renewal of "doctrine" in the life of the church, doctrine in the broader sense of teaching, teaching that inspires, challenges, and changes lives, teaching that is grounded in the biblical material. For doctrine, whether in Augustine's sense or in our sense, is in the end communicating authoritatively (*ethos*) the fundamental meaning of scripture (*logos*), so elucidating God's word and God's will as to get a response (*pathos*) in devotion (loving God) and in action (loving the neighbor).

2. Beyond That Gap: An Interim Report

Given that huge issues remain to be discussed in volume 2—issues such as the basis for Trinitarian theology in scripture—any conclusions outlined at this point are bound to be interim. But surely some historical and theological consequences may be sketched as a result of this attempt at redescribing the process whereby statements of doctrine emerged alongside scripture as central to the identity of Christianity. In chapter 1 we identified the currently perceived gap between scripture and doctrine, usually bridged by the model of "development" or the notion of "Hellenization." Can we move beyond these bridges, indeed, beyond the gap?

First, we need to articulate the presuppositions behind the gap. Both the "Hellenization" theory and the "development" account assume the post-Darwinian mindset—the paradigm of evolution—which is as all pervasive in modern culture as Platonism was in the world of the early church. Maybe what we are really dealing with is the gap between the empiricism of modernity and the intellectual culture of the ancients. This one-time empiricist has a vivid

---

31. Hill, *Teaching Christianity*, 162 n. 6.

recollection of listening to a student colleague back in the 1960s expounding Christian belief top-down, beginning with the Trinity, her inner reaction being profound resistance—surely you had to start where we are, look at the evidence, begin with scripture interpreted historically, and empirically trace subsequent doctrinal development.

Even if we stay within that paradigm for a moment we have made two crucial findings that put the two kinds of "development" theses into a somewhat different perspective:

1. The rule of faith—essentially a summary of the teaching delivered to aspiring Christians and enshrined in baptismal formulae—was received as apostolic along with the scriptures from very early on, and bears the marks of a Christian "in-language" shared with those who composed the New Testament scriptures. There never was a gap between scripture and basic Christian teaching.
2. So far from adopting "Hellenized" conceptions, the essentially biblical, yet profoundly countercultural, view of God as the transcendent Creator of everything rapidly became a crucial criterion for determining the appropriate formulation of Christian teaching—a fundamental point that would persist through the argumentation that produced the doctrine of the Trinity, as we shall see in volume 2.

Thus the historical process was not so much a "development"—certainly not an alien importation but rather the articulation within that particular intellectual context of what had been received from the apostles, and the identification of scripture's overarching unitive narrative, from the beginning to the end, as an account of fall and redemption under the providential oversight of the one true Creator God, to whom all human creatures are accountable. These findings, mere modifications of modernist historical accounts though they be, also expose a paradigm shift away from tracing the supposed evolution of tradition to an examination of questions asked, solutions proposed, and outcomes debated.

For the implicit paradigm adopted in this work is postmodern, focused as it is on discourse, language, and hermeneutics. Postmodernism is notoriously difficult to define, but as a reaction to modernist empiricism it focuses on the way human beings construct or negotiate meaning and identity through language and interpretation. And that is what we set out to do—to trace how the definition of doctrine came about through the endeavor to make sense of scripture in terms of the rationality of the time. The underlying motive for articulating the meaning of scripture in dogmatic propositions was the belief that these books constituted the word of God and it was vital to teach that word for the sake of human salvation. Scripture rightly interpreted offered divine pedagogy—the *doctrina* needed to become what God intended humankind to become. The doctrines deduced along the way were at the time assumed to be coinherent with their scriptural basis, to be an expression of the Spirit's intention—even those which were eventually determined in hindsight not to be orthodox, as in the case of Origen.

Construing scripture raised questions, then, particularly about the true meaning of this collection of books, and what we have observed is the resultant reading, interpreting, and summarizing—indeed, the restating in propositional terms with universal relevance—of scriptural prophecy and poetry, narrative and drama with its roles and characters. In other words, the rational and intellectual process of humans making sense within a particular intellectual culture of texts received as holy and as God-given, a process traceable in historical terms, possibly inspired, but that claim would take us beyond history to theology. Hopefully this has yielded for now a plausible account of the genesis of doctrine from scripture through the early church's search for a viable hermeneutic. What is remarkable, looking back over our journey through this volume, are the profound continuities, through to Cyril of Jerusalem and Augustine via Origen, from the initial second-century mapping of the basic shape of the scriptural narrative, with its fundamental focus on God's providential purposes through creation, fall, redemption, and eschaton. This also alerts us to the fact that dogmas were never discrete, never piecemeal, because it was the way they fit together into a coherent conception of the overarching biblical narrative that constantly shaped their formulation.

Of course, the developmental model was partially true, though we are perhaps more ready than Newman to admit that it might not have worked out that way after all; those other "options" (*haireseis*) might have prevailed and, as we noted in the opening chapter, the Monarchian solution still has cachet in some contemporary Christian circles. So what was it that prevented that outcome? Was it the quality of argument? Or was it the plausibility of the apostolic testimony? Or was it the coherence of these doctrines with the scriptural witness? All three might be Irenaeus's answer, but we may be in a better position to respond at the end of volume 2. Of course, the theory of Hellenization was also partially true—it was the demands of the pervading intellectual culture that raised the questions about the essential teaching (*doctrina*) of this ostensibly haphazard collection of books. But in this account we have not ignored the challenge offered to the pervading cultural milieu by Christian teaching derived from scripture. Notable has been a persistent emphasis on the goodness of the created material order and the creatureliness of even the spiritual and intellectual realm. In due course this would dramatically shift the Platonist tendencies of theologians such as Gregory of Nyssa and Augustine.[32]

Partially true though they be, those older approaches nevertheless had potentially negative implications: "Hellenization" seemed to mean the loss of the original primitive gospel, "development" some kind of automatic in-built evolution, like the proverbial oak growing from an acorn. Such potentially negative consequences have here been circumvented, while positive aspects of each approach have been taken up into the overall picture. For undoubtedly there was over time a process, an emergence of approved statements of doctrine shaped by then current intellectual frameworks, but it was the outcome of an implicit search for the truth, indeed for identity, through argument and by the exegesis of texts received as authoritative scripture.

So we may welcome the "postmodern turn," especially perhaps the perspectives offered by focusing not simply on the original or authorial meaning but on the text itself, on readers' responses, and on the future of the text, its formative impact as it becomes generative of new meaning. There is potential here for opening up ways of closing the gap, reducing the tensions between biblical scholarship and dogmatic argument, and reclaiming the perspective of the early Church on the coinherence of doctrine and scripture. The old historico-critical approach of modernity allowed the reader to sit in judgment over the text and its origins, sources, or veracity; now perhaps there is potential for nurturing a certain intellectual humility, for encouraging readers to receive from scripture and respond rather than seeking mastery of the text. The old approach generated that gap not just between doctrine and scripture but between scripture and liturgy. Now perhaps there is potential for enabling a renewed theological reading within the liturgy of the church and the devotion of the believer, along with a certain respect for the future of the text, namely, the canonical meaning within the doctrinal framework that the church over time has discerned as the essential sense of the biblical witness as a whole. To be able to reclaim from the early church the essential coinherence of scripture and doctrine could encourage greater ecumenical consensus about the unity of tradition and scripture, as well as gain what might be termed an ecumenism over time, a sense of continuity in identity across the centuries. This would surely mean accepting the discernment of the early church that the rule of faith provides the nugget that may be hammered out into the rich gold leaf of the

---

32. See my article "Creation and Human Being."

overarching scriptural narrative—the unifying story of fall and redemption in which all humankind can potentially find its meaning, its identity, and its future. Also it might mean perhaps finding a new appreciation of the imagination whereby biblical narratives and symbols were drawn through typology into a multilayered tapestry depicting God's providential artistry from creation to eschaton.[33]

But these reflections can only be a preliminary response—the beginning of an answer—for we have not yet faced up to questions such as whether the Christian doctrine of God as Trinity or the Chalcedonian definition of the nature of Christ can really be read out of scripture or defended as biblical. As noted in chapter 1, I have previously charged systematic theologians with just carrying on with trying to make sense of such formulations within our current intellectual culture without facing the fact that modern approaches to reading scripture are so fundamentally different to those of the past: Do they not need scriptural justification all over again?[34] Those central matters of doctrine surely demand further attention. We need to retrace the doctrinal deductions of the early church, reconsider the proofs they offered, and then perhaps ask how far they remain valid. Could such a review permit a return to doctrinal reading of scripture as a whole, centered on Christ and conceiving the one God as Trinity? This is the challenge to be faced in volume 2.

---

33. For possible developments along these lines see my *Construing the Cross* and *Brokenness and Blessing: Towards a Biblical Spirituality* (Grand Rapids: Baker Academic, 2007); see also Andrew Louth, *Discerning the Mystery: An Essay on the Nature of Theology* (Oxford: Clarendon, 1983), and Ephraim Radner, *Time and the Word: Figural Reading of the Christian Scriptures* (Grand Rapids: Eerdmans, 2016).

34. See my article "The 'Mind' of Scripture: Theological Readings of the Bible in the Fathers," *International Journal of Systematic Theology* 7 (2005): 126–41.

Bibliography

TEXTS AND TRANSLATIONS

Acts of the Christian Martyrs. Edited and translated by H. Musurillo. OECT. Oxford: Clarendon, 1972.
Apostolic Constitutions. Text in *Les constitutions apostoliques*. Edited by Marcel Metzger. 3 vols. SC 320, 329, 336. Paris: Cerf, 1985–1987.
The Apostolic Fathers. Edited and translated by R. H. Lightfoot. 2 vols. London: Macmillan, 1885, 1890.
Athanasius. *Contra Gentes and De Incarnatione*. Edited and translated by Robert W. Thomson. OECT. Oxford: Clarendon, 1971.
———. *The Incarnation of the Word of God: De Incarnatione Verbi Dei*. Translated by a religious of C. S. M. V. 2nd ed. London: Mowbray, 1953.
Athenagoras. *Legatio and De Resurrectione*. Edited and translated by William R. Schoedel. OECT. Oxford: Clarendon, 1972.
Augustine. *City of God*. Translated by Henry Bettenson. Edited by David Knowles. Harmondsworth: Penguin, 1972.
———. *De Civitate Dei libri viginti et duo*. Edited by Bernard Dombart and Alphonse Kalb. 2 vols. Leipzig: Teubner, 1928–1929.
———. *De Doctrina Christiana*. Edited and translated by R. P. H. Green. OECT. Oxford: Clarendon, 1995.
———. *On Christian Teaching*. Edited and translated by R. P. H. Green. Oxford: Oxford University Press, 1997.
———. *On Genesis: A Refutation of the Manichees*. Pages 39–102 in *On Genesis*. Translated by Edmund Hill. Edited by John E. Rotelle. The Works of Saint Augustine 1/13. Hyde Park: New City, 2002.

———. *Teaching Christianity: De Doctrina Christiana*. Translated with notes by Edmund Hill. Edited by John E. Rotelle. The Works of Saint Augustine 1/11. Hyde Park: New City, 1996.

———. *Unfinished Literal Commentary on Genesis*. Pages 114–51 in *On Genesis*. Translated by Edmund Hill. Edited by John E. Rotelle. The Works of Saint Augustine 1/13. Hyde Park: New City, 2002.

Cicero. *On the Nature of the Gods. Academics*. Edited and translated by H. Rackham. LCL. Cambridge: Harvard University Press, 1933.

Clement of Alexandria. *Stromata I–VI*. Edited by O. Stählin. GCS 15. Leipzig: Hinrichs, 1906.

Cyprian. *De Lapsis and De Ecclesiae Catholicae Unitate*. Edited and translated by Maurice Bévenot. Oxford: Clarendon, 1971.

Cyril of Alexandria. *Commentary on John*. Translation of selections in *Cyril of Alexandria*. Translated by Norman Russell. London: Routledge, 2000.

Cyril of Jerusalem. *Catechetical Orations*. Text in *S. Patris Nostri Cyrilli Hiersolymorum Archiepiscopi Opera quae supersunt Omnia*. Edited by W. K. Reischl and J. Rupp. Munich: Libraris Lentneriana, 1848–60. Translation of selections in *Cyril of Jerusalem*. Translated by Edward Yarnold, SJ. London: Routledge, 2000.

Epiphanius. *Ancoratus*. Text in Pages 1–149 of *Epiphanius I: Ancoratus und Panarion haer. 1–33*. Edited by Karl Holl, Marc Bergermann, and Christian-Friedrich Collatz. GCSNF 10.1. Berlin: de Gruyter, 2013.

———. *Panarion*. Text in *Epiphanius I: Ancoratus und Panarion haer. 1–33*. Edited by Karl Holl, Marc Bergermann, and Christian-Friedrich Collatz. GCSNF 10.1. Berlin: de Gruyter, 2013; *Epiphanius II: Panarion haer. 34–64*. Edited by Karl Holl and Jürgen Dummer. GCS 31. Berlin: Akademie Verlag, 1980; Pages 1–496 in *Epiphanius III: Panarion haer. 65–80; De fide*. Edited by Karl Holl and Jürgen Dummer. GCS 37. Berlin: Academie Verlag, 1985. English translation in *The Panarion of St. Epiphanius, Bishop of Salamis: Selected Passages*. Translated and edited by Philip R. Amidon, SJ. Oxford: Oxford University Press, 1990.

Eusebius. *Church History*. Text in *Eusebius Werke: Die Kirchengeschichte*. Edited by Eduard Schwartz. 2 vols. GCS 9. Leipzig: Hinricks, 1908. Translation in *The History of the Church*. Translated by G. A. Williamson. Harmondsworth: Penguin, 1965.

Gospel of Truth. Translations in *The Gnostic Scriptures: A New Translation with Annotations and Introductions*. Translated and edited by Bentley Layton. London: SCM, 1987; George W. MacRae. "The Gospel of Truth." Pages 37–49 in *The Nag Hammadi Library in English*. Edited by James M. Robinson. Leiden: Brill, 1977.

Gregory of Nazianzus. *Theological Orations.* In *Faith Gives Fullness to Reasoning: The Five Theological Orations of St. Gregory Nazianzen.* Edited by F. W. Norris with F. Williams and L. Wickham. VCSup 13. Leiden: Brill, 1991.

Gregory Thaumaturgus. *Oratio Panegyrica.* In *Grégoire de Thaumaturge: Remerciement à Origène suivi de la letter d'Origène à Grégoire.* Edited by H. Crouzel. SC 148. Paris: Cerf, 1969.

Hippolytus. *Refutatio omnium haeresium.* Text in *Hippolytus Werke: Refutatio omnium haeresium.* Edited by Paul Wendland. GCS 26. Leipzig: Hinrichs, 1916. Translation in Werner Foerster. *Gnosis: A Selection of Gnostic Texts.* Vol. 1. *Patristic Evidence.* Translated by R. McL. Wilson. Oxford: Oxford University Press, 1972.

(Ps.-)Hippolytus. *The Apostolic Tradition.* Text in B. Botte. *La tradition apostolique de saint Hippolyte: Essai de reconstitution.* Liturgiewissenschaftliche Quellen und Forschungen 39. Münster: Aschendorff, 1963. Translation in *On the Apostolic Tradition.* Translated by Alistair Stewart-Sykes. Crestwood, NY: St. Vladimir's Seminary Press, 2001.

Historia Philosophiae Graecae. Edited by H. Ritter and L. Preller. Gotha: Perthes, 1888.

Irenaeus. *Adversus Haereses.* Text in *Sancti Irenaei episcopi Lugdunensis libros quinque adversus Haereses.* Edited by W. W. Harvey. 2 vols. Cambridge: Typis Academis, 1857.

———. *On the Apostolic Preaching.* Translated and edited by John Behr. Crestwood, NY: St. Vladimir's Seminary Press, 1997.

Justin. *1 Apology.* Text in *Iustini Martyris Apologiae pro Christianis.* Edited by Miroslav Markovich. PTS 38. Berlin: de Gruyter, 1994. Translation in *Justin, Philosopher and Martyr: Apologies.* Edited and translated by Denis Minns and Paul Parvis. OECT. Oxford: Clarendon, 2009.

———. *Dialogue with Trypho.* Text in *Iustini Martyris Dialogus cum Tryphone.* Edited by Miroslav Markovich. PTS 47. Berlin: de Gruyter, 1994.

Maximus of Tyre. *Philosophical Orations.* Text in *Maximus Tyrius, Philosophoumena–Dialexeis.* Edited by George Leonidas. Berlin: de Gruyter, 1995. Translation in *The Philosophical Orations.* Translated by M. B. Trapp. Oxford: Clarendon, 1997.

Melito of Sardis. *On Pascha and Fragments.* Edited and translated by Stuart George Hall. OECT. Oxford: Clarendon, 1979. Translation in *On Pascha.* Translated and edited by Alistair Stewart-Sykes. Crestwood, NY: St. Vladimir's Seminary Press, 2001.

Nestorius. *First Homily against Theotokos.* Text in pages 249–64 in *Nestoriana: Die Fragmente des Nestorius.* Edited by Friedrich Loofs. Halle: Niemeyer,

1905. Translation in pages 123–31 in *The Christological Controversy*. Edited by R. A. Norris. Philadelphia: Fortress, 1980.

Numenius. *Fragments*. Edited by E. Des Places. Paris: Les Belles Lettres, 1973.

Origen. *Contra Celsum*. Text in *Die Schrift vom Martyrium, Buch I–IV gegen Celsus and Buch V–VIII gegen Celsus, Die Scrift vom Gebet*. Edited by P. Koetschau. Origenes Werke 1–2. GCS 2–3. Leipzig: Hinrichs, 1899. Translation in *Against Celsus*. Translated by Henry Chadwick. Cambridge: Cambridge University Press, 1965.

———. *De principiis*. Text in *De principiis*. Edited by P. Koetschau. Origenes Werke 5. GCS 22. Leipzig: Hinrichs, 1913. Translation in *On First Principles*. Translated by G. W. Butterworth. London: SPCK, 1936; Repr. Gloucester, MA: Smith, 1973; *On First Principles*. Edited and translated by John Behr. 2 vols. Oxford: Oxford University Press, 2019.

———. *Letter to Gregory*. Text in *Grégoire de Thaumaturge: Remerciement à Origène suivi de la letter d'Origène à Grégoire*. Edited by H. Crouzel. SC 148. Paris: Cerf, 1969.

Plutarch. *Moralia V*. Edited and translated by F. C. Babbitt. LCL. Cambridge: Harvard University Press, 1984.

Tertullian. *Adversus Marcionem*. Edited and translated by E. Evans. OECT. Oxford: Clarendon, 1972.

———. *Contre Hermogène*. Edited by Frédéric Chapot. SC 439. Paris: Cerf, 1999.

Theodoret of Cyrus. *Eranistes*. Edited by Gerard H. Ettlinger. Oxford: Clarendon, 1975.

———. *The Questions on the Octoteuch*. Edited by John F. Petruccione. Translated by Robert C. Hill. Washington, DC: Catholic University of America Press, 2007.

Theophilus. *Ad Autolycum*. Edited and translated by R. M. Grant. OECT. Oxford: Clarendon, 1970.

Secondary Literature

Babcock, W. S. "Caritas and Signification." Pages 145–63 in *De Doctrina Christiana: A Classic of Western Culture*. Edited by Duane W. H. Arnold and Pamela Bright. Notre Dame: University of Notre Dame Press, 1995.

Bauer, Walter. *Orthodoxy and Heresy in Early Christianity*. Edited and translated by Robert A. Kraft and Gerhard A. Kroedel. 2nd ed. Philadelphia: Fortress, 1971.

———. *Rechtgläubigkeit und Ketzerei in ältesten Christentum*. Tübingen: Mohr Siebeck, 1934.

Becker, E.-M., and M. Vinzent. "Marcion and the Dating of Mark and the Synoptic Gospels." StPatr 99 (2018): 5–33.
Behr, John. *The Formation of Christian Theology*. 3 vols. Crestwood, NY: St. Vladimir's Seminary Press, 2001–2004.
Bell, H. I. *Jews and Christians in Egypt*. London: British Museum, 1924.
Bigg, Charles. *The Christian Platonists of Alexandria*. Oxford: Oxford University Press, 1886.
Bokedal, Tomas. *The Foundation and Significance of the Christian Biblical Canon*. London: Bloomsbury, 2014.
Bradshaw, Paul F., Maxwell E. Johnson, and L. Edward Phillips. *The Apostolic Tradition: A Commentary*. Hermeneia. Minneapolis: Fortress, 2002.
Briggman, Anthony. *God and Christ in Irenaeus*. Oxford: Oxford University Press, 2019.
Brock, Sebastian. *The Luminous Eye: The Spiritual World Vision of Saint Ephrem the Syrian*. Collegeville, MN: Cistercian, 1992.
Brown, Peter. *Augustine of Hippo: A Biography*. London: Faber & Faber, 1967.
———. *The Body and Society: Men, Women and Sexual Renunciation in Early Christianity*. London: Faber & Faber, 1989.
Burtchaell, James Tunstead. *From Synagogue to Church: Public Services and Offices in the Earliest Christian Communities*. Cambridge: Cambridge University Press, 1992.
Chadwick, Henry. *Augustine*. Oxford: Oxford University Press, 1986.
Childs, B. S. *Introduction to the Old Testament as Scripture*. Philadelphia: Fortress, 1979.
Clark, Elizabeth A. *The Origenist Controversy: The Cultural Construction of an Early Christian Debate*. Princeton: Princeton University Press, 1992.
Crouzel, Henri, *Origen*. Translated by A. S. Worrall. Edinburgh: T&T Clark, 1980.
———. *Origène*. Paris: Aubier, 1962.
Daley, Brian E. *The Hope of the Early Church*. Cambridge: Cambridge University Press, 1991.
Daniélou, Jean. *Origen*. Translated by Walter Mitchell. New York: Sheed and Ward, 1955.
———. *Origène*. Paris: La Table Ronde, 1948.
Daube, David. "Rabbinic Methods of Interpretation and Hellenistic Rhetoric." *Hebrew Union College Annual* 22 (1949): 239–64.
Dawson, David. *Allegorical Readers and Cultural Revision in Ancient Alexandria*. Berkeley: University of California Press, 1992.
Dillon, John. *The Middle Platonists*. Rev. ed. London: Duckworth, 1996.
Dowden, Ken. *Religion and the Romans*. London: Duckworth, 1992.
Dunn, J. D. G. *Jesus, Paul and the Law*. London: SPCK, 1990.

———. *The Parting of the Ways between Christianity and Judaism and their Significance for the Character of Christianity*. London: SCM, 1991.

Edwards, Mark J. "Ammonius, Teacher of Origen." *JEH* 44 (1993): 169–81.

———. *Christians, Gnostics and Philosophers in Late Antiquity*. Farnham: Ashgate, 2012.

———. "Gnostics and Valentinians in the Church Fathers." *JTS* 40 (1989): 26–47.

———. *Origen against Plato*. Aldershot: Ashgate, 2002.

Farrar, Austin. *A Rebirth of Images: The Making of St. John's Apocalypse*. Westminster: Dacre, 1949.

Festugière, A. J. *Le Dieu Inconnu et la gnose*. Vol. 4 of *La Révelation d'Hermes trismégiste*. Paris: Gabalda, 1954.

Ford, David F. *The Gospel of John: A Theological Commentary*. Grand Rapids: Baker Academic, 2021.

Ford, David F., and Frances Young. *Meaning and Truth in 2 Corinthians*. London: SPCK, 1987.

Fredricksen, Paula. "Beyond the Body/Soul Dichotomy: Augustine's Answer to Mani, Plotinus, and Julian." Pages 227–51 in *Paul and the Legacies of Paul*. Edited by William S. Babcock. Dallas: Southern Methodist University Press, 1990.

Frend, W. H. C. *The Donatist Church*. Oxford: Clarendon, 1952.

———. *The Early Church*. London: Hodder and Stoughton, 1965.

Froehlich, K. *Biblical Interpretation in the Early Church*. Philadelphia: Fortress, 1984.

Gamble, Harry Y. *Books and Readers in the Early Church: A History of Early Christian Texts*. New Haven: Yale University Press, 1995.

Goodman, Martin. *Mission and Conversion: Proselytizing in the Religious History of the Roman Empire*. Oxford: Clarendon, 1994.

Greenblatt, Stephen. *The Rise and Fall of Adam and Eve*. London: The Bodley Head, 2017.

Greer, Rowan A., and Margaret M. Mitchell. *The 'Belly-Myther' of Endor: Interpretations of 1 Kings 28 in the Early Church*. Atlanta: SBL Press, 2007.

Harnack, Adolf von. *History of Dogma*. Translated by Neil Buchanan, James Millar, and E. B. Speirs. 7 vols. 3rd ed. London: Williams and Norgate, 1894–1898.

———. *The Mission and Expansion of Christianity in the First Three Centuries*. Translated by James Moffatt. London: Williams and Norgate, 1908.

Harrison, Carol. *The Art of Listening in the Early Church*. Oxford: Oxford University Press, 2013.

Harrison, Verna. "Gender, Generation and Virginity in Cappadocian Theology." *JTS* 47 (1996): 36–68.

Hatch, Edwin. *The Influence of Greek Ideas on Christianity*. New York: Harper and Brothers, 1957.
Heine, Ronald E. ed. *The Commentary of Origen on the Gospel of Matthew*. 2 vols. OECT. Oxford: Oxford University Press, 2018.
———. "The Introduction to Origen's *Commentary on John* Compared with the Introductions to the Ancient Philosophical Commentaries on Aristotle." Pages 3–12 in *Origeniana Sexta: Origène et la Bible. Actes du Colloquium Origenianum Sextum, Chantilly, 30 août–3 septembre 1993*. Edited by G. Dorival and A. Le Boulluec. BETL 118. Leuven: Peeters, 1995.
———. *Origen: Scholarship in the Service of the Church*. Oxford: Oxford University Press, 2010.
Heine, Ronald E., and Karen Jo Torjesen, eds. *The Oxford Handbook of Origen*. Oxford: Oxford University Press, 2022.
Hick, John, ed. *The Myth of God Incarnate*. London: SCM, 1977.
Hooker, Morna, and Frances Young. *Holiness and Mission: Learning from the Early Church about Mission in the City*. London: SCM, 2010.
Hurtado, Larry W. *The Earliest Christian Artifacts: Manuscripts and Christian Origins*. Grand Rapids: Eerdmans, 2006.
Jonas, Hans. *The Gnostic Religion: The Message of the Alien God and the Beginnings of Christianity*. Boston: Beacon, 1958.
Judge, E. A. "The Early Christians as a Scholastic Community." *Journal of Religious History* 1 (1960): 1–8, 124–37.
———. "St. Paul and Classical Society." *Jahrbuch für Antike und Christentum* 15 (1972): 19–38.
Kannengiesser, Charles. "The Interrupted *De doctrina christiana*." Pages 3–13 in *De Doctrina Christiana: A Classic of Western Culture*. Edited by Duane W. H. Arnold and Pamela Bright. Notre Dame: University of Notre Dame Press, 1995.
Kaster, R. A. *Guardians of Language: The Grammaticus and Society in Late Antiquity*. Berkeley: University of California Press, 1988.
Kelly, J. N. D. *Early Christian Creeds*. London: Longman, 1960.
———. *Early Christian Doctrines*. London: Black, 1960.
Kinneavy, James L. *Greek Rhetorical Origins of Christian Faith*. Oxford: Oxford University Press, 1987.
Koch, Hal. *Pronoia und Paedeusis*. Berlin: de Gruyter, 1932.
Lamberton, Robert. *Homer the Theologian*. Berkeley: University of California Press, 1986.
Lampe, Peter. *From Paul to Valentinus: Christians at Rome in the First Two Centuries*. Translated by Michael Steinhauser. London: T&T Clark, 2003.

Lash, Nicholas. *Newman on Development: The Search for an Explanation in History*. London: Sheed and Ward, 1975.
Levine, Lee I. *The Ancient Synagogue: The First Thousand Years*. New Haven: Yale University Press, 2000.
———. *Judaism and Hellenism in Antiquity*. Peabody: Hendrickson, 1998.
Lieberman, Saul. *Hellenism in Jewish Palestine*. New York: Jewish Theological Seminary of America, 1950.
Lieu, Judith M. *Marcion and the Making of a Heretic: God and Scripture in the Second Century*. Cambridge: Cambridge University Press, 2015.
Limberis, Vasiliki. "Resurrected Body and Immortal Flesh in Gregory of Nyssa." Pages 515–28 in *Jesus Christ in St Gregory of Nyssa's Theology: Minutes of the Ninth International Conference on Gregory of Nyssa (Athens 7–12 September 2000)*. Edited by Eliad D. Moutsoulas. Athens: University Press, 2005.
Lodge, David, ed. *Modern Criticism and Theory: A Reader*. Harlow: Longman, 1988.
Louth, Andrew. *Discerning the Mystery: An Essay on the Nature of Theology*. Oxford: Clarendon, 1983.
Malherbe, Abraham. *Paul and the Popular Philosophers*. Minneapolis: Fortress, 1989.
Markschies, Christoph. *Gnosis: An Introduction*. Translated by John Bowden. London: T&T Clark, 2003.
Markus, R. A. *Saeculum: History and Society in the Theology of St. Augustine*. Cambridge: Cambridge University Press, 1970.
Marrou, H. I. *A History of Education in Antiquity*. Translated by G. Lamb. New York: Sheed and Ward, 1956.
———. *L'histoire de l'éducation dans l'antiquité*. Paris: Seuil, 1948.
———. *Saint Augustin et la fin de la culture antique*. Paris: de Boccard, 1938.
Martens, Peter W. *Origen and Scripture: The Contours of the Exegetical Life*. Oxford Early Christian Studies. Oxford: Oxford University Press, 2012.
Martin, Dale B. *Slavery as Salvation: The Metaphor of Slavery in Pauline Christianity*. New Haven: Yale University Press, 1990.
May, Gerhard. *Creatio ex Nihilo: The Doctrine of Creation out of Nothing in Early Christian Thought*. Translated by A. S. Worrall. Edinburgh: T&T Clark, 1994.
Meeks, Wayne A. *The First Urban Christians: The Social Context of the Apostle Paul*. 2nd ed. New Haven: Yale University Press, 2003.
Merlan, P. "The Later Academy and Platonism." Pages 53–83 in *Cambridge History of Later Greek and Early Medieval Philosophy*. Edited by A. H. Armstrong. Cambridge: Cambridge University Press, 1967.
———. "The Pythagoreans." Pages 84–106 in *Cambridge History of Later Greek*

and Early Medieval Philosophy. Edited by A. H. Armstrong. Cambridge: Cambridge University Press, 1967.

Mitchell, Margaret M., and Frances M. Young, eds. *Origins to Constantine*. Vol. 1 of *Cambridge History of Christianity*. Cambridge: Cambridge University Press, 2006.

Morgan, Teresa. *Roman Faith and Christian Faith: Pistis and Fides in the Early Roman Empire and Early Churches*. Oxford: Oxford University Press, 2015.

Mühlenberg, E. *Die unendlichkeit Gottes bei Gregor von Nyssa*. Göttingen: Vandenhoeck and Ruprecht, 1966.

Newman, John Henry. *An Essay on the Development of Christian Doctrine*. Pelican Classics. Harmondsworth: Penguin, 1974.

Niehoff, Maren. *Jewish Exegesis and Homeric Scholarship in Alexandria*. Cambridge: Cambridge University Press, 2011.

O'Collins, Gerald, SJ. *Saint Augustine on the Resurrection of Christ: Teaching, Rhetoric, and Reception*. Oxford: Oxford University Press, 2017.

O'Donnell, James J. "*Doctrina Christiana, De*." Pages 278–80 in *Augustine through the Ages: An Encyclopedia*. Edited by Allan D. Fitzgerald, OSA. Grand Rapids: Eerdmans, 1999.

Norden, Eduard. *Agnōstos Theos*. Leipzig: Teubner, 1913.

Parker, David. *The Living Text of the New Testament*. Cambridge: Cambridge University Press, 1997.

Price, S. R. F. *Rituals and Power: The Roman Imperial Cult in Asia Minor*. Cambridge: Cambridge University Press, 1984.

Radner, Ephraim. *Time and the Word: Figural Reading of the Christian Scriptures*. Grand Rapids: Eerdmans, 2016.

Richardson, Alan. *Creeds in the Making*. London: SCM, 1935.

Roberts, C. H. "The Codex." *Proceedings of the British Academy* 40 (1954): 169–204.

Roberts, C. H., and T. H. Skeat. *The Birth of the Codex*. Oxford: Oxford University Press, 1983.

Sanders, E. P. *Paul and Palestinian Judaism*. London: SCM, 1977.

Schürer, Emil. *The History of the Jewish People in the Age of Jesus Christ*. Edited by Geza Vermes, Fergus Millar, and Matthew Black. Rev. ed. Edinburgh: T&T Clark, 1979.

Skarsaune, Oskar. *The Proof from Prophecy. A Study in Justin Martyr's Proof-text Tradition: Text-Type, Provenance, Theological Profile*. Leiden: Brill, 1987.

Steinhauser, Kenneth B. "Codex Leningradensis Q.v.I.3: Some Unresolved Problems." Pages 33–43 in *De Doctrina Christiana: A Classic of Western Culture*. Edited by Duane W. H. Arnold and Pamela Bright. Notre Dame: University of Notre Dame Press, 1995.

Stewart-Sykes, Alistair. *The Lamb's High Feast: Melito, Peri Pascha and the Quartodeciman Paschal Liturgy at Sardis*. Leiden: Brill, 1998.

Torjesen, Karen Jo. "'Body,' 'Soul,' and 'Spirit' in Origen's Theory of Exegesis." *Anglican Theological Review* 67.1 (1985): 17–30.

———. *Hermeneutical Procedure and Theological Method in Origen's Exegesis*. Berlin: de Gruyter, 1985.

Trigg, Joseph W. *Origen*. London: Routledge, 1998.

———. *Origen: The Bible and Philosophy in the Third-Century Church*. London: SCM, 1985.

Volgers, Annelie, and Claudio Zamagni, eds. *Erotapokriseis: Early Christian Question and Answer Literature in Context*. Leuven: Peeters, 2004.

Wendt, H. "Marcion the Shipmaster: Unlikely Religious Experts of the Roman World." StPatr 99 (2018): 55–74.

Widdicombe, Peter. *The Fatherhood of God from Origen to Athanasius*. Oxford: Oxford University Press, 2000.

Wiles, Maurice. 'Looking into the Sun." Pages 148–63 in *Working Papers in Doctrine*. London: SCM, 1976.

Williams, Rowan, *Arius: Heresy and Tradition*. London: Darton, Longman and Todd, 1987.

Young, Frances. "Adam and Christ: Human Solidarity before God." Pages 144–64 in *The Christian Doctrine of Humanity*. Edited by Oliver D. Crisp and Fred Sanders. Grand Rapids: Zondervan Academic, 2018.

———. "Allegory and the Ethics of Reading." Pages 103–20 in *The Open Text: New Directions for Biblical Studies?* Edited by Francis Watson. London: SCM, 1993.

———. *The Art of Performance: Towards a Theology of Holy Scripture*. London: DLT, 1990.

———. *Biblical Exegesis and the Formation of Christian Culture*. Cambridge: Cambridge University Press, 1997.

———. "Books and Their 'Aura': The Functions of Written Texts in Judaism, Paganism and Christianity during the First Centuries CE." Pages 535–52 in *Religious Identity and the Problem of Historical Foundation: The Foundational Character of Authoritative Sources in the History of Christianity and Judaism*. Edited by Judith Frishman, Willemien Otten, and Gerard Rouwhorst. Leiden: Brill, 2004.

———. *Brokenness and Blessing: Towards a Biblical Spirituality*. Grand Rapids: Baker Academic, 2007.

———. *Construing the Cross: Type, Sign, Symbol, Word, Action*. Eugene: Cascade, 2015.

———. "'Creatio Ex Nihilo': A Context for the Emergence of the Christian Doctrine of Creation." *SJT* 44 (1991): 139–52.

———. "Creation: A Catalyst Shaping Early Christian Life and Thought." Pages 23–33 in *Schools of Faith: Essays on Theology, Ethics and Education in Honour of Iain R. Torrance*. Edited by David Fergusson and Bruce McCormack. London: T&T Clark, 2019.

———. "Creation and Human Being: The Forging of a Distinct Christian Discourse." StPatr 44 (2010): 335–48.

———. "Did Epiphanius Know What He Meant by Heresy?" StPatr 17 (1982): 199–205.

———. *Exegesis and Theology in Early Christianity*. Farnham: Ashgate, 2012.

———. "The Fourth Century Reaction against Allegory." StPatr 30 (1997): 120–25.

———. "The God of the Greeks and the Nature of Religious Language." Pages 45–74 in *Early Christian Literature and the Classical Intellectual Tradition: In Honorem Robert M. Grant*. Edited by W. R. Schoedel and R. L. Wilken. Théologie Historique 53. Paris: Beauchesne, 1979.

———. *God's Presence: A Contemporary Recapitulation of Early Christianity*. Cambridge: Cambridge University Press, 2013.

———. *The Making of the Creeds*. London: SCM, 1991.

———. "Naked or Clothed? Eschatology and the Doctrine of Creation." Pages 1–19 in *The Church, the Afterlife and the Fate of the Soul: Papers Read at the 2007 Summer Meeting and the 2008 Winter Meeting of the Ecclesiastical History Society*. Edited by Peter D. Clarke and Tony Caldon. Woodbridge: Ecclesiastical History Society, 2009.

———. "Paideia and the Myth of Static Dogma." Pages 265–83 in *The Making and Remaking of Christian Doctrine: Essays in Honour of Maurice Wiles*. Edited by Sarah Coakley and David Pailin. Oxford: Clarendon, 1993.

———. "The Pastoral Epistles and the Ethics of Reading." JSNT 45 (1992): 105–20.

———. "Proverbs 8 in Interpretation (2): Wisdom Personified." Pages 102–15 in *Reading Texts, Seeking Wisdom*. Edited by David F. Ford and Graham Stanton. London: SCM, 2003.

———. "The Rhetorical Schools and Their Influence on Patristic Exegesis." Pages 182–99 in *The Making of Orthodoxy: Essays in Honour of Henry Chadwick*. Edited by Rowan Williams. Cambridge: Cambridge University Press, 1989.

———. "Riddles and Puzzles: God's Indirect Word in Patristic Hermeneutics." StPatr 91 (2017): 149–55.

———. "Teasing Out Meaning: Some Techniques and Procedures in Early Christian Exegesis." StPatr 100 (2020): 3–18.

———. *The Theology of the Pastoral Epistles*. Cambridge: Cambridge University Press, 1994.

———. "The Trinity and the New Testament." Pages 286–305 in *The Nature of*

New Testament Theology: Essays in Honour of Robert Morgan. Edited by Christopher Rowland and Christolpher Tuckett. Oxford: Blackwell, 2006.

———. "Typology." Pages 29–48 in *Crossing the Boundaries: Essays in Biblical Interpretation in Honour of Michael D. Goulder*. Edited by Stanley E. Porter, Paul Joyce, and David E. Orton. Leiden: Brill, 1994.

———. *The Use of Sacrificial Ideas in Greek Christian Writers from the New Testament to John Chrysostom*. Patristic Monograph Series 5. Cambridge: The Philadelphia Patristic Foundation, 1979.

———. *Virtuoso Theology: The Bible and Interpretation*. Cleveland: Pilgrim, 1993.

———. *Ways of Reading Scripture*. WUNT 369. Tübingen: Mohr Siebeck, 2018.

———. "Ways of Reading the Bible: Can We Relativize the Historico-Critical Method and Rediscover a Biblical Spirituality?" Pages 7–25 in *Reading Scripture for Living the Christian Life*. Edited by Bernard Treacy with Frances Young, J. Cecil McCullough, and Thomas Brodie. Dublin: Dominican, 2009.

Index of Authors

Alici, Luigi, 236n
Amidon, Philip R., 53n
Armstrong, A. H., 63n, 64n
Arnold, Duane W. H., 228n, 229n, 236n

Babbitt, F. C., 57n
Babcock, William S., 200n, 236n
Barthes, Roland, 241
Bauer, Walter, 30
Becker, E.-M., 50n
Behr, John, 10, 91n, 108, 143n, 225
Bell, H. I., 20n
Bettenson, Henry, 201n
Bévenot, Maurice, 216n
Bigg, Charles, 118
Birdsall, Neville, 96n
Black, Matthew, 19n
Blowers, Paul M., 109n
Bockmuehl, Markus, 91n
Bokedal, Tomas, 95–97, 109n
Botte, B., 94n
Bowden, John, 74n
Bradshaw, Paul F., 94n
Briggman, Anthony, 98
Bright, Pamela, 228n, 229n, 236n
Brock, Sebastian, 191n
Brodie, Thomas, 241n
Brown, Peter, 177, 219–20, 227n
Buchanan, Neil, 7n

Burtchaell, James Tunstead, 22n
Butterworth, G. W., 115n, 136n, 143n

Caldon, Tony, 168n
Chadwick, Henry, 36n, 200n
Chapot, Frédéric, 72n
Childs, Brevard S., 232
Clark, Elizabeth A., 222n
Clarke, Peter D., 168n
Coakley, Sarah, 113n, 118n
Crisp, Oliver D., 199n
Crouzel, Henri, 33n, 35n, 118–19

Daley, Brian E., 211n
Daniélou, Jean, 119n
Daube, David, 21n
Dawson, David, 87–88
Declerk, J. H., 224n
Deferrari, R. J., 216n
Dillon, John, 63n, 64n, 65n, 67n, 70n
Dombart, Bernard, 201n
Dorival, G., 26n
Dowden, Ken, 14n, 16n, 57n
Dunn, J. D. G., 48n

Eco, Umberto, 235, 236n
Edwards, Mark J., 35n, 68n, 69n, 87, 89n, 90n, 119–20
Ettlinger, Gerard H., 156n
Eubank, Nathan, 91n
Evans, E., 52n

261

INDEX OF AUTHORS

Farrar, Austin, 87n
Fergusson, David, 59n
Festugière, A. J., 65n, 68n
Fitzgerald, Allan D., 230n
Foerster, Werner, 71n
Ford, David F., 48n, 240n, 242n
Fredriksen, Paula, 200n
Frend, W. H. C., 219n, 220n
Frishman, Judith, 14n
Froehlich, Karlfried, 21n, 224n, 225n

Gamble, Harry Y., 20n, 21n, 46n, 47n
Goodman, Martin, 15n, 18n
Grant, Robert M., 72n, 178n
Green, R. P. H., 226n, 227n
Greenblatt, Stephen, 200n
Greer, Rowan A., 224n

Hall, Stuart George, 186n
Harnack, Adolf von, 7–11, 12, 19n, 37–41, 74, 76, 87
Harrison, Carol, 46n
Harrison, Verna, 177n
Harvey, W. W., 75n, 76
Hatch, Edwin, 14–15
Heine, Ronald E., 26n, 30n, 33n, 46n, 111, 171n, 223n
Hick, John, 10n
Hill, Edmund, 168n, 226n, 227n, 229n, 236n, 238n, 243n
Hill, Robert C., 52n
Holl, Karl, 53n, 222n
Hooker, Morna, 16n
Hurtado, Larry W., 96n

Jacob, Christian, 50n
Johnson, Maxwell E., 94n
Jonas, Hans, 74n
Joyce, Paul, 223n
Judge, E. A., 24–25

Kalb, Alphonse, 201n
Kannengiesser, Charles, 228, 229n
Kaster, R. A., 33n
Kelly, J. N. D., 156n, 216n, 220n
Kinneavy, James L., 240n
Knowles, David, 201n

Koch, Hal, 124n
Koetschau, P., 36n, 115n, 143n
Koniaris, George Leonidas, 66n
Kraft, Robert A., 30n
Kroedel, Gerhard A., 30n

Lamb, G., 33n, 50n
Lamberton, Robert, 122n
Lampe, Peter, 27–29
Lash, Nicholas, 3n, 4n, 10n
Layton, Bentley, 75n, 77, 82n
Le Boulluec, A., 26n
Levine, Lee I., 19n
Lieberman, Saul, 21n
Lieu, Judith M., 44–45, 52, 58–59, 62n, 63n
Lightfoot, R. H., 46n, 59n
Limberis, Vasiliki, 211n
Lodge, David, 241n
Loofs, Friedrich, 183n, 189n
Louis, Pierre, 67n
Louth, Andrew, 46n, 247n

MacRae, George W., 75n, 77n
Malherbe, Abraham, 25
Mariès, Louis, 224n
Markovich, Miroslav, 55–56n
Markschies, Christoph, 74n
Markus, R. A., 201n, 220n
Marrou, H. I., 33n, 50, 227n
Martens, Peter W., 114, 115n, 120n, 122–24, 135, 154
Martin, Dale B., 24n
May, Gerhard, 71n, 72n
McCormack, Bruce, 59n
McCullough, J. Cecil, 241n
Meeks, Wayne A., 22n
Merlan, P., 63n, 64n
Metzger, Marcel, 214n
Millar, Fergus, 19n
Minns, Denis, 55n
Mitchell, Margaret M., 31n, 224n
Mitchell, Walter, 119n
Moffatt, James, 19n
Morgan, Teresa, 18n, 38n, 39–41
Moutsoulas, Eliad D., 211n
Mühlenberg, E., 68n
Musurillo, H., 28n

Index of Authors

Newman, John Henry, 3–7, 10, 12, 108, 225, 226
Niehoff, Maren, 51
Norden, Eduard, 68n
Norris, Frederick W., 168n
Norris, R. A., 183n, 189n

O'Collins, Gerald, 194n, 211n
O'Donnell, James J., 230n
Orton, David E., 223n
Otten, Willemien, 14n

Pailin, David, 113n, 118n
Parker, David, 50n, 95n
Parvis, Paul, 55n
Petruccione, John F., 52n
Phillips, L. Edward, 94n
Places, E. des, 63n, 70n
Porter, Stanley E., 223n
Preller, L., 65n, 66n
Price, S. R. F., 17n

Rackham, H., 18n
Radner, Ephraim, 247n
Reischl, W. K., 157n
Richardson, Alan, 10n
Ritter, H., 65n, 66n
Roberts, C. H., 46n, 47n
Robinson, James M., 75n
Rotelle, John E., 168n, 227n
Rouwhorst, Gerard, 14n
Rowland, Christopher, 6n
Rupp, J., 157n
Russell, Norman, 191n

Sanders, E. P., 48n
Sanders, Fred, 199n
Schoedel, William R., 46n, 65n, 177n
Schürer, Emil, 19n, 20n
Schwartz, Eduard, 31n
Skarsaune, Oskar, 49n, 56n, 96

Skeat, T. H., 46n
Stählin, O., 116n
Staniforth, Maxwell, 46n, 59n
Stanton, Graham, 240n
Steinhauser, Michael, 27n
Stewart-Sykes, Alistair, 94n, 186n
Strecker, Georg, 30n
Swete, H. B., 225n

Thomson, Robert W., 199n
Torjesen, Karen Jo, 33n, 110–14, 223n
Trapp, M. B., 66n
Treacy, Bernard, 241n
Trigg, Joseph W., 36, 119, 136n
Tuckett, Christopher, 6n

Vermes, Geza, 19n
Vinzent, M., 50n
Volgers, Annelie, 50n

Wendland, Paul, 71n
Wendt, H., 29n
Whittaker, John, 67n
Wickham, Lionel, 168n
Widdicombe, Peter, 171n
Wiles, Maurice, 2–3
Wilken, R. L., 65n
Williams, Frederick, 168–69n
Williams, Rowan, 162n, 223n, 230–31, 234
Williamson, G. A., 31n
Wilson, R. McL., 71n
Worrall, A. S., 71n, 118n

Yarnold, Edward, 165n
Young, Frances M., 6n, 10n, 13n, 14n, 16n, 19n, 20n, 23n, 31n, 48n, 50n, 57n, 59n, 65n, 72n, 91n, 98n, 113n, 117n, 165n, 167n, 168n, 177n, 186n, 190n, 199n, 211n, 222n, 224n, 225n, 235n, 239n, 240n, 241n, 246n, 247n

Zamagni, Claudio, 50n

Index of Subjects

acculturation, 12–13, 37–41, 109
Achamoth, 86–87, 89
Adam: Adam-Christ typology, 186–87, 191, 201, 207, 209; Irenaeus on Christ's recapitulation of, 102–3; and sin, 185, 199, 201, 206–7, 209
agapē meals, 28
Alcinous, 65n, 66–67
Alexandria: anti-Semitism, 20; catechetical schools and the "fractionated" church, 29–37; Clement's catechetical school, 29, 32–33; Jewish biblical scholarship and "question and answer" tradition, 51; Origen's catechetical school, 30–37, 112, 228; Pantaenus's catechetical school, 29, 32–33
allegory: Antiochene reaction against, 221, 223–25; Gnostic reading of scripture, 73
Ambrose, 125, 227
Ambrosiaster, 51
Ambrosius, 32
Ammonius Saccas, 35
Anselm, 238
Antiochenes, 184, 191, 221, 223–25; and the reaction against allegory, 221, 223–25
Apelles, 28
apocalyptic literature, 88–90
apophatic theology, 64, 66–68, 85, 107, 169, 238–39; Augustine, 238–39; Clement of Alexandria's motif of revelatory concealment, 116–17; Cyril on God, 165; namelessness of God in Hellenistic Jewish theology, 69, 84, 89, 165, 239; Platonism/Neoplatonism, 167, 239
Apostles' Creed, 176
Apostolic Constitutions, 214–17
Apostolic Fathers, 62, 197–98
Apuleis, 66–67
Arian controversies, 156, 162, 164, 168–69, 171–72, 174, 175, 194, 222–23
Aristotle, 51, 126
Arius, 8, 162, 170, 222–23
Athanasius, 8, 9, 159, 189, 190, 199, 204, 216
Athenagoras, 70, 177, 210–11, 212
Augustine: on bodily resurrection, 211; on Christ's resurrection, 194–95; *The City of God*, 200–209, 211; on creation, 168, 203–5, 211; doctrine of original sin and free will, 199–209; and Donatist schism, 220; pedagogy, 240–43; "question and answer" tradition, 51; the *rhetor* and discernment (*inventio*) of the subject matter, 228–34, 240; sign theory and distinction between "things" and "signs," 228, 231, 234–40; *Teaching Christianity*, 227–43; on the Trinity, 230, 231, 237–39

baptism: Augustine on original sin and, 200; Cyril on sin and, 197; Matthew's Gospel, 94–95; Origen on baptismal lit-

urgy, 141; Pentecostal tradition, 1; threefold shape of the rule of faith according to Irenaeus, 93–97, 104, 160
Basileides, 30, 71–72, 123
Basil of Caesarea, 168, 217
book culture, early Christian, 46–49

Caesarea, Origen's teaching activities in, 33–34, 36, 112, 118–19
canon criticism, 98, 232–33
Cappadocians, 216
Carpocrates, 30
Celsus, 36, 39, 66–67
cento, Homeric, 98, 99
Cerdo, 28
Christian Platonists of Alexandria, The (Bigg), 114
church: and the *Apostolic Constitutions*, 214–17; Cyprian's *The Unity of the Catholic Church* and unity during heresies and schisms, 217–20; Cyril of Jerusalem and catholicity of, 213–20; image as Christ's body, 215–16; images deriving from scripture, 214–19; images of the household and the ship, 216–17; the word *ekklēsia*, 214, 215
Cicero, 17–18
Clement of Alexandria: catechetical school, 29, 32–33; Harnack on, 8, 9; motif of revelatory concealment (the hidden divine), 116–17; on Xenophanes's criticism of anthropomorphic gods, 65–66
Constantinople, creed of, 156, 176
creatio ex nihilo, doctrine of, 59, 69–73; Augustine, 204; Basileides, 71–72; *ex ouk ontōn*, 70–72; Gregory of Nyssa, 196; Origen, 150, 153; Philo, 70–71; Tertullian, 72; Theophilus of Antioch, 72. See also creation
creation: Augustine on, 168, 203–5, 211; Basileides on, 71–72; 1 Clement (late first century), 59–61; Cyril of Jerusalem on, 166–70, 212–13, 221; Irenaeus on, 100–101, 106–7; Origen on, 128–31, 149–52, 153, 203; Philo on, 64, 69, 70–71; Platonism/Neoplatonism, 70–73, 167–68; Plutarch,

70; second-century thinking on God and, 58–73; Tertullian on God and, 72, 76–77; Valentinian gnostic explanation of the material world, 86–87. See also *creatio ex nihilo*, doctrine of
creeds, 156–225; Constantinople, 156, 176; Cyril of Jerusalem on relationship between creed and scripture, 156, 157–221; Cyril's treatment of the ten "holy dogmas," 158–59, 161–62, 163–221; Epiphanius of Salamis on doctrine and reading of scripture, 156–57, 221–25; fourth-century doctrinal controversies over alternative readings of scripture, 161–63, 171–72, 174, 175, 182–83, 194, 196; Nicene, 156, 170, 176; as "tests of orthodoxy," 156. See also Cyril of Jerusalem's *Catechetical Homilies*; Epiphanius of Salamis; rule of faith
Cyprian, 219–20
Cyril of Alexandria, 190, 191, 216
Cyril of Jerusalem's *Catechetical Homilies*, 156–221; on the begetting, 171, 173–74; on bodily resurrection and eternal life, 209–13; on Christ, his divinity, relationship with the Father, and the incarnation, 161, 170–76; on Christ's resurrection and ascension, 191–95, 212, 223; on the church (the catholicity of), 213–20; on creation, 166–70, 212–13, 221; on creed as "summary" of scripture, 158–60; the cross and the passion of Christ, 183–91; on faith (two senses of), 159; and fourth-century doctrinal controversies over alternative readings of scripture, 161–63, 171–72, 174, 175, 182–83, 194, 196; on God, 163–70; on the incarnation, 176, 178, 181–83; on judgment, 195–97; scriptural proofs and quotations, 160–61; scriptural testimonies, 174–75, 182, 188–90, 192–93, 194, 213; on sin, 197–99; treatment of the "holy dogmas," 158–59, 161–62, 163–221; on the virgin birth, 161, 176–83

Decian persecution, 197, 217, 219
De doctrina christiana (Augustine). See *Teaching Christianity* (Augustine)

266 INDEX OF SUBJECTS

Delphic Oracle (Pythian priestess), 126–27
Demetrius, bishop, 31, 33
demiurge, 55, 61, 63–64, 131; of gnostic revelation, 69–70, 85, 87, 89
developmental model. *See* doctrinal developmental models
Diocletian, 219
Diodore (Antiochene), 224
Dionysus, 178
docetism, 70, 183, 223
doctrinal developmental models, 3–7, 243–46; Hellenization theory, 7–11, 12, 37–41, 74, 87, 108–9, 165, 243–46; Newman and continuity of development from the beginning, 2–7, 10, 12, 226
Donatist schism, 219–20

Eastern Orthodox tradition, 9
Ephrem the Syrian, 191
Epicureanism, 21–22, 35, 134
Epicurus, 126
Epiphanius of Salamis: on creedal doctrine and reading of scripture, 156–57, 221–23; on dogma and the Antiochene reaction against allegory, 221, 223–25; *Panarion* on Ptolemaeus's letter to Flora, 53–55
Epistle of Barnabas, 30, 96
Essay on the Development of Christian Doctrine (Newman), 3–7
"ethical reading," 13
Eucharist gatherings, 24, 28
Eunomis, 168–69
Eusebius, 30–33, 51–52, 124–25, 216
Eustathius, bishop of Antioch, 224

Formation of Christian Theology, The (Behr), 10
"fractionated" Roman church, 27–37, 45. *See also* school-like character of early Christian groups
free will, 199–203; Augustine on original sin and origin of evil, 199–203; Origen on, 149, 150, 199
From Paul to Valentinus (Lampe), 27–29

Galen, 28, 39, 177
Gnosticism, 7–8, 73, 74–109; Basileides on matter and creation, 71–72; canonical definition as response to, 85–90, 105–8; demiurge of gnostic revelation, 69–70, 85, 87, 89; Gospel of Truth, 75–85, 104–5; Harnack on Hellenization of the gospel and, 7–9, 11, 74, 87, 89–90, 108–9; and Irenaeus's *Demonstration of the Apostolic Preaching* and articulation of the canon of truth, 75, 90–105, 108–9, 181–82, 198–99, 201; Irenaeus's principal arguments against, 106–8; reading of scripture (symbolically and allegorically), 73; Valentinian tradition, 74, 85–90. *See also* Gospel of Truth (Nag Hammadi treatise); Irenaeus's *Demonstration of the Apostolic Preaching* (*Epideixis*); Marcion; Valentinus/Valentinian gnostic tradition
Gospel of Truth (Nag Hammadi treatise), 75–85, 104–5; allusions to Matthew's Gospel, 78, 79–80; and Irenaeus's *Demonstration*, 104–5; Jesus as revealer, 80–83; Johannine echoes and allusions, 78, 80, 82–83; metaphorical echoes of canonical Gospels, 78–80; names in the book of the living, 83–85, 104; overview, 76–77; scriptural reminiscences and allusions, 75–85; scripture as source of gnostic revelation, 87–90; and the Valentinian gnostic tradition, 85–90
grammaticus, 16, 31, 33, 50, 228
Gregory of Nazianzus, 168–70, 195
Gregory of Nyssa, 168, 196, 204, 211

Hellenization theory, 7–11, 12, 37–41, 74, 87, 89–90, 108–9, 165, 243–46; and Gnosticism, 7–9, 11, 74, 87, 89–90, 108–9; Harnack, 7–11, 12, 37–39, 74, 87, 89–90, 108–9
Heraclas, 31–32, 33
heresies: Cyprian and the unity of the church during schisms, 217–20; Cyril of Jerusalem and fourth-century doctrinal controversies, 161–63, 171–72, 174, 175, 182–83, 194, 196; Epiphanius's *Panarion* on Ptolemaeus's letter to Flora, 53–55; *haireseis* ("options"), 21, 38–40, 59, 64, 73, 122, 131, 134, 136, 149, 155, 159–60, 245; Origen on Christian sects, 134–36; and

orthodoxy, 30, 43. *See also* Gnosticism; Marcion; Valentinus/Valentinian gnostic tradition
Hermeneutical Procedure and Theological Method in Origen's Exegesis (Torjesen), 113–14
Hermogenes, 72
Herod, 56
Hesiod, 65–66, 100
Hippolytus, 7–8, 71, 89, 94
historical criticism (historico-critical method), 2–3, 98, 232–33, 236, 241–42, 246
History of Dogma (Harnack), 7–11
"holy dogmas" of Cyril of Jerusalem's *Catechetical Homilies*, 158–59, 161–62, 163–221; bodily resurrection and eternal life, 209–13; the catholicity of the church, 213–20; Christ as the Son of God, 161, 170–76; God, 163–70; judgment, 195–97; the passion of Christ, 183–91; the resurrection and ascension, 191–95, 212, 223; sin, 197–99; the virgin birth, 161, 176–83
Homer, 22, 51, 65–66, 98, 99, 122, 159
homoousios, 153, 159, 170–71, 176, 184
hypothesis of scripture: Irenaeus on the rule of faith as, 98–104, 108–9, 158, 160, 225, 230, 232–33; and the meaning of hypothesis in ancient literary theory, 98–99, 104

Ignatius, 45–46, 216
Influence of Greek Ideas on Christianity, The (Hatch), 14–15
Introduction to the Old Testament as Scripture (Childs), 232
Irenaeus: on creation, 100–101, 106–7; doctrine of recapitulation, 102–3, 107–8, 190–91, 232; image of the church as Christ's body, 216; principal arguments against Gnosticism, 106–8; on salvation and the incarnation, 190; on the scriptural canon, 108; on the virgin birth, 180–81, 183. *See also* Irenaeus's *Demonstration of the Apostolic Preaching* (*Epideixis*)
Irenaeus's *Demonstration of the Apostolic Preaching* (*Epideixis*), 75, 90–105, 108–9, 181–82, 198–99, 201; discovery of the manuscript, 91; and the gnostic Gospel of Truth, 104–5; on proof from prophecy, 92–93, 102, 105; and the rule of faith (canon of truth), 75, 90–105, 108–9, 181–82, 198–99, 201; on the rule of faith as the hypothesis of scripture, 98–104, 108–9, 158, 160, 225, 230, 232–33; summaries of apostolic preaching, 91–92; on the threefold shape of the rule of faith, 93–97, 104; on the three names of the rule of faith, 95–97, 104, 109, 160

Jerusalem temple, destruction of (70 CE), 17, 19
"Jesus only" Pentecostal tradition, 1–2, 95
Jewish apocalyptic literature, 88–90
Jewish Exegesis and Homeric Scholarship in Alexandria (Niehoff), 51
Jewish tradition: apocalyptic literature, 88–90; early Christian ambivalence in appropriation of Jewish scripture, 45–49; and the gnostic Gospel of Truth, 84, 88–90; Hellenistic influence on rabbinic interpretation and scholarship, 21–22; Ignatius on Christian appropriation of Jewish scripture, 45–46; Irenaeus on scriptural prophecies as proof for rule of faith, 92–93, 102, 105; negative theology and God's namelessness, 69, 84, 89, 165, 239; the synagogue as sociological model for early Christianity, 22–23; synagogues and schools (and school-like character of early Christian groups), 19–23, 38
John Chrysostom, 199
John the Baptist, 175, 184, 188
Josephus, 20
Julian the Apostate, 17
Justin Martyr, 94, 95, 107–8, 177; Christian worship in second-century Rome, 28–29; on the Creator God, 63–64; on Marcion's teaching, 62; reading of scripture, 49n, 55–58, 92; reading prophetic texts, 55–58, 179–80; on the resurrection and ascension, 194; on the virgin birth and the Greek myths, 178–80

Leningrad Codex, 229
Logos-theology, 8, 77, 171

Manichaeism, 165–66, 168, 202
Marcellus of Ancyra, 195–96
Marcianus, 91
Marcion, 29, 44–45, 49–55, 58–59, 62–70, 73, 166; biblical criticism and its context, 49–53; and Gnosticism, 73, 166; and Greek "question and answer" tradition, 50–53; and Luke's Gospel, 49–50, 95; Origen's critique of, 123, 131, 134, 135; the "other God" and Greek philosophical tradition, 64–69; rejection of the God of scripture, 44–45, 58–59, 62–64
Mariology, 177
Maximus of Tyre, 66
Melito of Sardis, 100, 186–87
metempsychosis, 119
Methodius, 215
modern perspectives on relationship between doctrine and scripture in the early church, 1–3, 11–13, 232–33, 241–47; hermeneutics, 12–13; historical criticism, 2–3, 98, 232–33, 236, 241–42, 246; linguistic philosophy, 12; postmodernism, 11–12, 226, 232, 244–46; sociology of knowledge, 12; structuralism, 12, 241–42; and "theological reading" of scripture, 242–43, 246
Monarchians, 1–2, 174, 175, 183, 245
Montanists, 28, 145
mystery cults (mystery religions), 17, 25, 28, 37–38
Myth of God Incarnate, The (Hick), 11

Nag Hammadi library, 75, 88. *See also* Gospel of Truth (Nag Hammadi treatise)
Neoplatonism, 6, 7, 68, 89–90, 149, 167–68. *See also* Platonism
Neopythagoreans, 63, 68
Nestorius, 182–83, 189, 191
Nicaea, council of (325), 156, 176
Nicene Creed, 156, 170, 176
Noah's ark, 188, 217, 218, 220
Numenius, 63, 66–67, 70

Ogdoad, 86, 90
"Oneness" Pentecostal tradition, 1–2, 95
Oratio Panegyrica, 33–34
Origen, 110–55; *Against Celsus*, 111–12, 117, 121, 124–36, 180–81, 194; Augustine and, 203; catechetical school in Alexandria, 30–37, 112, 228; catechetical school in Caesarea, 33–34, 36, 112, 118–19; on the concealed intent of the divine author, 114–17; concept of doctrine and scripture (divine pedagogy), 110–55; on creation, 128–31, 149–52, 153, 203; critique of Jewish literalism, 123; critiques of gnostics, 123; on different levels of Christians and the learning journey, 110–14; *First Principles* and attempt to articulate a "single body of doctrine," 136–52; and the fourth-century reaction against allegory, 224; on free will, 149, 150, 199; on God's incorporeality, 146–49, 239; on God's knowledge of us, 128–31; on God's pedagogical purpose, 154–55; on heresies among Christian sects, 134–36; homilies, 36, 111–12; image of the church as Christ's body, 216; Origenist controversies of the fourth century, 117–22, 162; on our knowledge of God, 131–34; and *paideia*, 36, 113–14, 117–22; philosophical studies, 34–36; and Platonism, 112–13, 117–22, 125, 129–30, 132, 148, 152–53; on a precosmic fall and restoration of creation, 149–52; on prophecy and its fulfillment, 125–28, 181; "question and answer" tradition, 52; on the resurrection and ascension, 194; on the rule of faith, 135–36, 137–49, 153; on salvation and the incarnation, 190; on the unitive *skopos*, 114–15, 159; on the virgin birth, 178–79, 180–81; on the wrath of God, 62–63
Origen and Scripture (Martens), 122–23
Origen's *Against Celsus*, 111–12, 117, 121, 124–36, 180–81, 194; on God's knowledge of us, 128–31; and heresies among Christians, 134–36; on oracles and prophecies, 125–28, 181; and Origen on Platonism, 125, 129–30, 132; on our knowledge of God, 131–34; and

the rule of faith, 135–36, 137–49, 153; the virgin birth, 178–79, 180–81

Origen's *First Principles*, 136–52; and creation out of nothing (*creatio ex nihilo*), 150, 153; on God and scripture, 145–49; the Holy Spirit, 141–45; and inquiries into meaning and truth, 139–40; pessimistic view of matter and bodies, 150–51; on a precosmic fall and restoration of creation, 149–52; on the rule of faith, 137–49; the three names of the rule of faith, 138–39, 160; toward a "single body of doctrine," 120, 136–39, 140

Orthodoxy and Heresy in Earliest Christianity (Bauer), 30

paideia, 26, 36, 113–14, 117–22
Pantaenus, 29, 32–33
Papias, 46
Paraclete (as name/title), 145
passion of Christ: Cyril of Jerusalem on the cross, 183–91; Gospel of Truth on the cross, 81; Melito and Passover typology of the cross, 186–87; universal redemption, 185
Pastoral Epistles, 23–24, 25–27, 40, 42–43, 216, 229
Pauline Epistles, 47–48, 77, 107, 207
Pelagians, 199–200
Pentecostal tradition, 1–2, 95
Peri Pascha (Melito of Sardis), 100, 186–87
Pharisees, 21, 38, 40, 81
Philo: *Allegorical Commentary*, 51; comparing synagogues to schools, 20; on creation and matter, 70–71; on God and creation, 64, 69; Hellenistic influence on Jewish scholarship, 21–22, 51; *Questions and Answers on Genesis and Exodus*, 51
pistis, 17–18, 39–40, 240–41
Plato: *Parmenides*, 63, 68; *Seventh Letter*, 68; *Sophist*, 70; *Symposium*, 68; *Timaeus*, 63
Platonism, 6, 16, 21–22, 39, 63–64, 67–68, 87, 122, 159, 169, 211; apophatic theology, 239; doctrine of transcendent God, 66–68; and the gnostic tradition, 87, 88;

Harnack on, 7; matter and creation, 70–73, 167–68; Origen and, 112–13, 117–22, 125, 129–30, 132, 148; and the Trinity, 6. *See also* Neoplatonism

plērōma, 76, 79, 86–87, 107
Plotinus, 35n, 68, 74, 87, 89
Plutarch: on creation and matter, 70; discussion of oracular riddles, 115–16; on God and the cosmos, 64; *Moralia*, 57, 116; *Pythian Dialogues*, 57; "question and answer" tradition, 50
Porphyry, 51–52
postmodernism, 11–12, 226, 232, 235–36, 244–46
Protestantism, 9–10
Pseudo-Aristotle, 72
Ptolemaeus, 53–55, 63, 64
Ptolemy, 56
Pythagoreans, 68, 117, 159

Quartodecimans, 186
"question and answer" tradition, 50–53

reader-response theory, 241–42
resurrection of Christ: Augustine on, 194–95; Cyril of Jerusalem on ascension and, 191–95, 212, 223; Irenaeus on the incarnation and, 103; scriptural testimonies of, 192–93, 213
resurrection of the body: Athenagoras on, 210–11, 212; Augustine on, 211; Cyril of Jerusalem on eternal life and, 209–13
Roman Catholic Church, 3, 8–9
Rufinus, 137, 142–43, 151
rule of faith, 156, 160, 176, 184, 221, 225, 233–34, 244; Augustine's *inventio* as expression of, 232; Irenaeus on the hypothesis of scripture, 98–104, 108–9, 158, 160, 225, 230, 232–33; Irenaeus on the threefold shape of, 93–97, 104; and Irenaeus's *Demonstration of the Apostolic Preaching* (*Epideixis*), 75, 90–105, 108–9, 181–82; Origen on, 135–36, 137–49, 153; three names of, 95–97, 104, 109, 138–39, 160

Sadducees, 21, 38
Samaritans, 210, 213

school-like character of early Christian groups, 14–43; acculturation as a network of schools, 37–38; Alexandrian catechetical schools, 29–37; and Augustine's *Teaching Christianity*, 227, 230; and Christianity's oddness when considered a religion in its social context, 15–19; the "fractionated" Roman church and the schools within, 27–37, 45; and Hellenization theory, 7–11, 12, 37–41, 74, 87, 89–90, 108–9, 165, 243–46; the household, 23–25, 28; the household-based *collegia*, 24–27; Jewish synagogues and schools, 19–23, 38; the rereading of scripture, 42–43; a school with a distinct identity, 38–41; the sociological approach to rethinking the early Christian context, 22–37
semiotics and Augustine's theory of "signs," 235–36
Sermon on the Mount, 198
Sibylline Oracles, 57
sign theory, Augustine's: distinction between "things" and "signs," 228, 231, 234–40; and postmodern semiotics, 235–36
Simon Magus, 166
sin, original: Adam-Christ typology, 199, 201, 207, 209; and Adam's fall, 185, 206–7; Apostolic Fathers on, 197–98; Augustine on baptism and, 200; Augustine's doctrine of free will and, 199–209; Cyril's doctrine of sin, 197–99; Pelagian controversy, 199–200
sociological approach to rethinking the early Christian context, 22–37; the "fractionated" Roman church and the schools within, 27–37, 45; the household-based *collegia*, 24–27; the household model, 23–25, 28; the Jewish synagogue, 22–23
sociology of knowledge, 12
Sophia (wisdom), Valentinian myth of, 86–87, 89, 90
Stoicism, 21–22, 32, 72, 87, 131, 147, 148
structuralism, 12, 241–42

supersessionism, 17, 214, 215
systematic theology, 6–7, 233, 247

Targum Onqelos, 57
Tatian, 28, 62, 211
Teaching Christianity (Augustine), 227–43; and Augustine's pedagogy, 240–43; composition and intended audience, 227–30; the *rhetor* and discernment (*inventio*) of the subject matter, 228–34, 240; sign theory, 228, 231, 234–40; title of, 227; on the Trinity, 230, 231, 237–39
Teaching of Peter, The, 146
Tertullian: critique of Marcion, 52, 62–63; on God and creation, 72, 76–77; opposition to Gnosticism, 7–8; presumption of divine impassibility, 183
Theodore (Antiochene), 224–25
Theodoret, 51–52, 176
"theological reading" of scripture, 242–43, 246
Theophilus of Antioch, 62, 72, 100
Trinitarianism, 1–2, 6, 104, 165, 220, 239, 243
Trinity: Augustine on, 230, 231, 237–39; Platonism and, 6
Tyconius's *Rules*, 237

Valentinus/Valentinian gnostic tradition, 28, 29–30, 32, 53, 74, 75, 85–90; explanation of the material world, 86–87; myth of *Sophia* (wisdom), 86–87, 89, 90; Origen's critique of, 123, 134, 135; scripture as source of gnostic revelation, 87–90
virgin birth, 176–83; and Christian ideal of virginity since second century, 177; and christological controversies, 182–83; Cyril of Jerusalem on the incarnation and, 176, 178, 181–83; and fulfillment of prophecy, 179–80, 181; and Greek myths, 178–81; Justin and, 178–80; Origen and, 178–79, 180–81; *parthenos*, 181

Xenophanes, 65

Zeus, 178, 179–80

Index of Scripture and Other Ancient Sources

Old Testament

Genesis
1	168
1:26	106
1:26–27	172
2–3	89
3:5	82
3:7	82
6:14	220
14:14	96n
18:27	161, 165
22:13	234
49:8–11	177n
49:9	192
49:10	57
49:10–12	56

Exodus
3:21–22	228
3:34	69
12:35–36	36, 121, 228
12:46	218
13:1–11	36
15:25	234
20:2	1
31:1–11	121
33:11	69
33:17–23	69
33:19	172
33:20	69, 166, 172, 239
33:22	182
33:23	169
34:4–7	172

Leviticus
8:3	214

Numbers
21:9	188
24:17	57

Deuteronomy
4:20	214
5:6–7	1
9:20	214
28:66	188

Joshua
2:19	218

2 Samuel
5:6–8	52

1 Kings
11:31	218
19:9	182

Job
36:27	165

Psalms
2:7	177n
2:9	177n
8:3	169
16:10	192
17:8	165
22	56, 194
24	194
30:1–3	192
31:19	198
32:5	198
33:4	165
33:6	106
33:9	106
35:10	146
36:7	170
36:8	129
45:1	171n
47:5	194
49:12	206

271

49:20	206
51:13	141
72:5–17	57
85:11	192
88	192
88:13	192
95	187n
104:24	167
110	194
110:1	172
110:4	175
111:10	243
115:3	106
139	198
139:6	170
146	165

Proverbs

2:5	148
20:27	61

Song of Songs

2:10–14	192
2:12	192
3:1	193
3:3–4	193n
3:11	188
4:12	192, 220
5:1	192, 193
6:7	222
6:9	217
6:11	192

Isaiah

6	142
7:10–14	177
7:14	56, 177, 179–80
9:6	56
10:17	151
11:1–4	57
11:2–3	243
14:12	202
20:22	165
26:19	209
34:4	196
40:12	210
42:5	142
44:6	1
44:13–17	68–69
45:7	166
53	184–85
53:9	185n, 186
55:8	239
55:8–9	69, 147n

Jeremiah

23:24	169

Ezekiel

1:28	166
37	210
37:7	216

Daniel

2:44	177
4:9	141
12	209

Micah

5:1–4	57
5:2	56, 177

Habakkuk

3:2	142

Zechariah

4:10	165
9:9	56, 177n

Deutero-canonical Books

Wisdom of Solomon

2:7	169
3:5	166

2 Maccabees

7:28	71n

Ancient Jewish Writers

Josephus

Against Apion

1.29	46n
1.176–182	20n

Jewish Antiquities

16.43	20n

New Testament

Matthew

4:11	172
5:8	132, 148
5:21–22	198
5:27–28	198
5:28	185
5:38–39	54
5:48	80, 165
6:19	79
7:11	79
7:16–20	79
7:24	217
9:12	80
11:27	105, 142, 148, 165, 171
12:11	78
12:30	218
12:32	143
13:36–43	111n
15	54
16:22–23	186
17:24	185n
18:12–14	78
19	54
20:28	81
23:37	165
24	196
28:19	1, 94–95, 141n

Mark

7:14–23	198

9:48	79	18:28	187n	1:15	211–12	
13:2	174	19:14	187n	1:18	185	
		19:23	218	1:25	185, 231	
Luke		19:24	218	1:27–29	130	
1:1–4	41	19:31	187n	2:4	125n	
1:35	141	19:36	187n	2:6	140n	
2:10–11	172	19:39	193	2:10	142, 165	
9:51	187	20:1	193	3:2–3	111–12	
10:22	172	20:21	217	3:7	229	
14:23	220	20:22	82, 141	3:14–15	195	
23:14	185n	21:15–17	217	4:15	174	
23:41	185n			5:6	231	
24:1	193	**Acts**		5:7	187n	
24:25–27	42	1:7	196	8:5	173	
24:41	193	2:16–17	144	8:5–6	43	
24:44–45	42	5:17	38	9:9–10	124n	
		8:18	141	9:12	173	
John		10:36	172	10:1–2	124n	
1:3	106	15:5	38	10:3–4	124n	
1:14	231	24:24	38	10:4	172	
1:18	82, 148, 164, 166	26:5	38	10:11	124n	
1:29	185, 187n	28:22	38	11:19	134, 218	
1:36	187n			12:3	141	
3:8	142	**Romans**		12:8–9	144	
3:14	188	1	148	15	81, 192	
3:31	78	1:1	24	15:16	195	
4:24	146n, 147	1:19–20	167	15:21	183	
5:23	174	1:20	231	15:25	195	
5:26	174	3:23	84	15:28	151, 152	
5:39	42n, 115	4	41	15:45–49	107	
5:45	42n	4:17	71n	15:50	212	
8:44	202	5:5	85n	15:50–57	81	
10:15	171	5:12	200			
10:16	218	5:12–17	107	**2 Corinthians**		
10:18	188	5:14	195	1:3	164	
10:30	1, 218	7:12	54	2:14	79	
12:23	187	8:3	82	4:4	89n	
12:31	89n	8:21	151	10:10	40	
12:32	83	10:14–15	84	12:4	132	
13:31	187	11:33	69n, 154n, 170, 239n			
14:6	78, 80	11:36	237	**Galatians**		
14:9	132	16:25–27	140n	2:23–24	215	
14:26–27	145			3:28	222	
16:12–14	145	**1 Corinthians**		4:21–24	124n	
17:5	188	1:10	218	4:24	225n	

4:26	124n, 214
5:17	207
5:22	142
5:32	215, 218
6:15	222

Ephesians

2:19	208
2:25	54
3:8	69n, 239n
3:9	80
4:2–3	218
4:4	217
4:5	197
4:6	106
4:27	79
5:22–6:9	23
5:23	217
5:27	219
5:28–32	215
5:31–32	124n
5:32	215

Philippians

3:20	208

Colossians

1:15	148
1:15–20	81
1:16	172
1:20	189
1:25	80, 81
1:25–26	80
2:3	115
2:14	81
2:16	124n
3:8	129
3:11	222
3:18–4:1	23

1 Thessalonians

1:9	43
1:9–10	59
5:23	106

2 Thessalonians

2	196

1 Timothy

2:5–6	26, 42
3:14–16	25–26
3:15	23
4:1–3	145
4:6	23
4:7–8	26
5:1–2	23
6:13–16	27
6:14	215
6:16	69n, 239n

2 Timothy

1:10	140n
3:14–17	26

Titus

1:1	24

Hebrews

2:1	81
5:12–14	111–12
6:1	140n
6:4–6	197
7:17	175
8:5	124n
9:17	81
10:1	124n
11:3	71n
11:37–38	127n
12:29	146n

James

1:17	164

1 Peter

2:4–6	155n
2:9	215
2:10	215
2:22	185n
2:22–23	186
2:24	189
4:17	23

2 Peter

2:22	79

1 John

1–4	41
1:5	146
2:1	145
5:7	218

Revelation

2:11	207
3:7	105
5	83
19:12	84
20:6	207
20:14	207
21:18	207
21:25	78

EARLY CHRISTIAN WRITINGS

Alcinous

The Handbook of Platonism

10	67
14	64n

Apostolic Constitutions

book 1	215
book 2	216
book 8	215, 216

Athanasius

Against the Pagans

46–47	190

On the Incarnation

6	189, 204

Index of Scripture and Other Ancient Sources

Athenagoras

Embassy for Christians
13–30	178n
30.5	178n
33	177n

On the Resurrection
2.2–3	210
10.6	210
14.6	212
15.2	210
18.1	210
18.2	212

Augustine

The City of God
7.29–31	201
9	201
9.5	201
9.15	201
10	201
11	201–3
11.1	202
11.2	202
11.13	202
11.14–15	202
11.17	203
11.22	203
11.23	203
11.34	203
12	203–6
12.1	204
12.2	204
12.3	204
12.4–5	204
12.6	204
12.7	205
12.8	205
12.9	205
12.10	205
12.13	205
12.15	205
12.19–20	211n
12.22	205
12.23	205
12.28	205
13	206–7
13.3	206
13.4	207
13.5	207
13.13	207
13.14	207
14	207–8
14.1	208
15–18	201, 208
19–22	208
19.13	202n
22.1	203n
22.1–3	211n
22.12–14	211n

Epistles
93	220n
173	220n

On Genesis against the Manichaeans
1.6	168
1.26	168

On the Literal Interpretation of Genesis
1.1	168

Retractions
2.4	229n

Teaching Christianity
1	228, 229, 230
1.4 [1.2.2]	234
1.5 [1.2.2]	234
1.8–9 [1.4.4]	231
1.10–12 [1.5.5]	237–38
1.13 [1.6.6]	238
1.14 [1.7.7]	238
1.22 [1.10.10]	231
1.23 [1.11.11]	231
1.26 [1.13.12]	231
1.27–30 [1.14.13]	232
1.31–38 [1.15.14–21.19]	232
2	228–29, 236–37
2.1 [2.1.1]	235
2.3 [2.2.3]	235
2.9 [2.5.6]	236
2.16–24 [2.7.9–11]	242–43
2.93 [2.24.37]	235
2.144–145 [2.40.60]	228n
3	228–29, 236–37
3.30–32 [3.9.13]	237
3.45	220n
3.45 [3.12.19]	235
3.47–49 [3.12.20]	235
3.52 [3.14.22]	235
3.60–61 [3.18.26–27]	235
3.67–74 [3.21.30–23.33]	235
3.108 [3.34.47]	237
3.133 [3.37.56]	237
4	228–29, 240
4.3 [4.1.2]	240
4.15 [4.4.6]	241
4.79 [4.13.29]	241
4.93 [4.16.33]	229
4.150 [4.26.58]	241
4.151–153 [4.27.59–60]	241
4.157 [4.28.61]	241
11.13–15 [2.6.8]	236

Basil of Caesarea

Letters
81	217
210	217

On the Holy Spirit
30.76	217

1 Clement
19–21	59–60
21	61
21.3	198
21.8–9	198
33	60
38	60
40–44	215
59–61	60–61

276 INDEX OF SCRIPTURE AND OTHER ANCIENT SOURCES

Clement of Alexandria

Stromateis
5.4	116
5.5–9	117
5.8	117
5.12	116

Cyprian

The Unity of the Catholic Church
1–4	217n
5–7	218n
8–11	218n
12–14	219

Cyril of Alexandria

Commentary on John
1.9	191

Cyril of Jerusalem

Catechetical Homilies
1	198
2	198
2.2	198
2.4	198
2.5–6	198
3	161, 198
3–5	161
4	161, 163–64, 165, 171, 191–92, 193–94, 209–10
4.2	158–59
4.4–6	163–64
4.7–8	171
4.10	184
4.11	184
4.12	191
4.13	194
4.17	157n
4.22–23	211
4.30	211
4.30–31	210
5.10–12	159
5.12	157n
6	161, 164–66
6.2–4	164–65
6.6	165
6.8	165
6.12–36	166
7	164
7.5	164
7.9–10	164
8	164
8.1–2	164
8.4	166
9	166–67
9.3	166
9.7	166
9.15–16	167
9.16	167
10	161
10.1	173
10.1–2	173
10.2	173
10.3	173, 175
10.3–5	172
10.5	172
10.6	172
10.7	172
10.7–8	172
10.9	172
10.10	172
10.11	174
10.14	175
10.15–17	175
10.19	175
10.50	173
11	171, 175
11.1–2	173
11.2	172n
11.3	173
11.4	172, 173
11.5	173
11.7	173
11.8–9	174
11.10	171
11.10–12	174
11.13	174
11.14	174
11.15	174
11.16	174
11.17–21	175
12	161
12–13	160
12.4	178
12.5–8	182
12.10–15	182
12.15	182
12.16	182
12.17–26	177
12.21–22	178
12.27	178
12.28–29	178
13	184–91
13.1	185
13.2	185
13.3	185
13.4	187
13.5	185
13.5–6	187
13.6	186
13.7	188
13.8	188
13.17	188
13.18	188
13.19	188
13.20	188
13.28	188
13.35	188
13.38	189
14	192–94
14.5	192
14.9	192
14.10–11	192
14.11	193
14.12	193n
14.15–20	193
14.21–23	193
14.24	193
14.24–30	194
15	195–97
15.1–4	196
15.4–9	196
15.13	196
15.22	196

15.23	197	33.3.7	54	21.3–5	75		
15.24–26	197	33.4.1	54	21.3–8	83		
15.27–33	195	33.4.14	54	21.11–14	83		
18	209–14	33.6.6	54	21.23	83		
18.1	210	33.7.5–6	55	21.25–34	83		
18.2–3	210	64	222n	22.4–7	83		
18.4–5	212			22.12–13	83		
18.6–18	212	**Epistle of Barnabas**		22.14–18	75		
18.10	213	9.7–8	96n	23.19–31	77		
18.11	213			24.9	80		
18.12–13	213	**Eusebius**		24.9–10	82		
18.14–16	213			27.9	80		
18.17	195	*Ecclesiastical History*		30.3–7	81–82		
18.23	213	3.39	46n	30.27–31.1	82		
18.24	214	4.36.2	124–25	30.35–31.35	80–83		
18.25–26	214	5.10	32	31–34	78–80		
18.25–27	214	5.11	32	31.1–7	82		
		5.24	186n	31.9–13	82		
Procatechesis		6.2	31	31.13–35	82		
1	221	6.3	31	31.20	84		
6	158	6.6	33	31.27–32.16	78		
7	197	6.12	32	32.18–34	78		
8	197	6.15	32	32.35–33.8	79		
11	157, 158	6.18	32, 33	33.11–21	79		
		6.19	35n	33.30–34	79		
Ephrem the Syrian		6.23	32	33.37–34.5	79		
Hymns on the Church		6.30	33	35–36	80		
51.8	191	9.9	18n	37.35–43.22	83–85		
		10.3	216	37.37–38	84		
				38.7	84		
Epiphanius				38.11–12	84		
Ancoratus		**Gospel of Truth**		38.14–24	84		
9	222	**(Nag Hammadi)**		38.25–32	84		
13	222n	16.34–17.1	76	39.3–5	84		
18	222	17.5–9	76	39.15–19	84		
19	222	17.10–21	76	42.25–29	84		
56–58	222n	18.7–20.2	80–83	43.5–7	85		
63	222n	18.7–21	80	43.10–13	85		
81	222	18.21–35	80	43.14–24	85		
86–87	222n	18.31	76				
		19.7	76	**Gregory of Nazianzus**			
Panarion		19.24–30	81				
33.3–7	53n	19.34–20.6	83	*Theological Orations*			
33.3.1	53	19.34–23.31	83–85	1.4	195		
33.3.4	53	20.10–27	81	22–31	170n		
33.3.5	53	20.28–32	81	28.2	169		

28.3	169	**Irenaeus**		28	102	
28.4–5	169			29–30	102	
28.6	169	*Against Heresies*		31	102–3	
28.8	169	1.7.2	176n	32	182	
28.9	169	1.8	99	32–34	103	
28.13	169	1.8.1	98	35–36	103	
28.16	169	1.9.4	98	38	103	
28.18	170	1.9.5	90n	40	103	
28.21	170	1.10.1	98–99	42	92, 104	
		1.22.1	106n	43–52	93	
Gregory of Nyssa		1.27.2	62n	47	107	
		2.1.2	62n, 107	53–85	93	
On the Making of Humankind		3.8.3	106n	86–87	93	
		3.11.19	75	100	93	
16.12	204	3.22	181			
23–24	196	4, preface 4	106n	**Justin**		
25–26	211n	4.4.2	107			
		4.7	216	*1 Apology*		
Hippolytus		4.20.2	105	21	179	
		4.28.1	105	22	179	
Apostolic Tradition		5.6.1	106	23	179	
21	94	5.6.2	107	26	58, 62	
		5.19–21	190	30–31	56	
Refutation of All Heresies		5.20.2	190	33	180	
5.21	89	6.1–7.3	107	45	194	
7.20	71	20.1–9	107	49	55n	
7.21	71			50	55	
9.12.22ff.	220n	*Demonstration of the Apostolic Preaching*		51	194	
10.10	71			58	58, 62	
		1	98	61	94	
Ignatius		1–2	97	66–67	28, 49n	
		3	93	67	46n	
To the Ephesians		3–10	97			
5.1	216	5	106n	*Dialogue with Trypho*		
15.3	198	6	91–92	43	178n	
		7	94	53	55n	
To the Philadelphians		11	100	67	178	
5	46n	12	100	68.3	58n	
8	46	17	100	71.2	58n	
		18–22	100	72	58n	
To the Smyrnaeans		22	101, 107	76	55	
6–7	46n	23	101	92.1	56	
		24	101	98–107	194	
To the Trallians		25	101	100	107–8, 182	
11.2	216	26	101	113.1	58n	
		27	101–2			

Index of Scripture and Other Ancient Sources 279

119.1	56	2.55–66	135	6.53	131		
123.7	58n	2.75	130	6.54–56	131		
		3.1	123n	6.56	129		
Maximus of Tyre		3.1–2	126n	6.61–65	134n		
		3.12	111	6.64	133		
Dissertations		3.12–13	134	6.65	131		
11	67n	3.15	126	6.70	147		
		3.28	121	6.73	135		
Philosophical Orations		3.49	111	6.79	216		
11	66	3.52	111	7.2–7	126		
		3.53–54	112	7.7	127		
Melito of Sardis		3.74	111, 112n	7.10	127–28		
		4.2–7	135	7.32–34	118n		
On Pascha		4.3	124n	7.41	112		
32	186	4.21	126	7.42	132		
54	186	4.26	130	7.59	112		
64	186	4.38	117	7.59–60	112		
68	187	4.39	117	7.60	113		
		4.44	124n	8.49–50	118n		
Methodius		4.49	124n	8.53	128		
		4.52	131				
Symposium		4.53	128	*Commentary on John*			
3	215n	4.57	118n, 135	1.15	115n		
		4.65–66	135	10.174	114n		
Origen		4.71	129	13.27	154n		
		4.72	129	13.30	154n		
Against Celsus		4.75	130				
1.2	125	4.83	121	*First Principles*			
1.4	121, 128	4.95	126n	1.pref.4	141		
1.9	37, 111n, 129	5.2–5	135	1.pref.4–8	138n		
1.9–11	39n	5.16	129n	1.pref.7	149		
1.21	131	5.18–20	118n	1.pref.8	145–46		
1.23	130	5.18–22	135	1.pref.9	146		
1.25	130	5.22	135, 136n	1.pref.10	136n		
1.32–35	135	5.60	123	1.1.1	146, 152n		
1.34	178n, 181	5.61	134, 135	1.1.2	147		
1.37	179, 180	6.1	36, 111	1.1.3	152n		
1.49	126	6.1–5	130n	1.1.4	147		
1.54–55	135	6.8	180	1.1.5	147		
1.62	37, 135, 153	6.32	134, 135	1.1.6	147–48		
2.2	124n	6.35	126	1.1.7	148		
2.7	124n	6.48	216	1.1.8	148		
2.8	136	6.49	130	1.1.9	148		
2.27	134	6.49–52	130n	1.3.1	141		
2.34–38	135	6.52	130	1.3.2	141, 143		
2.38	123n	6.52–53	135	1.3.3	141, 143n		
2.55–58	194						

1.3.4	142	4.2.9	115	**GRECO-ROMAN**	
1.3.6	121	4.3.5	115	**LITERATURE**	
1.3.7	143	4.3.14	154n		
1.3.8	143, 152n	4.4.6	151	**Cicero**	
1.5.3	150n	4.4.8	151, 151n		
1.5.5	152	*Homilies on Matthew*		*On the Nature of the Gods*	
1.6.1	140	16.12	115n	1.14	18
1.6.2	152n			3.5	17–18
1.6.4	151	*Homilies on Samuel*			
1.7.5	151	5.4	115n	**Justinian**	
1.8.1	151				
2.1–5	138n	**Shepherd of Hermas,**		*Letter to Menna*	143n
2.1.4	151	**Mandate**			
2.2.2	151	1	71n	**Plato**	
2.3.7	140				
2.6	138n			*Parmenides*	
2.6.7	140	**Tertullian**		142a	68
2.7	138n	*Against Hermogenes*	72	*Seventh Letter*	
2.7.2	144	*Against Marcion*		341c–d	68
2.7.3	145	1.19	63	*Sophist*	
2.8.4	140	2.20	62	238c	70
2.9.2	150	2.21	62		
2.9.3–6	149	2.23–24	62	*Symposium*	
2.9.8	150	2.25	62	210e–211b	68
2.10.1–3	151n	4.6	52		
2.10.8	151	4.9	52	*Timaeus*	
2.11.2	118n			28e	67
2.11.3	155	*To the Heathen*			
2.11.5–6	155	1.8	19n	**Plutarch**	
2.11.7	155				
3.3.5	150n	**Theodoret of Cyrus**		*The E at Delphi*	
3.5.4	152n			384	116
3.6.1	151	*Eranistes (Florilegium 2.7)*		385–386	116
3.6.3	152n		156n	406	116
3.6.4	151n	*The Questions on*			
3.6.6–7	151n	*the Octateuch*	51–52	*On Isis and Osiris*	57n
3.6.8	152n			378	116
3.6.9	151	**Theophilus**		382	116
3.11	115				
4.1.7	140	*To Autolycus*		*On the Failure of Oracles*	57n
4.2.1	118n	1.6–7	72n		
4.2.2–3	115	1.9ff.	178n	*On the Generation of*	
4.2.5	115	2.2–8	178n	*the Soul in the Timaeus*	
4.2.6	117–18	2.4	72n	1014b	70n
4.2.7	122	2.10	72n		
4.2.8	115	3.2–8	178n	*The Oracles at Delphi*	57n